GW00702180

The Which?
Wine Guide
2005

WHICH? BOOKS

Which? Books is the book publishing arm of Consumers' Association, which was set up in 1957 to improve the standards of goods and services available to the public. Everything Which? publishes aims to help consumers, by giving them the independent information they need to make informed decisions. These publications, known throughout Britain for their quality, integrity and impartiality, have been held in high regard for over four decades.

Independence does not come cheap: the guides carry no advertising; no wine merchant or producer can buy an entry in our wine guide; we also pay for the wine used in our tastings. This policy, and our practice of rigorously re-researching our guides for each edition, helps us to provide our readers with information of a standard and quality that cannot be surpassed.

About the author

Susan Keevil swapped her desk job, as editor of *Decanter* magazine, for a writing career roving the world's wine regions in 2000, and has since been exploring far and wide in the pursuit of new flavours and interesting wine estates. Favourite among her travels was a venture to Australia in 2001, where she enjoyed taking part in that year's Shiraz harvest and comparing winemaking notes in the Hunter and Barossa Valleys. Susan is a specialist in the wines of California and is not averse to sampling gutsy big red wines (usually Cabernet Sauvignon, Merlot and, her favourite, Petite Sirah) in Napa and Sonoma. Back home, she writes about these excursions (and more) for *Wine*, *Decanter*, and *Harpers* magazines and has a column in the American magazine *The Wine News*. Susan is co-author of *The Which? Wine Guide 2003*, winner of the prestigious Le Prix du Champagne Lanson 2003 Award for Annual Wine Guide of the Year.

The Which?
Wine Guide
2005

Susan Keevil

Which? Books are commissioned by
Consumers' Association and published by
Which? Ltd, 2 Marylebone Road, London NW1 4DF
Email: books@which.net

Distributed by The Penguin Group:
Penguin Books Ltd, 80 Strand, London WC2R 0RL

First edition 1981
This edition October 2004

British Library Cataloguing in Publication Data
A catalogue record for *The Which? Wine Guide 2005* is available from the British Library

ISBN 0 85202 982 9

For a full list of Which? books, please call 0800 252100, access our website at
www.which.net, or write to Which? Books, Freepost, PO Box 44, Hertford SG14 1SH

Senior contributing writers: Susy Atkins, Bill Evans

Additional contributors: Christine Austin, Dave Broom, Tom Cannavan, Rosalind Cooper,
David Furer, Jamie Goode, Natasha Hughes, Rowena Medlow, Michael Palij MW,
Maggie Rosen

Editorial and production: Lynn Bresler, Joanna Bregosz, Alethea Doran, Nithya Rae,
Mary Sunderland, Barbara Toft

Cover design by Price Watkins
Cover photograph by James Duncan

Typeset by Saxon Graphics Ltd, Derby
Printed and bound in Spain by Bookprint, S.L. Barcelona

The Which? Wine Guide voucher scheme
The Which? Wine Guide includes three £5 vouchers that readers can redeem against
a £50 wine purchase at participating merchants (look for the **£5** symbol in the
merchant reviews). Only one voucher may be used against a wine purchase of £50 or
more. Remember that your intention to use a voucher MUST be mentioned at the time
of buying. The vouchers may not be used in conjunction with any other discount, offer
or promotional scheme. Actual vouchers (not photocopies) must be presented. The
vouchers will be valid from 30 October 2004 to 30 October 2005.

Contents

Using the *Guide*
The 'Best wine-producing countries' section includes recommendations of top red and white wines. These are lists of readily available wines sourced from both expensive and more affordable price brackets, in order to represent the best of each region's wines. The wines listed in 'Simply the best', on pages 15 and 16, are perceived as some of the best in the world.

The prices given for the top red and white wines in 'Best wine-producing countries' are approximate and are intended to give only an indication of their cost: bear in mind that prices may vary from one retailer to another.

Introduction

Welcome to this year's all-new *Which? Wine Guide*. In this edition the *Guide* has adopted a radically different, at-a-glance style – to make the task of finding a great wine, or a new one, quicker and easier than ever. The country-by-country section brings you all the pertinent details from the world's wine regions, and highlights the best bottles to buy – as well as the stockists at which to buy them. It identifies which wine styles to avoid and which to embrace, and flags up any new and interesting wine enclaves to watch out for. The 'Where to buy wine' section has been refined still further this year, homing in on the top 150 outlets in the UK, now grouped by region. Our merchant reviews bring in even more useful information than before, including our selected Best Buys from each retailer. We hope you find them helpful.

The *Guide* has also been expanded to include the UK's best pubs and restaurants for wine. There's no reason why great wine discoveries should all be made at home, and – owing to the ever-increasing popularity of wine in this country – pubs and restaurants are taking their wine lists much more seriously these days. Good news indeed.

Believe it or not, we are consuming a massive 19.6 litres of wine per head each year in the UK – that's not quite as much as the French or Italians (56 and 51 litres apiece), but significantly more than the Americans (8.8 litres), and an increase of nearly three litres per head since 2000. Of this vast quantity, an ever-increasing proportion is red and sparkling wine, as well as – surprisingly – a growing amount of rosé. Plus, we Brits are showing more interest than ever in the wines of Spain, Italy and France. Rosé? Spain? Italy? Sound like a trip back to the seventies? Maybe it is, but fashions have a way of returning. And be assured that the quality of today's wines is distinctly better than it was 40 years ago …

Sub-£5 wallet-pleaser wines have got to go

… Better, that is, until you delve into some of the lower price ranges. With the steady upward tug of inflation, wine prices are slowly rising, and there are far fewer sub-£5 wines evident on wine merchants' lists than there used to be. Supermarkets and other retailers who ship their wines direct (SH Jones, for example – see page 157) tend to stock a number of different options, but in general under-£5 is becoming an increasingly difficult price point for producers to hit. Given the cost of a bottle, the cork, the label, the advertising and the marketing, on top of which is the UK tax (see page 20), it's a very small fraction of five pounds that actually goes on the wine itself.

What we at the *Guide* find disturbing is that many supermarkets are still asking growers to slash their prices below this level. Marks & Spencer reputedly asked its suppliers to take a 1.25 per cent price cut in 2004. Even making bulk quantities of wine (on the scale of Australia's Oxford Landing, say) will incur costs, and for every penny that big-muscle buyers such as M&S want to save, a corner must be cut in the winery somewhere. The resulting wine will taste worse.

So, the next time you buy a bargain sub-£5 cheapie, consider your purchase carefully. By making that choice, you may be encouraging a grower to accept yet another batch of sub-standard fruit, or helping a supermarket to stifle another quality check or stamp a quirky grape blend out of existence.

Big brands *versus* supermarket own-labels

If bargain-hunting is your thing, then the two main options open to you are big-name brands (the likes of Piat d'Or, Blossom Hill, Banrock Station or Kumala –

wines that are usually blended from a variety of regions to a specific flavour formula, with plenty of big-company money behind them) or own-label wines (sourced, say, by a supermarket from wherever it can buy most cheaply and plentifully).

John McLaren at Wines of California (the state is one of the biggest brand exporters to the UK) says that the more dependable of the two choices is the brand. 'For a start, the styles are becoming much more UK-orientated. Gallo Turning Leaf is far less sweet than it was, and the wine is attuned to the British palate. For supermarket own-labels, the buyers are much more pragmatic; they'll buy whichever wine is the cheapest for their generic Chardonnay or Merlot – and that often means sweeter local styles.'

Rumour has it that some of the big brand wines are refusing to accept supermarket price reductions, and are investing money back into their wines – *Harpers* magazine suggests that Oxford Landing, Jacob's Creek and Turning Leaf are the good guys in this regard. In the pages of this *Guide* you'll repeatedly find us bemoaning the dull uniformity of branded wines (by which we mean both own-label and bulk brands) – but where big companies make an effort to boost quality in this way, we can't complain.

GM: Great Management or Grape Messing?

Producers and consumers are showing an increasing interest in holistic winemaking methods – be they organic, biodynamic or GM-free. Growers in Mendocino (California's northernmost wine region) led the way recently by signing a pledge to keep their zone free of genetically modified vines – see page 108. It looks very likely that higher-profile Sonoma County and all its famous sub-regions will follow. On the face of it, this is a very good thing. We at the *Guide* think that the wine in our glasses should be as natural as possible a reflection of the landscape from which it hails.

But those who support GM would argue that new biotechnological methods can be used to prevent the effects of devastating diseases such as fan-leaf virus (which can stop a vine producing leaves and grapes) and Pierce's Disease (which attacks a vine's vascular system and effectively starves it to death). The latter has been known to wipe out whole wine regions. Fair point.

Be that as it may, growers in France have been up in arms recently to protest about the planting of trial vines in Alsace. They are worried about the contamination (through cross-pollination) of neighbouring 'normal' vines, and thereafter the ruin of years of clonal selection and vine evolution to generate the fine flavours we taste in these traditional wines today. The likes of Anne-Claude Leflaive (Domaine Leflaive, Puligny-Montrachet, Burgundy) and Aubert de Villaine (Domaine de la Romanée-Conti) have called for the government to halt all GM trials in order to preserve French wine at its finest, as it is. Only time will tell which is the best way forward.

Appellation shake-up

The French have been enraged by both proposed and actual changes to their wine laws this year. The *crus bourgeois* of Bordeaux have been given what many would argue was a much-needed weeding out, with furious consequences (see page 56), and there is to be a new level of excellence awarded to the country's finest vineyard enclaves, entitled the AOCE (see 'Does wine need rules?', page 10).

Depending on your point of view, these changes represent either an esoteric fuss about nothing or a sound move towards ensuring that a wine 'does exactly what it says on the tin'. Traditionalists (the *Guide* among them) believe that consumers should be able to have confidence in regional wine styles. If a wine says Burgundy, it should taste like Burgundy, and not like anything from cold tea to cherryish mouthwash. In other words, we should be able to have a good idea of the kind of flavours we'll find in a glass. The appellation guide on pages 33 to 34 gives some indication of wine styles that are typical of European regions.

The news on the street

The *Guide*'s merchant reviews this year (see the 'Where to buy wine' section) reveal a number of new findings, some of them surprising.

From their favoured countries this year (France, Spain and Italy), UK wine consumers are buying more wine from the Languedoc, Sicily and quirky Spanish regions such as Costers del Segre, Utiel-Requena and Somontano. In terms of style, 'in' are meaty Syrahs (from anywhere in the world), thirst-quenching (but gutsy) rosé, and Riesling – while Chardonnay and sherry are still out.

Australia is as popular as ever, and at long last the *Guide*'s rant about wine regions is being heeded. Consumers are beginning to take an interest in the differences between a McLaren Vale or Barossa Shiraz, and learning to compare Hunter Valley with Margaret River Semillon. Australia is one of the places in which Riesling fever is really taking hold – so that country is no longer just about Chardonnay, thank goodness. California is another matter: we're seeing more California wines than ever before in the UK, but many of them, unfortunately, are bargain brands rather than the wines that really show this state's winemaking colours.

Wines from the classic regions (Bordeaux, Burgundy, Tuscany and Rioja) continue to find favour in all their varied forms and vintages. But German wines and cheap gluggers from Eastern Europe are still right at the bottom of the pile. The profile of German wines may be inching upwards (see page 82), but the news clearly hasn't spread very far yet. And East European wines have a long way to go before regaining their 1980s good-value, juicy-fruited fame.

The world's best bargain wines now come instead from Portugal and southern Italy, where there is a wealth of oddly named grape varieties with rich, heart-warming intensity and highly individual flavours to discover. Greece has a similarly quirky array to choose from, particularly from the sensational 2003 vintage. See page 85 for a breakdown of the best Greek grape styles.

New 'icon' (top-of-the-range) wines causing a stir on the wine-show circuits (and among the media), while usually at the opposite price extreme, are offering good value from parts of South Africa, for example, where there are a great many new-wave producers awaiting international discovery. Their Cape Blends (based on Cabernet Sauvignon, Merlot, Pinotage and even Syrah grapes) are likely to be the big sensations of 2005. New prestige wines from Chile are expensive, but nonetheless remarkable for their concentration and rich fruit (see page 47) – proving that this country isn't just home to cheap and cheerful Merlot.

In short, there's still a lot out there to surprise us.

And finally …

If you find any further vinous surprises that you'd like to let us know about, please do not hesitate to get in touch. We value any feedback you can provide – and we'd especially like to hear your views on the merchants we list (and those we don't). Do they offer the kind of service and the kind of wines you'd expect? Do write (our address is on page 4), or you can email us your comments at books@which.net. We look forward to hearing from you.

Does wine need rules?

Susan Keevil questions the proposed new quality regulations for French wine, and asks if they will genuinely improve the calibre of wine on our shop shelves.

In 2005 we should be asking, 'Are rules and regulations any good for wine?'. The French are leading a drive back to the rule book with a proposed new appellation hierarchy designed to increase the stature of their best wines worldwide. The Spanish carried out a similar restructure in 2003. And the Italians introduced a new law in 1992 that attempted to bring order to an otherwise chaotic set of wines.

So are these appellation laws any use, or do they just complicate an already tricky subject? (See the chapters on France, Italy and Spain for an explanation of the appellation hierarchies in these countries.) Surely these classic wine-producing countries, with all their complex regional subdivisions, are confusing enough already – without all the laws governing wine style and quality that go with appellation status? Are these extra quality distinctions really going to help?

New-Worlders would argue, perhaps, that the wine world is better categorised by major grape variety. This would carve our wine shelves and lists into, say, eight simple-to-understand flavour sections – starting with Chardonnay and Cabernet Sauvignon and ending with Zinfandel. Easy enough. Some supermarkets do this already. But surely we'd still want to know how fat-and-buttery or flinty-and-dry our Chardonnay was going to be. Or how elegant or cassis-rich our Pinot Noir. Appellations can provide pointers to these essential distinctions. And if there is no way of knowing how good or bad a producer is, then surely some pre-assigned quality mark would be useful? This is where well-defined wine regions (rules) and quality accolades (regulations) come into play.

New French proposals

In addition to their existing countrywide system (see Glossary, page 241) the French are proposing a higher-quality category to help consumers decide on the wine they are choosing. AOCE, or *appellation d'origine contrôlée d'excellence*, will represent wines made from lower-yielding vines (which give more concentrated, better-quality fruit), and will call for more rigorous controls in the vineyard and winery. It is expected that these new reforms will be in place by the end of 2005. Wines awarded this category will reinforce the French notion of *terroir* – in which a wine is the perfect summation of the soil, geology, microclimate and human tradition that created it. *Terroir* wines don't just come from France; other parts of Europe and some New World growers also cultivate them. Their hallmark is that they offer unique flavours that reflect their own part of the landscape. The AOCE will – the authorities hope – present the country's *terroir* wines as a perfect set.

In reality, the French authority (the INAO – Institut National des Appellations d'Origine) is also making this change in order to boost its declining image. With a market share dropping rapidly in the face of competition – juicy-fruited, reliable wines from Australia, California, South Africa and Chile – the French now realise something must be done or they will be toppled from their position as leaders of the wine world, their Gallic noses severely out of joint. The AOCE level is intended to restore confidence, particularly at the quality end of the spectrum.

However, many producers don't like it. Growers are worried about Parisian bureaucrats and theoretical viticulturalists traipsing their land and passing judgement. Patrick Le Brun of the Syndicat Général des Vignerons de la

Champagne (representing Champagne's growers) claimed in *Harpers* magazine that it will spell disaster for his region within five years. Gonzague Lurton of the Syndicat de Margaux in Bordeaux has similar qualms about the extra rules and regulations and is dubious about whether individual appellations will be able to propose their own AOCE boundaries without INAO interference (*Wine* magazine, July 2004). Things could get heated. The French generally have no hang-ups about venting their feelings when they don't like something: witness the Languedoc producers who burnt down warehouses in protest against the enforced distillation of surplus wine in 2001.

The AOCE is an opportunity for growers to strive for further quality. Those that make good wines already won't have to worry, they'll be included in the glittering AOCE set. For others, there'll be a chance to prove themselves without having to resort to adopting a lower-status label (*vins de pays*) for attention-grabbing grape experiments. And it's also an opportunity for consumers to see the best wines clearly when these have been creamed off from the rest.

And if the AOCE genuinely represents better wines, then those four small letters on a bottle will be a tremendous help to all wine buyers. At the moment, the AOC wines are of such varied quality that they are no longer completely trusted: a good producer name is the only real guarantee of a good wine. As long as new AOCE rules are adhered to by selected growers (who, it is proposed, will be chosen by existing local committees) then their wines should present a new, trustworthy way to explore French regions.

The Italian job

The French should be warned by what happened in Italy. When the Italians introduced their similar DOCG law in 1963, they made two big mistakes. Firstly, this was to be a quality category with an extra level of excellence, one level above DOC, very much like the proposed French AOCE. But instead of being a reward for the best wines, it was awarded as a 'carrot' for wines with potential (rather than actual) quality. Secondly, it is alleged that certain unremarkable wines such as white Albana de Romagna were given the new super-gong because certain growers had close links with the right ministry. The result was patchy performance among the new DOCG set and it therefore became a system that consumers could not trust. In many regions these problems have been ironed out, but there still remain vestiges of doubt about the DOCG system.

The Italians had a better idea in 1992 when they introduced a new appellation (IGT) for regional wines that allowed growers to experiment with different grape varieties. It generated space for the illustrious and innovative new 'Super-Tuscan' wines without their producers having to call the results lowly *vini da tavola* (table wine), and its clarity meant that Joe-wine-consumer was left in no doubt as to which were the traditional regional wines, and which the new 'quality' set.

Spanish flair

The Spanish also have a similar system to AOCE in place: DOCa (*denominación de origen calificada*) was set up, in 1991, as Spain's highest wine category – featuring Rioja. And more recent categories have been introduced to accommodate basic wines clamouring for promotion, appellation wines aiming for quality, and estates with high standards that are not already covered by the existing system. These changes have been made so that the consumer doesn't have to know every page of a wine's history – nor whether every individual producer is good or bad. Instead, a quick glance at the bottle should reveal the quality of wine to be expected.

What the merchants think

The UK trade (never short of an opinion) is dubious about introducing new rules. Michael Palij MW, Italian wine importer, compared the proposed AOCE law with one of London's latest parking rules. 'First there was a single yellow line along the road and people ignored it; they still parked there. Then they painted a double yellow line, with not much more effect. Today they have double red lines, and so it goes on. You can keep on drawing lines but at some point you've got to say, The wine is good!'. Introduce too many rules and people will ignore them and come right back to the producer: find a good one and you know for sure that you'll get a good wine.'

Others think there are better ways to increase the world profile of the European countries than bureaucratic tweaking. Simon Field MW of Berry Brothers & Rudd commented: 'Settling in a new regulation is a lengthy process. Loss of market share needs to be addressed in rather more simplistic terms – at brand level, for example – rather than trying to complicate things with an extra level of hierarchy.' David Roberts MW of Lay & Wheeler has a similar opinion: 'The AOCE won't grab attention back from the New World because nothing beats New World simplicity; France should be like the New World and keep things simple too.'

Old World red tape *versus* New World simplicity

New laws such as the AOCE aren't so much a problem in themselves, it's their application that creates trouble. Ideally, after new regulations are set down, the judges should take a long holiday (say, to the Australian Outback for a few years) while the dust back home settles and their new rules kick in unimpeded. Unfortunately, life's not so simple. The complaints and repercussions that arise tend to mean that things fall apart. The bitterly contended reclassification of the Médoc's *crus bourgeois* (see page 56) is a case in point.

So are the New World countries any better off? In California, there's a sound system of AVAs (American Viticultural Areas) in place – but these govern only regional parameters, not wine style or quality. In setting simple (perhaps too simple) boundaries like this there's much less backlash from the growers, but the consumer is, at the end of the day, no further forward. He or she doesn't glean any further information about what the contents of that bottle are going to taste like.

The Australians took things a step further and set up appellation boundaries (governing a smaller, more geologically specific region than AVAs) around the precious red-earth *terroir* of Coonawarra, but there were disputes aplenty. The arguments were taken on board and, in 2002, the boundaries of Coonawarra were widened. So do we now trust the wines from this area to be true reflections of their origins? The honest answer is that, because of all the contention and changes of mind, consumers just aren't sure any more.

Generally, in the New World the best guidelines are producer or price (this book offers tips on the best to look out for). Simple grape variety definitions are not enough on their own. To really have a clear idea of the style of wine you'll be getting, appellations set good guidelines, even if hitches can arise in setting up new systems. A brief outline of the main appellations and their styles is given on pages 33 to 34.

So hats off to the French. The new AOCE might be inciting much anguished speculation – but if, at the end of the day, what we get in the bottle is a more reliable, more flavourful, more easy-to-predict wine, then the struggle has to be worth it.

Wine tastings for *Which?* magazine

Which? magazine – published, as is this Guide, *by Consumers' Association – has been running wine-tasting reports for several years. Susy Atkins, who has weathered* Which? *tasting panels for years and written many of the magazine articles, tells us how they work – and why they are essential reading for wine drinkers.*

In a perfect world, we would all get to taste every wine there is and pick our favourites before buying. There would be no excuse for staying stuck in a rut, buying the same old brand and/or grape varieties, and everyone would be able to drink new, exciting styles with confidence.

Of course, life isn't quite like that. This *Guide* will help you branch out and hunt down the star buys, just as *Which?* magazine does; however, precious little wine advice elsewhere is impartial and independent.

Many voices not one

A lot of people rely on recommendations in the press before trying a specific new bottle. But it's important to realise that wine columns in magazines and newspapers are based on a personal view. If the individual wine critic has quite different tastes from you, then he or she could recommend something you won't like.

This is why panel tastings are important. The wines recommended in *Which?* reports come from a wide-ranging group of experts, not an individual (with a perhaps idiosyncratic palate). We publish their consensus views to provide a unique insight into the most interesting, flavoursome and good-value wines.

Choosing a topic

So how do we do it? Each quarter, *Which?* picks a topic that our research tells us readers are interested in. Subjects include regions/countries (southern French reds or Italian whites, for example) and styles (sparkling wines or dessert wines, say). Often we focus on bottles within a certain price limit or compare wines at different cost levels.

Real-life bottles

Next we approach the major retailers and ask for nominations from their lists. We pick around 25 of these wines and buy as many as we can, anonymously and direct from the shop shelves. This last point is crucial and marks *Which?* panel tastings out from others. Other tastings (and individual columnists) almost always rely on wine samples that come direct from the retailer, importer or a public relations department. These bottles are usually stored in perfect conditions, as opposed to the situation in shops (where bottles are stacked upright, exposed to heat and light), and so their contents may well differ from the average high-street buy. Only by buying from the same shelves as the shopper, and not making any special payments, can we be sure to test wine that is in a similar state to the condition in which consumers are likely find it.

Rating the wines

Once they arrive, the wines are tested under the same strict conditions as other products at *Which?*. They are put before a panel of up to eight professional, independent wine tasters. We usually have at least one Master of Wine (MW) on the panel.

The wines are tasted 'blind' – the labels are covered up. The judges know the subject of the tasting and the price brackets, but nothing else. After sampling the candidates, each judge gives a mark for each wine and the average marks are calculated to provide overall rankings. Our famous 'Best Buys' are those wines most highly rated.

As well as giving a mark, our expert tasters write a clear, concise tasting note for each wine, and also give their general impression of the whole selection – whether they are good value or disappointing, as well as capturing any notable qualities, quirks or faults. The panel also compares the set of wines tasted with similar styles and price points around the world – for example, how did the southern French reds under £7 measure up, in its view, to close contenders from Spain, Australia or Chile?

Wine winners and losers revealed by *Which?*

Using the methods described, *Which?* has come up with some exciting, illuminating and occasionally controversial results.

- The September 1999 issue tested 39 widely available clarets (red Bordeaux) costing under £10. The panel was highly critical of the wines overall, and found only a few to recommend, with just one wine (priced at nearly £8) drawing much praise. This tasting confirmed the views of many at the time – that Bordeaux was performing poorly at the inexpensive end of the market.
- A December 2002 *Which?* champagne report received much national press coverage after revealing that a Tesco own-label champagne had beaten many top names. This was a compelling result, but perhaps not as surprising as some thought it to be. Own-label supermarket champagnes are supplied by major players who create the more famous brands locally, and are made under strict regulations. Why shouldn't an inexpensive champagne come up trumps? One reporter for a national newspaper suggested that *Which?* had been 'in bed' with Tesco over the results. In fact Tesco had no knowledge of the results until publication of that issue.
- When the same champagne was pitted against UK sparklers in June 2004 (it was included as a 'rogue' bottle among a group of English still and sparkling whites), interestingly several of the home-grown wines came out better – although the Tesco bottle's style could have changed in the 18 months between reports. The top wine was found to be Nyetimber Classic Cuvée 1996 for £19, an encouragingly positive result for England's bubbly (if not the still wines).
- The June 2003 issue braved a contentious subject in the wine industry when the panel compared bottles with screwcaps versus those with natural corks. The wines in the two groups were similar (same styles, same countries, same price points) except in their closure method. Although no earth-shattering differences emerged in the reds, interestingly the screwcapped whites were considered 'fresher, more characterful' and 'more vibrant' than those under cork. So our conclusions were that, if there's a style of dry white you like bottled under cork, it's likely to be more reliable with a screwcap.

Pushing the wine frontiers further

At the time of writing, the next panel tasting is imminent (Chilean whites under £7). Will this produce a plethora of Best Buys and a general thumbs-up, or will we find holes to pick instead? It remains to be seen – as do the results of a red Rioja tasting, a rosé tasting and a Burgundy report, all taking place over the next 12 months. Don't miss them!

To take out a subscription to *Which?* magazine, write to PO Box 44, Hertford X, SG14 1SH or call (0845) 307 4000. You can also check out the website at *www.which.co.uk* or email which@which.net

Simply the best

Everyone loves superlatives – especially those just dipping into a subject, or without much time on their hands. The following wines are some of the best in their field: worthy benchmarks for people who want to know how good wine can really be. A word of warning though – not all of them come cheap.

Chardonnay

Jean-Marie Raveneau, Chablis (Burgundy)
Bonneau du Martray, Corton-Charlemagne (Burgundy)
Leflaive, Puligny-Montrachet (Burgundy)
Comtes Lafon, Meursault (Burgundy)
Ramonet, Chassagne-Montrachet (Burgundy)
Penfold's, Yattarna (Australia)
Petaluma, Tier's Chardonnay (Australia)
Pierro, Margaret River Chardonnay (Australia)
Helen Turley, Marcassin (California)
Flowers, Sonoma Coast Chardonnay (California)

Sauvignon Blanc

Château Margaux, Pavilon Blanc (Bordeaux)
Château Smith-Haut-Lafitte, Blanc (Bordeaux)
Didier Dagueneau, Pur Sang Pouilly-Fumé (Loire Valley)
Vacheron, Sancerre (Loire Valley)
Palliser Estate, Martinborough Sauvignon Blanc (New Zealand)
Wairau River, Martinborough Sauvignon Blanc (New Zealand)
Tement, Styria Sauvignon Blanc (Austria)
Shaw & Smith, Adelaide Hills Sauvignon Blanc (Australia)
Mondavi, Tokalon Sauvignon Blanc (California)
Iona, Elgin Sauvignon Blanc (South Africa)

Riesling

Grosset, Clare Valley Riesling (Australia)
Petaluma, Clare Valley Riesling (Australia)
Henschke, Eden Valley Riesling (Australia)
Domaine Weinbach, Riesling (Alsace)
Hugel, Riesling (Alsace)
Weingut Bründlmayer, Kamptal Riesling (Austria)
F X Pichler, Wachau Riesling (Austria)
Maximin Grünhaus, Abtsberg Riesling Auslese, Ruwer (Germany)
Heymann-Löwenstein, Schieferterrassen dry Mosel Riesling (Germany)
Robert Weil, Gräfenberg Riesling, Rheingau (Germany)

Cabernet Sauvignon

Château Mouton-Rothschild, Pauillac (Bordeaux)
Château Cos d'Estournel, St-Estèphe (Bordeaux)
Château Léoville Las Cases, St-Julien (Bordeaux)
Château Haut-Brion, Pessac-Léognan (Bordeaux)
Château Palmer, Margaux (Bordeaux)
Stag's Leap Vineyards, Cask 23, Cabernet Sauvignon (California)
Robert Mondavi, Oakville District, Cabernet Sauvignon (California)
Cullen, Diana Madelaine, Cabernet Sauvignon (Australia)
Balnaves, The Tally, Cabernet Sauvignon (Australia)
Andrew Will, Cabernet Sauvignon (Washington)

Syrah/Shiraz

Penfold's Grange (Australia)
Henschke, Hill of Grace (Australia)
Peter Lehmann, Stonewell Shiraz, Barossa (Australia)
Veritas, Heysen Shiraz, Barossa (Australia)
Chapoutier, Hermitage (Rhône Valley)
Jaboulet Aîné, Hermitage La Chapelle (Rhône Valley)
Guigal, Côte-Rôtie (Rhône Valley)
Auguste Clape, Cornas (Rhône Valley)
Cayuse Winery, Walla Walla Syrah (Washington)
Montes Folly Syrah (Chile)

Pinot Noir

Anne, Gros'Vosne-Romanée (Burgundy)
Domaine de la Romanée-Conti, La Tâche (Burgundy)
Domaine Meo-Camuzet, Richebourg (Burgundy)
De Vogüé, Chambolle-Musigny (Burgundy)
Flowers Estate, Sonoma Pinot Noir (California)
Hanzell, Sonoma Pinot Noir (California)
Williams-Selyem, Russian River Pinot Noir (California)
Felton Road, Central Otago Pinot Noir (New Zealand)
Rippon Vineyard, Central Otago Pinot Noir (New Zealand)
Amity Pinot Noir (Oregon)

Merlot

Château Pétrus, Pomerol (Bordeaux)

Le Pin, Pomerol (Bordeaux)

Château Trotanoy, Pomerol (Bordeaux)

Château Lafleur, Pomerol (Bordeaux)

Casa Lapostolle, Clos Apalta Merlot (Chile)

Viña Carmen, Maipo Merlot (Chile)

Clos du Val, Napa Merlot (California)

Shafer, Stag's Leap District Merlot (California)

Hedges, Red Mountain Reserve (Washington)

Sileni, Hawke's Bay Merlot-Cabernet (NZ)

Quirky red wines

LA Cetto, Nebbiolo (Mexico)

Celliers de Meknès, Cabernet Sauvignon (Morocco)

Château La Roque, Pic St-Loup Mourvèdre (Languedoc)

Château Pech Redon, Carignan (Languedoc)

Domaine Ilarria, Irouléguy (South-west France)

Wines from the Nielluccio grape variety (Corsica)

Salice Salentino, Negroamaro Candido (Italy)

La Agricola, Mendoza Tempranillo (Argentina)

Gaia Winery, Notios Aghiorghitiko (Greece)

Kyr-Yianni, Ramnista Xinomavro (Greece)

Quirky white wines

Terredora, Fiano di Avellino (Italy)

Tenuta Capichera, Vermentino (Italy)

Domaine de l'Hortus, Pic St-Loup (Languedoc)

Domaine du Bellegarde, Jurançon (South-west France)

Boucassé, Pacherenc de Vic Bilh Moelleux (SW France)

Henschke, Eden Valley Pinot Gris (Australia)

F X Pichler, Wachau Grüner Veltliner (Austria)

Camel Valley Vineyard, Bacchus QW (England)

Sigalas, Assyrtico (Greece)

Tselepos, Moscofilero (Greece)

Rosé wines

Domaine Maby, Tavel Rosé (Rhône Valley)

André Méjan, Lirac Rosé (Rhône Valley)

Château Simone, Rosé (Provence)

Domaine Sauveroy, Anjou Rosé (Loire)

Marqués de Cáceres Rosé, Rioja (Spain)

Martinez-Bujanda Rosado, Rioja (Spain)

Valley Vineyards, Heritage Rosé NV (England)

Stella Bella, Margaret River Pink Muscat (Australia)

Charles Melton, Rose of Virginia Grenache Rosé (Australia)

Cantina Sociale di Santadi, Carignano del Sulcis (Italy)

Sweet wine

Château d'Yquem, Sauternes (Bordeaux)

Château Rieussec, Sauternes (Bordeaux)

Château de Fesles, Bonnezeaux (Loire Valley)

Royal Tokaji Wine Company, 6 Puttonyos Tokaji (Hungary)

Max Ferd Richter, Mosel Eiswein (Germany)

Paulinshof, Mosel Beerenauslesen (Germany)

Mount Horrocks, Cordon Cut sweet Riesling (Australia)

Campbell, Rutherglen Muscat (Australia)

González-Byass, Matusalem sweet oloroso sherry (Spain)

Mission Hill Icewine (Canada)

Sparkling wine

Krug, Grande Cuvée champagne

Dom Pérignon champagne

Louis Roederer Cristal champagne

Salon, Blanc de Blancs champagne

Veuve Clicquot, La Grande Dame champagne

Billecart-Salmon, Rosé champagne

Nyetimber, Classic Cuvée Brut (England)

Roederer Estate, Quartet sparkling wine (California)

Piper's Brook, Pirie sparkling wine (Australia)

Seppelt, sparkling Shiraz (Australia)

Vintages

2002 (Burgundy)

2001 (Rioja)

2000 (Bordeaux, Rhône Valley and Port)

1999 (Northern Rhône)

1997 (Italy)

1996 (Burgundy)

1994 (California and Port)

1993 (Tokaji and Champagne)

1988 (Champagne)

1982 (Bordeaux)

Wine regions to visit

Paarl and Stellenbosch (South Africa)

Saint-Emilion (Bordeaux)

Napa Valley (California)

Barossa Valley (Australia)

Margaret River (Australia)

Alsace (France)

Tuscany (Italy)

Jerez (Spain)

Cafayate and Salta (Argentina)

Champagne (France)

The Which? Wine Guide Awards for 2005

Choosing award winners was harder than ever this year. The UK's merchants are gaining so much confidence in their customers' willingness to experiment that they're happily stocking up wines of ever-increasing quality and complexity for them to try – and from a broader range of wine regions than ever before.

In particular they are now sourcing more bottles from Italy, southern France and Spain, where quality and excitement are increasing. Many of them have combined these European explorations with enthusiastic efforts to look deeper into Australia and California, seeking out wines from the regions as well as the main grape varieties. All these positive developments add diversity and breadth to the wines available on the shop shelves, and mean that there are many worthy contenders for the *Guide's* accolades.

The better supermarkets and high-street merchants in particular deserve praise for stocking these new-wave bottlings, as with an easy tide of customers to buy their wines, not all of the major outlets go to the trouble of seeking out something new. Supermarkets especially can be woefully unadventurous in their choices, and some culprit stores have been delisted from this edition of the *Guide*.

While wine should be regionally focused and flavoursome, it does not have to be expensive. This year we have introduced a new award for the merchant providing the best value in its wines – that is, quality and character at a price affordable for everyone.

Best Supermarket
Waitrose
Still by far the best range of supermarket wines in the country, proving that quality and good value can go hand in hand. Only Booth's comes remotely close.

Best High-Street Chain
Majestic Wine Warehouses
Majestic manages to balance upbeat New World wines with plenty of Old World classics (Bordeaux and champagne aplenty). The adventurously chosen, well-priced wines, together with the cheery in-store atmosphere, are bound to appeal.

Best Mail-Order Merchant
The Wine Society
With wines spanning all prices, styles and regions – from the most glamorous to the most obscure – it's a mystery how The Wine Society can deliver so many good bottles to so many customers. Choices are better than ever this year.

Most Innovative Wine Merchant
Noel Young Wines
It's not just the range of wines that is so special at Noel Young but the passion with which they're chosen. New World wines are selected with native insight, and unusual wine treasures celebrated with scant regard for fashion and rave reviews – only vibrancy of flavour.

Best-Value Wine Merchant
S H Jones

new award

Few merchants can take in such adventurous and interesting wines as S H Jones manages while keeping prices right down. Sub-£5 wines are common here, and far from dull. Even the Bordeaux section is home to bargains, with a stunning choice of second wines from the top châteaux.

Bordeaux Specialist
Bordeaux Index
As suppliers of Bordeaux in all its guises – from venerable old vintages to *en primeur* wines, and clarets from the most prestigious properties – Bordeaux Index offers an all-round service and plenty of guidance for consumers unsure of this illustrious ground.

Burgundy Specialist
Howard Ripley
However you wish to approach the complex subject of Burgundy, Howard Ripley knows how to assist. From small-scale growers to out-and-out stars, from grand vintages to lesser-known bargains, all the best wines are listed.

Rhône Specialist
Berry Bros & Rudd
The finest growers, vintages and appellations are under this merchant's roof, and it has an eye for up-and-coming new Rhône regions too, such as Vacqueyras and Cairanne. BB&R not only succeeds in spanning the styles, but also keeps the prices down.

German Specialist
Fortnum & Mason
The range and class of wines on offer at Fortnums is as impressive as ever, and the fine German selection is proof that quality matters here more than fashion.

Italian Specialist
Valvona & Crolla
With far and away the most exciting Italian list this year,

Valvona & Crolla takes on Italy's complex set of wines with a passion and exuberance that's both infectious and entirely fitting.

Spanish Specialist
The Halifax Wine Company
The Halifax Wine Company offers one of the broadest, most interesting wine lists in the country, and Spanish wines are covered with rare panache – no other merchant comes close. Classic Riojas and new-wave reds are all here.

New World Specialist
Vin du Van Wine Merchants
A virtually unmatched selection of Australian wines from this merchant demonstrates just how good the New World can be. This is more than glug-wine territory. Vin du Van's eccentric approach (and zany tasting notes) make choosing Aussie wine a crazy but completely pleasurable experience.

Fine Wine Specialist
Corney & Barrow
In terms of absolute quality, C&B's range can't be faulted. Whichever region its wines come from, the selection is peerless, with the finest ranges of all from Bordeaux and Burgundy.

Organic Wine Specialist
Vinceremos Wines & Spirits
Offering an increasingly wide choice from around the world, the organic and biodynamic wines on Vinceremos' list have shown dramatic quality improvements in the last two years. Value for money is as good as ever.

The basics

This section is designed to provide you with the essential tools for looking beyond special offers and trusty standbys, so you can explore the world of wine more fully. It will equip you with the basic know-how for choosing, buying, serving and slurping. You can flesh out your knowledge by reading about individual regions in the 'Best wine-producing countries' section.

Buying wine

Which wine to choose?

Knowledge is power. By the time you have read this book you will be equipped to survey the shelves of any supermarket or wine shop with a sharp eye for quality and value, and a good idea of what's corked up inside each bottle. But even before you know much about the way different grapes taste or the style of wine associated with a particular region – let alone the reputations of individual producers – you can determine the type of wine you're after. You will then be able to frame questions for wine merchants so they can point you in the right direction.

First, home in on what role you want the wine to fulfil. Is it something special for a romantic dinner, or to gulp down with a pizza in front of the TV? Do you want to take your taste buds on a journey into uncharted flavour territory? Are you hoping to match a particular food? Are you looking for something to lay down for a few years? How much are you happy to spend?

You also need to decide what sort of taste you are after. In terms of general style and flavour, the region and/or grape variety named on the label give plenty of clues. To learn more about grape varieties, see page 29 and the regional guides in the 'Best wine-producing countries' section. 'Appellations at a glance' on pages 33–34 gives you a key to what lies behind the names on French, Italian and Spanish labels.

Look also at the back label, if there is one. Charming stories and marketing hype don't explain much but many back labels give a fair idea of the flavour and some clues about how the wine was made. In moderation, oak treatment – whether the wine is barrel-fermented, matured in barrels or simply doused with oak chips (for which 'subtle oak integration' is the normal euphemism) – gives a rounder, softer character and adds vanilla and (in whites) butterscotch flavours. Any mention of modern techniques and temperature control suggests that the style is all about freshness, with an emphasis on

fruit. Lees stirring (or *bâtonnage*) is currently very fashionable for smart whites, and gives a rich, creamy texture. A long lecture on *terroir* may point to minerally complexity in the flavour. Hand-picking is generally a sign of quality, as is night- or dawn-harvesting in hot regions.

Certain objective measures of quality do exist. At the most basic level, the wine should taste clean and be free of faults (see page 26). The clarity and intensity of the flavour and the texture, balance and length are important; wine buffs also set store by less readily definable notions of complexity, individuality and integrity.

When it comes to ensuring high standards, the most important factor is the producer. Official quality categories like AC and DOC, fancy names and 'reserve' labels, well-known grape varieties and prestigious regions all count for nothing if the producer that made the wine is not dedicated to excellence. The 'Best wine-producing countries' section of this book is bursting with recommendations; look out also for reviews in the press or take advice from a merchant you trust. You can also glean much useful information on the Web – see page 248.

How much to pay

The most important factor is how much the wine appeals to you – there's no point in splashing out on a £50 bottle if you're not going to enjoy it. There is no magic price point at which 'good wine' starts. Budget bottles can be excellent value and expensive ones absolutely rotten.

Under £3 very little of what you pay goes on the wine itself: mostly you are covering the cost of the bottle, label and cork, transport and excise duty, which is charged at a uniform rate (£1.23 for still wines in 2004–05) whatever the value of the wine. The retailer typically adds a 30 per cent margin, and then there's VAT to pay. So cheap wines can't ever be anything more than basic – but there's a world of difference between well-made and shoddy offerings.

It follows that if you pay £5 or £6 you are getting considerably more value for your money. This will buy you grapes from better vineyards, or more expensive varieties, picked at lower yields to give more flavour and body. The wines will be made with greater care and may be matured in oak to give an extra dimension to the texture and flavour. However, while you can reliably find enjoyable drinks at these prices, it is rare to come across a wine with real individuality.

For £7 to £12 you should get a lovingly made wine that fully expresses the character of the grapes, the vineyard and the winemaker – but this sector of the market is full of pitfalls. In very competitive regions such as South America and southern France, quality generally continues to go up and you will start to find very well-crafted wines for this price from 'unfashionable' areas. However, in the prestigious appellations of Burgundy £10 will buy you only the humblest of bottles. The prices of big-brand wines from Australia are often inflated at this level, but they can represent good value when promotional discounts are applied.

Nor can you buy your way out of danger by spending over £12. Once you enter the premium wine market you start to pay for the reputation (or pretensions) of a region or a producer – the price of a bottle ceases to be related to the cost of production. Such reputations are founded on the producers' very best wines, which are often hugely expensive owing to the laws of supply and demand, and trailing an awful lot of undistinguished bottles in their wake. However, if you want to experience wines from the world's greatest vineyards you will have to venture into this territory.

Prices have a lot to do with location. The very best wines of lowly Sicily cost less than £30 while in the upper strata of Bordeaux and Burgundy that is pocket money, and you have to choose with care. A mature example of the most sought-after wines here will set you back hundreds of pounds. Sometimes a producer of a world-famous wine with an inflated price will have better-value alternatives. For example, the Australian producer Henschke's Hill of Grace Shiraz will set you back well over £100 a bottle, but their Mount Edelstone Shiraz, which is almost as good, comes in at under £30. In this category, be sure to take advice from books, magazines or a trusted merchant before parting with your money.

Getting the best out of the high street

- For a quick and easy introduction to a region, try an inexpensive bottle – don't expect fireworks, but it should give you some idea of what the local style is all about.
- Make the most of the huge ranges of modern fruity wines from £4 to £8.
- Take advantage of special promotions (as long as you like the wine).
- Look out for end-of-line discounts.
- Always return faulty bottles – most supermarkets have very generous replacement policies.

Getting the best out of specialist wine shops

- Ask for advice – the staff should really know their wines.
- Develop a relationship with the staff – discuss whether you enjoyed (or disliked) recent purchases.
- Expect to pay a bit more than at the supermarket … but to come away with a more interesting drink.
- Then again, shop elsewhere if the staff are always trying to make you spend more than you planned to.
- Look out for in-store tastings and tutored sessions with specialists or winemakers.
- Look out for bin-end offers.

Getting the best out of mail order and the Internet

- Look out for good-value mixed-case offers.
- If you are interested in a particular region, you may be able to find a supplier that is 100 per cent dedicated to that area.
- Don't stick to just one merchant – a few phone calls or mouse-clicks will give you a huge range to browse and enable you to compare prices.
- Check the company's terms and conditions carefully – if delivery is not included, the cost of this can wipe out the savings you thought you were making.
- If you are ordering online, always make sure you have real-world contact details, including a phone number, in case things go wrong.

Ethical wines

Organic and biodynamic wines

The wine industry as a whole is pulling back from excessive use of chemical fertilisers and pesticides, and an increasing number of vineyards follow a fully organic approach, which includes growing cover crops and other plants in the vineyard to maintain soil health and encourage natural predators. The most successful organic wines tend to come from hot, dry regions where pests and fungal infections are less common. Organic wine must be approved by an official certification body such as the Soil Association in the UK or Terre et Vie in France. For a wide range of organic wines, contact Vinceremos and Vintage Roots (see the 'Where to buy wine' section).

Biodynamics goes beyond the organic approach. It relies on ploughing and the application of natural products at very specific times of the year to create an 'energised' soil rich in micro-organisms. This is believed to create stronger vines with greater resistance to drought, pests and diseases. It is labour-intensive and the wines are often expensive. An increasing number of producers are adopting biodynamic techniques, primarily for quality rather than ethical reasons.

Vegetarian/vegan wine

Typically, animal-derived products including egg whites (acceptable to vegetarians), gelatin and isinglass – a fish protein – may be used to clarify wine after fermentation, although they leave no trace in the finished product. Vegan-approved wines use purely non-animal alternatives such as bentonite clay. Vintage Roots and Vinceremos (see above) indicate the vegetarian/vegan status of all their wines, and supermarkets often include relevant information on the back label.

Socially responsible wine

In South Africa and Chile, workers' empowerment initiatives within the wine industry have seen land turned over to vineyard workers, with additional support given through village development and education projects. South Africa's Wine Industry Ethical Trading Association (WIETA) promotes and monitors ethical practice (see *www.wosa.co.za*).

There is currently no official 'fair trade' certification for wines, but you will find information about the ethical background on some bottles, such as the Thandi range sold in Tesco. You can also find information and order wines from the Fairtrade Foundation at *www.fairtrade.org.uk* and Traidcraft at *www.traidcraft.co.uk*.

Wine in restaurants

Ordering wine in a restaurant can be a stressful experience. In part this is because the prices are usually far higher than you would pay in a shop, and so the stakes are raised. Unlike when eating at home, everyone tends to order different dishes, which complicates the choice of wine. And there's the ritual to endure of checking the wine when it is brought to your table …

Sticking to house wine makes life easy, but there's no guarantee it will be tasty. Fortunately more and more restaurants are offering a good range by the glass, which means everyone can pick something they like. Ordering a glass to start with also buys you time to peruse the full wine list at leisure. Don't worry excessively about matching the wine to the food (see page 27). Focus instead on finding something you will all enjoy at a price you are happy to pay.

Good red Burgundy is an amazingly adaptable partner for food, but it is very expensive. More affordable all-rounders are:

- Chilean reds
- Merlot from anywhere
- Languedoc reds
- unoaked Chardonnay
- New World Semillon
- Sauvignon Blanc
- dry Riesling
- Pinot Blanc from Alsace or Canada
- dry rosé, especially from Spain, southern France and the New World.

If the restaurant employs a wine waiter (or sommelier), make use of him or her. This person should be able to give useful suggestions if you explain what dishes you are ordering, the sorts of wine you like and your price range.

When the wine arrives the waiter should show you the label so that you can check it is what you ordered. Sometimes the vintage will be different from the one listed. If that is important to you (maybe the replacement is too young or the vintage is notoriously duff), order something else instead. When the waiter pours a drop for you to check, have a sniff and a quick taste to see if you notice any obvious faults (see page 26). If you are unsure, say so and ask for a second opinion from someone else at the table or from the waiter. Even if you don't notice a problem until the wine is poured, you are still perfectly entitled to ask for a replacement.

Wine for special occasions

Birthdays and Christmas, weddings and parties often call for special bottles or large quantities of wine, and for advance planning. Some general suggestions are given here.

Sparkling wines

Champagne is the obvious choice to kick off a celebration and, if you can afford it, goes down well throughout the entire meal (which simplifies your wine choice). Famous brands are expensive. Even on special offer they will set you back at least £17, so go for a good 'house' label (the ones from supermarkets and major merchants are mostly good and cost around £12 to £14 before discounts). Sparkling wines from other parts of France, the New World or even England can offer comparable quality at half the price, and often have a fruitier flavour that suits many people better. Spanish Cava is even more affordable but can be rather earthy, so try a sample to check that it tastes crisp and fresh. Otherwise you could serve refreshing whites – maybe some tangy Sauvignon Blanc, grapy Alsace Muscat or, for a sedate crowd, some Alsace Pinot Blanc.

Catering for your guests

When you are deciding what wine to provide and like the taste of something, check the alcohol level. Anything over 12.5 per cent is a bit heavy-duty for an aperitif.

Serving a different wine with each course of a meal is a major logistical feat. To make life simpler you can continue to offer the aperitif with the starter, then add a red option with the main course, or choose red and white all-rounders to serve throughout the meal (see 'Wine in restaurants', page 22, for some suggestions). Think about the likely preferences of the guests. Were they weaned on Jacob's Creek or are they more at home with drier, less pronounced European flavours? To suit a mixed crowd choose something fruity but go easy on tropical flavours and sweet vanilla oak.

The general rule on quantities is to allow half a bottle of wine per person for three hours of celebrating. Many people will drink less but a few will always gulp down more. Adjust accordingly for a longer party or a boozier crowd.

Weddings and bulk buys

For a wedding it is usual to order wine from the caterer providing the food. If you decide to search out something independently, remember that you will probably have to pay the caterer a corkage fee for handling the wine – this could be £5 to £8 per bottle or more. However this gives you more choice and the chance to save money. If a caterer offers a basic bottle or one that you don't like the sound of for £15, you could pay £5 for something better which would end up as £10 to £13 including corkage.

Buying by the case at wholesale prices or even factoring in the cost of a trip to the discount outlets in Calais can give you good value (and better quality than you might get from a caterer's list). Be sure to arrange sale or return terms to avoid being left with cases of unopened wine.

Your rights when things go wrong

Faulty wine

If you believe that a wine is faulty the retailer, restaurant or shop should replace it. If they refuse, it is up to them, for the first six months after purchase, to prove there is nothing wrong with it. Under the Sale of Goods Act 1979 (as amended) you have a right to a replacement, even if you have stored the wine for some time before opening it – but in this case you must inform the shop or wine merchant as soon as you know there is a problem.

If for some reason a restaurant refuses to replace a wine your only option is to pay for it. Say you are doing so 'under protest' and record this in writing on the receipt. Take the bottle away to be checked by an independent expert such as a local wine merchant. If he or she agrees that the wine is defective then you are entitled to your money back plus any extra costs incurred.

Mail-order misery

If any bottles are missing from your order or broken, the merchant will replace them as long as you give notice within a reasonable time – this varies and is usually specified in the terms and conditions. Signing a delivery note does not mean that you have inspected or accepted the wine as delivered. If the wrong wine turns up by mistake it is the merchant's responsibility to arrange for it to be collected and replaced with the correct order. Always read the terms and conditions before placing your order.

You don't like the wine

If the wine is perfectly good but you just don't like it you may be able to exchange unopened bottles for something else … but there's no guarantee, and you are essentially dependent on the good nature of the merchant.

With 'distance selling' purchases, using mail-order or the Internet, the law entitles you to a seven-day cooling-off period after the goods are delivered, during which time you can send them back for a refund.

Opening and serving wine

A corkscrew and some proper wine glasses are the only essential kit for enjoying wine. Otherwise it's a matter of treating the wine well to get the best out of it.

Corkscrews and foil cutters

Good leverage and a slender, open spiral that won't crumble the cork are the functional points to look for in a corkscrew. The Screwpull brand (you keep turning these until the cork is fully out) has long been lauded for the use of high-quality materials that give a silky-smooth action. They're great for natural corks but aren't well suited to some of the plastic stoppers. The traditional 'waiter's friend' corkscrew – the type that folds up like a penknife – is very convenient, and rarely fails once you have the knack of using it. Smart modern ones incorporate a neat foil cutter (rather than the traditional knife) for trimming the metal or plastic capsule off the top of the bottle. It's well worth having one of these devices – the cutter makes it so much neater than tearing the foil off by hand or ploughing through it with a corkscrew.

Opening sparkling wine

Remove the foil and the wire cage that keeps the cork safely in place. Immediately grip the cork – don't let go until the bottle is open because it is liable to pop out at high speed and could injure somebody. Whether you twist the cork or the bottle doesn't matter: once the cork starts to move the pressure in the bottle does the work, so simply keep a firm grip on the cork and allow it to ease out slowly. Have a glass ready to catch any initial surge of foam. Half-fill all the glasses, then top them up once the bubbles have calmed down.

Breathing and decanting

There is no great mystery here: when a bottle is opened the wine starts to react with oxygen in the air and this helps to release the aromas and flavours in the wine – although after time (minutes, hours or even days, depending on the wine) it will tire and lose its character. There's no need for breathing or decanting with cheap-and-cheerful bottles or with wines that are meant to taste fresh and zippy, but complex and heavyweight wines – both red and white – can really shine with a bit of aeration.

Simply uncorking the bottle has very little immediate effect; it's much better to pour off a glass to expose a larger surface area. Sloshing the wine into a decanter, carafe or jug has a significantly more dramatic impact – but don't do this with expensive old wines. Remember that wine keeps on breathing in the glass, and a quick swirl does a lot to release the aromas.

Decanting also separates the wine from sediment in the bottle. Stand the bottle upright for a day or more to allow the sediment to settle, then pull the cork very gently. Set up a lamp or torch to shine through the neck of the bottle as you pour the wine slowly into a decanter or a jug. Stop pouring as soon as you see the sediment flowing into the neck.

Serving temperatures

The flavours of wine fall apart when it is too warm, and equally they can be impenetrable when it is too cold. The ideal temperature depends on the style of the wine. Normal room temperature (20°C) suits only the fullest-flavoured reds and fortified wines. The lightest reds and rosés should be served cool (around 12°C), but not very chilled unless it's a blazing summer's day. Not all

Corks *versus* screwcaps

An increasing number of wines are being sold in screwcap bottles, and a public debate has been raging about the relative merits of Stelvin closures (as screwcaps are properly called) versus traditional corks. Some very smart wines are now in screwcap bottles and only a snob would reject them on principle. They keep wine very fresh, so are particularly favoured for zingy whites like Sauvignon and Riesling, and they remove the risk of tainted flavours associated with faulty corks. On the other hand, corks allow a wine to develop over time because of the tiny amount of air that passes through, which can be a good thing – especially with expensive reds.

All sorts of different plastic bungs have been tried as alternatives to cork. They guarantee a fresh flavour in the short term, but some have proved unsuitable for longer periods of storage.

whites need to be chilled: indeed, complex, full-bodied whites should be only gently cooled. Save the heavy fridge treatment for light, neutral or very fresh-flavoured whites, fino sherry and of course champagne styles.

If you need to cool a bottle in a hurry, you can use an ice bucket filled half with ice, half with water. A couple of big spoonfuls of salt in the mix will make it even more effective. If a wine needs warming the best approach is to pour it and cradle a glass in your hands.

Leftover wine

Wine won't lose all its flavour overnight, especially if the bottle is still fairly full. Recork any leftover bottles and pop them in the fridge for finishing over the next two or three days. You could consider buying half bottles to reduce the amount of excess wine. Special devices to suck out the air, such as the Vacuvin system, do help, as do the ones that deposit a blanket of neutral gas (for example, Wine Saver), but they're not strictly necessary.

Glasses

Any glass will do for everyday quaffers, but for a wine to tell its full story the vessel you choose should do justice to its colour, aroma and texture as well as its basic flavour. Go for tulip-shaped glasses made of clear glass, and when you pour the wine fill them only one-third full to leave room for the aromas to swirl around. The ideal size varies according to the weight and complexity of the wine but a good all-round size is 30–35cl. For sparkling wine the bubbles last longest in tall, narrow flutes. There is no need to buy expensive glasses as the shape is the important thing, although smarter ones will

have a finer lip, which upgrades the whole sipping experience.

Wine glasses need to be clean and odour-free to perform well. Detergent residues alter the aromas of the wine and can kill the bubbles in sparkling wine. So whether you wash them conventionally or use a dishwasher, rinse your glasses thoroughly with hot water and dry them with a clean linen cloth. Store glasses upright so they don't develop stale odours. Any that have been on the shelf for a while, especially if they have been sitting in a cardboard box, will benefit from a rinse before use.

Tasting wine

Wine tasting is not complicated. It simply means paying a bit more attention to what's in the glass so that you can obtain even greater pleasure from drinking it. It's the best way to learn your way around the world of wine flavours and to gain confidence when choosing wine. Many wine merchants organise regular tutored tastings, but even if you don't attend these, every glass of wine is an opportunity to develop your tasting skills.

Advantages of tasting

If you take up proper wine tasting, you will:

- learn to compare different wines
- become more aware of the styles that you like and where to find them
- feel confident about spotting faults
- become better able to communicate what you want when ordering wine
- perceive the finer nuances that make the best wines worth the money.

How to taste wine

You will need a proper wine glass, filled no more than a third full (see 'Glasses', page 25). Begin by looking at the wine. Note whether the colour is dark or light. Tilt it against a white background to reveal the range of colours from the core of the wine to the rim. You can discover much about the age and style of a wine this way. For example, red wines gradually change from purple when newly made to ruby and finally to brick-red when very old, and the rim becomes wider and paler as each year goes by. Whites, conversely, darken with age.

Swirl the wine in the glass to release its aromas and take a sniff. This can tell you whether the wine is in good condition or faulty, as well as revealing its character. You may be able to recognise the grape variety or region just from the smell of the wine – see coverage of grape varieties (pages 29–33) for aromas to expect.

Take a sip and sloosh the wine around your mouth so it gets to all parts of your tongue, to your cheeks and your gums. Then hold it in your mouth and gently suck air over it through pursed lips. This releases the aromas to important sensors at the back of the mouth. Consider the flavour and the texture, and also the balance of the basic components of acidity, sweetness, tannin, fruit and alcohol (see box).

If you are tasting a lot of different wines, spit them out so that you can stay sober. Otherwise, swallow and enjoy the lingering aftertaste of the wine. Evaluate the wine both subjectively (Do I like it?) and objectively (Is it a good example of this style?).

Cork taint and other faults

Most faults in wine can be detected by smell. The taste will usually confirm what your nose suspects. The following are some of the most common offenders.

- **Musty 'off' smells** Cork is prone to TCA infection which can ruin any wine – sometimes it merely dulls the flavour. Roughly 5 per cent of all corks are affected.
- **Cloudy wine** This is a sign of poor winemaking and very rare nowadays. (Cloudiness caused by stirred-up sediment will clear if the wine is left to stand.)
- **Vinegary or nail-varnishy smells** Signs that the bacteria that convert wine into vinegar are gaining the upper hand.
- **Sherry-like smells** Wine exposed to oxygen or stored somewhere hot becomes 'tired' and loses its fruit flavours. It tends to look slightly browned as well. Sherry and madeira are exceptions because they rely on oxidisation to develop their special character.

The basic components of wine

To get started on tasting it's useful to have some reference points for comparing wines.

Acidity
Acids are what make fruit taste crisp and refreshing. Excessive acid in unripe fruit makes for sharp or sour flavours, while too little makes for dull eating. The same goes for wine.

Sweetness
All but the very driest wines contain small quantities of unfermented sugar. It's worth noting any sweetness you detect on the tip of your tongue as you first sip the wine.

Tannin
This is the stuff in red wine that coats and dries your mouth and can taste bitter. It contributes texture and flavour and mellows as the wine ages.

Fruit
Fruit flavours are an important part of both the smell and the taste of a wine. Some wines are overtly fruity, but note that high-quality wines often don't have much aroma when they are young.

Alcohol
Table wines can have anything from 8% to 15% alcohol. In terms of tasting, high alcohol levels give a fuller body but can have a bitter 'burn'.

- **Rotten eggs or burnt rubber smells** These are caused by sulphur compounds. Sometimes the fault can be corrected by dropping a copper coin into the wine.

No cause for complaint

Some apparent problems are harmless and shouldn't affect your enjoyment of the wine.

- **White crystals** Tartrate crystals occasionally form in the bottle but do not affect the flavour of the wine.
- **Cork crumbs** These have nothing to do with cork taint and can simply be removed from the glass.
- **Sediment** This forms naturally in red wines as the tannins soften over time. To deal with sediment see 'Breathing and decanting', page 24.
- **Burnt match smells** Caused by sulphur dioxide, a preservative used in virtually all wines, this smell usually dissipates once the bottle has been open for half an hour.

Storing wine

Most wines are intended for drinking, not for long-term cellaring, and are best consumed within a couple of years of production. None the less, any wine that you store in your home for more than a few days will benefit from being properly kept. There's no need to dig out a cellar or buy an expensive storage cabinet, but some common principles apply.

Wine is happiest when it is in a cool, dark place free from sudden changes in temperature. So at the very least avoid stashing it on a kitchen windowsill or close to a radiator, and it should be content for a

few weeks. But don't store it in the fridge as the flavours tend to dissipate.

Wines for cellaring

Some wines are slow starters and do not show their best until a few years after the vintage. Their flavours are not the same as the fresh fruit of ready-to-drink wines, but more evolved – combining fruit with gamey, earthy, leathery, spicy or honeyed qualities. For recommendations on where to buy wines that will keep well, and ageing times, see the box on page 28 for reasonably priced suggestions, or refer to the vintage guides in the regional section.

So where to keep them? In addition to avoiding heat and light, for ideal storage keep such wines free from vibration and somewhere moderately humid, but with enough ventilation to avoid mustiness. A cellar is the perfect place but for the majority not lucky enough to possess one, an understairs cupboard or a disused fireplace is ideal, and failing that a bottom drawer that isn't disturbed too often. Garages and lofts tend to experience excessive highs and lows of temperature over the year and so are to be avoided. If the wine has a natural cork it is important to lay it on its side so that the cork doesn't dry out and shrink, which allows the wine to oxidise.

Any good wine merchant will be able to tell you when the wines you have bought should be at their best, and may also offer suitable storage space in optimal conditions for a small annual fee. Wine bought as an investment should always be stored this way to maximise its resale value. If you take up this option, make sure your cases are properly identified and stored away from the merchant's main stock, and that you get a stock certificate.

Affordable wines for cellaring

The classic wines for ageing are expensive: top red and white Bordeaux and Burgundy, northern Italy's Barolo, and vintage port and vintage champagne. Here are some more affordable suggestions:

- Riesling from anywhere
- Australian Semillon and Shiraz
- southern French reds such as Coteaux de Languedoc and Costières de Nîmes
- Côtes du Rhône-Villages
- Douro reds from Portugal
- Spanish Rioja
- Sweet Loire Chenin Blanc.

Once fine wine is ready to drink, don't guzzle it all at once. If you have a number of cases, try one bottle from each case every year so you can gauge how the wine is progressing and establish the age when you like it most. Learn from every mistake and don't get too precious about your wine. It is there to be drunk, not worshipped.

Wine with food

The wine-and-food-matching rule book went out of the window years ago, so don't fret too much about finding the ideal wine to partner a particular dish, just savour the moment when you do come across a perfect combination. With a little bit of thought you can find a wide range of wines that will be happy enough beside your meal; genuinely unpleasant clashes are mercifully rare.

Basic principles

Acidity, tannin and sweetness (see page 26) are the three main areas to keep in mind – the rest will inevitably be a journey of discovery. Consider matching the acidity of a dish with a complementary wine (for example, citrus or fruit flavours with crisp white wines or light reds). Think also about contrasts. The same crisp whites could equally cut a refreshing swathe through creamy or oily dishes. Ensure that tannin, that mouth-furring component of robust and full-flavoured red wines, is paired off only with rich and robust foods, usually red meats. And for simplicity's sake partner sweet food with similarly sweet wines.

Another good rule of thumb is to choose a wine with a cultural link with the dish you are preparing or choosing. Mediterranean cooking goes well with southern French, Italian and Spanish reds. For pasta and pizza stay in Italy. French regional food has traditional links with many wines, manzanilla sherry and tapas suit each other, and so on. Modern fusion or spicy foods are somewhat trickier, but often this is where you can safely start with New World wines.

Problem foods

The foods listed below can make the majority of wines taste dull or harsh – but these combinations will see you through.

- **Eggs** Try a not-too-oaky Chardonnay.
- **Tomatoes** Try matching the acidity of the tomato with Sauvignon Blanc.
- **Smoked fish** Smoked salmon is fine with Chablis or champagne. With oilier fish (mackerel, kippers) go for something lighter still, and more acidic, such as Sauvignon or Muscadet – or try fino sherry.
- **Spinach and artichokes** These make wine taste metallic (in a similar way to red wine combined with fish). See 'Seasoning tricks', below, for how to avoid this.
- **Chinese and Thai food** Crisp, aromatic whites are the best accompaniment – Riesling, Alsace Gewurztraminer or (especially when there's lemongrass in the dish) New Zealand Sauvignon Blanc. Light reds such as Pinot Noir are also a possibility.
- **Indian food** Richly flavoured New World whites, such as Chardonnay, Semillon or Verdelho are excellent, or try New World Zinfandel, Shiraz or Merlot.
- **Chocolate** Dessert Muscat wines are the best bet, or try ripe New World Cabernet Sauvignon with dark chocolate.
- **Puddings and cakes** Match the sweetness in the wine to that in the food. Sweet, frothy Asti is a good alternative to sticky dessert wines.

Seasoning tricks

To combat clashes, try adding a condiment of some kind – by doing this, you expand your wine choices.

Salt makes tannic wines seem even more so, but grind or shake some black pepper on to your steak, for example, and the wine will seem smoother and fruitier right away. You can add salt to a dish to balance a particularly crisp wine, such as a young

---

Perfect matches

For a taster of the best food-and-wine combinations, eat fresh-cooked prawns or langoustine with a buttery Chardonnay; goat's cheese with Sancerre; lamb and rosemary with top Bordeaux; Sauternes with Roquefort cheese; fino sherry with sushi; and port with Stilton. Plus, if you get the chance, champagne and oysters.

Sauvignon. Lemon juice will temper the metallic taste of spinach (or you can soften it by stirring in cream). Coriander in a dish can lift the fruitiness of many a dull Soave, and rosemary or mint can ease the relationship between many a Cabernet and its platter (Pinot Noir too, for that matter).

Grape varieties

The grape variety is one of the key factors in determining the style of a wine, and wines are increasingly named accordingly. The best grapes for making wine come from the *Vitis vinifera* family, amounting to some 1,500 varieties. This overview introduces 50 of the most significant varieties. You will find more information on the styles of wine produced from these grapes in individual regions in 'Best wine-producing countries'.

The classic grapes

At the top of the tree are a select band of all-time classics. They are primarily associated with particular regions of France (and in one case Germany), where their cultivation has been honed over the centuries. But they are also the grapes that first inspired the winemakers of the New World and gave them the raw material to lead the wine revolution of the twentieth century. Today, they are familiar names on wine labels from all countries and at all price levels.

Red

Cabernet Sauvignon

The world's favourite red grape delivers wines with deep colour, blackcurrant aromas and flavours, and firm tannins. Capsicum, blackcurrant leaf and coffee beans are other common flavours, with cedar, cigar box and lead pencil shavings the hallmark of mature premium examples. From its origins in Bordeaux it has been successfully adopted all around the wine-producing world. Cabernet works best as a solo grape in places where it delivers ripe, pure fruit flavours, as in Chile. Otherwise it benefits from blending to balance its backbone with lusher characteristics.

Merlot

Another of the major Bordeaux varieties, Merlot is softer and fruitier than Cabernet Sauvignon and hence an ideal partner in a blend, where it gives a lovely plummy quality. At the premium level Merlot is a firmly tannic, long-lived wine and following the lead of Chile it has reached new heights of popularity in irresistible wines bursting with ripe berry fruit and minty flavours. However, many examples from hot vineyard areas lack that bright-eyed fruit.

Pinot Noir

The smooth-textured, strawberryish summer flavours of young Pinot Noir turn exotic and mushroomy with age. It is the leading grape of Burgundy where it is valued for its ability to reflect the subtle differences between vineyards – including some very small plots. Pinot Noir is expensive and even on its home ground doesn't reliably deliver those sought-after flavours. It is an important constituent of champagne and other sparkling wines.

Syrah/Shiraz

This smoky, spicy, blackberryish grape produces full-bodied, robust reds. Syrah is its French name while the term Shiraz was popularised in Australia. Wines from its original home in the northern Rhône tend to have more finesse and smoke, and the best New World examples increasingly emulate this model (and increasingly adopt the French version of the name), while the rich, chocolaty, sweet-fruited Australian style is much imitated at the budget level.

White

Chardonnay

The runaway global success of Chardonnay stems from the brilliance of the best examples from Burgundy. Depending on where it is grown, its flavours range from lean apple, subtle melon or white peach to ultra-ripe pineapple and tinned peaches. Chardonnay responds to fermentation and ageing in small oak barrels to produce fuller-bodied wines with creamy, nutty or butterscotch flavours. In cooler vineyards it produces prime raw material for champagne and other sparkling wines. But beware: the name on the label is no guarantee of quality.

Riesling

The honeyed, steely acidity of Riesling immediately sets it apart from other varieties, yet it is gaining mainstream popularity as consumers seek alternatives to Chardonnay and Sauvignon Blanc. Fruit flavours are typically lime and apple, but

Riesling lovers tend to be more interested in the minerally qualities it gains from different types of soil and the intriguing petrolly aroma that can develop with age. Alsace and New World examples are generally dry while in Germany it is often sweet.

Sauvignon Blanc

The instantly recognisable flavours of gooseberry and nettle combined with invigorating fresh acidity made New Zealand Sauvignon a hit. Few of the countries that have followed in its wake can match the style so reliably. New World flavours can be wildly tropical, but Sauvignon from Sancerre and neighbouring areas of France is less overt and more minerally, while Bordeaux does a good tasty budget version as well as using it for serious dry and sweet whites. Hot regions of southern France rarely come up with the goods. Oaked versions do exist, but mostly this conflicts with the zesty nature of the grape.

Other important varieties

The following grape varieties are capable of producing wines to match those from the leading varieties but they have never achieved quite the same level of global popularity – maybe because they're best in blends, or because they really thrive only in their native region. Others are oddballs whose flavour has not yet won widespread affection. However, from the ranks of these varieties a number of newly fashionable grapes have emerged.

Red

Cabernet Franc

A major but unsung grape in Bordeaux, Cabernet Franc has earned its reputation in the Loire Valley. In these cool conditions it produces elegant wines redolent of summer fruits and with appealing earthy and leafy flavours.

Grenache/Garnacha

Grenache thrives in hot climates and delivers ripe, sweet-fruited flavours with a twist of peppery spice and a good slap of alcohol. It frequently crops up in blends rather than as a single varietal and is a major player in the southern Rhône, including Châteauneuf-du-Pape, while in Spanish guise as Garnacha it plumps up many a Rioja and hits the heights in Priorat. Grenache is a good grape for rosé, while at the other end of the spectrum it produces super-concentrated old-vine reds in Australia.

Malbec

Argentina's great red success can make light, fruity wines but owes its reputation to deep-coloured, rich, velvety, oak-aged versions with delicious black-cherry fruit. In France it is a minor constituent of red Bordeaux and the basis of robust, deep-flavoured Cahors.

Nebbiolo

One of the most highly rated grapes in the world but one that doesn't generally fare too well outside its Piedmont base, Nebbiolo is the variety responsible for the wines of Barolo and Barbaresco. It can be tannic and hard to enjoy when young, but mature examples blossom to reveal complex aromas and flavours combining prunes, chocolate, cherries, herbs, tobacco and, famously, the extreme contrast of tar and roses.

Sangiovese

Tuscany's chief grape variety delivers a good rasp of cherry and plum fruit with a distinctly Italian twist of herbs and tealeaf. Quality varies dramatically and good versions range from light, varietally labelled wines to the long-lived heavyweights of Brunello di Montalcino, while the classic Sangiovese-based wine is Chianti. The grape is not widely grown internationally.

Tempranillo

Travelling under a host of pseudonyms, Tempranillo is the source of the leathery, strawberryish flavours in many of the best Spanish reds. It is the mainstay of Rioja and Ribera del Duero. Argentinian versions can be vibrantly fruity.

Touriga Nacional

One of the prime grapes used in port production, Touriga has emerged as an exciting variety for dry red wines in Portugal, combining firm tannins with intense red-fruit flavours.

Zinfandel/Primitivo

California for long claimed Zinfandel as its own invention but the grape's origins have been traced back to southern Italy – where it is known as Primitivo – and beyond. This grape produces heady, brambly, idiosyncratic reds, often outrageously high in alcohol, as well as oceans of insipid, sweetish, pink 'blush' wines.

White

Chenin Blanc

Along the Loire Valley Chenin is used for everything from bracing fizz to unctuous sweet wines. Its contradictory flavours, setting honey and quince sweetness against steely, minerally acidity, are not always easy to love, especially as much bulk-produced Chenin is poorly made. Barrel-fermentation and ageing hold out the promise of more mainstream appeal. In South Africa it is used for budget quaffers, but increasingly serious wines are emerging.

Gewürztraminer
The antithesis of crisp, neutral dry white wine, Gewürztraminer's exotic aromas of lychees, roses and spice explode out of the glass as a prelude to a rich, oily texture that is rarely fully dry. It is a variety to love or hate with a passion. Alsace produces the most extreme flavours.

Grüner Veltliner
Austria's best white is suddenly attracting international attention as a star to rival top Chardonnays. On an everyday level it offers appealing peppery and limey flavours.

Marsanne
This Rhône variety delivers rich, peachy, floral-scented wines, and is starting to be more widely grown. It is often blended with the similar Roussanne.

Muscat
Muscat is pretty much the only variety that produces wines that smell and taste like grapes. It is used widely for sweet wines and delicious light fizz such as Asti, and occasionally comes as a refreshing dry wine.

Pinot Gris
In Alsace this grape produces potent, earthy, honeyed wines but in general its character is more gentle – particularly in Italy where it is known as Pinot Grigio. It also appears in Germany under the name Grauburgunder, producing oak-aged versions that give Alsace a run for its money. It is starting to be fashionable in the New World.

Sémillon
The best flavours of Sémillon emerge only with time, as it evolves from crisp, neutral and unexceptional tastes into fat, creamy, complex maturity. It is important for both dry and sweet wines in Bordeaux and is a classic variety in Australia.

Viognier
Touted by some as the new Chardonnay, Viognier has only recently been planted in any quantity outside its Rhône home of Condrieu. Its great strength is a beguiling apricoty and floral aroma backed up by a lush, full-bodied texture. Only a few of the copycats come close to these heights, but they reliably deliver something fairly aromatic with a good weight of alcohol.

Best of the rest
These grapes are a mixed bag of highly localised specialities and less prestigious varieties that are none the less important in blends and everyday wines.

Red

Barbera
A widely planted grape from northern Italy, Barbera makes fruity reds. Often tasting of redcurrants and cranberries, the wines can be high in acidity and low in tannins. Some producers use oak to round out its character. Argentinian versions are soft and fruity.

Carignan
The plodding workhorse of southern France has recently shown that it is a worthwhile variety when treated well. It produces rich, earthy, spicy reds from old vines in the Languedoc and is known as Cariñena or Mazuelo in Spain.

Cinsaut
Usually part of a blend in southern France, Cinsaut makes light, fresh and occasionally characterful reds.

Dolcetto
The 'little sweet one' produces some of Italy's most gluggable wines – refreshing, fruity and smooth, with a slightly sour, cherryish twist on the finish. It is seldom seen outside Piedmont.

Gamay
The Beaujolais grape typically produces vibrant, strawberry-fresh wines for early consumption, although richer versions from *cru* villages can age well. Versions from the Loire can be attractive.

Mourvèdre
Although it has Spanish origins (where it is known as Monastrell), Mourvèdre has its moment of glory in Bandol in Provence where it produces rich, thick wines with deep herbal and blackberry flavours. It also appears as Mataro in Australia.

Negroamaro
Literally 'black and bitter', this grape actually produces ripe, chocolaty Salice Salentino

from the heel of Italy. Wines develop warm, chestnutty qualities with age.

Nero d'Avola
The best grape of Sicily and southern Italy manages to retain good acidity and vibrancy despite the broiling heat, backed up by rich, spicy fruit. It is good in blends and occasionally excellent alone.

Periquita
Southern Portugal is home to this smoky, spicy, cherryish grape, also known as Castelão.

Petite Sirah
Not the same as Syrah/Shiraz, this variety is a source of powerful reds high in alcohol from California and Mexico. Durif is a similar grape grown in southern France and Australia.

Petit Verdot
A minor 'seasoning' constituent of the red Bordeaux blend, Petit Verdot adds deep colour, tannin and a violet fragrance. It is now appearing as a good-value and characterful varietal in Australia.

Pinotage
A South African speciality, this crossing of Pinot Noir and Cinsaut produces wines that range from light and fruity (with unusual banana-marshmallow flavours) through to serious heavyweights that need cellaring.

Tannat
Madiran in South-west France is the home base for this dark, tannic grape. Wines are typically powerful and need years to mature. It is softer and fruitier in Uruguay.

White

Albariño
This is the grape behind the fragrant and expensive wines of Rías Baixas in north-west Spain. The best are soft and apricoty or peachy, but still wonderfully fresh. Some versions have a leaner profile. It is used for Portugal's Vinho Verde (as Alvarinho).

Colombard
This neutral-tasting grape is often used for budget blends in southern France and New World countries. Colombard can have an attractive, floral quality and in Gascony produces enjoyable crisp quaffers.

Garganega
All the best Soave uses a high proportion of Garganega, and it is also produced as a varietal

in north-east Italy. It can have fresh acidity and attractive nutty and appley aromas.

Macabeo/Viura
Fresh, fairly neutral gluggers from Spain and the Languedoc owe a lot to this grape, which is also the source of unusual but attractive white Rioja when blended with Malvasia.

Malvasia
Malvasia crops up in many Italian regions. It gives good Frascati its creamy, nutty character and it also produces rich, sweet dessert wines. In Spain, it can add richness to white Rioja. In Madeira it is known as Malmsey and produces some of the finest sweet fortified wines. There is also a red version.

Melon de Bourgogne
The Muscadet region's grape is known for light, brisk quaffers to gulp with seafood but dedicated producers prove that it can have some depth and character.

Muller-Thürgau
The workhorse grape of Germany is generally responsible for sweetish, vaguely floral wines of no particular charm.

Palomino
In Spain the neutral-tasting, unexciting white wines from this grape are transformed by the sherry production process into dry, yeasty, fascinating fortified wine.

Pinot Blanc
Light, creamy, appley Pinot Blanc from Alsace and northern Italy (where it is called Pinot Bianco) makes a refreshing alternative to straightforward Chardonnay. It also appears as very good peachy, nutty Weissburgunder in Germany.

Torrontés
Argentina has made this its 'signature' white grape. At best it creates headily aromatic, grapey wine.

Trebbiano/Ugni Blanc
The pan-European workhorse *par excellence*, from Italy to Spain this variety delivers volume, not flavour and is often used to bulk up quantities of wines from more interesting varieties.

Verdelho
One of the finest grapes in Madeira, Verdelho produces smoky, fruity, semi-sweet fortified wines. It is also an increasingly popular source of rich, lime-juice-flavoured dry whites from Australia.

Vermentino
Light, dry, nutty Sardinian whites from this grape are great value. Producers in southern France also use it, generally under the name of Rolle.

Vernacchia
Tuscany's oldest white variety at best makes charming, characterful wines with soft, nutty, angelica flavours, but most versions are flabby and dull.

Appellations at a glance

In the case of European wines, the appellation name on the label is often the only clue to the style of the wine. This table lists commonly encountered appellations (with the relevant region in brackets), along with a brief summary of the main styles and grape varieties. You will find more detail on these wines in 'Best wine-producing countries'.

France

- Aloxe-Corton (Burgundy)
  Powerful Pinot Noir reds
- Bandol (Provence)
  Dense, rich, herby Mourvèdre-based reds
- Beaujolais (Burgundy)
  Light, fruity reds from Gamay
- Beaune (Burgundy)
  Fruity, firm Pinot Noir reds
- Bergerac (South-west)
  Lighter, cheaper, Bordeaux-style reds and whites
- Bonnezeaux (Loire)
  High-quality sweet Chenin Blanc
- Bourgueil (Loire)
  Subtle reds from Cabernet Franc
- Brouilly (Burgundy)
  Beaujolais *cru* with perfumed, fruity Gamay reds
- Cahors (South-west)
  Deep Malbec-based reds
- Chablis (Burgundy)
  Crisp, steely whites from Chardonnay
- Chambolle-Musigny (Burgundy)
  Light, perfumed Pinot Noir reds
- Chassagne-Montrachet (Burgundy)
  Rich, premium whites from Chardonnay
- Châteauneuf-du-Pape (Rhône)
  Powerful herb-and-spice red blend
- Condrieu (Rhône)
  Perfumed white from Viognier

- Corbières (Languedoc)
  Spicy, earthy red blend
- Cornas (Rhône)
  Dark, rich Syrah reds
- Costières de Nîmes (Languedoc)
  Rich, spicy red blend
- Côte-Rôtie (Rhône)
  Dark yet perfumed Syrah reds
- Coteaux du Layon (Loire)
  Honeyed, sweet Chenin Blanc
- Crozes-Hermitage (Rhône)
  Supple, smoky Syrah reds
- Entre-Deux-Mers (Bordeaux)
  Crisp, dry Sauvignon-based whites
- Faugères (Languedoc)
  Spicy, earthy red blend
- Fitou (Languedoc)
  Spicy, earthy red blend
- Fleurie (Burgundy)
  Beaujolais *cru*: fruity Gamay reds
- Gevrey-Chambertin (Burgundy)
  Powerful and perfumed Pinot Noir reds
- Gigondas (Rhône)
  Powerful, herby Grenache-based reds
- Givry (Burgundy)
  Rich, fruity Pinot Noir reds
- Graves (Bordeaux)
  Classic, blackcurranty Cabernet-based reds; long-lived Sémillon/Sauvignon whites
- Hermitage (Rhône)
  Powerful, slow-maturing Syrah reds
- Juliénas (Burgundy)
  Beaujolais *cru*: solid, supple Gamay reds
- Mâcon-Villages (Burgundy)
  Gentle, unoaked Chardonnay
- Margaux (Bordeaux)
  Classic blackcurrant Cabernet-based reds
- Médoc/Haut-Médoc (Bordeaux)
  Classic blackcurrant Cabernet-based reds
- Mercurey (Burgundy)
  Rich, fruity Pinot Noir reds
- Meursault (Burgundy)
  Rich, premium whites from Chardonnay
- Minervois (Languedoc)
  Rich, spicy red blends
- Montagny (Burgundy)
  Lean Chardonnay whites
- Morey-St-Denis (Burgundy)
  Light, perfumed Pinot Noir reds
- Morgon (Burgundy)
  Beaujolais *cru*: firm, fruity Gamay reds
- Moulin-à-Vent (Burgundy)
  Sturdiest of the Beaujolais *crus*

- Muscadet (Loire)
  Crisp, light whites from Melon de Bourgogne
- Nuits-St-Georges (Burgundy)
  Firm, slow-maturing Pinot Noir reds
- Pauillac (Bordeaux)
  Classic blackcurrant Cabernet-based reds
- Pessac-Léognan (Bordeaux)
  Classic blackcurrant Cabernet-based reds; long-lived Sémillon/Sauvignon whites
- Pomerol (Bordeaux)
  Classic plummy Merlot-based reds
- Pommard (Burgundy)
  Powerful Pinot Noir reds
- Pouilly-Fuissé (Burgundy)
  Rich, creamy whites from Chardonnay
- Pouilly-Fumé (Loire)
  Flinty whites from Sauvignon Blanc
- Puligny-Montrachet (Burgundy)
  Rich premium whites from Chardonnay
- Rully (Burgundy)
  Fruity Chardonnay whites
- St-Amour (Burgundy)
  Beaujolais *cru* with attractive, light Gamay reds
- St-Chinian (Languedoc)
  Rich, spicy red blends
- St-Emilion (Bordeaux)
  Classic plummy Merlot-based reds
- St-Estèphe (Bordeaux)
  Classic blackcurrant Cabernet-based reds
- St-Joseph (Rhône)
  Smoky Syrah reds
- St-Julien (Bordeaux)
  Classic blackcurrant Cabernet-based reds
- St-Véran (Burgundy)
  Rich, creamy whites from Chardonnay
- Sancerre (Loire)
  Gooseberry/minerally whites from Sauvignon Blanc
- Saumur-Champigny (Loire)
  Subtle reds from Cabernet Franc
- Sauternes (Bordeaux)
  Classic Sémillon/Sauvignon sweet wines
- Savennières (Loire)
  Intense dry Chenin Blanc whites
- Vacqueyras (Rhône)
  Powerful, herby Grenache-based reds
- Volnay (Burgundy)
  Elegant Pinot Noir reds
- Vosne-Romanée (Burgundy)
  Light, perfumed Pinot Noir reds

- Vouvray (Loire)
  Crisp, elegant Chenin Blanc whites (dry or sweet)

Italy

- Asti (North-west)
  Light, grapey Muscat fizz
- Barbaresco (North-west)
  Elegant, perfumed tannic reds from Nebbiolo
- Barolo (North-west)
  Elegant, perfumed tannic reds from Nebbiolo
- Brunello di Montalcino (Central)
  Long-lived herby, tannic Sangiovese-based reds
- Chianti (Central)
  Cherry-fruited, herby Sangiovese-based reds
- Frascati (Central)
  Light Trebbiano white, perfumed when Malvasia added
- Gavi (North-west)
  Light, crisp whites from Cortese
- Orvieto (Central)
  Dull Trebbiano white
- Soave (North-east)
  Light, nutty, appley Garganega/Trebbiano white
- Valpolicella (North-east)
  Light, cherryish red blend
- Vino Nobile di Montepulciano
  Herby, cherry-fruited tannic Sangiovese-based reds (Central)

Spain

- Priorat
  Concentrated, herby Garnacha reds
- Rías Baixas
  Perfumed Albariño whites
- Ribera del Duero
  Powerful, black-fruited Tempranillo-based reds
- Rioja
  Oaky, strawberryish Tempranillo-based reds; neutral or nutty Viura whites
- Rueda
  Fresh, dry whites from Verdejo/Sauvignon Blanc
- Toro
  Gutsy Tempranillo-based reds
- Valdepeñas
  Soft, leathery Tempranillo-based reds

Best wine-producing countries

Argentina

Quality is on the up in Argentina: a revolution is happening in the vineyards and wineries with better, more intense wines the result

What's hot ✔ ripe, concentrated, damsony Malbecs – particularly from old-vine plantings in Lujan de Cuyo and Salta ✔ soft, spicy Syrah and new-wave Tempranillo from small producers

What's not ✘ thin, acidic wine from Bonarda grapes ✘ over-oaked reds

Why buy Argentine wine?

Argentine wine has all the advantages of the New World – plentiful sunshine, vast areas of vineyard land, flexibility for winemakers to make exactly the style they wish – plus a uniquely wide range of Old World grape varieties from which to choose and blend. Successive waves of European immigrants in the early 1900s brought their favourite vines with them, which thrived. Today, no other country can draw so liberally from mature old vines of Spanish Tempranillo and Torrontés; French Malbec, Tannat, Syrah, Merlot and Sauvignon; Italian Sangiovese, Barbera, Bonarda; and many more. The country's wisest wineries make full use of this spectrum – but all too many make the mistake of sticking with mere Cabernet and Chardonnay.

The primary asset of this country's wines is diversity. The secondary is good value, enabled by low labour costs and a need for export success. Thirdly, ideal growing conditions (vineyards are well-watered by snow-melt from the neighbouring Andes, with desert heat and all-year sunshine to promote growth) ensure wide availability.

Argentina: the state of play

This is the largest wine producer in South America (it also ranks fifth in the world), and until recently the local population consumed most of its produce. Following its collapse in December 2001, Argentina's economy is in a precarious state, and the country now has to export to survive.

Argentine wines on the UK market are characterised by deep, often forceful fruit but sometimes lack personality. This could be the result of too much heat (temperatures of 40°C are not unusual in Mendoza, the main growing area), water (Andean snow-melt is

> ### New this year
> - San Pedro de Yacochuya: top-notch high-altitude wines
> - ambitious, quality-focused winery Clos de Los Siete
> - flavour-packed bush-vine Tempranillo from O'Fournier
> - Uco Valley Merlot and Chardonnay

often used too generously), or grapes (over-cropping follows from all the above). However, all this could change. Investment is flooding in from around the world, accompanied by winemaking expertise and a global marketing approach. Foreign investors are driving the search for new regions like the cool-climate Uco Valley, where slow ripening leads to positive aromas and elegant fruit in the wines. It is likely that when Argentina produces an 'icon' wine, it will come from this region. In addition, local companies such as Catena, Zuccardi, Canale and La Riojana are quietly updating themselves to meet the challenge of international markets.

Top grape varieties
❦ Malbec
Argentina's most widely planted red grape is known for deep, lush, damsony flavours which it never quite achieves in its French home town (Cahors). Common in Mendoza, it does best in areas where night-time temperatures fall sharply, retaining acidity in the wine. Old vines in Lujan de Cuyo and Salta make particularly good wines which show ageing potential.

❦ Bonarda
Widely planted, particularly in San Rafael, Bonarda produces a light, fruity quaffing

Top red wines

- Humberto Canale, Black River Malbec 1999 (Rio Negro) £8
- Lurton, Malbec Reserva 1999 (Mendoza) £9
- O'Fournier, A Crux 2001 (Uco Valley) £15
- Catena Alta, Malbec 2000 (Mendoza) £20
- San Pedro de Yacochuya, Malbec 2000 (Salta) £20

Top white wines

- Michel Torino, Cafayate, Torrontés 2003 (Salta) £6
- Norton, Barrel Select Sauvignon Blanc 2003 (Mendoza) £7
- Santa Julia, La Agricola, Viognier 2003 (Mendoza) £7
- Terrazas, Chardonnay Reserva 2000 (Mendoza) £8
- Familia Zuccardi, Q Chardonnay 2002 (Mendoza) £8

wine, which can be served chilled. It may be related to the Bonarda of Piedmont, or be the same grape as California's Charbono.

Cabernet Sauvignon

Everyone is planting this grape: it has quadrupled its hectarage in the last decade. Particularly popular in Mendoza and San Juan, it can give big, positive wines which blend well with Malbec. Less elegant than Chile's.

Syrah

Syrah is found mostly in cooler areas such as the Uco Valley, where producers are learning to make the most of its spicy character.

Merlot

This grape is strong in the Uco Valley. As yet, it is not quite as lush and balanced as Chile's Merlot, but could have potential.

Tempranillo

Old-style Argentine viticulture tended to over-crop this variety, leading to unremarkable, soft red wines. Now many unsuitable sites have been uprooted and new investment is reviving quality, especially in the cooler areas where it retains vital acidity.

Sangiovese

The classic grape of Italy has been over-stretched in Argentina for a century.

However, producers such as Benegas are learning how to combine concentration with character from old vines.

Pinot Noir

A newcomer to Argentina, Pinot is being planted experimentally in many areas – Patagonia most recently.

Moscatel de Alejandra and Pedro Gimenez

Boring, bland varieties dominating Argentina's whites: not used for quality wines.

Torrontés

This white grape is widely planted but rapidly being pulled up in favour of reds. Without proper attention it loses its light, aromatic style and becomes over-cropped and weak. In Salta, it develops tropical-fruit aromas combined with crisp acidity.

Chardonnay

Examples from the Uco Valley show promise, with light, peachy fruit; however there is a widespread tendency to over-oak.

Sauvignon Blanc

This variety shows the most rapid growth in plantings, although overall it still represents a tiny area. Examples from Rio Negro have good fresh, nettley flavours.

Wine regions

Salta

This region 1,000 kilometres north of Mendoza (see overleaf) has the perfect climate and altitude for growing grapes – temperatures drop at night, leading to complex aromas; high UV factors develop intense colour and tannins – but is too inaccessible to be a major producer. Torrontés occupies 90 per cent of the vineyard, although old Cabernet and Malbec vines produce excellent wines.

La Rioja

One of Argentina's oldest wine-producing regions, La Rioja is hot, dry and dependent on irrigation. Torrontés is the main grape but Bonarda, Cabernet Sauvignon, Barbera and Syrah are also significant. Quality is gradually improving as irrigation and pruning become more controlled.

San Juan

Scorching hot and blasted by a dry wind, this is where grapes for fortified wines are grown. El Pedernal Valley in the south is showing great promise for quality Chardonnay, Sauvignon Blanc, Merlot and Malbec.

Mendoza

This region is responsible for 75 per cent of Argentina's production. It spreads out from the city of Mendoza, encompassing land from the foothills of the Andes to the flat plains of San Rafael, and is divided into five areas.

North Mendoza has poor soils and salinity. It produces light wines for early drinking from Torrontés, Chenin Blanc, Bonarda and Sangiovese. Close to the city, mountains and river, **Upper Mendoza River** has long been regarded as one of the best places to grow grapes. Century-old vines at Lujan de Cuyo are still in production, while new vineyards of Malbec and Cabernet Sauvignon produce fine aromas and flavours. Further east, Malbec is important in Maipu. The **Uco Valley**, about 100 kilometres south of Mendoza, is the focus of new investment money. Close up against the Andes at around 1,000 metres, it enjoys cool temperatures which create quality wines: new holdings here herald sophisticated flavours and style. Lower down, the flat, warm land of **East Mendoza** is the bulk-wine region for Bonarda, Malbec and Sangiovese. Hail is a major problem in **South Mendoza**. Bonarda and Torrontés prevail but there is new interest in Cabernet Sauvignon, Merlot, Sauvignon Blanc and Pinot Noir.

Rio Negro

On the edge of Patagonia, this desert area has been brought to life by a large, diverted river. Warm days and cool nights produce soft, ripe reds from Merlot, Malbec and Syrah, and fresh-tasting whites from Chardonnay and Sauvignon Blanc.

Pick of the producers

Benegas An old family company in Mendoza, undergoing revival: the aim is to make a Bordeaux blend. A future star.

Humberto Canale Rio Negro pioneer making great strides in quality. Intense fruit flavours, now with added complexity.

Catena Argentina's biggest wine empire (Mendoza-based): bottles range from entry-level to a top-flight Rothschild collaboration. Can lack a little excitement.

Familia Zuccardi Innovation is the key at this Mendoza winery (aka La Agricola, Santa Julia or 'FZ'), with many grapes put through their paces. Soft, peachy Viognier is a great success, as is a deep-flavoured Tempranillo.

Finca La Celia New backing and new investment in these Uco Valley vineyards and

---

> ## Vintage
>
> **When to drink**
> - **reds** – usually ready to drink when bought; some will keep a year or so. Top wines such as Clos de Los Siete and San Pedro de Yacochuya will probably need some age
> - **whites** – drink all as young as possible; even oak-aged versions don't as yet have staying power

---

winery are giving well-made reds under the La Consulta brand with deep, rounded fruit.

Lurton Mendoza outpost of the Lurton flying winemaking empire. Piedra Negra Malbec has concentration, but overall wines could do with more Argentine personality.

Norton A recent facelift in the vineyards and winery is showing good results from this long-established Mendoza company. Malbec is the grape to watch.

O'Fournier A new, Spanish-backed investment in the Uco Valley, concentrating on bush-vine Tempranillo. Great results with early wines A Crux and B Crux.

La Riojana Surprisingly good wines from this huge, La Rioja-based co-operative now expanding into the Uco Valley and beyond. Organic Inti Malbec and Eden Collection Torrontés show big doesn't always mean bad.

Salentin Uco Valley pioneers, now beginning to get some dimension into their wines. Well-balanced, velvety Merlot and restrained, soft Pinot Noir.

San Pedro de Yacochuya 80-year-old vines, an extremely high-altitude vineyard in Salta and the combined forces of Michel Rolland and the Echart family are the factors that are likely to drive this new wine to icon status.

Clos de Los Siete A no-expense-spared project in the Uco Valley with wine guru Michel Rolland among the investors. Watch out for Argentina's long-awaited 'icon' wine.

> ## Top UK merchants
>
> - The Halifax Wine Company
> - Harrods
> - Inspired Wines
> - Vintage Roots
> - The Wine Society

Australia

The UK's number-one source of wine: bland, cheaper brands and niche producers seeking distinctive terroir fight for market share

What's hot   ✔ cool-climate regions producing complex, classy wines ✔ Victoria's Heathcote – the up-and-coming sub-region of Bendigo ✔ screwcaps, especially for white wines ✔ consistent and classy Riesling ✔ Shiraz – from straightforward and fruity to complex and rich blends becoming more popular

What's not   ✘ dull, uninteresting branded wines ✘ celebrity-endorsed wines ✘ over-priced top-level wines

Why buy Australian wine?

There's a reason why the British buy more wine from Australia than from anywhere else in the world. Brand Australia has been built on reliability, consistency and quality right from the beginning.

Australia's growing season, with its long, sunny days, is virtually guaranteed to produce ripe grapes just clamouring to be turned into fruity, accessible wines. And, when it comes to the finished product, there are few nasty surprises: the grape varieties are clearly marked on the labels. By and large, Australian wines do what they say on the tin. In short, it's easy.

Beware, however – the bottom end of the market is dominated by predictable, bland examples of winemaking-by-numbers. Investing the extra pound or two to take you into the £6–£10 price range pays rich dividends in terms of class and complexity.

Australia: the state of play

Although Australia has consolidated its hold on the UK market, all is not well in this vinous paradise. Recent years have seen major companies in turmoil. One of the biggest players, Southcorp Wines, was forced to call a halt to its share trading in May 2003. Meanwhile BRL Hardy was taken over by Constellation Wines, creating the biggest wine brand in the world.

The shake-up partly reflects the pressure big brands are under from UK retailers to slash prices. While this might appear to be good news for the consumer, in the long term this strategy benefits no one. Cut-price wine means cutting corners, and less choice on our shelves.

New this year

* Stella Bella, Pink Muscat 2003 (Margaret River)/half bottle £7
* Nepenthe, Pinot Gris 2002 (Adelaide Hills) £10
* Yering Station, Reserve, Shiraz/ Viognier 2001 £25

Thankfully, the country has a thriving culture of maverick, idiosyncratic producers (some funded by the companies whose cheap brands swamp our shelves) who are spicing things up in ways as diverse as the *terroirs* they cultivate. Some have tapped into Australia's cool-climate areas, where fruit of depth and finesse thrives. Others are investing in a slew of untraditional grapes, including Italian varietals. Blends are also growing in popularity, particularly those inspired by the Rhône.

The search for *terroir* is a driving force: Australians are becoming increasingly interested in incorporating a sense of place in their wines. In a country this vast, however, the picture is never simple, and there's been a smaller counter-movement towards creating classy trans-regional blends.

Another shift has been the increasing use of screwcaps, especially for aromatic whites. Evidence suggests that wines intended to be drunk young thrive when sealed this way, and this closure method has gained in popularity (despite a backlash on home turf). We can expect to see more bottles that won't be spoiled by rotten corks appearing in the UK.

Top red wines

- Pipers Brook, Pinot Noir 2001 (Tasmania) £15
- Stonier Reserve Pinot Noir 2001 (Mornington Peninsula) £16
- D'Arenberg, The Dead Arm, Shiraz 2001 (McLaren Vale) £20
- Cullen, Diana Madelaine Cabernet Sauvignon/Merlot 2001 (Margaret River) £30
- Peter Lehmann, Stonewell Shiraz 1998 (Barossa) £30
- Balnaves, The Tally Cabernet Sauvignon 2000 (Coonawarra) £48
- Henschke, Hill of Grace 1998 £185+
- Penfolds, Grange 1998 (South Australia) £200+

Top white wines

- Houghton Wines, Riesling 2002 (Frankland River) £9
- Nepenthe, Sauvignon Blanc 2003 (Adelaide Hills) £9
- Petaluma, Riesling 2003 (Clare Valley) £10
- Shaw and Smith, M3 Vineyard, Chardonnay 2002 (Adelaide Hills) £16
- Suckfizzle, Sauvignon/Semillon 2002 (Margaret River) £16
- Penfolds, Yattarna, Chardonnay 2000 £40

Top grape varieties

Shiraz

Shiraz is still deservedly king of Australia's red grape varieties, demonstrating a range of styles according to where it is planted: in the Hunter Valley of New South Wales it tends towards the rich and leathery; further south, in Victoria, it approaches an almost Rhône-like pepperiness; the heat of South Australia results in ripe, upfront chocolate- and berry-scented wines; and the cooler-climate regions of Western Australia produce Shiraz of great elegance.

Cabernet Sauvignon

This variety is still the country's number-two red draw. The cooler the climate the grapes are grown in, the greater the tendency towards finesse and complexity in the resulting wine.

Pinot Noir

In the past, the track record of Pinot Noir has been a bit patchy, but some cracking examples are now being made in Australia's cool regions – Tasmania, South Australia's Adelaide Hills and Victoria have had the greatest success with the grape.

Grenache and Mourvèdre (Mataro)

Winemakers are increasingly experimenting with non-mainstream varieties. South Australia, in particular, has had great success with Rhône reds such as Grenache and Mourvèdre (known here as Mataro). While these are seldom vinified alone, they are scoring huge successes in blends with their traditional partner, Shiraz.

Blends

Shiraz/Viognier blends, based on the traditional Côte Rôtie model, are becoming increasingly common, but may be a passing trend. Bordeaux-style blends of Cabernet Sauvignon with Merlot, Cabernet Franc and, occasionally, Petit Verdot or Malbec, are also growing in popularity.

Italian varietals

The search for the right *terroir* for Italian varietals is beginning to bear fruit as wines made from Barbera, Sangiovese and even Nebbiolo and Dolcetto come on stream. Although these varieties have yet to make much impact in terms of sales, their future looks promising.

Chardonnay

Sadly for the ABC (Anything But Chardonnay) brigade, Australia's love affair with the variety shows little sign of waning. It is still, by far, the most widely planted white grape. Thankfully, unsubtle, heavy oaking and flabby, over-ripe grapes are less prevalent. The move towards Chardonnay grown in cooler climates is bearing fruit, in more ways than one.

Semillon

Semillon's link with the Hunter Valley is as strong as ever, at best producing (after a bit of time maturing in the cellar) elegant, minerally wines. Riper examples are made in South Australia, while Western Australian versions can tend towards a green grassiness. Late-harvest and *botrytis*-affected Semillon grapes from New South Wales, South Australia and Victoria can make delicious dessert wines. Semillon is often successfully blended with either Chardonnay or Sauvignon Blanc.

❦ Sauvignon Blanc

This variety has had problems establishing itself in Australia, especially in warmer areas, where it produces flabby wines bereft of the acidity that provides its characteristic zinginess. But yet again, cooler climates are coming to the rescue and some impressive examples have been made in Margaret River, the Adelaide Hills and parts of Victoria.

❦ Riesling

Riesling is growing in popularity. It made its reputation in the Clare and Eden Valleys of South Australia, but is equally at home in Western Australia. Being bone dry, Australian Rieslings have little in common with traditional sweet or off-dry German styles. The very best examples exhibit a jolt of limey acidity, often backed up by more complex honey and kerosene notes.

❦ White Rhône grapes

Viognier, Marsanne and Roussanne have a small but dedicated band of followers – they thrive best in South Australia and Victoria's Goulburn Valley.

❦ Verdelho and Pinot Gris

Fresh, fruity examples of this old Australian grape now abound, as does an increasing volume of heady, spicy Pinot Gris.

Wine regions

New South Wales

The most established growing area in New South Wales is the **Lower Hunter Valley**, which majors in Semillon (at its rich, waxy best with a few years of bottle age) and Shiraz. The **Upper Hunter** is better known for its Chardonnay. More excitement, however, is being generated by the cooler-climate areas of **Orange** and **Mudgee**, as well as a number of areas around the Australian Capital Territory. All kinds of grapes have been planted here, and Cabernet Sauvignon, Shiraz, Chardonnay and even Pinot Noir and Sauvignon Blanc are all showing promise.

Victoria

It's difficult to generalise about wines from Victoria. Whatever style of wine you're after, if you look hard enough you'll find one from this state that fits the bill. Of mainstream interest are the fortified Muscats made in Victoria's **Rutherglen** district, the sparkling wines of the **Alpine Valleys**, Shiraz from the warmer vineyards of

Bendigo and the wines of the **Yarra Valley**. Almost everywhere you look in the state you'll find a small pocket of *terroir* where winemakers have established a toehold and are producing fascinating and diverse wines.

Tasmania

The temperamental cool Tasmanian climate holds risks for wine growers, but while volumes are small, this is the source of some of Australia's classiest Pinot Noir and sparkling wines. Tasmanian Riesling and Pinot Gris are both showing huge promise, too.

South Australia

South Australia not only produces more wine than any other region in Australia, it's also home to most of the country's biggest regional names. The hot, dry vineyards of the **Barossa Valley**, north of Adelaide, are the source of iconic ripe, fruit-dense Shiraz and other Rhône reds. The **Clare** and **Eden Valleys** are best known for their classy, acidity-streaked Rieslings, while to the south, **Coonawarra**'s prized, and hotly disputed, 'terra rossa' soils produce powerful Cabernet Sauvignon. **McLaren Vale** is best known for its reds – Cabernet Sauvignon and Shiraz in particular – while the cool **Adelaide Hills** have had great success with a wide range of white varieties, including crisp, fresh, Sauvignon Blanc, as well as the pernickety Pinot Noir grape.

Western Australia

Although Western Australia produces only about three per cent of the country's total annual crush, it more than makes up for its low output with high quality – about 20 per cent of the country's top wines are made in the state. While **Margaret River** is the most established growing region, areas such as **Pemberton, Frankland River** and **Mount Barker** are beginning to fulfil their early promise. By Australian standards, these are cool-climate regions, their temperatures moderated by coastal breezes. Of particular interest are Bordeaux-style blends of Cabernet Sauvignon and Merlot as well as Semillon and Sauvignon Blanc. Chardonnay thrives here, as do Riesling and Shiraz.

Pick of the producers

d'Arenberg The South Australian iconoclasts manage to turn out exciting wines at relatively rock-bottom prices year after year. Rhône grapes, both red and white, are a speciality.

Brokenwood Indisputably in the top tier of Lower Hunter Valley producers: of particular note are the Gravewood Shiraz and powerful Semillon wines.

Brown Brothers Although quality varies, 'BB' of Victoria deserve a following for their exotic varietal experiments. Accomplished sweet Muscats and a value-for-money fizz made from Chardonnay/Pinot Noir also impress.

Cape Mentelle Western Australian enterprise owned, like New Zealand's Cloudy Bay, by Veuve Clicquot – a vote of confidence for the consistent quality and elegance of the wines.

Capel Vale A superb range of wines. Bottles that stand out include Whispering Hill Riesling from the Mount Barker region, and Cabernet Sauvignon-based reds.

Clonakilla Elegant, Côte-Rôtie-style blends of Shiraz and Viognier from the Canberra area. The varietal Viognier is also good.

Cullen Vanya Cullen continues to make exemplary wines at her family winery in Western Australia. The Cabernet/Merlot blend is widely acknowledged to be one of the country's finest wines.

Devil's Lair Another Southcorp outpost, 'DL' in Western Australia is known for its complex, elegant Chardonnay and a powerful Cabernet/Merlot blend.

Dromana Estate On Victoria's Mornington Peninsula, winemaker Garry Crittenden experiments (usually successfully) with Italian varietals under the 'I' label bearing his name. The Dromana Estate wines are consistent, if not terribly exciting.

Grosset Spectacular Riesling and fine Chardonnay under the helmsmanship of Jeffrey Grosset in South Australia (Clare Valley).

Henschke If Penfolds' Grange is Australia's top Shiraz, Henschke's Hill of Grace is almost equally favoured. The South Australian winery also produces rich, complex Semillon plus classy Cabernet (and blends).

Houghton Wines Mainly aimed at the mass market, Houghton is beginning to make a number of premium wines. Its Frankland River Riesling is particularly good, as is the Pemberton Sauvignon Blanc.

Jasper Hill Undoubtedly Victoria's top Shiraz. A project is under way with Syrah specialist Chapoutier of the Rhône Valley.

Katnook Estate Coonwarra-based Katnook is best known for its superlative Cabernets, which show great elegance.

Knappstein Lenswood Wines are still made by Tim Knappstein, though the company is owned by Petaluma. Notable whites, especially a fabulous Gewürztraminer and a rich, elegant Semillon; a well-structured Merlot/Malbec/Cabernet blend is top red. Knappstein's own-label Clare Valley Riesling stands out.

Peter Lehmann A no-nonsense approach pays dividends. The playing-card series offers great value for money at £6–£8, while top-of-the-range Stonewell Shiraz sets a Barossa benchmark.

Leeuwin Estate One of Western Australia's most established wineries. The Art Series wines are consistently good.

Mitchelton Vintners A strong range of Rhône-style blends from the Goulburn Valley (Victoria), plus a delicious varietal Roussanne.

Mount Horrocks Home of fabulous Riesling (dry, and sumptuous sweet Cordon Cut) plus Chardonnay and Shiraz.

Nepenthe Spicy Pinot Gris, a limpid Riesling and an exotic blend of Cabernet, Tempranillo and Zinfandel spark interest in the Adelaide hills.

Penfolds Apparently untouched by ructions at parent company Southcorp, Penfolds continues to turn out high-quality wines in South Australia. While Grange sets the pace, 707 Cabernet and RWT (Red Wine Trial) are not far behind. Yattarna, the top Chardonnay, is settling into its stride after an overly oaky debut, and even entry-level wines hold their own.

Petaluma Innovative Brian Croser is the presiding genius behind Petaluma. Perhaps best-known for its iconic Rieslings, this South Australian label also makes great Chardonnay and Merlot.

Pipers Brook Quite probably Tasmania's premium winery, making spectacular Pinot Noir as well as some cracking aromatic whites and good-quality sparkling wine. Second label Ninth Island is great value.

Rosemount Estate Although now merged with Southcorp, family-owned Rosemount still makes one of Australia's classic Chardonnays – the Roxburgh – in the Upper Hunter; the cool-climate Orange Chardonnay and Balmoral Shiraz (McLaren Vale) are acclaimed, and even the bottom end of the range shows consistency and quality.

St Hallet Perhaps best known for its range of Shiraz, especially the Old Block, which comes from super-concentrated, low-yielding old vines. Some good-quality South Australian Riesling.

Shaw and Smith Based in the Adelaide Hills, this winery's Sauvignon Blanc and Shiraz show all the markers of cool-climate quality.

Stella Bella Targeting the Generation X-ers that hang out in its home town of Margaret River, Stella Bella's range includes a quirky, sweet pink Muscat and a mouthwatering Sauvignon Blanc.

Stonier Winery in Victoria's Mornington Peninsula, noted for its cool-climate Chardonnay and voluptuous, silky Pinot Noir.

Suckfizzle Sister winery to Stella Bella, with an equally exotic name, Suckfizzle of Western Australia makes an elegant Semillon/Sauvignon blend as well as a 100 per cent Cabernet Sauvignon.

Tyrrells A long-established Hunter Valley winery. Sometimes inconsistent, the wines are rich and complex at their best.

Yalumba Coonawarra winery producing, among others, some fabulous Cabernet-based wines and selling them for very reasonable prices. Also makes Australia's best Viognier.

Yarra Yerring Quirky, interesting red blends from Victoria. Wines usually repay a bit of bottle age.

Vintage guide

When to drink

- **reds** – top Shiraz, sparkling Shiraz and Cabernet can mature for many years. Drink the rest within 5 years
- **whites** – drink within 2 years, or 10 for top Hunter Valley Semillons, Clare Valley Rieslings and sweet wines

2004 Refreshing winter rains followed by even heat in spring and summer led to bumper crops of consistently high quality across Australia

2003 A very hot year. Great for Clare Valley and Eden Valley Riesling, but signs of heat stress in Western and South Australia

2002 One of the coolest years on record. Good whites from Margaret River, Clare and Eden Valleys; good reds from the Barossa and McLaren Vale. Sensational all round in Hunter Valley

2001 A hot year: Shiraz benefited in South Australia, Margaret River Cabernets are possibly the best ever

2000 Good in Margaret River but poor across the board in South Australia. Great for Hunter Valley Shiraz, and Victoria's cooler areas

Top UK merchants for Australian wine

- Nidderdale Fine Wines
- Noel Young Wines
- Philglas & Swiggot
- Sommelier Wine Company
- Vin du Van Wine Merchants
- The Wright Wine Company

Austria

Dry whites from Grüner Veltliner and Riesling deserve wider acclaim

What's hot ✔ Grüner Veltliner ✔ Minerally Rieslings ✔ Burgenland's sweet wines

What's not ✘ sometimes over-ambitious oaky red wines

New this year

- Weingut Stadt Krems, a historic old winery making headlines with Fritz Miesbauer's first vintage in 2003
- Austrian red wines continue to be in huge demand

Why buy Austrian wine?

Many consumers don't realise that Austria makes some brilliant, world-class dry white wines from Riesling and Grüner Veltliner. The reason they're not better-known abroad is because the domestic market greedily snaps up most of the good stuff, and keeps the prices high. Indeed, Austria doesn't actually make that much wine. But the word is out: the best Austrian whites are a match for any, and increasing numbers of wine buffs are switching on to them in the USA and UK. In particular, Grüner Veltliner (GV) is gaining more of the attention that it deserves. It's Austria's most abundant grape variety – some ten times more common than Riesling – and makes versatile, expressive white wines. The new Chardonnay? That might be stretching things a bit, but with its food-friendliness and capacity to gain complexity with age, GV looks set to gain more friends.

Austria: the state of play

At a famous blind tasting in London in 2002, Austria's leading GVs and Chardonnays were pitched against top Chardonnays from around the world. Remarkably, the panel voted for Austrian wines in seven out of the top ten places – not a surprise to those who know Austria's true quality.

While whites get most of the attention, reds have quietly been improving. Where they aren't over-oaked or forced, they can be surprisingly good, although they are still quite rare in the UK.

Generally, the price of Austrian wines remains a stumbling block that relegates them to niche status in the UK. While their value is reasonable considering the quality, there's not much choice under a tenner.

Top grape varieties

🍇 Grüner Veltliner

Austria's own variety makes complex, full-flavoured, spicy whites, often with a distinctive white-flower and cracked-pepper edge. GV has just as much to offer as Riesling, and there's a lot more of it. Wines drink well young, yet can age, and are marvellously food-friendly. Worth discovering!

🍇 Riesling

Riesling performs very well here, making generally dry wines that have more precision than their Alsace counterparts and more weight than those from Germany's Mosel. The variety is justifiably highly regarded.

🍇 Weissburgunder

This is what Austrians call Pinot Blanc. It makes lovely, gently aromatic, dry whites in southern regions such as Südsteiermark.

🍇 Welschriesling

Austria's second most-planted white grape is Welschriesling (not related to true Riesling). Fresh, simple, fruity dry whites are the norm, but it can also make sensational sweet wines.

🍇 Zweigelt

The most abundant red grape, Zwiegelt makes good wines ranging from simple, cherry fruit gluggers to more substantial reds.

🍇 Blaufränkisch

Common in Burgenland, this variety makes spicy, sturdy, berry-fruited reds with some tannic structure.

🍇 Blauer Portugieser

This red grape makes soft, approachable, juicy wines, mainly for early consumption.

Top red wines

- Graff Hardegg, 'S' Syrah 1999 (Weinviertel) £15
- Weninger Blaufränkisch Dürrau 2000 (Burgenland) £15
- Umathum Frauenkirchener Ried Hallebühl '98 (N'siedlersee) £30

Top white wines

- Schloss Gobelsburg, GV Tradition 2001 (Kamptal) £15
- Erich & Walter Polz, Hochgrassnitzberg Morillon 1999 (Südsteiermark) £18
- Bründlmayer Zöbinger Heiligenstein, Riesling Alte Reben 2002 (Kamptal) £25
- Prager Weissenkirchen Achleiten, Riesling Smaragd 1999 (Wachau)
- Kracher, Grande Cuvée TBA No. 10 Nouvelle Vague, 1998 (Neusiedlersee)/half bottle £26
- FX Pichler, Grüner Veltliner Smaragd 'M' 2002 (Wachau) £38

Emmerich Knoll One of Wachau's leading estates. Tight, minerally wines can be underwhelming young, but age fabulously.

Kracher Alois Kracher is famous for his fantastic sweet wines from the Neusiedlersee: arguably among the world's finest.

Fred Loimer An emerging Kamptal star for superb Grüner Veltliner and Riesling.

Nikolaihof Minerally, long-lived white wines are the calling card of this Wachau estate, run along biodynamic lines by the Saahs family.

Willi Opitz Specialist in much-loved late-harvest sweet wines from the Neusiedlersee.

Erich & Walter Polz Erich and Walter fashion stylish, food-friendly whites from well-appointed vineyard sites in Stryia.

FX Pichler Probably the Wachau's finest producer, making intense, concentrated wines that are highly sought after.

Prager Wachau Riesling is the speciality.

Schloss Gobelsburg Company owned by a Cistercian monastery, making some of the Kamptal's most impressive Grüner Veltliner.

Weninger Red wines are the speciality at this Burgenland estate. The Blaufränkisch grape excels, producing powerful, mineralic wines.

Wine regions

Wachau-Kremstal-Kamptal

These three neighbouring regions in **lower Austria** are best for Grüner Veltliner and Riesling. Most of the country's leading dry whites come from here.

Burgenland

On the Hungarian border, this area is famous for its sensational sweet wines from the **Neusiedlersee** and increasingly good reds.

Südsteiermark

This southern region neighbouring **Slovenia** is good for aromatic, savoury white wines from Weissburgunder, Chardonnay (Morillon) and Sauvignon.

Pick of the producers

Leo Alzinger Rising Wachau star making impressive Grüner Veltliner and Riesling.

Bründlmayer Willi Bründlmayer is probably the best producer in the Kamptal, and has a sizeable 60 hectares of vines.

Franz Hirtzberger Top Wachau grower making superb Riesling and Grüner Veltliner.

Jurtschitsch Sonnhof Run by three brothers from the Jurstschitsch family, producing impressively concentrated Kamptal wines.

Vintage guide

When to drink

- **reds** – drink from 2–5 years of age
- **whites** – drink cheaper whites on release. Grüner Veltliner is fine for a decade or more. Rieslings need a couple of years to open up

2003 Hot summer led to brilliant reds; some good whites

2002 A good year despite widespread flooding in August

2001 Fairly good whites despite September rains

2000 A hot, dry successful vintage

1999 Superb wines all round

Top UK merchants

- Bennetts Wines
- Raeburn Fine Wines
- Savage Selection
- T&W Wines
- Noel Young Wines

45

Canada

At last shrugging off its 'too-cold-for-normal-wines' image

What's hot ✔ Icewine: a dessert wine speciality ✔ Riesling in dry, late-harvest and Icewine styles ✔ Aromatic white grapes such as Pinot Gris and Pinot Blanc

What's not ✘ fake Icewine ✘ Cabernet Sauvignon ✘ American grape varieties

---

New this year

- Sparkling Icewine: buy it if you see it!

Why buy Canadian wine?

In 1988, the government sponsored a vinepull scheme to eradicate native American vines and enable Canada to compete on a world scale, growing the likes of Chardonnay, Riesling and Pinot Noir. New smaller wineries then began to plant vineyards and work towards regional identity.

The country's stunning sweet Icewines – richer than German *Eiswein*, with heady citrus and apricot fruit, plus brisk acidity – fetch high prices but can't sustain the industry. The 2000 harvest saw only 3,400 litres of Icewine produced against 10.3 million litres table wine, of which the best are from aromatic white grapes (Riesling, Pinot Gris and Gewurztraminer); only the best Canadian vintages can fully ripen red grapes.

Top red wines

- Château des Charmes, Pinot Noir 2000 (Ontario) £9
- Inniskillin Reserve Pinot Noir 1999 (Ontario) £14

Top white wines

- Mission Hill Chardonnay 2001 (British Columbia) £6
- Ch des Charmes, Late-Harvest Riesling 1999 (Ontario) £10
- Mission Hill Icewine 1998 (British Columbia) £14
- Inniskillin Silver Icewine 2002 (Ontario) £46

Wine regions

Ontario's wine regions are **Niagara Peninsula**, **Lake Erie North Shore** and **Pelee Island**. Niagara in particular turns out fine Riesling, and (in better vintages) tangy reds. British Columbia's **Okanagan Valley** on the Washington State border is technically semi-desert.

Hot and dry, the vineyards are good for red wines. Its cool northern extreme is best for aromatic whites. **Vancouver Island** is making some good Pinot Noir and Pinot Gris.

Top grapes and Icewine

The quick onset of the Canadian winter means **Cabernet Sauvignon** runs the risk of not ripening, but **Cabernet Franc**, **Merlot**, **Gamay**, **Pinot Noir** and even **Syrah** are developing well. Some whites (**Chardonnay**) still see too much oak; better bets are the impressive **Sauvignons**, plus **Riesling**, **Pinot Gris** and **Pinot Blanc**.

Grapes for **Icewine** undergo a series of freeze–thaw cycles during their autumn hang-time which creates intricate flavours in the concentrated juice. Temperatures must drop to −8°C and the grapes freeze solid during the crush to ensure that no water dilutes the wine. Diagnostic tests can now distinguish real Icewines from fakes.

Pick of the producers

Blue Mountain, Burrowing Owl, Cave Spring, Château des Charmes, Henry of Pelham, Hillebrand, Inniskillin, Jackson-Triggs, Malivoire, Mission Hill, Peninsula Ridge, Sumac Ridge, Thirty Bench, Vinelands.

Top UK Merchant

- Red or White

Chile

Chile has shown it can do pure, fruity wines at good-value prices: it is now moving upmarket and providing wines with depth, character and complexity

What's hot ✔ crisp Sauvignons from Casablanca ✔ rich, smooth Merlots from Colchagua ✔ deep-flavoured Carmenère from Maipo ✔ elegant Pinot Noir and Chardonnay from Leyda ✔ complex, Bordeaux-style icon wines ✔ new organic wines

What's not ✘ overstretched, dilute Sauvignon Blanc ✘ clumsy, over-oaked Cabernets

Why buy Chilean wine?

It's quite simple: Chilean wine offers pure fruit flavour at good-value prices. Tucked away behind the Andes, with its head in the desert and its toes in the Antarctic, Chile has reliable, sunny weather with rainfall mainly in winter. Water for irrigation sits conveniently on top of the snow-capped Andes, providing melt-water to most vineyard areas while those too far away benefit from bore-holes.

All the major international grapes grow well, from cassis-laden Cabernet Sauvignon to soft, velvety Merlot, crisp, lively Sauvignons and ripe, elegant Chardonnays. The weak-flavoured Sauvignonasse which for years masqueraded as Sauvignon Blanc has largely been replaced with the real thing, while Carmenère (the long-lost Bordeaux variety) has been identified and is now carving out a reputation for soft, plummy wines. Syrah shows promise, particularly in Colchagua, while Viognier, Gewürztraminer and Sangiovese are beginning to add diversity to Chile's range.

New this year

- Viña Ventisquero: an extensive estate based in Rancagua focusing on quality organic production
- Viña Indomita: showpiece Casablanca winery
- Viña Anakena: good Rapel whites
- delicate Pinot Noir from Leyda and crisp, minerally Chardonnay from Limarí Valley

Chile: the state of play

The revolution in Chile's wine industry started about ten years ago, with a rush to plant vines – in some cases without enough attention to vineyard site, planting density or clonal selection – before a proper market for the wines had been developed. Investment in wineries followed: many of these were state of the art and capable of processing vast quantities of grapes (albeit perhaps without finesse). The wines were good and full of Chilean natural fruit character but over-production led to low prices, and for a while it seemed as if Chile would permanently occupy the 'good-value' slot in international markets.

These early mistakes are now being corrected and today there is a second wave of investment, this time a lot more considered than the first. Vineyards are now being planted on hillsides where shade, breeze, sunshine and water availability get the most from each grape variety. Some of these are now producing deeper-flavoured, more complex wines that allow Chile to challenge the upper price brackets. 'Icon' wines, such as Almaviva, Seña and Montes M point the way to the future. As yet, none is a world-beater in terms of complexity and ageing capability, but they show that Chile has the potential to produce top-quality wine.

Chile is a natural place for organic grape production – with fewer natural pests and diseases than many other wine-producing countries, there is less need to spray. Ventisquero and Aguatierra lead the way while biodynamic viticulture is yielding excellent results at Viñedos Organicos Emiliana.

Top red wines

- Alvaro Espinoza, Antiyal 2001 (Maipo) £20
- Montes Folly, Syrah 2001 (Colchagua) £20
- Viñedo Chadwick, Cabernet Sauvignon 1999 (Maipo) £30
- Casa Lapostolle, Clos Apalta, Cabernet Sauvignon/Carmenère/ Merlot 2000 (Colchagua) £40
- Concha y Toro/Baron Philippe de Rothschild, Almaviva, Cabernet/ Carmenère 2000 £45

Top white wines

- Concha y Toro, Trio, Sauvignon Blanc 2004 (Casablanca) £6
- Viña Casablanca, Santa Isabel, Sauvignon Blanc 2003 £7
- Casa Lapostolle, Tanao Blanc 2001 (Colchagua) £10
- Concha y Toro, Amelia, Chardonnay 2003 (Casablanca) £12

Top grape varieties

☙ Cabernet Sauvignon

Chile's most-planted red variety is still increasing in hectarage. Even at high yields it manages lush, cassis-laden fruit, and can achieve deep tobacco and minty notes. At its best in Maipo but also good in Colchagua.

☙ Merlot

Chile's flagship variety, now clearly separated from Carmenère, achieves deep, velvety, ripe-raspberry flavours. Plantations have tripled in the last five years and it is now the second most-planted variety. It is particularly good in Colchagua and Curicó.

☙ Carmenère

Until 1994 this was confused with Merlot so was never picked at its best harvest date: the wines were disappointing as a result. Now acquiring a reputation for soft, plummy flavours, and a distinctive red-pepper character. Grows well in Rapel and Maule.

☙ Syrah

Showing promise with deep, spicy wines, particularly in Aconcagua and Colchagua.

☙ Pinot Noir

Still searching for its ideal location, the variety has had success in Colchagua, and is now thriving in Casablanca and the San Antonio Valley. Wines are soft and full of strawberry fruit although deeper, more complex flavours have yet to be achieved.

☙ Malbec

Considered to be an Argentine speciality, Malbec grows well in Chile too (notably Colchagua) and is often blended with Cabernet.

☙ Chardonnay

Chardonnay, the most widespread white grape variety, is widely planted in Curicó and Colchagua, and finds balance and fine expression in Casablanca and San Antonio.

☙ Sauvignon Blanc

Now Casablanca's vineyards have acquired some age, the Sauvignon from this region is astonishingly good. The cool areas around Molina and Teno in the north of Curicó produce fresh, lively examples too.

☙ Semillon

Widely planted in former days, Semillon is being replaced by Sauvignon and Chardonnay. It makes luscious, late-harvest wines.

☙ Viognier

Makes peachy, quaffable wines.

Wine regions

Chile's vineyards spread from north to south in the valleys formed between the Andes and the coastal mountain range, and in transverse valleys which cross the coastal range. The cool Humboldt ocean current runs from the Antarctic northwards, and can lower temperatures by as much as 10°C. Cold air falling off the Andes has a dramatic effect in some inland vineyard regions, particularly at night. There are four main wine regions.

Coquimbo

This northern region is close to the coast where wine production started a decade ago. **Limarí Valley** is the only significant sub-region, producing small quantities of Chardonnay and Cabernet Sauvignon.

Aconcagua

Aconcagua Valley, cooled by afternoon sea breezes, is historically important as a producer of Cabernet Sauvignon and is now home to icon wine Seña. **Casablanca**'s cool climate is appreciated by Sauvignon Blanc and Chardonnay; **San Antonio Valley** is a cool-climate region now providing crisp, balanced Chardonnays and elegant Pinot Noir.

Central Valley

Divided into four sub-regions. **Maipo Valley**, the traditional home of Chile's wine industry, is recognised for its high-quality red wines, particularly Cabernet Sauvignon. **Rapel Valley** is divided into Cachapoal and Colchagua Valley; both have potential and are planted with 80 per cent red varieties. Cabernet Sauvignon is significant in Cachapoal while Carmenère and now Syrah develop rich, deep, concentrated flavours in Colchagua.

Curicó is the powerhouse of Chilean wine production and the source of many good-value wines from the plains around Lontué. Cabernet Sauvignon is most widely planted, although Sauvignon Blanc production around Molina and Teno is exceptional.

Maule is the largest area. Its wide, flat, fertile plains are suited to bulk production of Cabernet and Merlot; Carmenère does well, developing rich, spicy flavours.

Southern region

The **Itata Valley**, **Bío-Bío** and **Malleco** regions are dominated by local varieties such as País and Alexandria Muscatel, but are also important new ground for quality Chardonnay and Pinot Noir. Rot can be a problem.

Pick of the producers

Casa Lapostolle Chic Colchagua winery where Michel Rolland is consultant: quality just keeps going up. Cuvée Alexandre Merlot and Clos Apalta are among Chile's best.

Concha y Toro Chile's largest wine company, with vineyards in all major regions. From basic level up to Terrunyo, Amelia and Don Melchor, the wine is exemplary. Cono Sur is a separate holding for some of Chile's brightest, most accessible wines. Viñedos Organicos Emiliana (VOE) is its label for organic wines. With France's Baron Philippe de Rothschild it makes icon wine Almaviva.

Cousiño-Macul New vineyards and new winery plus less emphasis on oak and more on deep, rich fruit are giving good results. Antiguas Reservas is the Cabernet-based best.

Errázuriz Historic company at the forefront of development, with site-specific varieties and top-notch Cabernet Don Maximiano. Deep, chocolate-style Syrah and elegant Sangiovese now form part of the main range. It also owns Caliterra (good barrel-aged reds) and partners the Mondavis of California to make premium wine Seña.

Montes Pioneering winery whose best vineyards in Colchagua produce stunning Syrah and Merlot. Estates in Curicó, Casablanca and at Marchigue produce all-round excellence. Alpha is the upmarket range, while Syrah-based Montes Folly has incredible concentration.

Viña la Rosa Old family company, recently revived by winemaker José Ignacio Cancino. Its Rapel vineyards suit Carmenère, Merlot and Cabernet Sauvignon. Wines have lush, soft fruit: La Palmeria is the brand.

Santa Carolina Consistently good wines from all regions, particularly Chardonnay and Merlot. Linked with Viña Casablanca, which makes bright, lively, herbaceous Sauvignon.

Santa Rita A large, historic, Maipo-based company making waves with the excellent fruit-driven Floresta range, plus good basics such as Santa Rita Reserva. Also owns next-door organic property Viña Carmen.

Veramonte Startlingly modern winery in Casablanca, now shaking off its California style and developing real fruit flavours and complexity. Primus is the top-notch label.

England

Decent Chardonnay and red wine is now made but sparkling is England's best bet for quality

What's hot ✔ sparkling traditional-method wine from Pinot Noir and Chardonnay ✔ red wines from Pinot Noir and Dornfelder grapes ✔ English sweet wines

What's not ✗ anything labelled 'UK Table Wine' (it has failed the English wine quality test)

New this year

- surge in Chardonnay and Pinot Noir plantings
- 'English Quality Wine': all wines must, since 2003, pass rigorous taste tests to prove their quality
- English Icewine from Northamptonshire – grapes are artificially frozen, but the wine tastes fantastic

Why buy English wine?

Wine has been grown in the UK since Roman times, but plantings had mostly died out by the twentieth century. After a 1950s revival there are now 115 wineries. These are mostly in southern England and Wales: warmer sites owing to the influence of the Gulf Stream. Low overall temperatures, however, mean harvests can vary in their success – grapes coming in as late as November. Fruit is at real risk from frost and rot, but the latter means English vineyards can benefit from *botrytis*. The natural acidity of grapes in UK conditions perfectly balances the sweetness of botrytised fruit.

With the right investment and careful winemaking, English wine shows its best. Sparkling wines notably succeed (see opposite). Surprisingly, red wines are faring well too. Less rot-prone clones, warmer weather and wineries prepared to take a risk have resulted in some juicy, fruity reds customers readily buy up. Plus a brand celebrating the 'quirkier' English grape varieties (Curious Grape, from Chapel Down) seems to be hitting its stride. This is good news as producers could uncover some ripe-fruited, genuinely interesting flavours. Who really needs another Chardonnay after all?

Since 2003, all bottles labelled 'English Quality Wine' or 'English Regional Wine' must pass a rigorous taste test as part of a new national quality assessment scheme (the same applies in Wales). Wines that fail are called 'UK Table Wine'.

Top red wines

- Valley Vineyards, Heritage Rosé NV (Berkshire) £12
- Chapel Down Vineyard, Curious Grape, Pinot Noir 2002 (Kent) £14

Top white wines

- Chapel Down Vineyard New Wave Wines, Curious Grape, Flint Dry 2001 (Kent) £6
- Three Choirs Vineyard, Estate Reserve Bacchus 2003 (Gloucestershire) £8
- Camel Valley Vineyard, Bacchus QW 2002 (Cornwall) £9
- Valley Vineyards, Fumé (oaked white) 1999 (Berkshire) £9
- Three Choirs Vineyard, Reserve Noble Rot 2003 (Gloucestershire) £15

Top sparkling wines

- Ridgeview, Cuvée Merret Bloomsbury 2000 (West Sussex) £15
- Nyetimber, Classic Cuvée Brut 1996 (West Sussex) £19

Top grape varieties

Warmer vintages are seeing real success with **Chardonnay** (rich, rounded oaked versions!), **Riesling** and even **Pinot Noir** and **Merlot**. Plantings of Chardonnay and Pinot Noir have trebled since the warm vintage of 2003. In reality, Germanic varieties bred to resist cold succeed most here: **Bacchus** (like Sauvignon Blanc), **Reichensteiner**, **Huxelrebe** and **Schönburger**, plus **Madeleine Angevine**, **Seyval Blanc**, **Müller-Thurgau** and **Optima** make dry or medium, light-bodied aromatic wines.

Red grapes doing well with some oak (to flesh them out) are **Dornfelder**, **Pinot Noir**, **Rondo** (like Syrah) and **Triomphe** (tannic) – creating the potential for decent blends in good vintages.

Sparkling wine

UK vineyards are one degree latitude north of Champagne's, so grape-growing conditions are very similar. Winemaking skills (using the traditional Champagne method) are improving dramatically: growers now rest wines on their lees to gain complexity and warm toasty, nutty characteristics, just as the Champenoise do. Offered at similar prices to the 'real thing', English sparklers have been confused not only with everyday champagnes, but *prestige cuvées* too. Sparkling rosé is equally tasty, but as with white, it's always more successful when made from the traditional grape varieties.

Top UK merchants for English wines

- The English Wine Centre
- Fortnum and Mason
- Laithwaites
- Majestic Wine Warehouses
- Tesco Stores
- Waitrose

Pick of the producers

Table wines: Bearsted, Breaky Bottom, Chapel Down (aka Curious Grape), Denbies, Hidden Spring, Sharpham, Shawsgate, Three Choirs.

Sparkling: Camel Valley, Nyetimber, Ridgeview, Valley Vineyards.

France: Alsace

Alsace is dedicated to unoaked white wines with great varietal character. Every adventurous drinker should explore its unique flavours

What's hot ✔ biodynamics in the vineyards ✔ matching Alsace wines with Asian cuisines ✔ good-value wines from the co-operatives ✔ Pinot Gris

What's not ✘ sweetness levels not always clearly marked on the bottle ✘ confusing proprietary names like Cuvée Theo and Réserve Personnelle

New this year

- Turckheim co-op Reserve range £6–£8
- Ribeauvillé co-op 'Bio' organic range £6–£10
- Clément Klur, Vieilles Vignes, Pinot Gris £11

Why buy Alsace wine?

Alsace has grapes and flavours you won't find elsewhere in France, yet its (mostly white) wines are made with a typically French focus on food. They are not only great partners for the rich local cooking, they have also found unexpected gastronomic bedfellows in India, Thailand, Vietnam and China. Alsace is also a dab hand at aperitif wines (both sparkling and still) and succulent dessert wines. And yet the wines from this region are a closed book to most UK wine drinkers, who see the jumble of long Germanic words on the label, and look away. This is a shame, as – being labelled clearly, by grape variety – they are some of the easiest to understand in France.

A quirk of geography gives Alsace its unique strengths as a wine region. The Vosges mountains to the west protect the region from rainfall and guarantee wines plentiful sunshine, while the geological upheavals that created them have left a patchwork of soils ideal for growing grapes, all lending individual characteristics to the wines.

Fermentation and maturation in oak is virtually unheard of; Alsace producers are concerned with harnessing the pure character of the grapes and the soil in which they are grown. So if oak is not your thing then Alsace could well be your place.

Alsace wine styles and labelling

Alsace is not as complicated as other parts of France. The wines are labelled simply **Alsace** or **Alsace Grand Cru** with no further regional subdivisions – the 50 best vineyard sites have been designated *grand cru* in the manner of Burgundy, and wines from these locations have more character and intensity. Alsace wines are also kept simple because the grape variety is named on the label. **Crémant d'Alsace** is sparkling wine from the region, made using the traditional method.

Sweetness levels can be a source of confusion. Supposedly dry styles, particularly of Pinot Gris and Gewurztraminer, can turn out to be off-dry (slightly sweet). Sweetness was not formerly mentioned on labels, but the 2003 vintage has seen the introduction of the term *moelleux*, which should be used to indicate the sweeter styles.

Vendange tardive (or 'late harvest') wines – riper, richer and rarer than standard styles – range from dry and potent to sweet and luscious depending on the producer. *Sélection de Grains Nobles (SGN)* wines are concentrated, sweet and made from grapes shrivelled by noble rot. They are rare, expensive and often delicious.

Alsace: the state of play

Not a great deal of Alsace wine is sold in the UK, but what we do see is good-to-excellent. Local co-operatives are generally progressive and focus on quality. They supply own-label wines for several of the UK supermarket chains, which make an excellent starting point for getting to know the region and its grape varieties.

Biodynamics is the buzzword at the moment, and producers who have embraced this harmony-with-nature approach are making significantly riper, more characterful wines. Quality overall has seen a boost in the wake of a recent tightening of already strict production regulations.

Most producers set out their stall with a range of basic varietals that display the fundamental character of the grapes and signal the house style. Above these stand wines of increasing refinement, made from old vines or special vineyards. The *grands crus* are now going through a shake-up whereby the very best hope to establish a firmer grip on the world's imagination: local committees can impose more stringent production standards and vary the grape varieties permitted for *grand cru* wines (Riesling, Gewurztraminer, Pinot Gris and Muscat). A number of producers, including leading names Hugel and Trimbach, refuse to

acknowledge the *grand cru* system, so those two words on the label are not a foolproof guide to the better wines. Consult a clued-up merchant to help you distinguish.

Red wine from Alsace has always meant light Pinot Noir of no great merit, but better vines and experimental winemaking techniques are having a positive effect.

Top grape varieties

Riesling

Alsace produces Riesling in a dry style, unlike neighbouring Germany. It makes refined, subtle, minerally wines with taut acidity and hints of citrus and apple fruit. With age the better examples develop intriguing petrolly aromas. Some everyday versions now emphasise vibrant, limey fruit in a more international style, but serious Alsace Riesling is about *terroir* and reflects vineyard character.

Gewurztraminer

Voluptuous, heady, perfumed, spicy, exotic… Gewurztraminer can overload the senses with its swirling bouquet of rose petals, lychees, Turkish delight, face cream and gingery spice. Nowhere in the world has yet managed to approach the sheer audacity Alsace attains with this grape.

Pinot Gris

This grape used to be known as Tokay and the name is still widely used despite the protestations of the Tokaji region of Hungary and the efforts of the EU's killjoy bureaucracy. The double-barrelled compromise Tokay-Pinot Gris is common. Wines are rich, full-bodied and deeply coloured, with earthy, smoky and honeyed qualities overlying fruit that can be peachy, or orangey like Cointreau.

Pinot Blanc

Pinot Blanc makes easy-going 'anytime' wines; at best, fresh-tasting and creamy-textured with light, appley or floral fruit. It is the main variety used in sparkling Crémant d'Alsace for an appealing, fresh character.

Muscat

This variety is fairly rare, but its aromatic dry wines with the smell and taste of fresh grapes make great aperitifs and are worth seeking out.

Top white wines

- Albert Mann, Vieilles Vignes Pinot Blanc/Auxerrois 2003 £8
- Pfaffenheim co-op, Tokay-Pinot Gris 2002 £7
- René Muré, Cuvée Oscar, Sylvaner 2001 £10
- Schlumberger, Les Princes Abbés, Riesling 2000 £10
- Turckheim, Grand Cru Brand, Gewurztraminer 1999 £12
- Hugel, Jubilee, Gewurztraminer 2000 £16
- JosMeyer, 1854 Fondation, Pinot Gris 1997 £21
- Paul Blanck, Grand Cru Schlossberg, Riesling 2000 £17
- Zind-Humbrecht, Clos Windsbuhl, Gewurztraminer 2002 £32
- Weinbach, Grand Cru Schlossberg, Cuvée Ste-Cathérine, Riesling 2001 £24
- Trimbach, Cuvée Frédéric-Emile, Riesling 1999 £23
- Albert Mann, Grand Cru Furstentum Sélection de Grains Nobles, Gewurztraminer 2000 37.5cl £27

Pick of the producers

Paul Blanck A huge and exciting range of wines, starting with rich, easy-drinking basics. *Grand cru* wines are superb.

Deiss Visionary, controversial producer. Complex top wines – named according to vineyard not variety – emphasise *terroir*; many have marked levels of sugar. Ripe and well made, down to the appealing 'ordinary' varietals.

Hugel Ancient company, for years the chief ambassador of Alsace abroad. Blended Gentil and standard Tradition wines, once a bit dull, are on the up. The quality Jubilee range benefits from cellaring.

JosMeyer Quality is going from strength to strength here alongside a conversion to biodynamics in the vineyard. Wines are exceptionally pure, with restrained but finely focused flavours.

Albert Mann Wines at this energetic organic estate are ripe and full-bodied, so suitable to enjoy young as well as to cellar.

René Muré Three ranges are produced: basics under the René Muré label, Côte de Rouffach, and Clos St-Landelin wines from the family's prime vineyard. Good fizz and an unusually accomplished Sylvaner Cuvée Oscar are worth a look.

Schoffit Regular wines are delicious and fruity, but the trump cards are Riesling and Gewurztraminer from Clos St-Théobald in the Grand Cru range.

Schlumberger This estate has an embarrassment of *grand cru* land, and many grapes find their way into the excellent ready-drinking Princes Abbés range. Gewurztraminer is the star.

Trimbach Like Hugel, a long-established, traditional company. Basic wines are very dry and rather hard work. Riesling is the focus, with wonderfully poised Cuvée Frederic-Emile and world-beating Clos St-Hune.

Weinbach The Faller sisters have a magical touch, producing rich, concentrated wines that taste terrific at any age, with food or without. Once you crack the code of family and vineyard names, quality is high across the board.

Zind-Humbrecht World-class wines from Olivier Humbrecht. *Terroir* is top of his agenda; *grands crus* and named vineyards are run along biodynamic lines. Some bottles have considerable levels of unfermented sugar.

Vintage guide

When to drink

- whites – drink Pinot Blanc and Muscat young and fresh. Gewurztraminer doesn't need much cellaring but Riesling and Pinot Gris benefit from 3 or more years. Drink grand cru wines up to 7 years old; premium bottles even later
- **2003** Lots of powerful wines, but few elegant ones
- **2002** Reasonably good vintage, best for Riesling
- **2001** Variable: stick to reliable producers
- **2000** Good-quality vintage all round

Top UK merchants for Alsace wine

- The Halifax Wine Company
- Handford Wines
- Harrods
- Noel Young Wines
- Reid Wines
- Sommelier Wine Company

France: Bordeaux

Despite the top reds' reputation for excellence, there is a vast lake of unexceptional, overpriced wine on the market. Bargain hunters beware!

What's hot ✔ a lot of good wine around from 1998, 1999 and 2000 ✔ value for money and dynamic winemaking in Bordeaux satellite regions ✔ second wines from top châteaux ✔ top 2001 wines recapturing classic Bordeaux elegance and refinement ✔ dry whites from Graves and Pessac-Léognan

What's not ✘ mediocre, badly-made wine trading on the Bordeaux name ✘ ridiculous price hikes for top-end wines ✘ patchy 2002 and 2003 vintages ✘ the *crus bourgeois* reclassification ✘ big brand wines from négociants

---

New this year

- more organically produced Bordeaux
- quality 1996 wines, beginning to hit their stride
- châteaux returning to the 'traditional' fold

Why buy Bordeaux?

Bordeaux provides a Chinese puzzle: despite the region's prestigious reputation, unless you buy carefully a £6–£10 bottle (significantly higher than the average UK bottle spend) can prove a bewildering disappointment. Too often your investment will reward you with a thin, tannic wine with little of the sheer, fruity pleasure of a New World wine at the same price.

If you're prepared to dig deep (very deep) into your pockets, the best wines of Bordeaux can provide a drinking experience that gives pleasure to both the senses and the intellect. The trouble is that such quality is unlikely to cost you less than £20 a bottle – unless you know where to look for the bargains. So if you don't have the budget of a billionaire, you need to do your homework.

To a large extent, the style of the wines made in Bordeaux over recent years has been governed by two factors: competition from New World wineries and critics' opinions. The influence of the American Robert Parker in particular has skewed the Bordeaux style towards bigger, fruitier, oakier wines. Many bemoan the resulting

decrease in traditional elegance, although there are signs that this is returning.

Broadly, wines from the Right Bank (Saint-Emilion, Pomerol) are dominated by the Merlot grape; these are softer and more accessible than wines from the Cabernet Sauvignon-dominated Left Bank (Médoc), which tend to have a sterner structure. The tannins which give these wines their sometimes formidable astringency in their youth, however, are what permit the wines to grow old as gracefully as they do. In their maturity these wines are breathtaking and exquisite.

Bordeaux: the state of play

Bordeaux's producers, who have long rested on their laurels, have finally begun to wake up to the fact that they are losing out, big time, to winemakers elsewhere. They have been caught on the hop by the aggressive strategies of big New World producers making inroads into the region's traditional market. These wines' reliable and consistent nature, as well as their value for money, have swung many consumers away from French wines in general, and those of Bordeaux in particular.

It's taken a long time for the penny to drop; however, many Bordelais producers are now making a concerted effort to raise their game and are opening their eyes to new ideas and techniques – from improved vineyard practices to more savvy marketing – in order to repair the region's damaged reputation. But there's a lot of hard work to be done before the region can regain the trust of the buying public.

Some big *négociants* have developed brands to compete directly with New World rivals: for example, Dourthe's No1, Yvon Mau's

The Bordeaux hierarchy

In 1855, Napoleon ordered the ranking of Bordeaux's Left Bank top châteaux according to quality. The resulting five-tier system (based on price) has proved remarkably enduring. At its apex lie the five *premiers crus* (first growths): châteaux Lafite, Latour, Mouton-Rothschild, Margaux (all from the Médoc) and Haut-Brion (from Pessac-Léognan). Below the *premiers crus* are the **second**, **third**, **fourth** and **fifth classed growths**, and then the *crus bourgeois*. (Note that some fifth growths can equal or outclass third growths, and some *crus bourgeois* hold their own with the classed growths.)

All 16 reds and dry whites of the Graves are listed as *crus classés*. The dessert wines of Sauternes and Barsac were classified in 1855 into three levels: *premier cru supérieur*, *premier cru* and *deuxième cru*. Of all the 'fine wine' communes, only Pomerol has never developed an official classification system, although Château Pétrus is unofficially ranked alongside the first growths.

Heralded in advance as a process to prune dead wood, the reclassification Médoc's *crus bourgeois* in June 2003 has been hotly disputed. Only 247 out of 490 châteaux were awarded the status of *cru bourgeois exceptionnel*, *crus bourgeois superieur* or *crus bourgeois*. Owners of properties that lost out accused the 18-strong panel of cronyism and the new system was overturned, only to be reinstated in February 2004 by a majority vote. The debate looks set to simmer until the current classification is revisited in 2013.

Over on the Right Bank, classification was introduced as late as 1955, with the last review in 1996. Saint-Emilion wines can apply for the **Saint-Emilion** or **Saint-Emilion** *grand cru* rating. Producers awarded the latter can submit their wines to be considered for a further award of *grand cru classé* or *premier grand cru classé* (subdivided into A or B). The two *premiers grands crus classé A* are châteaux Cheval Blanc and Ausone.

Exigence and Sichel's Sirius. Perhaps too successful in emulating their role models, they tend to be bland and safe rather than challenging or exciting. Better value is to be had elsewhere.

The recent debacle over the reclassification of the Médoc's *crus bourgeois* exemplifies the prevalence of infighting and politics in the region (see box, left).

Top red wines

- Château Troplong-Mondot 2001 (St-Emilion) £35
- Château La Dominique 1998 (St-Emilion) £45
- Château Palmer 2001 (Margaux) £52
- Château Lafite-Rothschild 2001 (Pauillac) £103
- Château Cheval Blanc (St-Emilion) 1989 £250
- Château La Mondotte (St-Emilion) 1998 £500
- Château d'Aiguilhe, Seigneurs d'Aiguilhe 2001 (Côtes de Castillon) £9
- Chevalier de Falfas 2001 (Côtes de Bourg) £15
- Château Pichon-Lalande, Réserve de la Comtesse 1999 (Pauillac) £18
- Château Palmer, Alter Ego de Palmer 1999 (Margaux) £20
- Domaine de l'A 2001 (Côtes de Castillon) £24

Top white wines

Dry whites
- Smith-Haut-Lafite Blanc 2001 (Martillac) £25
- Domaine de Chevalier Blanc 2001 (Pessac-Léognan) £35+
- Haut-Brion Blanc 2000 (Pessac-Léognan) £125+

Sweet whites
- Château Coutet 1996 (Barsac) £12
- Château Guiraud 1997 (Sauternes) £40
- Château Suduiraut 1997 (Sauternes) £41
- Château Climens 1999 (Barsac) £42
- Château d'Yquem 1997 (Sauternes) half bottle £85

Top grape varieties

❦ Cabernet Sauvignon

Cabernet is king of the Left Bank, and with good reason. At home in the stony soils and hot, dry microclimate of the Médoc and Graves vineyards, the grapes ripen in the best years to produce wines with intense flavours of blackcurrant, cedar and cigars and an elegant, if powerful, tannic structure. This grape usually dominates Left Bank blends.

❦ Merlot

If Cabernet is the king of the Left Bank, Merlot is the queen of the Right. The somewhat damper, clayey soils of St-Emilion and Pomerol can produce plum-and-spice-perfumed Merlots of exquisite depth and balance.

❦ Cabernet Franc

Cabernet Franc is often used as a blending grape in Bordeaux, and rarely takes centre stage. The one exception of note is St-Emilion superstar Château Cheval Blanc, where it dominates. If not ripened properly, it can smell unattractively herbaceous, but at its best it lends a violet-tinged elegance to the wines it graces.

❦ Petit Verdot

This classic Bordeaux blending grape is seeing a bit of a revival of late. Although it can be difficult to ripen successfully, in hot years it gives wine a spicy richness and concentrated, tannic structure.

❦ Sauvignon Blanc

Bordeaux-style Sauvignon makes a richer, fruitier wine than its Loire-grown counterparts, although it can still possess herbaceousness and piercing acidity. It is usually blended with Sémillon (and sometimes Muscadelle) to make dry and sweet whites.

❦ Sémillon

Sémillon lends Bordeaux's whites – both sweet and dry – honeyed richness, weight and depth. Its susceptibility to *botrytis* makes it the cornerstone of the most elegant sweet wines of Sauternes.

Wine regions

In order to understand Bordeaux as a whole, you have to get to grips with its geography. Fifty-seven appellations for red, dry white, sweet white and rosé wines (as well as small quantities of sparkling *crémant*) cluster around the Garonne and Dordogne Rivers

as they open into the Atlantic. The most basic are the Bordeaux and Bordeaux Supérieur appellations, which account for a significant proportion of production and are the source of much of the region's branded wine. The most prestigious appellations are divided into regions roughly defined as Left Bank, Right Bank, satellite appellations and Sauternes (along with a number of other, lesser appellations that produce sweet white wines).

Left Bank

The powerhouse that drove Bordeaux's prestige is made up of **Graves** and **Pessac-Léognan**, plus the communes of the Médoc (**Médoc, Haut-Médoc, Listrac, Moulis**, and top-of-the-heap: **Saint-Estèphe, Pauillac, Saint-Julien** and **Margaux**).

Left Bank reds tend to be dominated by Cabernet Sauvignon, which can ripen fully on its gravel-strewn soils, although grapes such as Merlot, Cabernet Franc and Petit Verdot are also grown here for blending. Bordeaux's classiest dry white wines are made in Graves and Pessac-Léognan.

If you can't face the steep prices of the top wines (expect to pay at least £100 a bottle) but still want something pretty special, look to the so-called 'second wines' of the top producers. Although these tend to be made from younger vines, and benefit from less new oak than the top *cuvées*, they usually provide a good approximation of the real thing at a significantly lower price.

Pick of the producers

Angludet (Margaux) They may never set the world alight, but Angludet's wines are reliable, pleasant and easy-going.

Chasse-Spleen (Moulis) Although a *cru bourgeois*, Chasse-Spleen tends to punch well above its weight.

Domaine de Chevalier (Pessac Léognan) Reds are consistently good; dry whites are often superb – both are worth ageing for a few years.

Cos d'Estournel (St-Estèphe) One of the most supple and accessible of the St-Estèphe *crus classés*.

Haut-Bages Libéral (Pauillac) Given the *terroir* (the vineyards lie next to those of châteaux Latour and Pichon-Lalande), wines produced here offer relatively good value.

Haut-Brion (Pessac-Léognan) The wines of this first growth – both white and red – are consistently elegant. The second wine,

Bahans-Haut-Brion, offers a cut-price window on the top *cuvée*.

Lafite-Rothschild (Pauillac) Wines of this first growth need time in bottle before opening out into the polished finesse of full maturity. The château's second wine is Carruades de Lafite-Rothschild.

Latour (Pauillac) A powerhouse of a wine that epitomises the Pauillac *terroir*. Les Forts de Latour is the second wine.

Léoville-Barton (St-Julien) Château loved as much for its espousal of fair pricing as for its rich, perfumed wines. La Réserve de Léoville-Barton is the second wine.

Léoville-Las-Cases (St-Julien) Intense, complex clarets are the hallmark of this property.

Margaux (Margaux) Margaux never fails to charm with its perfumed elegance. The second wine is Pavilon Rouge.

Montrose (St-Estèphe) Powerful, dense wines that repay ageing.

Mouton-Rothschild (Pauillac) Often the most expensive of the first growths. If you have the cash, Mouton's inky, Cabernet-dominated (80-per-cent-plus) wine has both force and structure. The second wine is Le Second Vin de Mouton-Rothschild.

Palmer (Margaux) Sumptuous, fruity wines of great class and depth, especially since the mid-90s. The second wine, Alter Ego de Palmer, is a star at the price.

Pichon-Longueville-Baron (Pauillac) This property's reputation has got better and better since the late 1980s. The second wine is Les Tourelles de Longueville.

Pichon-Longueville-Comtesse-de-Lalande (Pauillac) Consistently supple and graceful, the Comtesse is a wine of great charm and finesse. La Réserve de la Comtesse is the second wine.

Pontet-Canet (Pauillac) In the doldrums for a while, this property is finally beginning to flex its muscles.

Preuillac (Haut-Médoc) The Mau family took over in the 1990s, and successfully appealed against declassification in the recent *cru bourgeois* reshuffle.

Rauzan-Ségla (Margaux) Big investment in both the vineyard and the winery over the past few years are now paying dividends.

Rollan de By (Médoc) Another Médoc property on the rise, offering good value for money.

Smith-Haut-Lafitte (Pessac-Léognan) With truly great dry whites and elegant reds, Smith-Haut-Lafitte doesn't put a foot wrong.

Sociando-Mallet (Haut-Médoc) Power and elegance that almost outperforms the potential of its *terroir*. A property known for consistency and reasonable prices.

Right Bank

Saint-Emilion, Pomerol and their surrounding communes are collectively known as the Right Bank. Soils here are made up of clay and chalk, where Merlot ripens to perfection but Cabernet grapes can struggle in cooler years. Right Bank Merlot-based wines tend to be softer and rounder than those of the Left Bank and mature sooner, thanks to a lower tannin profile.

Because of the tiny size of these appellations, the relative scarcity of their wines can drive prices skywards. The Right Bank is also home to the so-called '*garagistes*', who produce turbo-charged, super-concentrated wines in minuscule quantities and price them as highly as precious jewels.

Pick of the producers

Angélus (St-Emilion) Ripe, fleshy, hedonistic Right Bank wines.

Ausone (St-Emilion) Like Cheval Blanc a *premier grand cru classé A*, Ausone is perhaps more typically St-Emilion as it is based on the appellation's premier grape, Merlot.

Canon-la-Gaffelière (St-Emilion) Consistent property whose wines are relatively light on Merlot, heavy on intense, concentrated Cabernet Franc.

Cheval Blanc (St-Emilion) One of two premier wines of St-Emilion (the other is Ausone), Cheval Blanc is known for its silky elegance. Cabernet Franc is the dominant grape in the blend.

La Conseillante (Pomerol) Fleshy and ripe in their infancy, the wines become very elegant when mature.

Grand-Corbin-Despagne (St-Emilion) Huge improvements during the 1990s made this a name to watch.

Grandes Murailles (St-Emilion) With only two hectares of vineyards, there's not much of this red around. What there is tends to be worth the price thanks to its concentration and complexity.

La Mondotte (St-Emilion) You'll have to pay a king's ransom to sample this wine's dense, fleshy fruit.

Pétrus (Pomerol) Perhaps the greatest of the Pomerol properties, Pétrus is dense, weighty and intended to be drunk at full maturity. Prices are stratospheric.

Le Pin (Pomerol) If Pétrus is king of Pomerol, Le Pin is queen. Sensual, delicate and charming, it fetches eye-wateringly high prices.

Trotanoy (Pomerol) It takes time for the tight structure of this wine to unwind into the complex, elegant beauty of its maturity. Classic Pomerol.

Vieux-Château-Certan (Pomerol) With more Cabernet than most Pomerols, this wine is also more structured. It retains both charm and finesse.

Bordeaux satellites

Bordeaux's 'satellite' appellations are the places to look for bargains. **Côtes de Castillon, Lalande-de-Pomerol, Fronsac, Canon-Fronsac**, the **Côtes de Bourg, Franc** and **Blaye, Montagne-St-Emilion, Lussac-St-Emilion, St-Georges-St-Emilion** and **Puisseguin-St-Emilion** are all based on the Right Bank of the Gironde estuary. Here, lower prices for land – and probably lower expectations, too – have allowed producers to experiment with low yields, novel methods of vinification and other methods to improve their wines, while still charging reasonable prices (for Bordeaux) of £8–£15 a bottle.

Pick of the producers

Domaine de l'A (Côtes de Castillon) This biodynamic property makes sumptuously fleshy, appealing wines.

d'Aiguilhe (Côtes de Castillon) Wines from this promising property offer great value for money. The second wine, Seigneurs d'Auguilhe, is worth a try.

Falfas (Côtes de Bourg) Biodynamic château making waves with very reasonable, stylish wines.

Fontenil (Fronsac) Stellar flying winemaker Michel Rolland runs this property with his wife, Dany. The wines are potent and well balanced.

De Gaspard (Côtes de Castillon) Mellow, classic Bordeaux just made to match a meal.

Lafleur de Bouard (Lalande-de-Pomerol) An underrated wine that's well worth tracking down for its value and potency.

Marsau (Côtes de Franc) A well-made wine that punches well above weight in terms of both quality and price.

Puygueraud (Côtes de Francs) Vigorous, fruit-packed wines. In the best vintages, the property produces the top Cuvée Georges.

Roc de Cambes (Côtes de Bourg) Full-bodied and well-balanced, with good fruit: a lot of wine for your cash.

La Vielle Cure (Fronsac) Soft, fruity wines that offer great value for money.

Sauternes and other sweet white appellations

Sauternes and **Barsac**, plus the lesser appellations for sweet whites (**Cadillac, Loupiac, Cérons** and **Ste-Croix du Mont**) are clustered tightly around the north and south banks of the Garonne River. Of them all, Sauternes is by far the most prestigious, and the wines of its top property, Château d'Yquem, command fabulous prices.

In this area producers pray each year for rain, for with its arrival in late autumn *botrytis* spreads among the vineyards planted with Sémillon and Sauvignon Blanc. It causes the sugars within the grapes to concentrate, creating the super-sweet essence that characterises these wines.

Pick of the producers

Bastor-Lamontagne (Sauternes) While not in the premier league, Bastor-Lamontagne consistently produces well-made wines at reasonable prices.

Climens (Barsac) One of Barsac's two best properties, Climens has plenty of fruit linked to a perfectly balanced structure.

Coutet (Barsac) The other star of the Barsac appellation, Coutet has elegant, citrussy finesse.

Doisy-Daëne (Barsac) Rich, sweet Sémillon-based wines from this property on the up.

Doisy-Védrines (Barsac) A bit too unctuous to be truly top-class.

De Fargues (Sauternes) The Lur-Saluces family also own Château d'Yquem; this is its bargain-basement cousin.

Guiraud (Sauternes) The sumptuous apricot-fruit flavours of Guiraud command top prices. If you're prepared to fork out, you'll be rewarded with a rich, classy wine.

Liot (Barsac) Good-value sweet whites that are made to be drunk young.

Vintage guide

When to drink

It's difficult to predict when Bordeaux will be drinking its best (vintage variation, the quality of the wine and personal taste all play a part). Generally:

- **reds** – drink lesser reds after 2 years, and the best after 8–15 years (more for top vintages)
- **whites** – drink dry whites anywhere between 1 year (cheaper versions) and 10 years (the best). Top sweet whites (notably Château d'Yquem) don't hit their stride until 10–15 years old; lesser ones can be drunk sooner

2003 Ripe, fleshy reds from a very hot year. Dry whites may lack acidity, but sweet wines will be good

2002 Better on the Left Bank than on the Right. Dry whites patchy in quality; sweet whites did well

2001 Rainy: reds moved away from modern super-ripeness back to traditional Bordeaux elegance. Good vintage in Sauternes

2000 A stellar vintage at astronomical prices. Reds are powerful, rich and concentrated; dry whites are equally good. Sweet whites rather poor

1999 Bad weather. Left Bank properties fared best. Treat Right Bank wines and dry whites with caution. Good year for Sauternes

1998 Better on Right Bank than Left. Dry whites have low acidity, but quality wines made in Sauternes

1997 Overpriced on release, reds are now reasonably priced and drinking well. Dry whites fared badly, but Sauternes excelled

1996 Quality vintage, just beginning to show well; slightly better on the Left Bank than Right. Another great Sauternes year

1995 A powerful vintage for the Right Bank, possibly less so for the Left. Classic Sauternes

1994 The tail end of a series of indifferent-to-poor vintages

1993 A rainy growing season resulted in poor quality. Drink up now, if you have any left

1992 Disastrous on the Left Bank and mediocre on the Right. Eminently forgettable in Sauternes

1991 A terrible year on the Right Bank and only barely acceptable on the Left

1990 Classic Left and Right Bank reds. Dry whites and Sauternes also did well

Rieussec (Sauternes) One of the premier wines of Sauternes, Rieussec is rich and opulent in style.

Suduiraut (Sauternes) A property going from strength to strength, with heady, unctuous wines.

d'Yquem (Sauternes) The fairy at the top of the Sauternes Christmas tree, d'Yquem never fails to dazzle – or to command stellar prices.

Top UK merchants for Bordeaux

- Bordeaux Index
- Corney & Barrow
- Farr Vintners
- Fine & Rare Wines
- Lea & Sandeman
- Roberson Wine Merchant
- The Wine Society

France: Burgundy

Burgundy is famed for uniquely elegant Chardonnays and Pinot Noirs, reflecting individual vineyard character; with flavours this fine there's little need to blend the grapes

What's hot ✔ 2002 wines, particularly the whites ✔ 2003 temperatures, creating quality but low yields ✔ Mâconnais wines (St-Véran, Pouilly-Fuissé and Pouilly-Vinzelles) ✔ organic/biodynamic wines

What's not ✘ genetically modified anything ✘ too much intervention – the best wines are left to ferment naturally ✘ complacency: Burgundians need to compete with New World prices and quality

Why buy Burgundy?

Burgundy's wines are world benchmarks, emulated by winemakers from California to the Cape. Pinot Noir (the main red grape) offers summer-fruit flavours that evolve into a heady fireside luxury of chocolate, smoke and leather when allowed to mature. And white Burgundies, made from Chardonnay, range from the haughtiest steel-and-flint wines to the most sumptuous apple, hazelnut and creamy butter versions. Burgundians believe their grapes are merely the catalyst through which the spirit of *terroir* (a meeting of soil, land, weather and grower know-how) is carried.

Some diehard fans say there are no bad Burgundy vintages, only bad producers. And to some extent, this is true. A continental climate, with cold winters (even snow) and a shortish growing season, means the vines are vulnerable to floods, hail, frost, rot and just about anything else that can ruin a good crop. Yet pernickety Pinot Noir, while playing havoc with growers' emotions elsewhere in the world, seems to thrive here as does Chardonnay. Even in bad years, careful picking and judicious vinification go a long way towards making a seriously good wine. In good years, it can be magical. Thus a talented producer is worth his or her weight in gold.

Burgundy: the state of play

Beneath the cheerfully coloured roof tiles, in cool stone cellars and on the variegated patchwork of rolling slopes that stretches from Dijon to Lyon, there's something

New this year

- Bourgogne Côte du Couchois (red) and Saint Bris (white): two new appellations worth watching
- Blason de Bourgogne: a promising group of co-ops aiming to make Burgundy less complicated for the buyer
- Château Bellevue, rejuvenated by Louis Jadot and making some serious Beaujolais
- The Bret Brothers making distinctive and excellent-value Pouilly-Vinzelles (Mâconnais) at their Domaine de la Soufrandière

fermenting – and it's not just wine. Tradition is butting heads with innovation: the old-guard patriarchs are at odds with a well-travelled, business-schooled generation, who insist that the New World is eating Burgundy's lunch, and if something isn't done about it, everyone will go hungry.

It's no wonder there's trouble. The region comprises some 185 kilometres, five growing districts, four French *départements* (political administrative areas), over 100 *appellation d'origine côntrolées* (AOCs), and thousands of landowners. Although it produces only three per cent of France's total output and a quarter of the volume of Bordeaux, it is prized as highly as that region and has the prices to show for it. Burgundy needs to measure up to the New World, yet various different approaches to winemaking exist,

Top red wines

- J Moreau et Fils, Bourgogne Pinot Noir £9
- Sylvie Esmonin, Côte de Nuits-Villages 2000 £11
- Château des Jacques, Louis Jadot, Moulin-à-Vent 2001 £12
- Perrot Minot, Gevrey-Chambertin 2000 £14
- Joseph Roty, Marsannay 2000 £14
- Château des Jacques, Louis Jadot, Moulin-à-Vent Grand Clos de Rochegrés 1999 £15
- Domaine Fourrier, Morey-St-Denis Clos Solon 2002 £16
- Nicolas Potel, Volnay Vieilles Vignes 2002 £19
- Domaine Dujac, Bonne-Mares 2001 £75
- Domaine Ponsot, Clos de la Roche Vieilles Vignes 2001 £75
- Armand Rousseau, Le Chambertin 2001 £85
- Domaine Jean Grivot, Richebourg 2001 £125
- Emmanuel Rouget, Echézeaux 2001 £125
- Comte Georges de Vögué, Musigny Vieilles Vignes £165
- Domaine Leroy, Romanée St-Vivant 2001 £200
- Anne Gros, Richebourg 2001 approx price: £200
- Domaine Meo-Camuzet, Richebourg 2001 £250
- Domaine de la Romanée-Conti, Romanée-Conti 2001 £1,000+

Top white wines

- Blason de Bourgogne, St Veran 2001 £7
- Cave de Viré, Viré-Clessé Vieilles Vignes 2002 £7
- William Fèvre, Petit Chablis 2002 £7
- Blason de Bourgogne, Crémant de Bourgogne £9
- Louis Jadot, Bourgogne 2001 £10
- Domaine Pinson, Chablis 2002 £12
- Daniel Barraud, La Roche Pouilly-Fuissé 2002 £16
- Domaine des Comtes Lafon, Meursault 2001 £30
- Réné and Vincent Dauvissat, Chablis Les Clos 2001 £30
- François Jobard, Meursault 2001 £33
- Jean-Marie Raveneau, Chablis Les Clos 2002 £100
- Domaine Jean-François Coche-Dury, Corton Charlemagne 2001 £200
- Domaine Ramonet, Le Montrachet 2001 £375

generating an impression of inconsistency and unreliability. Just as hand-sorting of grapes makes a better wine, so Burgundy is undergoing a painful culling process wherein smaller and more rustic growers in particular (but really anyone who strives for less than perfection) will eventually fall away – such growers are increasingly selling land to more efficient producers. This trend is being accelerated by the continued overlap in the roles of the growers and *négociants* (merchants).

In addition to buying in grapes, the *négociants* (such as Bouchard Père et Fils, Joseph Drouhin, François Faiveley, Louis Jadot, Michel Laroche and Louis Latour) vinify, bottle and sell wine from their own not inconsiderable holdings in recent years. Their turf has been encroached upon by new '*micro-négociants*', who offer growers a financial incentive to do more work in the vineyards, thus raising the quality of the grapes, and then divert supplies away from traditional *négociants*.

Happily for consumers, the ongoing shake-up seems to be having a positive impact on the whole region – most notably in the middle (*village*) and bottom (regional) portion of the packed appellation pyramid.

It's worth keeping tabs on some of the less fashionable and, for now, cheaper Burgundian areas – especially wines from the 2002 vintage, which has from its first release offered consistent good quality across the board. There are bargains to be had within this group. There is tension, however, about the 2003 vintage: one of the hottest, earliest and smallest in memory. Early tastings have raised alarms about the Pinot Noir being barely recognisable as such (too jammy and super-ripe), and Chardonnay being rich and ripe, but lacking in freshness. Critics predict a mixed bag, so it's best to buy from a reliable grower.

The Burgundy hierarchy

Top of the quality pile are the *grands crus* (39 in total, 24 of which are for red wine), some covering less than an hectare. Next the 562 *premiers crus*: these link their name on to the village name (e.g. Puligny-Montrachet 'Folatières', where Folatières is the name of the *premier cru*), or if no linked name is mentioned they will be a blend from several *premiers crus* sites. After this come the *village* wines (such as Meursault, Givry and Chambolle-Musigny). Then, lastly: **Bourgogne Rouge**, **Bourgogne Blanc**, **Bourgogne Passetoutgrains** (blended Pinot Noir and Gamay), and **Bourgogne Grande Ordinaire**.

Top grape varieties

Pinot Noir

Possibly the first, and widely considered the epitome, of the world's Pinot Noirs, Burgundy's version is the mainstay of wines from humble Bourgogne Rouge right up to stellar to-die- (and pay) for wines such as Domaine de la Romanée-Conti. Good young wines taste of fresh black and red fruits, while fine older ones will develop secondary flavours of smoke, game, chocolate, and much more. The character is all down to the *terroir*.

Gamay

Burgundy's second grape, Gamay (officially Gamay Noir à Jus Blanc) reigns supreme in Beaujolais, where it makes light, gluggable cherry- and berry-flavoured wines at the *villages* level and below, and some more interesting higher-end *crus*. Gamay is also used in Mâcon, where it is blended with Pinot Noir to make Bourgogne Passe-Tout-Grains appellations.

Chardonnay

Chardonnay is at its best in Burgundy, from flinty Chablis (in the north) to buttery Meursault and steely Mâcon (in the south), and is by far the region's most widely planted white grape. Sometimes it seems too rich and honeyed (as in Chassagne-Montrachet) to possibly be a dry wine. Chardonnay sings a different note for every parcel of land it grows on. It tastes delicious young, yet manages to age gracefully for several years.

Aligoté

While not as distinguished or versatile as Chardonnay, Aligoté is nonetheless a classic white Burgundy grape, used in wines labelled Bourgogne Aligoté AC or (if from the eponymous Chalonnaise village), Bourgogne Aligoté de Bourzeron AC. Older vines can produce wines with hazelnut and citrus notes. It's the grape used to make proper Kir.

Sauvignon Blanc

This is grown only in the newly appointed, little-known appellation of St-Bris (formerly Sauvignon de St-Bris), south-west of Chablis. The wines have muted green, almost grassy aromas, and a crisp finish.

Wine regions

Burgundy has five wine districts – from north to south: Chablis, the Côte d'Or, the Côte Chalonnaise, the Mâconnais and Beaujolais.

Red Burgundy

Red wine territory starts just south of Dijon. Here begins the Côte d'Or, a 65-kilometre, north-to-south band along which no fewer than 56 *grands crus* and hundreds of *premier cru* vineyards occupy some of the most valuable land on earth. The northern appellations (usually referred to as the Côte de Nuits) begin with **Marsannay** (known mainly for rosés) and finish with **Nuits-St-Georges**.

Côte de Nuits wines are the world benchmarks for Pinot Noir. They range from rich, full-bodied heavyweights, such as the iconic Chambertin – one of nine *grands crus* from the village of **Gevrey-Chambertin** (try those being made by rising stars such as Denis Mortet and Jean-Marie Fourrier) – to still-powerful but more perfumed styles typical of **Morey-St-Denis** (home to elegant Clos de Lambrays and Domaine Hubert Lignier), **Chambolle-Musigny** (Confuron-Cotedidot and Pierre Bertheau make delicious versions) and **Vosne-Romanée** (best known for Domaine de la Romanée-Conti and the almost chimeral Domaine Leroy). Regardless of vintage, only tiny amounts of these wines are made. Lastly come the wines of **Nuits-St-Georges**, which need more time to open out than their northerly cousins (try the better-quality *premier cru* wines).

Reds from the Côte de Beaune, which stretches from the town of Beaune (the heart of the wine industry) to Maranges, are considered slightly less fabulous, more feminine and more affordable. Among them are a host of well-known *premiers crus* like powerful **Pommard** and elegant **Volnay**, and one *grand cru*, **Corton** – reportedly on the ascent again thanks to winemaker Didier Dubois. **Savigny, Aloxe-Corton, Pernand-Vergelesses, Ladoix** and **Chorey-lès-Beaune** are simpler, good-value wines with potential.

The Côte Chalonnaise is discussed below (see 'Good-value appellations', page 65), while Mâcon, which mainly uses Gamay, is a better bet for whites.

Beaujolais, the southernmost region – where Gamay rules – is slowly showing the world there's more to it than Beaujolais Nouveau. Owing to a different fermentation technique and different grape from that of its northerly neighbours, the wines are lighter in weight, though intensely coloured (sometimes purple) and redolent of strawberries and raspberries.

Of the 13 Beaujolais appellations, ten are specific village *crus*. Some consider **Moulin-à-Vent, Morgon** and **Chénas** the most superior. The others are: St-Amour, Brouilly, Côte de Brouilly, Chicoubles, Fleurie, Juliénas and Regnié. While Georges Duboeuf rules the quantity roost, Louis Jadot has made a bid for quality from Château des Jacques and Château Bellevue. Try also straightforward Beaujolais (not *villages* or *crus*) from Alain Chatoux.

Pick of the producers

Boisset, La Famille des Grands Vins Family-owned and run, Burgundy's largest (and France's third-largest) company proves that bigger can be beautiful by hiring top winemakers for its handful of domaines (including Bouchard-Aîné, Jaffelin, Ropiteau and Domaine de la Vougeraie) and letting them do their own thing.

Chauvenet-Chopin Seriously stylish, modern wine at prices that are expensive, but just about within reach.

Robert Chevillon One of the great names in the Nuits, Chevillon is a family domaine that has benefited from input from both older and newer generations.

Confuron-Côtetidot One of the hottest young growers in the Côtes, Yves Confuron makes wonderfully concentrated, increasingly interesting red wines that can be drunk young or aged for future fascination.

Domaine Dujac Father and son Jacques and Jeremy Seysses make silky, voluptuous wines in Morey-St-Denis – including three top-notch *grand crus*.

Maison Louis Jadot The estate of this *négociant*-turned-grower-and-winemaker produces consistently excellent Beaujolais and Burgundies at all price levels.

Domaine Ponsot Family-owned since the 1870s, this biodynamic domaine adheres to low yields and a brutal particularity at pruning and harvest. Excellent Côte de Nuits wines from *village* right up to *grand cru* level are the result.

Domaine de la Romanée-Conti Long considered one of the greatest estates in Burgundy, this domaine consistently produces what its founder – the Prince of Conti – sought: the most exquisite wine of which France is capable.

Domaine Rouget Everything he knows about wine, Emmanuel Rouget learned from his uncle, the legendary Henri Jayer; Rouget's prized reds are distinguished by low yields and time in all-new oak.

Domaine Comte Georges de Vogüé Sophisticated, elegant wine: about the best Chambolle-Musigny has to offer.

White Burgundy

Whereas red burgundy may have an adversary in Bordeaux, its classy whites are unique. **Chablis**, the most northerly wine appellation, is vulnerable to cold and frost which can impede Chardonnay's ripening, but growers have tricks to safeguard their seven *grands crus* and 40 *premiers crus,* as well as the straightforward Chablis and Petit Chablis.

All the wines are notably dry (including the *grands crus* such as those from Domaine Raveneau and Domaine René & Vincent Dauvissat, which are aged in oak *barriques*), and known for a flinty, or chalky flavour imparted by their *terroir*. Indeed, tasters often describe the Chablis experience as sucking on flint – and these are positive flavour traits. Newer-style Chablis spends more time in stainless steel than oak, resulting in strong fruit flavours: characteristically, rhubarb and apple.

Moving back down to the Côte de Beaune – where most superlative white Burgundy is made – Chardonnay takes on a whole new persona. Usually aged in oak, the wines are fuller and rounder, with flavours of honey and peaches in the best **Meursault** (top wines come from Guy Roulot and François Jaubard). More floral, treacley qualities reside in top **Montrachets**: these divide into rich **Chassagne-Montrachet** and refined, elegant **Puligny-Montrachet**. (Top producers include Joseph Drouhin and Domaine Ramonet.) Another iconic white is honeyed, steely **Corton-Charlemagne** (as from Vincent Girardin Fonneau du Mortray and Jean-François Coche-Dury). As with the best reds, only a minuscule quantity is produced – Coche-Dury, for instance, only makes 50 cases a year – so prices can be very high. More affordable whites are made in the Mâconnais (see 'Good-value appellations', right).

Also worth a sip, particularly on a hot summer day, is the sparkling **Crémant de Bourgogne**, which, like champagne, is made from Pinot Noir and Chardonnay, and by the same process.

Pick of the producers

Domaine Jean-Francois Coche-Dury Worth watching for *village* Meursaults and Bourgogne Blancs that won't break the bank, right up to top Corton-Charlemagne wines.

René and Vincent Dauvissat Considered 'demi-gods' in Chablis, their wines are highly sought-after classics that benefit from ageing; their lesser wines (e.g. Petit Chablis) are excellent value.

Vincent Girardin Well-respected for his Santenays, Girardin uses rather more new oak than some of his compatriots, though not at the expense of fruit flavour.

François Jobard Meursault specialist whose wines love ageing. Lesser-ranking wines make a great start for anyone stepping on to the Burgundy ladder.

Domaine des Comtes Lafon A more modern-style Burgundy producer, most famous for his Meursault and his Montrachet (a Holy Grail).

Domaine Leflaive Biodynamic Puligny estate for wines with great ageing potential (co-owned by Olivier Leflaive, whose eponymous wines are sold through a separate *négociant* business).

Domaine Leroy The iconoclastic, infamous Lalou Bize-Leroy makes infinitesimal quantities of super-intense wines considered unique in Burgundy – and not just for their high price.

Ramonet Reportedly more consistent after some ups and downs, André Ramonet seeks a classic Burgundy harmony of fruit and farmyard.

Jean-Marie Raveneau Top-notch, but surprisingly affordable, Chablis. Experts suggest ageing for five years whether the wines are oaked or not.

Domaine Roulot One of Meursault's finest and longest-standing producers, turning out consistently impressive wines, from *village* up to *premier cru* level.

Good-value appellations

Contrary to appearances, exploring Burgundy requires neither a heist nor a hefty inheritance. Lesser appellation wines from the big-name winemakers, reliable *négociants* and co-ops can provide insight into why Burgundy can be such a joy – particularly in good years like 2002, when almost any regional appellation can delight without causing bankruptcy. Try basic **Bourgogne Rouge**, **Blanc** or **Aligoté** from growers like Patrick Javiller, Coche-Dury, Robert Chevillon, Etienne Grivot and Domaine Roulot.

No longer the well-guarded secret they once were, the Chalonnaise reds – particularly *premier crus* from **Givry** and **Mercurey** – offer quintessential Pinot Noir at much more modest prices than the more important appellations. Bouzeron's Aligoté makes a superb Kir or summer apéritif on its own, as does (sparkling) Crémant de Bourgogne. Likewise, Mâconnais whites can be delicious and terrific value. With aromas of fresh honeysuckle and apples, examples from **Pouilly-Fuissé** (Daniel Barraud), bargain-basement **Pouilly-Vinzelle**, **Saint-Véran** and **Saint-Auban**, as well as **Mâcon-Villages** and **Mâcon-Lugny** all offer a thirst-quenching glass for a relative pittance.

Pick of the producers

Blason de Bourgogne (red and white) A co-op comprised of other co-ops, Blason de Bourgogne produces very affordable, ready-to-drink Chablis and lesser-known appellation wines.

Bret Brothers (white) Promise from the Mâconnais (Pouilly-Vinzelles). Jean-Guillaume and Jean-Philippe Bret make high-end wines to lay down, and an extremely affordable no-oak *cuvée* to drink immediately.

Chandon de Briailles (red and white) Claude Drouhin's Pernand-Vergelesses wines have purity and delicacy, achieved with a 'non-interventionalist' technique. Between Aloxe-Corton and Savigny-lès-Beaune, the region is best known for its illustrious and pricy Cortons, but also offers excellent-value *village* wines.

Christophe Cordier (white) Tipped as a 'grower to watch', Christophe Cordier makes some of the best Mâcons around at amazingly decent prices.

Sylvie Esmonin (red) A producer who won't remain in the shadows for much longer. Her charming and supple wines (Gevrey-Chambertin and Côtes de Nuits) express classic Pinot Noir and have great ageing potential.

Patrick Javillier (white) An exacting winemaker, Javillier likes to extract maximum finesse from some excellent-value wines including Meursault. The Bourgogne Blanc is among Burgundy's best.

Domaine Hubert Lamy (red and white) Benchmark St-Aubin – one of the great bargain regions, particularly for white Burgundy.

Domaine Pavelot (red and white) Jean-Marc Pavelot makes stylish, juicy aromatic *village* and *premier cru* wines typical of Savigny-lès-Beaune, at prices to fit every budget.

Jean Thévenet (white) A superhero of well-priced Mâconnais, Thévenet's time and energy in the vineyard enable him to pick his grapes later than most, which maximises ripeness.

Vintage guide

When to drink
- **reds** – the higher-quality the appellation, the longer the wine should keep. Côte de Beaune reds mature sooner than more muscular Côte de Nuits. Drink lighter wines at 2–3 years; quality wines wait for 10–15 years
- **whites** – drink lesser wines at 2–3 years, top-quality *crus* at up to 10 years

2003 Reds will fare better than whites; both are for drinking sooner rather than later

2002 A generally fantastic year: many wines will drink young, the top tier may keep into their teenage years

2001 Fine-quality vintage. Top reds may last 10 years or more

2000 A top white wine vintage and some excellent Côte de Nuits reds

1999 Quality reds across the board, with long ageing potential. Modest white wine vintage

1998 A challenging year: some good-to-excellent reds if you choose carefully. Whites should be drunk up soon

1997 Good, reliable vintage for red and white wines

1996 Complex elegant reds and whites that will repay further keeping

Top UK merchants for Burgundy

- Domaine Direct
- Harrods
- Haynes Hanson & Clark
- Howard Ripley
- Montrachet Fine Wine Merchants

France: Champagne

Champagne is the world's ultimate branded wine. The real thing (only made here) is one of life's luxuries and a fabulous accompaniment to most cuisine

What's hot ✔ pink champagne ✔ great discounts on the high street
✔ the excellent 1996 vintage ✔ affordable own-label champagne

What's not ✗ sky-high prices for de-luxe brands

New this year

- Krug, Clos du Mesnil 1992, from a single walled vineyard in the Côte des Blancs
- 1998 Henriot Rosé, a delicious and fragrant pink fizz
- Vilmart, Grande Cuvée 1998, for lovers of all things organic

Why buy champagne?

Put simply, champagne is a hand-made wine in a mass-market world. It's an affordable luxury that deserves a place at the table, not just at special celebrations. It is a fiercely guarded brand, the product of vines grown on chalky soils in a cool climate, and its full flavour comes from sophisticated blending of several wines and grape types, plus the all-important second fermentation in bottle (see 'How champagne is made').

Champagne should be served chilled, but not too cold – stand the bottle in a bucket of crushed ice and water. The classic champagne flute showcases the beauty of the *mousse*: the fine stream of bubbles rising in the glass.

Champagne: the state of play

For the champagne trade 2003 was a record year. Around the world over 290 million bottles were consumed: most in France, while British drinkers came second, upping their intake substantially.

It can't all be cracked over racing cars or downed at Henley Regatta, so what is the enduring charm of champagne for the British? First, it (almost) always delivers on its promise. Second, champagne is actually affordable these days thanks to price wars on the high street. Today's purchasers have a strong notion of which champagne houses are fanciable, too, with Veuve Clicquot heading the list (according to a trade poll), followed by Moët & Chandon, Lanson, Bollinger and Laurent-Perrier. These wines represent a vast range of different styles. Forty-seven per cent of us buy for a special occasion, and only 10 per cent are influenced entirely by cost. So this is a very special wine – it can name its price and still sell well.

Rosé champagne is now cool after years of eclipse, and interest in all things eco-friendly has extended to the region. Growers, and houses that own vineyards, are adopting organic methods across the board. Champagne house Vilmart leads the way.

Own-label champagnes are becoming more fashionable, too. Many smart London bars have an own-label: the wines may be cheaper but often offer no less quality than from the big houses (often sourced from family growers, they may be organically produced too).

How champagne is made

Méthode champenoise (or *méthode traditionelle* outside the region) begins with thin, rather acidic wines (as come from this cold northerly region of France) and may include both red and white grape varieties. These wines are fermented to dryness, then bottled with a little yeast and sugar ready to undergo the second fermentation. The characteristic sparkle is created as the gas from fermentation is trapped within the bottle. The settled yeast deposits then impart champagne's special 'biscuity' character (in a reaction known as autolysis) before being collected in the neck of the bottle (by gently twisting it and inverting it over time). The yeast is frozen and expelled, then replaced by a mixture of sweetened wine which adjusts the wine style. The bottle is then re-sealed, and left to settle again before sale.

Top champagnes

- Heidsieck, Dry Monopole NV £18
- Mumm, Cordon Rouge NV £20
- Canard-Duchêne, NV £20
- Deutz, Classic NV £23
- Vilmart, Grande Reserve NV £23
- Henriot, Blanc Souverain NV £25
- Veuve Clicquot, Yellow Label NV £25
- Ayala, Blanc de Blancs 1998 £30
- Bollinger, NV £30
- Krug, NV £75

Top pink champagnes

- Lanson, Rosé NV £20
- Ayala, Rosé NV £23
- Moët & Chandon, Rosé NV £27
- Billecart-Salmon, Rosé NV £30
- Laurent Perrier, Rosé NV £36

Top grape varieties

🍇 Pinot Noir

Pressed quickly, so that only white juice is released, Pinot Noir is blended with Chardonnay and Pinot Meunier and gives body, structure and quality to the champagne blend. The best Pinot Noir comes from the Montagne de Reims.

🍇 Pinot Meunier

Pinot Meunier adds balance and fragrance to standard champagne blends. It is often left out of the better wines and vintage champagnes, being considered something of a workhorse grape. The best comes from the region of Bouzy.

🍇 Chardonnay

The Chardonnay grape, cultivated on chalky subsoils here, brings delicacy and finesse to champagnes. The most sought-after Chardonnay flourishes on the Côte des Blancs and adds not only a light, floral elegance, but also a firmness that softens and adds complexity with age.

Wine regions

Montagne de Reims

A heartland for the black grape varieties, this area just below the forest line is famed for producing acidic wines that work perfectly in the champagne process. The more famous villages include **Bouzy** and **Dizy**, plus **Verzenay** and **Verzy**, which yield subtle wines with great ageing potential.

Côte des Blancs

Home of the ever-popular Blanc de Blancs style, this Chardonnay zone is centred around **Epernay**. Villages like **Cramant** and **Avize** are a byword for delicate, intricate examples of the art. Try a bottle of Salon de Mesnil (if you can find one) to appreciate Chardonnay at its most refined.

Vallée de la Marne

Family producers offer wines at affordable prices here. It is a happy hunting ground for wine merchants, and some fine wines are now available on the mass market. As the slopes face south the wines are fuller and riper, with an almost New World style in top years.

Pick of the producers

Billecart-Salmon Small, family-owned house noted for elegant champagne. Particularly renowned for its rosé and vintage *cuvée* Elizabeth Salmon.

Bollinger Detractors believe this magnificent wine's pungent, forceful style (from barrel fermentation and long ageing) is over-the-top, but most champagne aficionados are devoted fans. Try an RD (Recently Disgorged) or the Grande Année vintage wine, made with two-thirds Pinot Noir.

Charles Heidsieck A dense and aromatic range, with vintage wines drinking well in youth as well as at full maturity.

Krug The 'haute couture' champagne house that makes its wine by hand (first fermentation takes place in oak barrel). The results show great complexity and depth of flavour. Confidently expensive, particularly the single-vineyard *cuvée* Blanc de Blancs Clos du Mesnil.

Lanson The reliable Black Label is as dependable as ever. Vintage Lanson wines age particularly well.

Laurent-Perrier A house known for its elegant yet affordable bottlings, and a stylish rosé fizz.

Moët & Chandon High-profile, reliable brand, whose vintage and non-vintage wines can be excellent, despite the prolific scale on which they are produced. Do not drink the fragrant yet powerful prestige wine, Dom Pérignon, too young.

Pol Roger Much-loved family house with a refined range, including classy blanc de blancs and long-lived luxury *cuvée* Sir Winston Churchill.

Louis Roederer High-performing house, with top blend Cristal a legend among de-luxe champagnes. Try the blanc de blancs if you can find it.

Ruinart This ancient house (founded 1729) has full, meaty champagnes in a clear and distinctive style that give game dishes a run for their money.

Taittinger Fashionable, Chardonnay-rich wines, especially blanc de blancs Comtes de Champagne. NV is good lately.

Veuve Clicquot Ponsardin A byword for reliability and consistency, this is one of the greatest houses, making wines of stature, breeding and longevity.

Vilmart An exciting house, given new life by recent modernisation. Vilmart is now a cult, with a woody style and great ageing potential.

Champagne styles

Blanc de blancs Champagne made entirely from white Chardonnay grapes. Typically fresh, elegant and creamy.

Blanc de noirs White champagne made from the juice of red grapes (Pinots Noir and Meunier). Usually firm, fruity wine.

Brut Dry champagne, with less than 15g/l residual sugar. Most champagne sold in the UK is Brut.

Demi-sec Confusingly, this means sweet.

Extra-dry Dry, but not as dry as Brut.

Mono-cru Single-vineyard wine: the expression of one particular plot of land. These wines reveal the importance of the individual components that make up a great champagne blend. Drappier's Grande Sendrée and Salon are good examples.

Non-vintage (NV) The producer's standard blend. Not to be maligned, this is the true reflection of a house style. NV can be as young as one year old, but quality houses aim for a minimum of three. Top blends draw from base-wines many years older. Basic examples will not improve with age; the best wines may.

Prestige cuvée / luxury cuvée The top champagne in a house range, and the most expensive. These wines have a more powerful, complex character than everyday champagnes, and benefit from some age. Moët & Chandon's Dom Pérignon is the most famous example.

Rosé Pink champagne: usually made by adding small amounts of red wine (Pinot Noir or Pinot Meunier) to the blend.

Vintage Champagne from a good-quality year. In lesser years, none is released. The best are more complex and have fuller flavour than NV; they should age very well. Look for the oldest possible, released around five years after the harvest. Young vintages can taste raw and unready.

Vintage guide

When to drink
Drink **non-vintage wines** at 3 years from date of purchase, **vintage wines** at 5–20 years, and **rosés** at 3–10 years

1996 Many bottles are still to be released: promise of a fine, full-flavoured harvest

1995 Great blanc de blancs; good wines in general

1993 A delicious year overall, with wonderfully subtle Chardonnay

1992 Not great wines, but very drinkable and soft

1990 Warm conditions and a classic vintage: long-lived, powerful wines all round

1989 A vintage of exceptional quality: rich, full-bodied wines

1988 Superb, complex and long-lived champagnes

1985 Perfect balance. Wines with longevity

1976 Full of ripe fruit, just right to open

1975 A full-flavoured year; great for drinking now

Top UK merchants for champagne

- Fortnum & Mason
- Fine & Rare Wines
- Harrods
- Majestic Wine Warehouses
- The Oxford Wine Company

France: Languedoc-Roussillon

Dramatic change has transformed this region into one of France's most dynamic, forward-thinking and fashionable sources of wine

What's hot ✔ value-for-money appellation wines ✔ good *vins de pays*, from basic level to top-end prestige wines ✔ classy old-vine Carignan and Grenache (particularly in 2003) ✔ some fantastic 2002 wines – but avoid those affected by heavy rains and hail ✔ delicious *vins doux naturels* from Rivesaltes, Maury and Banyuls ✔ some of France's best rosés

What's not ✗ incredibly ripe wines from 2003's hot summer are unlikely to age well ✗ sub-£5 appellation wine – pay a pound or two extra for class and character ✗ lack of style definition: it can be hard to tell whether a wine will be elegant or rustic before you open the bottle

Why buy Languedoc-Roussillon wine?

For many years, the *vignerons* of the Languedoc have endured a reputation for producing weak, sharp wines whose only redeeming feature was their cheapness. The era of bulk-produced, indifferent *vin de table* is long gone, however, and has now been replaced by a dynamic, go-ahead attitude. An increasing focus on *terroir*- and quality-driven winemaking now prevails.

It's become a bit of a cliché, but the buzz is that this is where the Old World meets the New. Long, hot summers virtually guaranteed to bring grapes to full ripeness most years and a relaxation of the often-rigid French attitudes to winemaking have

New this year

- Roussillon's Fénouillèdes region (traditionally home to *vins doux naturels*, now with much more on offer)
- old-vine plantings of Carignan and Mourvèdre producing rich, distinctive red wines
- unoaked white wines from the Languedoc, with plenty of tangy, herbaceous flavours of the '*garrigue*' landscape

helped. Add to this the fact that outside influences and finances – from as far afield as Australia and as close to hand as Bordeaux – have been invested in the area and, in theory, you have a recipe for success.

Languedoc-Roussillon: the state of play

Although things are looking up in the Languedoc, there are still many battles to be won before the region achieves the kind of recognition it deserves. Many producers' yields are down as they embrace change. Planting is taking place on the less-accessible (but often higher-quality) slopes instead of the coastal plains, and *vignerons* have begun to value old-vine plantings (particularly Syrah, Grenache and Carignan) for the super-concentrated, super-rich wines they create. In the winery, forward-looking producers are cutting back on oak and developing a wider range of unoaked wines.

The fly in the ointment is the survival of the entrenched, backward-looking attitude of some of the old-style co-operatives. In addition, high-street retailers are still putting pressure on producers to make generic appellation wine at sub-£5 levels (with the best will in the world, it's difficult to produce quality wine in France at these prices).

If the Languedoc is facing an uphill struggle, Roussillon, its southern neighbour, barely registers as a blip on most consumers' radar screens. This is a shame as the appellation wines, in particular, can be very good indeed. Styles range from velvety, elegant reds to zesty, fruit-driven rosés and headily aromatic whites – look out for wines from Roussillon's up-and-coming Fénouillèdes area. Traditionally, the region is best-known for its *vins doux naturels*: rich, sweet fortified wines based on Grenache and Muscat that are as much at home served as an apéritif as they are with pudding.

Top grape varieties

⚜ Syrah

Often the dominant grape in red blends from the area, Syrah adds class and elegance to the mix. Its taste can vary from peppery spiciness to rich, leathery bramble fruit.

⚜ Grenache Noir

Known as Garnacha just over the border in Spain, this is another key grape for red blends. It can give wine a herby, red-fruit character but if not carefully vinified tends

to be overly hot and alcoholic. It is also used to make some superb fortified wines.

⚜ Mourvèdre

The growling beast behind the sometimes smoky, meaty character of the region's red wines. It can be tannic and chewy, so is usually blended.

⚜ Carignan

Once-maligned, this variety is becoming increasingly appreciated as *vignerons* realise that, if cropped at low yields and correctly vinified, it can create wines of amazing depth and potency. It often expresses itself with notes of dark chocolate and herbs; tannins may be drying.

⚜ Chardonnay

The only unblended dry white AOC wine in the Languedoc is found in the cool hills around Limoux. The same appellation also uses the grape, with Mauzac, Chenin Blanc and sometimes a splash of Pinot Noir, to create sparkling Crémant.

⚜ Muscat

Muscat is used to make a number of sweet wines, both in the Languedoc, where there are four appellations for sweet whites – Lunel, Frontignan, St-Jean-de-Minervois and Mireval – and in Roussillon.

⚜ Grenache Blanc, Roussanne and Marsanne

These varieties are traditionally blended together to make richly aromatic dry whites that often have a peachy, floral character.

⚜ Picpoul

This variety makes a crisp, dry white with high acidity that goes down a treat with seafood. The appellation to look for is Picpoul de Pinet.

Wine regions

As wine lovers develop ever more interest in individual *terroirs*, the region's appellations are coming under ever-closer scrutiny. The Languedoc, in particular, has a number of sub-appellations that are hovering on the verge of full appellation status. Within the sprawling appellation of the **Côteaux du Languedoc**, for example, the areas of **La Clape**, **Picpoul de Pinet**, **Pic-Saint-Loup**, **Montpeyroux** and **Saint-Saturnin** are considered to have their own characteristic *terroirs*. Meanwhile, the **Corbières** region has eleven distinct *terroirs*, one of which, **Boutenac**, is hotly tipped for appellation status within the next couple of

Top red wines

- Château Villerambert-Jullien, Rosé 2002 (Minervois) £7
- Vignerons Catalans, Cuvée Extreme 2001 (Côtes du Roussillon Villages) £9
- Mas Amiel, Maury (sweet) 2001 £11
- Abbotts Cordis 2001 (Minervois) £14
- Jacques et François Lurton, Château des Erles 2001 (Fitou) £16
- Mas de Daumas Gassac Rouge, Vin de Pays de l'Hérault 2001 £18
- Domaine de la Grange des Pères Rouge, Vin de Pays de l'Hérault 2000 £35

Top white wines

- Les Vignerons de Baixas, Château Les Pins 2001 (Roussillon) £7
- Sieur d'Arques, Toques et Clochers Haute Vallée 2002 (Limoux) £8
- Château la Liquière, Les Schistes 2001 (Côteaux du Languedoc) £9
- Mas Jullien Blanc 2000 (Vin de Pays de l'Hérault) £16
- Domaine Piquemal, Muscat Coup de Foudre (sweet) 2001 (Rivesaltes) 50cl £17

years. Another *cru* rapidly gaining a reputation is **Minervois la Livinière**, which lies within the boundaries of the **Minervois** appellation, although it has appellation status in its own right.

Confused? You're not alone. The plethora of appellations, sub-appellations and distinct *terroirs* – in a region that has failed to outline stylistic variations between existing appellations – only serves to increase bewilderment.

Pick of the producers

Abbotts *Négociant* making waves with well-made *vins de pays* and some fascinating stars, particularly the Syrah-based Cumulo Nimbus and Cumulus. Cordis, made from old-vine Carignan, is liquid proof that this variety deserves more respect.

Mas Amiel Top-class Maury *par excellence*; also some pretty decent Muscat de Rivesaltes.

Gérard Bertrand One of the Languedoc's top *négociants*, whose range of *terroir* wines pack plenty of bang for your buck. Top wines La Forge, Le Viala and l'Hospitalita are rich, powerful reflections of *terroir* (though a bit over-priced).

Domaine Borie de Maurel Stunning wines from the Minervois la Livinière sub-appellation.

Mas de Daumas Gassac Top-of-the-range *vins de pays* at premium prices. The top red is based on Cabernet Sauvignon spiked with up to 17 other varieties; the top white an aromatic mix of some 16 grapes including Chardonnay, Viognier and Petit Manseng.

Ermitage du Pic-St-Loup Elegant wines reflect the cooler microclimate of the Pic-St-Loup area. Sumptuous Cuvée St Agnes is the star attraction.

Domaine Gauby A renowned biodynamic producer. The Vieilles Vignes wines (white and red) are rich, potent expressions of *terroir*.

Domaine de la Grange des Pères Gives its neighbour Mas de Daumas Gassac a run for its money in terms of quality and pricing. The silky, elegant red easily compares with any of France's prestigious wines.

Jacques et François Lurton Château des Erles, a sublimely rich and concentrated AOC Fitou, is the top *cuvée* of this Languedoc producer also making *vins de pays*.

Château Massamier la Mignarde Cuvée Domus Maximus is a spot-on example of why Minervois la Livinière is attracting so much attention.

Mont Tauch Fitou-based working model for what the co-operatives can achieve when they abandon hidebound attitudes. One of its best *cuvées*, Les Douze, is well worth its £5.99 price tag.

Domaine Piquemal Producer of an exceptional sweet Muscat, Coup de Foudre.

Domaine de la Rectorie The brothers Parcé ensure quality in Roussillon. Among the best are the Collioure and Banyuls appellation wines.

Sieur d'Arques Toques et Clochers Chardonnays from four Limoux areas provide textbook examples of *terroir*. Haute Vallée consistently demonstrates the best balance.

Les Vignerons de Baixas A fairly wide range of wines, the best of which are the red and white Château les Pins.

Vignerons Catalans The area's biggest exporter to the UK. Quality is consistent; *terroir*-driven Haute Coutume wines from Côtes du Roussillon Villages stand out (Cuvée Extreme is available at M&S).

Vignobles Lorgeril Producer of various Languedoc appellation wines, notably Cabardès, l'Esprit de la Bastide – a blend of Syrah and Cot (aka Malbec).

Vintage guide

When to drink
- **reds** – top reds will age 10 years and more; drink others within 5
- **whites** – drink all but the top wines within 4 years

2000 Good to great wines, drinking well
2001 Some fine wines made, but a tendency to dryness
2002 Wines have good structure and ripeness
2003 A drought-ridden summer led to over-ripeness and unbalanced wines

---

Top UK merchants for Languedoc-Roussillon wines

- Baton Rouge
- Berry Bros & Rudd
- Great Western Wine Company
- Lay & Wheeler
- Stone, Vine & Sun

France: Loire Valley

Bastion of Old World elegance with some top-quality wines at a fraction of the price of Bordeaux or Burgundy

What's hot ✔ classic minerally Sauvignon Blanc ✔ 2003 reds ✔ new-wave Anjou Blanc ✔ experimental *vins de pays* ✔ excellent value, especially for Sauvignon from Touraine

What's not ✘ insipid or overpriced rosé ✘ inconsistent quality ✘ unpredictable sweetness levels

Why buy Loire wines?

The Loire's calling cards are subtlety and finesse. Drink these wines when you have had enough of bumptious southern hemisphere brutes: their brisk acidity and reserved flavours have earned them a fine reputation as food partners; wines that seduce rather than shout. Minerally *terroir* character is an important factor, but they are fruity too – gently, fragrantly fruity, without a hint of anything tropical.

The Loire is a region of great variety. The river runs for over 600 miles from the Massif Central to the Atlantic coast, with the major vineyards concentrated in its second half between Pouilly-sur-Loire, home of the famous Pouilly-Fumé, and Nantes, centre of the Muscadet region. It takes in emphatically dry whites as well as some of the world's greatest sweet wines, good fizz, charming reds from light quaffers to long-lived classics, and sometimes a decent rosé.

With the exception of one or two famous appellations, Loire wines are tremendous value for money. Stick with established producers or take advice from a merchant with a passion for the region.

Loire Valley: the state of play

Loire wines fell out of fashion dramatically in the early 1990s but the region has licked its wounds and is gathering momentum thanks to the efforts of committed new producers who are improving vineyard management.

Chenin Blanc, long the least-loved of the major grape varieties, is emerging from the shadows despite the existence of some mediocre and unpleasant examples. In part this is due to its improving presence in South Africa, but also to the cleaner-tasting, more drinker-friendly wines from quality-conscious producers in Anjou, many of them revelling in the creamy lustre of new oak. The now annual Rendez-vous du Chenin, held in the Loire Valley, should see its profile continue to rise. A mismatch remains, however, between the Loire tradition of varying the sweetness of the wine according to the vintage (without giving any clues on the label) and modern demands for consistency.

Experiments with Chardonnay and rarer varieties like Sauvignon Gris and Petit Manseng are seeing very exciting wines appear under the *vin de pays* and *vin de table* classifications from former Muscadet vineyards.

Meanwhile, the classic minerally Sauvignons of Sancerre and its neighbours continue to command high prices and to resist fruity New World styles. Touraine Sauvignon is finding favour as a halfway house and remains refreshingly cheap.

Rosés, dry or sweetish and made from Cabernet Franc grapes, have the potential to delight, but too much is made from the characterless, cloddish Grolleau. Sancerre's pink Pinot Noir rarely measures up to the price tag.

New this year

- Atlantique, Sauvignon Blanc 2003 (Touraine) £5
- Domaine de la Monnaie 2001 (Savennières) £12
- Ampelidae, PN1328 Pinot Noir 2003 (Vin de Pays de la Vienne) £15

Top white wines

- Domaine de l'Ecu, Muscadet Sèvre-et-Maine Granite 2002 £6
- Bernard Germain, Anjou Barrel-fermented 2002 £7
- Domaine des Ballandors Quincy 2002 £8
- Domaine Ogereau, Anjou Cuvée Prestige 2000 £9
- Henry Pellé, Sancerre Croix au Garde 2002 £10
- Château Pierre-Bise, Savennières Clos de Coulaine 2001 £10
- Huët L'Echansonne, Vouvray le Haut-Lieu demi-sec 2002 £12
- Vacheron Sancerre 2002 £14
- Domaine Richou, Coteaux de l'Aubance les Trois Demoiselles 2001 £19
- Domaine des Baumard, Côteaux du Layon Clos Ste-Cathérine 1997 £29
- Nicolas Joly, Savennières Clos de la Coulée de Serrant 2001 £35

Top red wines

- Pierre-Jacques Druet, Bourgueil les Cents Boisselées 2002 £7
- Château du Hureau, Saumur-Champigny Cuvée Lisagathe 2002 £14
- Domaine des Roches-Neuves, Saumur-Champigny Terres-Chaudes 2001 £15
- Alphonse Mellot, Sancerre Génération XIX 2001 £45

Top grape varieties

❦ Sauvignon Blanc

Sauvignon's hallmark refreshing acidity zips through all its Loire wines. Minerally elegance is the pinnacle of the Central Vineyards style, with herbaceous flavours playing a supporting role. Touraine produces less intense versions with delightful nettle and gooseberry fruit character.

❦ Chenin Blanc

Nowhere can match the Loire's expertise with this chameleon grape, used for wines ranging from searingly dry (Anjou, Savennières) to unctuously sweet (Coteaux du Layon, Bonnezeaux); from light and bright – including refreshing, appley fizz in

Saumur – to lusciously full-bodied. Vouvray offers all styles. The grape's strikingly high acidity renders many a poor example eye-wateringly undrinkable, but skilled makers know how to bring out the honeyish, nutty, apple, quince and greengage fruit.

❦ Cabernet Franc

It's difficult to get red wine right in the cool climate of the Loire. The best wines (Chinon, Bourgueil, St-Nicolas-de-Bourgueil) combine summer-fruit flavours with an appealing lick of warm earth and refreshing blackcurrant leaf.

Wine regions

The overall *vin de pays* classification for the Loire is 'Vin de Pays du Jardin de la France'. Higher-quality wines from the appellations generally come from four regions.

Central Vineyards

Sancerre and **Pouilly-Fumé** are the Loire's best-known and most highly valued (i.e. expensive for the quality) appellations. Their reputation is based on minerally Sauvignon Blanc. **Menetou-Salon**, **Quincy** and **Reuilly** are similar, cheaper and generally better value. Reds from Pinot Noir also feature (the best are expensive).

Touraine and Anjou-Saumur

Sauvignon also appears in these château-strewn stretches of the valley, under the generic **Touraine Sauvignon** label, but Chenin Blanc is the leading white variety. At the summit of the dry wines is full-bodied, long-lived **Savennières**. **Vouvray** and **Montlouis** are far lighter and come in varying levels of sweetness. **Anjou Blanc** is a generic label for dry whites and many are poor wines, but producers of sweet wines from the Layon Valley use it for dry Chenins that rival Savennières. The honey-quince-sweet yet fresh wines from the **Coteaux du Layon** (including sub-appellations such as **Bonnezeaux**) and from Vouvray can be among the world's best. Good ones also appear from the **Coteaux de l'Aubance**.

Saumur has some classy dry Chenin but is better-known for fizz and for elegant, summer-fruited (and occasionally long-lived) Cabernet Franc reds. The best of these traditionally hail from **Chinon** and **Bourgueil**, along with neighbour **St-Nicolas-de-Bourgueil**, but in **Saumur-Champigny** a number of estates are pioneering richer, riper and more powerful examples.

Atlantic Vineyards

Dry, lemon-fresh seafood-partner Muscadet is the chief appellation here and quality, once poor, is now better than ever. The best wines are **Muscadet Sèvre-et-Maine** with the words *sur lie* (referring to the production process, which adds creamy and spritzy notes) on the bottle.

Vintage guide

When to drink

- **reds** – most Cabernet Franc producers make a range: some to drink young, some to keep for 4 years or more. Drink Gamay and most Pinot Noir young
- **whites** – drink Touraine Sauvignon and Muscadet young, Sancerre at 2 years: keep the best bottles longer. Chenin often benefits from ageing for several years; the best sweet wines live on for 40+ years

2003 A heatwave year. Brilliant for reds. Whites can be super but many lack refreshing acidity

2002 Good quality all round

2001 Reasonably good dry wines, superb sweet wines

2000 Decent dry wines

Pick of the producers

Philippe Alliet Excellent small Chinon estate for wines with marvellous pure fruit.

Yanick Amirault Leading estate in both Bourgueil and St-Nicolas de Bourgueil. The Quartiers and Graviers can be enjoyed young but the Petite Cave and Malgagnes need cellaring.

Bernard Baudry Current joint champion in Chinon with Philippe Alliet. Enjoyable and affordable basic Chinon to premium red and white Croix Boisée.

Domaine des Baumard Fastidious producer of sweet Coteaux du Layon and Quarts de Chaume, with a sideline in fine Savennières. Reds more of a mixed bag.

Didier Dagueneau Producer ahead of the pack in Pouilly-Fumé for years. His brilliant but expensive range takes in minerally Chailloux, flinty Buisson-Renard and complex top wines Silex and Pur Sang.

Pierre-Jacques Druet Idiosyncratic Bourgueil producer. His wines have lovely fragrant fruit and very supple tannins.

Huët l'Echansonne Biodynamic producer and a long-standing benchmark in Vouvray. Wines can be sweet, dry or in between depending on the year.

Domaine de l'Ecu Biodynamic producer Guy Bossard bottles some characterful Muscadet and also produces a lovely red quaffer.

Château du Hureau Established Saumur-Champigny producer, surging forward with its Cuvée Lisagathe red. The white is delightful and scented.

Nicolas Joly Biodynamics guru making intense, long-lived and expensive Savennières. Joly allows each vintage to express itself to the full, so the wines can vary from year to year.

Alphonse Mellot Quality-obsessed producer of red and white Sancerre. Basic la Moussière white is well above average, while top-of-the range red and white Génération XIX are currently the appellation's best wines.

Domaine du Clos Naudin Philippe Foreau's Vouvrays are on a par with those from Huët, with generally more open flavours.

Château de la Ragotière/Frères Couillaud Dynamic producer whose Muscadet is spot-on and can age well (especially premium wine 'M'). There's also good Chardonnay.

Domaine Richou A touchstone of reliability in Anjou. Well-balanced sweet Coteaux de l'Aubance heads a large range that includes dry whites and good Gamay reds.

Domaine des Roches-Neuves Thierry Germain has raised the quality bar in Saumur-Champigny. The standard red is bright and savoury, while Terres Chaudes and Marginale have plentiful tannins and need time. L'Insolite Chenin is intriguing.

Vacheron Top-notch Sancerre domaine known as much for reds such as La Belle Dame as for its immaculate whites.

Château de Villeneuve Leader in Saumur-Champigny alongside Roches-Neuves. Intense Grand Clos (red) and Les Cormiers (white) top the range and need time; even standard bottles show good quality.

Top UK merchants

- Gauntleys of Nottingham
- The Halifax Wine Company
- The Nobody Inn
- Stone, Vine & Sun
- Yapp Brothers

France: Rhône Valley

A top-ranking classic region: the source of gutsy, great-value reds, classic whites from the peachy Viognier grape and high-brow, long-lasting vintages

What's hot ✔ great-value regional Côtes-du-Rhône bottlings ✔ Gigondas that rivals the power and depth of Châteauneuf-du-Pape ✔ up-and-coming Côtes du Rhône-Villages wines from Rasteau and Cairanne ✔ well-structured, complex *vins de pays*

What's not ✘ Châteauneuf-du-Papes that don't merit the price tag
✘ the 2002 vintage (a disappointment to many after a string of superb years)

Why buy Rhône wine?

Not only does it produce some of France's (and the world's) most highly prized reds and whites, the Rhône Valley is today turning out some of the most reliable wines you can buy for under £10. This is a region for all palates, with bottlings ranging from great-value, lively blends for everyday drinking to complex, ageworthy wines that satisfy the most demanding of wine-lovers. At the top end, elegantly fruited Viogniers are probably the best examples of the variety on the planet. And the much-aped Syrahs from the northern Rhône show similar world-beating qualities – bold, with fruit and plenty of power but more restraint and elegance than bruiser Australian Shiraz. In the Rhône, these varieties show a structure, complexity and ageworthiness that bottlings from other countries can't match. Everyday Rhône wines tend to have all the up-front fruit and spicy boldness of their superior cousins, with less intensity.

The Northern and Southern Rhône differ immensely in topography – the northern vineyards are steeper-sloping and cooler, the southern ones flatter and more arid – and this is reflected in the grapes grown. In the north Syrah reigns, and in the south it's Grenache, joined by a multitude of other traditional varieties (Châteauneuf-du-Pape producers have an exhausting choice of 13). This means that while the northern appellation reds have very distinctive varietal characteristics, those from the south can differ greatly, albeit demonstrating the same robust character.

The Rhône Valley: the state of play

This year, the availability of highly affordable regional reds is impressive. Lively, spicy Côtes-du-Rhônes for under £5 are easy to find and provide consistently enjoyable, no-nonsense drinking. An appealing new guard of *vins de pays* is also worth hunting out, taking in both traditional local varieties and the ubiquitous Chardonnay and Cabernet Sauvignon.

Three factors keep the prices down here: firstly, reasonable land prices in this part of France; secondly, the fact that a high percentage of wine comes from large-scale co-operatives (responsible for around 70 per cent of all regional Côtes du Rhône); thirdly, a youthful band of *vignerons* who are striving for quality vine-growing and winemaking.

New stars are rising amid the *village* appellations, too. Producers in Gigondas have been fighting hard to shift their region out of the shadow of fellow Southern Rhône legend Châteauneuf-du-Pape, and are achieving noteworthy results. While

> ### New this year
> - Jaboulet, Parallèle 45, Rosé 2002 (Côtes du Rhône) £5
> - Château de Saint Cosme, Great Rocks and Hot Rocks (Côtes du Rhône-Villages) £6
> - Château de Saint Cosme, Rhône Ranger 2002 (Côtes du Rhône-Villages) £6

Châteauneuf producers are still resting on their laurels, Gigondas' have been making wines to rival the power and weight of the best of them. Some Gigondas prices reflect this, but buyers can be confident that they are paying for the quality of the wine, rather than celebrity of the appellation.

The latest vintages also reveal that the quest for top quality has caught on in the Côtes du Rhônes-Villages of Rasteau and Cairanne too, which are tipped for great things. Relative un-heard-ofs Coteaux du Tricastin and Costières de Nîmes (with a host of red-cherry and dark-berry flavours to look forward to) are also set to join the Rhône wine establishment. These less-traditional appellations are now becoming reliable sources of well-priced, fruit-forward, early-drinking bottles.

Organic wines are providing an increasing buzz across the spectrum of categories. Organic, and even-more-intriguing biodynamic, winemaking practices have been fervently championed in the Rhône

for over a decade now. Each year, more growers are turning their backs on fertilisers and chemical sprays and embracing natural techniques to protect their vines, promote quality fruit growth, and get back in touch with the natural character of the grape. Rhône reds are now a permanent feature of supermarkets' organic aisles, and a staple of organic specialists.

Grape varieties
🌱 Syrah
The only red variety permitted in the northern Rhône appellations shows its top form here. It is typically dark in colour, with intense red- or black-berry fruit, and an array of flavours such as truffles and leather when aged. It can be austere and brutish in a young Côte-Rôtie, or fleshy with burgeoning fruit flavours in a youthful Crozes-Hermitage. Syrah is blended increasingly into the fiery wines of the Southern Rhône.

🌱 Grenache
Grenache is at its powerful, spicy best from the harsh, dry and windswept Southern Rhône. It is by far the most prolific variety of the south. Unlike Syrah it is mostly blended (except on rare occasions), as firmer grapes are needed to boost its pale colour and soft structure. Châteauneuf-du-Pape is the variety's showcase. It also shines in the inimitable richest rosés of Tavel.

🌱 Mourvèdre
This southern staple produces flavour-packed, weighty, long-lasting wines when well nurtured in the vineyard, but it can be harsh if allowed to over-crop. It is greatly appreciated among southern winemakers for its compatibility with Grenache, to which it imparts both backbone and deep colour.

🌱 Viognier
The northern Rhône is home to the region's only white appellations, Condrieu and Château Grillet, in which the world's finest examples of Viognier are to be found. Unlike the more blowsy imitations around the globe, these Viogniers have luscious hints of pears, peaches and apricots plus a firmness of structure and fine length. Small percentages are also commonly used to give an aromatic lift to the reds of Côte-Rôtie.

🌱 Roussanne
Roussanne (along with its more significant partner Marsanne) is the other traditional

---

Top red wines

- Perrin et Fils, Côtes du Rhône Nature 2001 (Southern Rhône) £9
- Domaine de Grangeneuve, Coteaux du Tricastin Cuvée de la Truffière 1998 (Southern Rhône) £11
- Domaine Rabasse Charavin, Côtes du Rhône-Villages 2001 (Southern Rhône) £11
- Chapoutier, Crozes-Hermitage Les Meysonniers 2001 (Northern Rhône) £13
- Château de Beaucastel, Coudoulet de Beaucastel 2000 (Southern Rhône) £13
- Château du Trignon, Gigondas 2001 (Southern Rhône) £13
- Jean-Luc Colombo, Cornas (Northern Rhône) £30

Top white wines

- La Vieille Ferme, Côtes du Luberon 2002 (Southern Rhône) £6
- Georges Vernay, Vin de Pays des Collines Rhodaniennes Le Pied de Samson 2002 (Southern Rhône) £19
- M Chapoutier, Condrieu 2001 (Northern Rhône) £20

white grape of the Rhône. It gives both tightness of structure and perfumed aromas to Northern Rhône reds, but its heartland is the Southern Rhône. In Châteauneuf-du-Pape it appears with Grenache Blanc and any of the half-dozen other varieties permitted in the making of the appellation's power-packed whites. It is sometimes bottled alone as a single varietal in more modern *vins de pays*.

Marsanne

Marsanne is well regarded for the weight and roundness it gives to Northern Rhône reds, but it is not unusual to find it bottled alone in cutting-edge *vins de pays*. In the south, it is often blended into the lively, spicy regional whites, where it can be joined by Roussanne, Grenache Blanc, Clairette and Viognier.

Wine regions

Due to the distinct differences in topography and resulting styles of wine, the Rhône Valley is usually divided into the Northern Rhône and Southern Rhône, with the town of Montélimar lying between the two.

Northern Rhône

The northern vineyards are the origin of the Rhône's most serious, ageworthy and expensive red wines. Steep slopes that loom up above the river, lined with terrace upon terrace of vines, are among the key promoters of quality grape growth here. Some white wine is produced, but this is truly the land of the Syrah grape.

The classic wines of **Hermitage** and **Côte-Rôtie** are firmly structured, complex and long-lasting, with layers of aroma and flavour to discover, despite being quite unapproachable when young. Moving south, the bold, tannic wines of **Cornas** are equally austere in their youth and have been much-maligned for their rusticity of late. Efforts to round off any rough edges and infuse the wines with star quality are, however, apparent. **Saint-Joseph** and **Crozes-Hermitage** reds are traditionally fruit-forward and less structured than those of other northern *crus*, but some rival the weight and finesse of their more revered peers.

Of the few Rhône white wines, **Condrieu** can be exemplary. Made from 100 per cent Viognier, this grape's luscious apricot and peach notes are coupled with a formidable structure and length here. Dissecting Condrieu's vineyards is Château-

Grillet, a tiny appellation covering just over seven acres (part of the eponymous estate) producing rare, ageworthy Viogniers.

The appellations of **Saint-Péray**, south of Cornas on the banks of the Rhône, and **Diois**, which follows the contours of the River Drôme to the south-east, produce refreshing sparkling wines brimming with ripe fruit, in both classic (Saint-Péray and Crémant de Die) and local styles (Clairette de Die and Clairette de Die Tradition). Diois is also home to two appellations producing easy-drinking modern still reds and whites: **Châtillon-en-Diois**, centred on Burgundian varieties (Chardonnay, Pinot Noir), and **Coteaux de Die**, a very young appellation for ripe-fruited Clairettes.

Southern Rhône

Sited on gentler, lower slopes under a harsher Mediterranean sun, this is a region of more laid-back, easy-drinking wine styles. The majority of the lively, spicy, fruit-forward 'regional' Côtes du Rhône wines are made in the Southern Rhône, as are the generally better-structured Côtes du Rhônes-Villages.

Regional wines make up a substantial percentage of this region's production, but *village* wines are also an important feature. One of the most famous is **Châteauneuf-du-Pape**. Taking its name from the 'new' papal castle built here in the fourteenth century, its power-driven, highly spiced bottlings are living legends and traditionally bear a cross-keyed logo on the bottle – look out too for the lesser-known white wines. Take care to avoid paying high prices for names with similar designs that do not live up to this high reputation.

Neighbouring appellations include the red-wine villages **Gigondas**, **Vacqueyras** and **Lirac**, the source of spiced, sweet-fruited, Grenache-rich bottlings. Close by sits an anomaly of the southern Rhône, **Tavel** – the origin of one of the wine world's richest rosé styles. Equally individual fortified reds and whites (*vins doux naturels* – VDN), deeply rooted in tradition, are made in and around the villages of **Rasteau** and **Beaumes-de-Venise**, both of which have recently been elevated to *cru* status.

Surrounding the Côtes du Rhône vineyard areas are the newer appellations of **Coteaux du Tricastin**, **Côtes du Ventoux**, **Côtes du Luberon** and **Costières de Nîmes**. The majority of bottlings here are red, typically characterised by prominent fruit flavours – from dark forest berries to ripe red cherries – and a warming, spicy edge. While they can be a touch astringent, the best have their tannins in check and linger impressively on the finish.

Pick of the producers

Northern Rhône

M Chapoutier Despite ventures now reaching as far as South Australia, Michel Chapoutier is still firmly entrenched in his home appellation, Hermitage. He makes bold, richly fruited, complex examples, labelled 'Ermitage'.

Domaine Jean-Louis Chave Jean-Louis Chave has more than five centuries of family winemaking history behind him in Hermitage. His red and white wines are among the elite of their appellation.

Jean-Luc Colombo A shining star of Cornas, accredited with revamping the appellation's wine style, bringing more balance, weight of fruit and finesse to its bottlings.

Château-Grillet The sole owner of these top Viognier vineyards in the eponymous northern Rhône appellation for white wines.

E Guigal Pioneer of single-vineyard Côte-Rôtie, Guigal is the appellation's champion. His La Landonne, La Mouline and La Turque vineyard bottlings are considered among the best of the Rhône *crus*.

Paul Jaboulet Aîné Hermitage 'la Chapelle' is the masterpiece of this winemaker respected for his achievements throughout the northern Rhône. His more affordable Crozes-Hermitages are worth seeking out too.

Georges Vernay Renowned for his achievements with Viognier, Vernay has not only raised the Condrieu benchmark but has also turned his hand to making *vins de pays* Viogniers that challenge the rest of this top appellation.

Southern Rhône

Château de Beaucastel Some of the most powerful Châteauneuf-du-Papes, from extensive vineyards. Very old vines are responsible for two prized *cuvées*: 'Hommage à Jacques Perrin' (made mostly from Mourvèdre, only in exceptional years), and the white 'Vieilles Vignes' – 100 per cent Roussanne.

Domaine Henri Bonneau One of the elite Châteauneuf wineries: *cuvée* 'Réserve des Célestins' is the pinnacle of Bonneau's achievements with Grenache-rich reds.

Perrin et Fils An old Rhône Valley family, producing justly famous wines. Perrin's

Châteauneuf bottlings are in a class of their own.

Château de Rayas One of the most sought-after Châteauneuf-du-Papes. The key to Château de Rayas's success is single-varietal bottlings of Grenache harvested from extremely low-yielding vines.

Château de Saint-Cosme As capable at the good-value end as the high end, this producer's interests range Rhône-wide, but it is the Gigondas that really gets people talking.

Château du Trignon Renowned producer of Gigondas and other southern wines. Typically among the most strongly fruited and long-lasting of their appellations.

Domaine du Vieux-Télégraphe An expansive Châteauneuf estate where vines average over 50 years old. Both red and white bottlings are standard-bearers for this legendary appellation.

Vintage guide

When to drink

- **reds** – everyday wines are drinkable when purchased. Age top wines for at least 5 years; the best call for 10 or more
- **whites** – drink most crisp and young. Well-structured *village* wines need cellaring for at least 3 years (5 or more for top Viognier)

2002 Patchier quality than in previous years

2001 Power-packed wines; still very youthful

2000 High quality, with punchy reds for the long term

1999 Intense reds, coming into their own now

1998 Succulent reds developing beautifully

Top UK merchants for Rhône wines

- Berry Bros & Rudd
- Corney & Barrow
- Handford Wines
- Yapp Brothers

France: South-west

Though hard to find, wines from this diverse region suit all tastes/budgets

What's hot ✔ wines increasingly made by organic methods ✔ deep-flavoured, long-lived reds and crisp, clean whites ✔ superb sweet whites ✔ skilled winemaking is now taming the region's once-ferociously tannic red wines

What's not ✗ the hot, dry summer of 2003 caused baked fruit flavours

New this year

- Medieval-style Black Wine of Cahors from Clos Triguedina
- Revived interest in sweet white

Why buy South-west wines?

South-west France is an umbrella designation for a diverse wine-producing region that runs south from Bergerac (close to Bordeaux in style and location), through the tannin-rich *terroirs* of Madiran and Cahors down to Irouléguy in Basque country, and east to the versatile Côtes du Frontonnais and Gaillac.

During the Middle Ages, South-west wines were preferred to those of Bordeaux: that city's jealous merchants ensured their decline by introducing a range of protectionist tactics. The wines now fight for a foothold in the UK: because of their scarcity, they remain the domain of intrepid wine buyers prepared to seek them out.

Top grape varieties

A plethora of arcane and unusual grapes is grown in addition to the more conventional. **Fer**, **Len de l'El**, **Arrufiac** and **Duras** offer a fabulous opportunity to escape the straitjacket of Cabernet Sauvignon etc. Star varieties include the **Auxerrois** (Malbec) of Cahors, Madiran's tannic **Tannat**, and the **Gros** and **Petit Manseng** of Jurançon.

Wine regions

Appellations such as **Bergerac**, **Buzet**, the **Côtes du Marmandais** and **de Duras** grow traditional Bordeaux Cabernets Sauvignon and Franc, as well as Merlot. Dry whites use Sauvignon Blanc and Sémillon, as do the sweet whites of Sauternes-like appellations **Monbazillac** and **Saussignac**.

Cahors is known for Malbec-based wines (tasting of smoke and game), while **Gaillac** and **Frontonnais** use diverse grapes. The white *vins de pays* of the **Côtes de Gascogne** are crisp, clean and great value. **Madiran** (red) and **Pacherenc-du-Vic-Bilh** (sweet and dry whites) are idiosyncratic stars. Dry whites are now fashionable in **Jurançon**, whose sweet whites are still prized for their honey tones shot with citrus. Often tannic and acidic, **Irouléguy's** wines can be perfumed and sophisticated.

Pick of the producers

Domaines de l'Ancienne Cure, Berthoumieu, Alain Brumont, de Tariquet, les Tres Cantous; Ch'x du Cèdre, Tour des Gendres, Plaisance, Clos Lapeyre; Producteurs Plaimont; Clos Trigeudina; Clos d'Yvigne.

Top red wines

- Château du Cèdre 2001 (Cahors)
- Ch Tour des Gendres, Moulin des Dames Rouge 2000 (Bergerac)
- Clos d'Yvigne, Rouge et Noir 2000 (Bergerac)

Top white wines

- Clos Lapeyre, Vintage Vielh Sec 2001 (Jurançon)
- Domaine les Tres Cantous, Robert Plageoles Mauzac en Vert 2002
- Alain Brumont, Brumaire Pacherenc-du-Vic-Bilh Moelleux 2000

Top UK merchants

- Great Western Wine Company
- Stone, Vine & Sun

France: Provence, Corsica, Jura, Savoie and Bugey

Provence

The best wines come from **Bandol**, the most serious appellation, with robust, herbal, blackberry reds from Mourvèdre vineyards overlooking the Mediterranean; they need at least eight years to mature. **Les Baux-de-Provence** follows closely, with fruity, grippy reds, many of them organically grown (up to 20 per cent Cabernet is allowed; Syrah and Grenache make up the rest). **Coteaux d'Aix en Provence** is mainly rosé, but also has some interesting reds from Counoise, plus Cabernet and Mourvèdre. **Coteaux Varois** (inland, with higher, cooler vineyards) focuses on Cinsaut and Grenache; **Côtes de Provence** is a vast region producing 80 per cent rosé (Cinsaut and Grenache), plus more interesting reds from Syrah, Cabernet and Mourvèdre. For white wines, look to **Cassis** (fresh, low-acid white wines from Marsanne and Clairette) and **Côtes de Lubéron** (nutty Vermentino). **Bellet** creates fresh, aromatic Vermentino whites plus Italian red grapes such as Folle Noire and Braquet, and **Palette** makes firm, minerally whites – some even needing bottle age – from local grapes Clairette, Grenache Blanc, Ugni Blanc and Muscat (Château Simone's are best by far).

Pick of the producers: *Domaine des Béates, Domaine Bunan, Domaine de la Courtade, Château d'Estoublon, Gros Noré, Château de Pibarnon, Domaine Rabiega, Château Routas, Clos Sainte Magdeleine, Château Simone, Domaine Tempier, Domaine de Trévallon, Domaine de Triennes, Château Vignelaure.*

Corsica

Corsica is a mountainous island 170km off the coast of France: its hot, dry conditions and strong winds are ideal for fending off disease, so this is a haven for organic viticulture. Its appellations include the generic Vin de Corse, which has five sub-regions: **Calvi**, **Sartène**, **Figari**, **Porto-Vecchio** and **Coteaux du Cap Corse**. **Ajaccio** is an AC for Sciacarello, Patrimonio and powerful Nielluccio reds. Not much of this wine makes it to UK shores but islanders have recently begun to take great pride in their local varieties, releasing them as tangy single varietals under the 'Vins de l'Ille de Beauté' label. Vermentino is the main white grape, for aromatic whites; Bianco Gentile is another important white to watch for the future. Reds and rosés come from Grenache, Carignan and Cinsaut, as well as local Nielluccio (the same as Sangiovese from Tuscany) and Sciacarello.

Pick of the producers: *Domaines Antoines Arena, Culombu, Figari, Fiumicicoli, Gentile, Leccia, Orenga de Gaffory, Renucci, Torraccia, Tanella and Canaralli.*

Jura, Savoie and Bugey

As they're near to Burgundy, all three regions plant Chardonnay and Pinot Noir, but the real specialities are from **Jura**: red Arbois (based on Pinot Noir and local grapes Poulsard and Trousseau); Vin Jaune (long-lived, nutty-tasting, unusual wine from l'Etoile and Château-Chalon); sweet Vin de Paille (made from grapes dried out on straw mats); and Côtes de Jura (red, rosé or white).

The Alpine wines of **Savoie** and **Bugey** are reds from the smoky-tasting Mondeuse grape, and whites from Jacquère (the most interesting variety – look out for the wines of Abymes and Apremont), Roussanne (dry white Chignin Bergeron), Chasselas and Altesse. Plus there's a fairly decent sparkling wine called Seyssel.

Pick of the producers: *Château d'Arlay, Pierre Boniface, Jean Bourdy, Château de l'Etoile, Raymond Quénard, Château Ripaille, Rolet Père et Fils, Varichon et Clerc, Philippe Viallet.*

Germany

Spurred on by a run of superb vintages, Germany is producing some of the world's finest white wines from the newly fashionable Riesling grape

What's hot ✔ Rieslings from top producers in the Mosel, Nahe, Pfalz and Rheingau ✔ New World-influenced brands, freshly packaged with export markets in mind ✔ drier (trocken-style), food-compatible Rieslings ✔ top wines from the brilliantly successful 2001 vintage

What's not ✘ supermarket Hock, Liebfraumilch and Piesporter ✘ Blue Nun and Black Tower: amazingly, these are still selling well in the UK! ✘ non-Riesling whites, especially Müller-Thurgau

---

New this year

- Schneider, Terrassen Riesling Alte Reben 2003 (Rheingau) £15
- Paulinshof, Brauneberger Kammer Riesling *Auslese Trocken* 2003 (Mosel-Saar-Ruwer) £16
- Max Ferd Richter, Brauneberger Juffer Sonnenuhr Riesling *Auslese* 2003 (Mosel-Saar-Ruwer) £21

Why buy German wine?

A spectacular run of vintages over the last decade has spurred a German revival. Top German wines, at their best among the world's most thrilling whites and sources of the most distinctive expressions of the Riesling grape, are now hot property.

The strength of German Riesling is its versatility. You want it sweet? You got it. Dry? No problem. Light, crisp and minerally? Fine. Fuller-flavoured and savoury? It can do that too. You can drink it young; you can drink it old. Riesling can make light, fresh wines for uncomplicated summer drinking as well as more substantial versions for long ageing. It's also a grape that easily captures the character of the vineyard where it is grown. Germany's other worthy wine style is red from the Spätburgunder (Pinot Noir) grape, with a lot of fans of late.

The good news is that German wines are still relatively affordable – if you can understand the label (see box opposite). The best purchasing strategy is to go on the producer's reputation or take the advice of a trusted independent merchant with a good selection to try.

Germany: the state of play

German wine in the UK marketplace is still a bit schizophrenic. At one end sits cheap supermarket Liebfraumilch, Hock and Piesporter, distinguished only by its low price (the average bottle price of German wine sold here is a woeful £2.48). At the other end, top estate wines are flying off the shelves of the independents and specialist mail-order merchants.

Despite an overall decrease for Germany in market share, mid-range brands such as Devil's Rock, Fire Mountain and Kendermanns – clean, drier-style wines that have dispensed with the traditional bottle shape and are modelled on New World brands – are doing well. The industry now needs to shift away from the cheap and nasty towards these wines which give an inkling of why top German wines are so special.

Top grape varieties

🍇 Müller-Thurgau
Also known as Rivaner, this variety was Germany's most widely planted grape until recently overtaken by Riesling. It is mostly dull and usually of little merit.

🍇 Riesling
Riesling vies with Chardonnay for the title of 'world's greatest white grape' and in Germany the scales seem to be tipping in its favour. It is capable of making a variety of wine styles, from crisp, minerally and limey to rich and ripe with flavours of melons and apricots. If affected by *botrytis*, it makes fantastically rich and complex sweet wines with good natural acidity.

German wine labelling

German wines fall into different categories depending on their style and vineyard location. Recently introduced classifications include 'Classic' (everyday wines made from single grape varieties considered typical of a region); 'Selection' wines, which must meet more rigorous criteria; and *Erstes Gewächs* – quality wines from 'first growth' vineyards.

Under the German QmP system, wines are classified according to their sugar levels at harvest. *Kabinett* wines tend to dryness and *Spätlese* are dry to off-dry (with a richer texture), while *Auslese* (richer again) are dry to medium-sweet. All may be made in sweet or dry wine styles. *Beerenauslese* and *Trockenbeerenauslese* (made from specially selected berries concentrated by noble rot) are sweet and very sweet respectively, while the rare and expensive *Eiswein* wines – made from grapes frozen on the vines and crushed before the ice can melt – have intense, sweet flavours.

Grauburgunder/Rülander

Known elsewhere as Pinot Gris or Pinot Grigio, this variety does best in the southerly regions where it makes fat, savoury whites with rich textures.

Weissburgunder

This is Germany's version of Pinot Blanc, capable of making rich, nutty whites.

Spätburgunder

This is Germany's name for Pinot Noir – an increasingly popular choice for expressive red wines with flavours of cherry and berry fruits, sometimes herbs and undergrowth.

Dornfelder

This widely planted red grape typically makes soft, fruity, approachable wines.

Wine regions

Mosel-Saar-Ruwer

One of Germany's great wine regions, Mosel-Saar-Ruwer is named after the three interconnecting rivers along whose banks the vineyards are sited. It's a northerly region, and so the site of a vineyard is the key to quality here. Top locations include **Wehlener Sonnenuhr, Juffer Sonnenuhr, Urziger Würzgarten** and

Top red wines

- Rudolf Fürst, Bürgstadter Centgrafenberg Frühburgunder 'R' 1999 (Franken) £23

Top white wines

- JJ Christoffel, Ürziger Würzgarten Riesling *Auslese* 2001 (Mosel-Saar-Ruwer) £14
- Horst Sauer, Eschendorfer Lump Silvaner *Auslese* 1999 (Franken) £15
- JJ Christoffel, Ürziger Würzgarten Riesling *Auslese* 1999 (Mosel-Saar-Ruwer) £18
- Fritz Haag, Brauneberger Juffer Sonnenuhr Riesling *Auslese* 2002 (Mosel-Saar-Ruwer) £18
- Markus Molitor, Riesling *Trocken* Alte Reben 2002 (Mosel-Saar-Ruwer) £18
- Maximin Grünhaus, Abstberg Riesling *Auslese* 1995 (Mosel-Saar-Ruwer) £20
- Dr Loosen, Wehlener Sonnenuhr Riesling *Auslese* 1998 (Mosel-Saar-Ruwer) £20
- Hermann Dönnhoff, Oberhäser Brücke Riesling *Spätlese* 2002 (Nahe) £21
- Schlossgut Diel, Dorsheimer Pittermännchen Riesling *Auslese* 2001 (Nahe) £24
- Maximin Grünhaus, Abtsberg Riesling *Auslese* No 145 2001 (Mosel-Saar-Ruwer) £31

Graacher Domprobst. The best wines are made from Riesling grapes grown on the steep hillsides overlooking the river. These wines are fresh, delicate and mineralic, with racy acidity and low alcohol levels; frequently there will be some sweetness to counter the acidity.

Nahe

Small and fragmented, this region generally keeps a low profile. With a slightly warmer climate than the north, it makes some lovely, intense Rieslings that lie somewhere in between the minerally raciness of the Mosel and the fuller-bodied style of the Rheingau. The best wines come from the hillside sites.

Pfalz

This southerly region is Germany's most productive. Although many of the vineyards here make inexpensive commercial wines of the sort that has given the industry such a poor reputation, sub-regions such as the **Mittelhardt** do produce high-quality wines, mainly from the Riesling grape. These Rieslings are fuller-bodied and more substantial than the classic Mosel versions.

Rheingau

This small region on the north bank of the Rhine near Mainz is Germany's most aristocratic wine-growing area. The south-facing hillside vineyards produce some of the world's greatest expressions of the Riesling grape, which need long ageing to show their best and are a little fuller than the wines of the Mosel-Saar-Ruwer.

Rheinhessen

Immediately south of the Rheingau, on the other side of the Rhine, this large region makes wines of hugely varying quality. It has some top-quality estates but is sadly responsible for half of all Liebfraumilch.

Baden-Württemberg

This large region runs along the French border, just across the Rhine from Alsace. Despite its southerly location the wines rarely hit the peaks, though they are frequently soft and reliable. The key varieties are Müller-Thurgau, Spätburgunder, Weissburgunder and Grauburgunder, and Riesling is just a minor player. Unlike the other German regions, Baden's wines are mostly dry in style.

Franken

Don't let the squat *bocksbeutel* bottle shape put you off exploring the wines of Franken. The Silvaner grape variety is the speciality here.

Pick of the producers

JJ Christoffel Seriously good Mosel Riesling with great clarity and purity of fruit.

Hermann Dönnhoff His Nahe Rieslings have deservedly achieved cult status in recent years.

Maximin Grünhaus/von Schubert Sublime Rieslings from the Abtsberg vineyard in the Ruwer, with laser-like precision and lightness of texture.

Fritz Haag Wilhem Haag is making serious, brilliantly poised Rieslings from the Juffer-Sonnenuhr vineyard in Mosel's Brauneberg.

Dr Loosen Media-friendly Ernst Loosen makes richly flavoured, powerful wines that are among the Mosel's best.

Markus Molitor Concentrated, rich Mosel Rieslings with good balancing acidity. An estate on the up.

Egon Müller-Scharzhof One of Germany's most famous domaines, known for its rare, expensive sweet Saar wines.

JJ Prüm Manfred Prüm's famous Mosel estate makes intense, minerally Rieslings that repay long ageing.

Willi Schaefer Pure, intense, expressive Rieslings from Mosel vineyards in Graach.

Schlossgut Diel Journalist Armin Diel makes seductive, powerful wines from the Nahe that turn critics' heads with their forward style.

Schneider Young Markus Schneider has taken over winemaking here in the Rheingau and is turning out some impressive, minerally Rieslings from old-vine vineyards.

Vintage guide

When to drink
- **reds** – best drunk from 2–5 years
- **whites** – Riesling needs a year in bottle to settle. *Kabinetts* and *Spätlese* will survive for a decade or more. *Auslese* and above are best at 5+ years; many live for 40

2003 The hottest German vintage for centuries. Wines show good ripeness but low acidity. Ageing potential as yet unclear

2002 A very good year in between two potentially exceptional ones. Wines are ripe and generally well balanced, with good acidity

2001 The vintage of the century. Successful almost everywhere. Store the best wines away and let them mature

2000 Late rains. A high-yielding year. Only top growers excelled

1999 A warm growing season with reasonable wines overall

1998 Alternating heat and rain, but generally good wines resulted

---

Top UK merchants

- Fortnum & Mason
- The Halifax Wine Company
- Hedley Wright Wine Merchants
- Howard Ripley
- Stone, Vine & Sun

Greece

Home to delicious aromatic whites and tangy, herbaceous reds

What's hot ✔ concentrated wines from hot 2003 ✔ Greece's own varieties, loved at last for their quirky character ✔ Tangy Moscophilero, Roditis and Assyrtico

What's not ✘ aromatic whites smothered by oak flavours ✘ poor wines from rained-on 2002 ✘ not all bottlings have fully translated labels

Why buy Greek wine?

For a start, it's no longer as expensive as it used to be – there are plenty of bottles for £5 or £6. Secondly, retsina and oxidised taverna wines no longer dominate the industry. Instead, Greece's grape varieties are holding their own and becoming more intense as new wineries get into their stride. Greece has over 250 varieties, and a dozen or so now rightly head up native blends without the support of foreigners.

Top grape varieties

Aromatic white **Moscophilero** is similar to Gewürztraminer, with a Turkish Delight perfume; **Roditis** is full of toasty, herbaceous flavours (which are even better without adding pine resin, for retsina); and **Lagorthi** is fruity, with aromas of dry herbs. **Malagousia** has a herb-and-lemon-peel character, while **Assyrtico** – full of honeysuckle and citrus – is warm and lemony from Macedonia, and crisp and salty from Santorini. It is the perfect base for honeyed, sweet Vinssanto. **Robola** produces fleshy wines with a hint of lime.

Of the reds, **Aghiorghitiko** resembles Cabernet Franc, making everything from juicy, sappy rosés to brambly black wines. Cabernet and Merlot thrive in neighbouring vineyards, as does **Mavrodaphne** for robust, tannic reds. **Xinomavro** is like Pinot Noir with strawberry and tomato flavours. Beefy **Limnio** has a delicate hint of sage and laurel.

Wine regions

Peloponnese vineyards are suited to crisp whites (Mantinia appellation Moscophilero) and warmer richer reds (Nemea for Aghiorghitiko). **Macedonia**, in the north, houses Naoussa and Goumenissa, appellations for Xinomavro. **Maroneia**, across the

northern Aegean coast, is reviving some of Greece's oldest vineyards. **Central Greece** has patches of quality and the **Islands** have tangy whites from Robola and Assyrtico.

Pick of the producers

Gaia, Gerovassilou, Ktima Alpha, Kyr-Yianni, Constantin Lazaridis, Oenoforos, Sigalas, Tselepos, Vassiliou.

New this year

- Greek wines in Marks & Spencer

Top red wines

- Kyr-Yianni, Yiannakohori, Merlot/ Xinomavro 2002 (Macedonia) £12
- Biblia Chora, Merlot/Cabernet Sauvignon 2002 (Macedonia) £13
- Gaia, single-vineyard Aghiorghitiko 2000 (Peloponnese) £17
- Gerovassilou, Syrah 2000 (Macedonia) £25

Top white wines

- Hatzidakis, Aidani-Assyrtico (Santorini) £10
- Sigalas, Assyrtico '03 (Santorini) £10
- Tselepos, Mantinia 2003 (Peloponnese) £12

Top UK merchants

- Fortnum & Mason
- Oddbins
- Lay & Wheeler

Hungary

Among many varieties and wine styles are affordable hidden gems

What's hot ✔ Tokaji Aszú ✔ affordable reds from traditional and French varieties ✔ 1993 and 1999 vintage Tokaji

What's not ✗ over-cropped or oxidised reds ✗ high-acid whites picked too early

Why buy Hungarian wine?

This land-locked country boasts indigenous, French and German varieties, and can blend the lot. While many good reds are made, two-thirds of production is white, with a tiny percentage of sparkling wines. German company Henkell owns Hungary's largest winery group and exports under the Chapel Ridge label. While the brand is well priced, more concentrated flavours would establish a reputation for quality. Hungary's finest asset is sweet, sumptuous Tokaji.

Top red wines

* Tibor Gal, Pinot Noir 2002 (Eger) £7

Top white wines

* Akos Kamocsay, Irsai Oliver 2003 (Duna) £4
* Domaine Szeremely, Pinot Gris 2001 (Badacsony) £5
* Château Vincent, Crystal Dry NV Sparkling Wine £8

Top Tokaji wines

* Oremus, Furmint Noble Late Harvest 2000 (Tokaji) £9
* Royal Tokaji, Blue Label Tokaji Aszú 1999 (5 Puttonyos) £17
* Crown Estates, Tokaji Aszú Eszencia 1993 (Szarvas) £54

Top grape varieties

Once an export staple, Egri Bikavér ('Bull's Blood'), a blend of **Medoc Noir** (Merlot),
Kadarka and **Kékfrankos**, does little for the nation. Better wines can be found in **Pinot Noir**, **Zweigelt**, and **Cabernets Franc** and **Sauvignon**. Or try the superior dry white wines of **Szuerkebarat** (Pinot Gris), **Irsai Oliver**, **Riesling**, **Zenit**, **Juhfark** and **Furmint** (the principle grape of Tokaji).

Wine regions

There are 22 in all (a sensible reduction to eight has been proposed). The ones to watch are **Badacsony**, **Balatonfuered-Csopak**, **Balatonboglár**, **Balatonfelvidek** and **Balatonmelleke**. ('Balaton' in the name generally signifies white wines grown on volcanic soils near Lake Balaton. Nice medium-bodied reds are also found here.) **Szekszard** is dominated by red grapes that show potential. **Sopron**, at the Austrian border, can fashion crisp, lively whites.

Pick of the producers

Tibor Gál, Heimann, Château Megyer, Oremus, Royal Tokaji, István Szepsy, Domaine Szeremely, Château Vincent.

Tokaji wines

These honeyed-but-tangy botrytised wines grown on volcanic, hillside soils in the eastern Tokaji-Hegyalja region are some of the world's finest and longest-lived. Since 1990, over £55 million has been invested here, with capital from the US, France, Spain and the UK.

Winemakers remain divided as to the primacy of the oxidised version associated with Communist times or the more modern, clean-fruited fashion. Tokajis Aszú, Aszú Eszencia and Eszencia have enjoyed the spotlight in recent years. Their richness is measured in 'puttonyos' – three for the lightest, up to seven for the most concentrated.

Italy

With 3,000 years of winemaking experience, lots of native grape varieties and wines that innately match food, Italy has a style for everyone – from the everyday to the sublime

What's hot ✔ modern examples of stunning Chianti and Soave ✔ anything made from the Nero d'Avola grape ✔ hearty reds from sun-drenched Puglia ✔ unoaked whites from Italy's Verdicchio, Fiano and Greco grape varieties ✔ wonderfully complete 1999 Brunello di Montalcino

What's not ✘ Italy's old stock-in-trade: £2.99 Soave and Chianti ✘ dull-as-ditchwater Pinot Grigio ✘ reds from the difficult 2002 vintage ✘ over-priced Super-Tuscans ✘ oak-dominated Barolo and Barbaresco

New this year

- Sicily: the ancient island's vineyards have the perfect climate, plus stunning native grapes at reasonable prices
- giant Sicilian co-op Settesoli, making wines under the Inycon and Mandrarossa labels
- Calatrasi, an enormous Sicilian producer – Allora and d'Istinto both offer exceptional value
- fantastic new-wave wines from Sicilian producers Cusumano, Donnafugata, Planeta and Valle dell'Acate

Why buy Italian wine?

The new Italy is a mouth-watering prospect: all that Italian creativity harnessed to a viticultural paradise that includes dozens of native grape varieties, high-altitude vineyards and long, hot summers. It is Italy's diversity that truly sets it apart. On offer is a dizzying array including sparkling, fortified and light wines that runs the gamut from Sicily's finest reds to the racy Sauvignons of the Alto Adige. Italian innovations such as Asti, Vin Santo, Recioto and Amarone complete a glittering display of vinous originality. Judged on quality alone Italy can now compete with the best wines from anywhere in the world – even the best from Bordeaux, as far as the Super-Tuscans, led by Sassicaia, are concerned.

Ten years ago one in six bottles of Italian wine sold in the UK was Lambrusco: today this wine isn't even on the radar but Italy's reputation continues to suffer from a 'pile it high, sell it cheap' image. But while it's true that much of Italy's leviathan production (second in volume only to France) is utterly forgettable, with the new generation of winemakers the absurdly high yields and sloppy winemaking of yesteryear are well and truly over.

Italian wine classifications

The lowest grade is **vino da tavola (VdT)**: since 1996 these wines may not list region, grape variety or vintage. Some producers still release top wines as VdT to bypass restrictions on higher levels. Most top *vini da tavola* and Super-Tuscans fall under **Indicazione geografica tipica (IGT)** – similar to French *vins de pays* – which imposes some rules about grape varieties and production; some newly qualify for higher **Denominazione di origine controllata (DOC)** status. DOC wines face more stringent restrictions, while **DOCG** adds a '*garantita*' and generally means higher-quality wines.

Italy: the state of play

The last ten years have witnessed a sharp decline in Italian exports as consumers increasingly embrace the reliable charms of New World wines. This has been mirrored by a similar drop in domestic consumption among discerning drinkers. Faced with a stark reality – either increase quality or go out of business – the response has been dramatic: from Piedmont to Puglia producers have cut yields, invested in new technology and fashioned wines with international appeal. At the top end, wines such as Amarone, Barolo and Brunello have benefited from reduced ageing time in new oak and a string of brilliant vintages in the late 1990s, although prices have crept higher. At the lower end, Italy's entry-level wines have never looked stronger.

However, Italy still needs greater consistency to compete on the world stage. Inexpensive wines from traditional appellations such as Chianti, Soave and Valpolicella are the worst offenders. Riding on once-lofty reputations they continue to besmirch Italy's good name. In the industrial north, soaring land values have effectively put the £2.99 price point beyond reach. This cut-price Soave and Chianti are possible only through either appallingly high yields or, worse still, illegal blending with cheap wines from the south. The good news is that excellent value can still be found from traditional regions in the £5–£10 bracket.

Spending truly vast sums on Italian wine does not guarantee quality; extremely expensive *cuvées* – often from Tuscany and fashioned from international varieties – seldom justify their exalted prices. The key is to find a reliable producer.

Although quality production remains focused on Piedmont, Tuscany and the Veneto, the deep south offers perhaps the best value of all. Despite the deeply engrained culture of overproduction, recent investment has worked a minor miracle. Stainless steel vats and temperature control have unlocked this area's fabulous potential and there are plenty of concentrated, characterful wines to be had for under a fiver. Sicily and Puglia, in particular, have shed their reputation for dull and oxidised wines. Shining new examples of Primitivo, Nero d'Avola and Inzolia reflect the south's blissful marriage of grape and *terroir*.

Top grape varieties

❦ Nebbiolo
Nebbiolo produces Italy's most ageworthy reds. In structure and flavour it's like a cross between Pinot Noir and Sangiovese: sinewy and stylish, with the acidity and tannin necessary to develop for decades. Liquorice,

Top red wines
- Morgante, Don Antonio, Nero d'Avola IGT Sicilia (Sicily) £8
- Castello di Bossi, Berardo, Chianti Classico Riserva DOCG (Tuscany) £18
- Feudi di San Gregorio, Patrimo IGT (Campania) £25
- Montepeloso, Nardo IGT (Tuscany) £30
- Siro Pacenti, Brunello di Montalcino DOCG (Tuscany) £35
- Corte Sant'Alda, Amarone della Valpolicella DOC (Veneto) £35
- Paolo Scavino, Cannubi, Barolo DOCG (Piedmont) £50

Top white wines
- Cusumano, Cubia, Inzolia IGT (Sicily) £8
- San Michele Appiano Sanct Valentin Sauvignon Blanc DOC (Alto Adige) £10
- La Monacesca, Mirum, Verdicchio di Matelica DOC (Marche) £11
- Inama, Vigneti di Foscarino, Soave DOC (Veneto) £12
- Schiopetto, Pinot Grigio Collio DOC (Friuli) £12
- Planeta, Cometa IGT (Sicily) £15
- Borgo del Tiglio, Tocai Ronco della Chiesa, Collio DOC (Friuli) £18

roses, bitter chocolate, redcurrant, hay and tobacco are common descriptions, but 'perfumed' best summarises Nebbiolo's ineffable charms. Its home is Piedmont's Langhe but it also appears as Chiavennasca in Lombardy's Valtellina.

❦ Sangiovese
Sangiovese's aggressive character used to be softened with more accommodating varieties such as Canaiolo and Trebbiano, but better trellising and shorter macerations have recently brought out the best of its sour-cherry character, elegance and longevity. Sangiovese's apotheosis is in Brunello, a majestic and immortal red, but it is better known for its lead role in Chianti.

❦ Barbera
Barbera vies with Sangiovese for most widely planted red grape variety, and is prized for its prolific yields and mordant

acidity. New-wave Barberas, given heavy clay soils, low yields and a lick of new oak, can muster wines with soft, red-fruit flavours, low tannin and a certain rustic appeal.

Nero d'Avola

Virtually unknown until Sicily burst on to the world stage less than a decade ago, Nero d'Avola is slowly being recognised as one of Italy's finest indigenous grapes. Its malleable mulberry and liquorice spiciness is shown to equally good effect blended with Cabernet, Syrah or the local Frappato.

Aglianico

Of Greek origin, Aglianico thrives in the scant, volcanic soils of Italy's deep south, particularly around Vesuvius in Campania, where it produces the south's only red DOCG, Taurasi. Its intense flavour of sour cherry overlaid with violets, coupled with fine tannins and high acidity, make it one of Italy's most enduring reds.

Greco

A white Campanian grape of Greek origin, Greco's polished elegance and racy acidity are characterised by pear, quince and apple aromas. Seldom oaked, it is the mainstay of the Greco di Tufo DOCG but also appears in Sicily, Puglia and Calabria, and is thought to be related to Soave's Garganega.

Fiano

Fiano maintains a haughty austerity for a year or two before slowly revealing layers of melon, cinnamon and an eventual honeyed complexity reminiscent of Burgundy. Its apogee is the eponymous DOCG, Fiano d'Avellino, in Campania, but it travels well and this white grape is now planted in both Sicily and Puglia.

Garganega

Long before the introduction of the ubiquitous Chardonnay and Trebbiano to the Veneto, Garganega's enticing floral and almond aromas were synonymous with Soave and, indeed, Italian white wines. A naturally generous yielder, Garganega needs a firm hand and well-drained, volcanic soils to show at its best. Proper Soave has enticing flowery notes and an austere minerality.

Trebbiano

Italy's most widely planted white grape is a perennial underachiever. Its ubiquity and neutral, easy style have led to universal loathing. Given a chance, however, in its only DOCs (Lugana and Trebbiano d'Abruzzo) it is occasionally rewarding.

Verdicchio

Proper Verdicchio is unoaked and combines high alcohol with firm acidity. In its youth this white variety is both citrusy and faintly herbal; age confers nutty gravitas. The backwaters of the Marche (Verdicchio's home on the Adriatic coast) reveal plenty of surprisingly ageworthy examples.

Wine regions
The north-west

This region comprises **Piedmont**, **Lombardy**, **Valle d'Aosta** and **Liguria**, and despite its northern, Alpine setting, is predominantly red-wine country. Nebbiolo, Barbera and Dolcetto thrive in central Piedmont's limestone soils, occasionally making thrilling wine. Lofty names such as **Barolo DOCG** and **Barbaresco DOCG** command a premium, but the best Barbera (from **Asti DOC** and **Monferrato DOC**) and Dolcetto (from **Dogliani DOCG**) offer a more affordable introduction to both grape and region. If it must be Nebbiolo then look out for **Langhe Nebbiolo DOC** (often, declassified Barolo) or head north in search of **Roero DOC**, **Ghemme DOCG** and **Gattinara DOCG** – or even into Lombardy's remote **Valtellina** where powerful Nebbiolo, known locally as Chiavennasca, is still produced from dried grapes in the Sforzato tradition.

Although the north-west's reputation rests on its reds, at 70 million bottles a year volume is dominated by production of sweet, frothy, summer-drinking **Asti DOCG** and the superior **Moscato d'Asti DOCG**. More serious sparkling wine is produced using the traditional method in the DOCG of **Franciacorta**. Still white wines, including **Gavi DOCG**, are invariably breezy and unoaked.

Pick of the producers

Gaja Angelo Gaja resurrected not only Barbaresco's but also Piedmont's reputation. Magnificent older vintages (of Barbaresco and Barolo) are testimony to his skill and to Nebbiolo's potential.

Giacomo Conterno Traditional need not mean staid. Roberto Conterno's Barolo 'Monfortino' remains a paragon of ageworthy Piedmont Nebbiolo.

Giuseppe Mascarello Ultra-traditional and therefore often overlooked, the Mascarellos have been creating ageworthy Piedmont classics for over a century.

Luciano Sandrone A self-taught virtuoso, Luciano Sandrone has developed a reputation for uncompromising quality over 30 years – his Barolo Cannubi Boschis is the proof.

Paolo Scavino Piedmont producer of impeccable standing, with a host of famous Barolos. His more affordable Barbera and Dolcetto also warrant a look.

Triacca In Valtellina, Domenico Triacca crafts beautifully balanced, traditional Sforzato from carefully air-dried Nebbiolo grapes. The Valtellina Sassella is also excellent.

Uberti The Uberti family have been making a superb range of traditional-method sparklers since the inception of Franciacorta DOCG.

The north-east

The centre of Italian quality wine production, the **Veneto** produces more DOC and DOCG wine than any other region. Oceans of ordinary **Soave** and **Valpolicella**, the twin props of Italian wine exports, pour into the UK, but fine examples are now available as the ranks of quality producers grow.

Having fashioned itself as the home of whites, **Friuli** continues to demand vast sums of money for rather ordinary fare. Better value can often be found in the friendly Alpine **Trentino** and **Alto Adige**. Despite the predominance of red grape varieties including Schiava, Lagrein and Teroldego, it is the whites that warrant a second look. Crisp and aromatic expressions of Pinot Bianco, Sauvignon, Riesling and proper Pinot Grigio all offer excellent value under various DOCs including Trentino, Alto Adige and **Valdadige**.

Pick of the producers

Allegrini Quality at this Valpolicella institution remains high despite record sales. The style is modern and seductive with a smoky, concentrated Amarone setting the pace.

Borgo del Tiglio Nicolo Manferrari pays scrupulous attention to detail: his Tocai Ronco della Chiesa from the Collio DOC is one of the very best and his Malvasia and Chardonnay are also superb.

Cantina Produttori San Michele Appiano This vast, well-managed co-op turns out prodigious volumes of consistently delicious varietals including Sauvignon, Chardonnay and Pinot Grigio.

Corte Sant'Alda Festooned with awards, the self-effacing Marinella Camerani produces wonderful wines, including an immense Amarone and a decadent Recioto.

Foradori Elisabetta Foradori is the undisputed queen of Teroldego, a Trentino native offering a truly Burgundian blend of elegance and power. Her best wine is Granato but even the basic Teroldego is marvellous.

Inama Stefano Inama has established himself as a leading exponent of Soave with two stunning, single-vineyard wines: Vigneti di Foscarino and Vigneto du Lot.

Pieropan In Soave's darkest moments Leonildo Pieropan kept the flame of quality alight. His La Rocca remains a sublime example of Garganega at its most graceful.

Schiopetto A family-run conscientious estate, responsible for a range of Friulian classics that actually justify their lofty prices.

Villa Russiz Run with skill, enthusiasm and confidence by Gianni Menotti, Friulian Villa Russiz enjoys a deserved reputation for its powerful and aromatic whites crafted from Sauvignon Blanc, Pinot Grigio, Ribolla Gialla and Tocai Friulano.

Central Italy

Tuscany, quite rightly, claims the lion's share of attention although neighbouring **Umbria**, **Lazio** and the **Marche** are important contributors to the nation's viticultural mosaic. Sangiovese is synonymous both with Tuscany and with **Chianti DOCG**, Italy's most famous viticultural export. Chianti runs the gamut from wicker-wrapped abominations to the truly sublime. The latter usually hail from the Classico zone, and are increasingly aged in *barriques* rather than traditional *botte* (large oak casks).

Sangiovese's finest moment is the sultry black fruit and mineral complexity of **Brunello di Montalcino DOCG**. Neighbouring **Vino Nobile di Montepulciano** and **Morellino di Scansano** also look to Sangiovese for inspiration but never mange to scale the heights of Montalcino.

South of Pisa the Bordeaux-inspired vineyards of Sassicaia, Tua Rita and Ornellaia dot the coastal DOCs of **Bolgheri** and **Suvereto** in the **Maremma** area. Wines such as Sassicaia and Tignanello were the first 'Super-Tuscans' and threw down the gauntlet to the best of Chianti and Brunello. Their success spawned a host of (often overpriced) imitators and forced a radical overhaul of Italian wine legislation. Bordeaux varieties are found in neighbouring Umbria too, although this is the birthplace of Sagrantino, a structured red variety with characteristic black-cherry aromas.

Orvieto DOC is Umbria's other wine of note but most is white, neutral and utterly forgettable. On the Adriatic coast the Marche produces crisp, citrusy Verdicchio from two DOCs, **Castelli di Jesi** and **Matellica**. The vineyards of **Rosso Cónero DOC** cling to the vertiginous slopes of Monte Cónero just south of Ancona; this is the northern limit for Montepulciano, a grape capable of intensity and gamey flashes of brilliance, both here and in the Abruzzo.

Pick of the producers

Caprai A lone voice in the Umbrian wilderness, Arnaldo Caprai was the first to harness the potential of Sagrantino and still sets the standard.

Castello di Bossi Over 20 years Marco Bacci has completely turned around the fortunes of this Tuscan producer. The Super-Tuscan Corbaia is a nimble blend of Cabernet and Sangiovese.

Castello dei Rampolla Rampolla's Cabernet-dominated d'Alceo is legendary but graceful Chianti Classico and a raft of other wines from this Tuscan celebrity are consistently impressive.

Fonterutoli The Mazzei family have been making wine in Tuscany since 1435. Although the 50:50 Sangiovese/Merlot blend Siepi receives most accolades, the concentrated and unashamedly modern Chianti Classico is perhaps more interesting.

Fontodi One of the first estates to release a 100 per cent Sangiovese from Chianti Classico vineyards. In 1981 this was against the DOCG regulations so outlaw Flaccianello della Pieve was made a humble *vino da tavola*.

La Monacesca The real thing: Verdicchio of rare power and balance, epitomised in Aldo Cifola's single-vineyard Mirum.

Montepeloso Wines of the hyped Maremma are usually expensive and predictable. Fabio Chiarellotto's intensely concentrated Nardo showcases the region's potential.

Siro Pacenti This is Brunello at its finest: lashings of concentrated black fruit, fine

tannins, powerful alcohol and the capacity to mature gently for decades.

The south and islands

Volume aside, the south has for long lagged behind the north. Not any more. From the smooth, creamy elegance of **Fiano d'Avellino DOCG** in **Campania** to the dense and earthy charms of Nero d'Avola from Sicily's **Eloro DOC** the south now sets the standard for chic affordability. The weak links are **Lazio** (some decent Frascati but little else); the **Abruzzo** (tedious Trebbiano and monotonous Montepulciano); **Basilicata** (just one DOC – **Aglianico del Vulture**) and **Calabria** (**Cirò** – a lonely DOC struggling to develop a personality).

Puglia has completely re-invented itself as a hotbed of viticultural excellence. Primitivo and Negro Amaro grapes are star performers in DOCs such as **Salice Salentino**, **Brindisi** and **Manduria**. Flavours are as bold as they are original, with jammy opulence countering bitter-sweet elegance.

Sardinia appears to be continually on the verge of making a breakthrough, but despite extremely promising **Carignano del Sulcis DOC** (from the Languedoc's Carignan) and **Vermentino di Gallura DOCG** it struggles to shake off its sleepy backwater image. Italy's other major island region, **Sicily**, has no such difficulties. Everybody from the local co-op to dozens of emerging estates are cashing in on this viticultural paradise. Native grapes such as Nero d'Avola, Frappato, Nerello Mascalese, Inzolia, Grillo and Catarratto grow alongside Chardonnay and Syrah in a happy muddle of new and old. The results are extraordinarily encouraging, and it's worth noting that Sicily is the only Italian region with both the volume and the climate necessary to build a significant international presence.

Pick of the producers

Cusumano Thoroughly modern wines reflect the passion of Diego Cusumano, a young Sicilian proud of his island's viticultural heritage. Cubía, a 100 per cent Inzolia aged in steel, is one of Sicily's pre-eminent whites.

CS di Santadi A large co-op in Santadi, a sleepy backwater of Sardinia, which turns out good-value reds including the satisfyingly gamey Terre Brune.

Donnafugata The Rallo family make the most of Sicily's craze for light wines fashioned from clever blends of native and international varieties. Top performers include Milleuna Notte.

Feudi di San Gregorio A vast Campanian concern run with enthusiasm by consultant oenologist, Riccardo Cotarella. Patrimo, crafted from ancient Merlot, is the star.

Leone de Castris The Leone de Castris family have been growing grapes here since 1665. Their elegant, aromatic rosé Five Roses is unsurpassed while Salice Salentino Riserva is Puglia at its robust and gluggable best.

Morgante Carmelo Morgante turns out one of the south's most compelling reds: the taut, concentrated Nero d'Avola Don Antonio.

Planeta Before Diego Planeta's pioneering efforts with award-winning Chardonnay and Cabernet, few would have thought Sicily capable of such viticultural genius.

Terredora A rising star in Italy's deep south, run by Lucio Mastroberardino and his family. With over a century of experience, their range of Fiano, Greco and Taurasi is one of the best.

Vintage guide

When to drink
- **reds** – a reputation for indestructibility is justified by new-breed Barolo, Barbaresco, Chianti, Brunello and Taurasi. Most need 3–5 years; some need 5–10 years to really strut their stuff
- **whites** – the best surprise with layers of flavour and ageing potential. Top examples of Soave, Verdicchio and Frascati will improve in bottle for 5 years or more; cheaper wines rather less

2003 Hottest and earliest harvest on record. Expect New World-style wines, rich in alcohol and flavour. Only the finest will last

2002 Damp and cold: best reds in the south, whites in the north

2000/ Two textbook vintages that
2001 made fantastic wines

1999/ A much-prized pair of cooler
1998 vintages whose elegant reds will repay cellaring

1997 A lush vintage with correspondingly appealing wines – many top reds are already drinking well

Top UK merchants for Italian wines

- Ballantynes Wine Merchants
- Bennetts Wines
- Berry Bros & Rudd
- Ceci Paolo
- Jeroboams
- Liberty Wines
- Valvona & Crolla

New Zealand

New Zealand doesn't do cheap wines, but its aromatic whites, elegant and fruity reds, and decent sparklers are often worth the price

What's hot ✔ Sauvignon Blanc and Riesling from Marlborough
✔ ripe, smooth Pinot Noirs ✔ good-value fizz ✔ Merlot and Syrah from Hawke's Bay ✔ premium wines in screwcap bottles

What's not ✗ a few green, under-ripe reds linger on ✗ avoid over-priced Pinot Noir from Central Otago

Why buy New Zealand wine?

There is simply nothing like Sauvignon Blanc from Marlborough, with its distinctive, outrageous, perfumed blast of fresh gooseberry, chopped grass, tomato leaf and green asparagus. Compare Sauvignons from Nelson, Martinborough and Waipara, and give other aromatic whites a whirl (especially Riesling and Gewurztraminer) to taste some truly vibrant flavours emerging. The high standard of New Zealand's white wines is partly down to the country's relatively cool climate. The warm – but not scorching – daytime sun, and a sharp dip in temperature in night, result in a long, slow ripening season, with plenty of fresh, crisp acidity in the finished wines.

Chardonnay can be well-balanced, clean and fresh, especially from Marlborough, Gisborne and Hawke's Bay. That goes for sparklers too: again, bright, pure fruit shines through. Red wines have improved: they used to be under-ripe and stalky, but better site selection, more attention in the vineyard, and a new emphasis on Pinot Noir and Merlot (instead of Cabernet) has helped a great deal. Syrah also looks promising, but don't expect Australian-style blockbusters. The best Kiwi reds display a bright, modern fruitiness with Old World complexity and elegance.

NZ: the state of play

The average price per bottle of Kiwi wine in the UK is now over £6 – higher than any other country. Very few cheap wines exist (avoid those you do find). That said, New Zealand's reliable, fruity wines are well worth the price at the middle and premium end of the market.

New this year

- Matua Valley's premium Paretai, Sauvignon Blanc 2003 (Marlborough) £9
- Craggy Range Sauvignon Blancs (from Te Muna Road in Martinborough, or Old Renwick and Avery in Marlborough) £10–£12
- Villa Maria's single-vineyard range (Marlborough) £10–£20
- Gravitas, Sauvignon Blanc 2003 £12
- Cable Bay, Bordeaux blend 2003 (Waiheke Island) £13
- Riesling from Kahurangi in Nelson

A predicted grape glut may pull the average price down. In 2002, there were 391 wineries; now there are 460. The wine industry has seen a frenzy of planting, and vineyard expansion has doubled since 1996. This puts pressure on the producers and may result in the emergence of cheaper wines, even sub-£4.99 Sauvignon Blancs. The losers will be the smaller, less well-established boutique wineries with over-priced, over-hyped wines – notably those in the 'gold rush' winelands of Central Otago.

All this could be good news for the consumer, provided quality stays high. But the ocean of wine about to pour out of New Zealand may have been overestimated. This is a cool-climate country, and severe frost often affects the harvest (the 2003 crop was seriously dented).

In another major change, a high number of premium bottlings sport screwcaps. New Zealand's winemakers believe that unoaked, aromatic whites – their forte – are particularly susceptible to cork taint. Many have thrown out the corks forever.

Top red wines

- Palliser Estate, Pinot Noir 2002 (Martinborough) £13
- Sileni, Estate Selection Merlot/ Cabernet 2000 (Hawke's Bay) £14
- Te Mata, Bullnose Syrah 2002 (Hawke's Bay) £16
- Felton Road, Pinot Noir 2002 (Central Otago) £19
- Craggy Range, Gimblett Gravels Vineyard Block 14, Syrah 2002 (Hawke's Bay) £20
- Te Mata, Coleraine Cabernet/ Merlot 2002 (Hawke's Bay) £25
- Esk Valley, The Terraces 2002 (Hawke's Bay) £50+

Top white wines

- Jackson Estate, Riesling 2001 (Marlborough) £8
- Villa Maria, Private Bin Sauvignon Blanc 2003 (Marlborough) £8
- Lawson's Dry Hills Gewurztraminer 2003 (Marlborough) £9
- Hunter's, Sauvignon Blanc 2003 (Marlborough) £11
- Babich, Irongate Chardonnay 2000 (Hawke's Bay) £12
- Cloudy Bay, Sauvignon Blanc 2003 (Marlborough) £13
- Neudorf, Chardonnay 2002 (Nelson) £14
- Cloudy Bay, Chardonnay 2002 (Marlborough) £15
- Seresin, Pinot Gris 2003 (Marlborough) £16

Top sparkling wines

- Deutz, NV (Marlborough) £11
- Cloudy Bay, Pelorus NV (Marlborough) £13
- Hunter's, Miru Miru Brut 2001 (Marlborough) £13
- Cloudy Bay, Pelorus Vintage 1999 (Marlborough) £15
- Huia, Brut 1999 (Marlborough) £18

Top grape varieties

Sauvignon Blanc

This grape put New Zealand on the map in the 1980s. Its richly fruity gooseberry, citrus and passionfruit flavours, with highly aromatic notes of grass, herbs, tomato and even tomcat, are unforgettable. Some styles are now more subtle, but perhaps Kiwi Sauvignon Blanc is meant to be an extrovert, in-your-face style. Most still come from stony Marlborough, but try wines from Nelson, Waipara or Martinborough (Wairarapa) too. Beware poor, dilute vintages.

Chardonnay

It's easy to overlook New Zealand's Chardonnays. But these can be excellent, with lovely, fresh citrus fruit flavours and elegance. Bigger, rich and oaky wines come mainly from warmer areas like Hawke's Bay.

Riesling

Currently creating considerable excitement, Riesling produces clean, limey and appley wines that age reasonably well. Good-to-great dry Riesling is found in Martinborough and the South Island regions. Botrytised sweet Riesling is delicious, but at present can't be imported into the UK for arcane legal reasons.

Pinot Noir

Much Pinot is used to make sparkling wine, but the still wines have been impressive of late; some are wonderfully silky reds with vibrant cherry-berry fruit and a hint of nuttiness. Most are made in Martinborough, Marlborough and Central Otago. Beware over-priced, disappointingly simple bottlings.

Bordeaux varieties

The breakthrough hot 1998 vintage produced better, riper reds than ever before. Merlot took precedence as it can cope with cooler temperatures than Cabernet (now firmly the junior partner in most Bordeaux blends). Quality is improving, and the ripe, concentrated wines of Hawke's Bay and Waiheke Island have an exciting future.

Others

Pinot Gris is being talked up; only a few so far have impressed, but it could eventually do well here. A few Chenins, Semillons and Viogniers have proved attractive. As for reds, Syrah is now one of the most exciting varieties, specifically in Hawke's Bay, which is providing most of the serious, ripe, Rhône-style reds.

Sparkling wines

New Zealand fizz is good value (in the medium-price bracket) and has a lovely refreshing, fruity quality which makes up for a lack of complexity. The best bubblies come, unsurprisingly, from the relatively cool-climate region of Marlborough.

Wine regions

North Island

Waiheke Island, a short ferry ride from Auckland, is a warm spot renowned for some of the country's richest reds. A few boutique wineries around Auckland, especially to the north in **Matakana**, are starting to impress.

Gisborne, to the east, has widespread plantings and is a fine source of Chardonnay. Further south, on the east coast by the art-deco city of Napier, **Hawke's Bay** is where some of the best wines are made, particularly Syrah, Bordeaux reds and Chardonnay. Many top wines come from its **Gimblett Gravels** sub-region. At the south-east tip is **Martinborough** (also known as **Wairarapa**), which has a reputation for smooth, classy Pinot Noir and whites.

South Island

Marlborough, in the north-east, is New Zealand's most widely known region. Its sunny, cool climate and stony soils yield some of the best fruit in the land, and it is here that Sauvignon Blanc developed its distinctive style. Look out for Pinot Noir, other aromatic whites and sparkling wines too.

Neighbouring region **Nelson** has a few fine wineries, and Christchurch makes notably fresh, elegant whites and some Pinot. The **Waipara** sub-region here is the most promising. Then there's beautiful **Central Otago**, the most southerly region, where some great wineries are producing complex, characterful wines, especially from Pinot Noir.

Pick of the producers

Alpha Domus Superb reds from Hawke's Bay, including the wonderfully concentrated Bordeaux blend The Aviator.

Babich High quality across the range. This includes Irongate Chardonnay and Cabernet, and the Patriarch label.

Cloudy Bay New Zealand's most famous winery, in Marlborough, maintains high standards with benchmark Sauvignon Blanc and Chardonnay, fine Pelorus fizz and juicy Pinot Noir. However, not everyone likes new oaked Sauvignon Te Koko.

Craggy Range Steve Smith's new mega-winery in Hawke's Bay looks set for cult status. Single-vineyard wines impress; watch out for more to join the portfolio.

Felton Road Central Otago star performer putting out top Pinot and Chardonnay. Using screwcaps even for premium wines.

Montana Hugely reliable giant of the New Zealand wine trade. Country-wide vineyards make excellent entry-level wines, more complex reserves, and stars such as the single-vineyard labels and top fizz Deutz.

Palliser Estate Top Martinborough winery for delicious, rich Pinot Noir, Chardonnay and Sauvignon.

Te Mata Long-established Hawke's Bay winery, on top form with reds (try the Coleraine label); also Elston Chardonnay.

Villa Maria A big outfit that also owns Esk Valley and Vidal wineries. Villa's range is near-impeccable, from bottom (Private Bin) to top. Esk's Hawke's Bay reds are top notch.

Vintage guide

When to drink
- reds – most Pinots can be enjoyed immediately but will keep a few years; cellar top Bordeaux-style reds for up to 10 years
- whites – drink most young; the richest will keep several years

2004 Solid performance so far, with fair-to-good quality

2003 Spring frosts restricted quantities but wine was high-quality

2002 Big harvest of acceptable quality, but not the most exciting wines

2001 Martinborough and the south fared better than the north

2000 Small crop of intensely flavoured Marlborough wines; reds varied

1999 Good to very good for whites, less so for reds

1998 Hot, dry weather led to ripe, full reds; some still drinking well

Top UK merchants for NZ

- Fine Wines of New Zealand
- Lay & Wheeler
- Majestic Wine Warehouses
- Noel Young Wines
- Waitrose
- The Wine Society

Portugal

Amid a sea of international taste-alikes, Portugal offers rapidly improving red wines from unusual grape varieties, and crisp, food-friendly whites

What's hot ✔ high-end table wines from the Douro ✔ affordable, full-flavoured wines from the Ribatejo and Estremadura ✔ ripe, fruit-filled reds from the sunny Alentejo ✔ Touriga Nacional

What's not ✗ ubiquitous rustic, old-style wines from the Dão, Bairrada and the Douro ✗ cheap Vinho Verde: with its vicious acidity it will strip your tooth enamel ✗ label design: commonly still stuck in the 1970s

---

New this year

- Pintas 2001 (Douro)
- Poeira 2001 (Douro)
- Quinta do Macedos 2000 (Douro)
- Niepoort, Dado 2000 (Dão/Douro)

Why buy Portuguese wine?

Portugal's trump card is that it offers something different to consumers bored with international-style wines made from the usual suspects of Chardonnay, Sauvignon Blanc, Cabernet Sauvignon, Merlot and Shiraz. The relative isolation of Portuguese wines, and the industry's slowness to modernise, have helped to preserve the unique grape varieties and wine styles that are now being recognised as the country's distinctive selling point.

For such a small country, Portugal offers an amazing diversity of wine flavours – from the rich, ripe New-World-style reds of the sunny Alentejo, through the elegant, expressive table wines of the Douro, to the crisp, high-acid whites of the Minho. Like its neighbour Spain, Portugal is primarily red wine country, though, and this is where its strengths lie. Another plus point is that winemakers tend to recognise that blends usually work better than wines made from a single variety.

Whatever your budget, you'll find something of interest. At the bottom end, the southern and central regions of Alentejo, Ribatejo and Estremadura make ripe, juicy, food-friendly wines that over-deliver in terms of quality. Further north, the Douro, Dão and Bairrada regions are the place to go for high-end *terroir* wines that possess a real sense of place. Underpinning all these wines is a strong sense of nationality and individuality.

Portugal: the state of play

The Portuguese wine industry is currently going through an extremely dynamic phase, with lots of exciting new wines appearing and an increase in quality across the board. A decade ago old-fashioned rustic, oxidised wines were the norm and you'd have been hard pressed to identify as many as a dozen Portuguese wines that could truly compete on an international stage. Now there are at least 30, with each new vintage seeing the launch of another handful of cult wines from ambitious new producers. Producers are proving adept at meeting the demand of export markets for quality wines. A handful of bottles are still of the old-school type, but encouragingly there are far more hits than misses.

It would be wrong to paint too positive a picture, though. Portuguese wines are still seen by many in the UK trade as bargain-basement material, and it's unfair to expect too much quality in a bottle if you are only willing to pay £3. Given a choice between spending £6 on an Australian brand and the same amount on a new-wave Portuguese red though, it's a fairly sure bet you'll have a more interesting drinking experience with the latter. At the top end, domestic demand for the jewels of the Portuguese wine scene is so strong that they have become expensive. Wines such as Batuta and Quinta do Vale Meão are being sold in the UK for over £35 in only their second vintage (they cost even more in Portugal, where they enjoy cult status).

Top grape varieties

☙ Touriga Nacional

Portugal's star grape, Touriga Nacional, is grown just about everywhere but flourishes best in the Douro and Dão regions. It produces concentrated, expressive, spicy wines with distinctive, perfumed black fruits – sometimes with an almost floral streak widely described as 'violety' – and a firm tannic structure.

☙ Aragonez/Tinto Roriz

The same variety as Spain's Tempranillo, this red grape makes classy wines with tight, red-berry fruits, and has an affinity for new oak. It has a tendency to low acidity and is sensitive to vintage variations.

☙ Trincadeira

Known in the Douro as Tinta Amarela, Trincadeira is a brilliant red variety that is probably the most widely planted grape in Portugal. Particularly successful in the Alentejo and Ribatejo, it makes fruity, aromatic wines.

☙ Touriga Franca

Known commonly by its old name of Touriga Francesa, this reliable workhorse is the most abundant grape in the Douro. It does well in warm sites, producing wines that have a floral, aromatic edge to their red-fruit character yet lack something of the oomph of Touriga Nacional.

☙ Tinta Cão

This high-quality red grape makes wines of concentration and balance, and is one of the Douro's five recommended varieties for port. It is a low yielder so not widely planted, but deserves to be more so.

Madeira

Portugal's second-most-famous fortified wine is madeira. Avoid the sweet rich or pale dry versions but indulge instead in the classic styles: Sercial (dry), Verdelho (nutty, medium dry), Bual (medium-sweet, raisiny) and Malmsey (sweet, very rich). Good labels are: Blandy's, Cossart Gordon, Henriques & Henriques, H M Borges and Barbeito.

Wine regions

The Douro

In a relatively short period of time, the Douro has established itself as Portugal's premium red-wine region. It's hard to overstate the scale and pace of change that is taking place here. The steeply terraced vineyards' potential for top table wine production (as opposed to port) is just being realised and a pioneering spirit prevails, with many new premium wines in only their first or second vintage. Given this region's high labour costs and low yields, its wines occupy the top price ranges.

Bairrada

Unusually for Portugal, this region is dominated by just one grape: the often-maligned Baga. Thick-skinned, highly acidic and tannic, it has the potential to make tough, challenging wines – especially given the common practice of leaving the stems in the fermentation vat. While many wines are overly astringent, there are few really good producers. Proceed with caution.

Dão

Located inland, the Dão has cold, wet winters but mild, dry summers. The granite-

---

Top red wines

- Dão Sul, Quinta Sá de Baixo, Grande Eschola 2000 (Douro) £20
- Quinta das Maias, Black Label 2000 (Dão) £20
- Chryseia 2000 (Douro) £25
- Niepoort, Redoma 2001 (Douro) £25
- Pintas 2001 (Douro) £25
- Poeira 2001 (Douro) £25
- Quinta do Crasto, Vina Maria Teresa 1998 (Douro) £25
- Quinta do Vale Meão 2000 (Douro) £35
- Zambujeiro 2000 (Alentejo) £35

Top white wines

- Quinta do Ameal, Escolha 2001 (Minho) £10
- Quinta dos Roques, Encruzado 2001 (Dão) £12
- Niepoort, Redoma Branco 2001 (Douro) £14

soiled vineyards are at altitude, resulting in ripe grapes with good acidity and the potential for elegant, expressive red wines. In some ways, it's Portugal's Burgundy. Over the last decade massive improvement has taken place, raising the standard above the tough and tannic wines that were the norm.

Alentejo

The Alentejo has led the way in Portugal's wine revolution. It produces red wines in two distinctive styles: traditional ones with complex leathery, herby, spicy flavours; and modern, fruit-forward, almost New-World-style wines that have recently proved a huge commercial success.

Ribatejo

The Ribatejo's fertile alluvial soils on the banks of the River Tagus produce soft-textured, ripe, drinkable reds in the sorts of quantities and at price points that excite supermarket buyers (it's been a provider of bulk wine for a long time). Unlike most other Portuguese regions, foreign varieties such as Cabernet Sauvignon and Merlot are quite common here.

Estremadura

A long, thin region running up the Atlantic coast from Lisbon, Estremadura has struggled in the past as a producer of bulk wine from tired co-operatives. While the region is still quite a mixed bag, some impressive wines are emerging at both ends of the market.

Minho

This is Portugal's most northerly region, and the home of Vinho Verde. At their best, the light white wines from this area are refreshing, crisp and nicely tart; pick a bad one and the excessive acidity will leave you wincing. Good bottles make great summer drinking but can typically be hard going for those weaned on Australian Chardonnay.

Pick of the producers

Dão Sul An impressive producer based at Quinta da Cabriz in the Dão making very assured wines at all price points, principally from the Dão and Douro.

Mouchão An estate making impressive, long-lived Alentejo wines with a higher-than-normal proportion of the *teinturier* (red-fleshed) Alicante Bouschet grape.

Niepoort In Charme, Batuta and Redoma, Dirk Niepoort makes some of the Douro's (and Portugal's) best red wines; Redoma Branco is also superb.

Quinta do Vale Dona Maria Christiano van Zeller's brilliantly situated Douro estate is turning out impressive, expressive reds: the latest release (2001) is the best yet.

Quinta do Vale Meão A new arrival on the Douro scene; already one of Portugal's most sought-after names. Supple, rich, concentrated reds from vineyards that produced the legendary Barca Velha.

Quinta dos Roques Impressive, concentrated, modern-styled Dão expressions including a fine white from Encruzado. Sister estate Quinta das Maias is a top performer.

Prats & Symington A partnership between Bruno Prats of Bordeaux fame and the port house Symington makes Chryseia, a top-quality new-wave red from the Douro.

Zambujeiro This ambitious new producer makes super-ripe, concentrated Alentejo red wines.

Vintage guide

When to drink

Most new-wave Portuguese wines haven't yet established a track record for ageing. As a general rule:

- **reds** – drink cheaper reds within 3 years, and higher-priced reds from Douro, Dão and Bairrada within 5–10 years
- **whites** – drink within 2 years

2003 Abnormally hot, so riper flavours than usual. Some real hits and a few misses

2002 A tricky vintage – disastrous in Bairrada, Vinho Verde and the Douro. Proceed carefully

2001 One of best vintages in recent years, matching quantity with quality. Douro reds were better than in 2000

2000 Hugely successful, particularly in the Douro, Dão and Bairrada

---

Top UK merchants for Portuguese wine

- Great Northern Wine
- Handford Wines
- R&R Fine Wines

Portugal: port

A unique fortified wine style from Portugal's spectacular Douro Valley

What's hot ✔ 2000 vintage port ✔ single quinta port ✔ 20-year-old tawny

What's not ✗ white port ✗ cheap ruby and vintage character ports

Why buy port?

Port is made by adding spirit to still-sweet, part-fermented grape must. It comes in two different styles: the **bottle-matured** vintage and single quinta ports (sweet, dark, tannic and richly fruited), and the **cask-matured** tawny and Colheita ports – lighter-coloured, soft and spicy, with less overt fruitiness.

Port: the state of play

The hot 2003 season may be a vintage declaration (see 'Port styles'). Demand for vintage and single quinta wines is strong. Unfortunately, lesser wines tend to sell on price not quality. Interest across the Atlantic has pushed up recent prices – consider buying mature vintages to drink now.

Port styles

Vintage ports are 'declared' about four times a decade: the very best are blended and bottled after two years in cask. Expensive, intense, sweet and very tannic when young, they hit their prime after about 20 years. They need decanting. While vintages are blended from different vineyard sources, **single quinta** ports are made from single estates and often offer the best value.

Ruby ports are bottled after two to three years' maturing in wooden vats and have fiery, cherryish fruit. **Crusted ports** (typically blends from different vintages) are bottled after three or four years and are reasonably priced. **Late bottled vintage (LBV)** ports, bottled after five or six years in cask can be uninspiring, but **'traditional' LBVs**, bottled earlier, offer vintage character at a fraction of the price. **Tawny ports** derive their flavour from extended ageing in cask. Good ones are up to 40 years old with lovely nutty, spicy complexity. A **Colheita** is a tawny port from a single vintage: they can be brilliant. **White ports** are made from white grapes and are generally mediocre: serve them chilled.

Top ports

- Warre 2000 £40
- Niepoort Vintage 2000 £45
- Graham Vintage 2000 £50
- Fonseca Vintage 2000 £50
- Taylor Vintage 2000 £55
- Quinta do Noval Nacional 2000 £270

Pick of the producers

Churchill, Dow, Fonseca, Graham, Niepoort, Noval, Smith Woodhouse, Taylor, Warre.

Vintage guide

When to drink
- **vintage ports** – start drinking at 15 years (they will last 50+)
- **single quinta** ports – best at 10–20 years
- **late-bottled vintage, tawny and Colheita** – drink on release or soon

2003 Unusually hot. Superb wines
2002 Fairly disastrous, with almost constant rain
2001 Good but unexceptional. Fine single quinta wines
2000 Stunning, concentrated ports
1999 Rainy. Some good ports
1998 Unsettled harvest weather. Some fine single quinta wines
1997 Very good, but not great
Other good vintages 1994, 1992, 1991, 1985, 1983, 1980, 1977

Top UK merchants for port

- Farr Vintners
- Fine & Rare Wines
- Fortnum & Mason
- Reid Wines

South Africa

Some of the most beautiful vineyards in the world, and wine that is improving to match the scenery

What's hot ✔ bright, zesty Sauvignons from Elim ✔ ripe, spicy Shiraz from Wellington ✔ elegant Pinot Noir from Walker Bay ✔ rich-tasting, complex Pinotage-based Cape Blends

What's not ✘ overstretched, dilute-tasting Chenin Blanc ✘ old-style heavy Pinotage

Why buy South African wine?

The ten years since apartheid have seen a transformation in South Africa's wine industry. Where once wines showed a lack of international polish, vineyards were planted with the wrong varieties and the organisation of the industry was heavy-handed and slow, there is now a buzz of enterprise across the winelands. New companies are springing up, new vineyards are being planted and the positive influence of visiting winemakers (from France and the New World) is beginning to make itself felt. Where whites used to be thin and green there are now zesty, zingy flavours. The reds that were dull and heavy are now full of ripe dollops of fruit. Oak is being used to enhance, not kill the flavours, and the talk is of new areas, micro-climates, lower yields and yet more ripeness.

South Africa's wines offer good value for money. There are still a few unexciting wines at the base-line between £3 and £4, however for £4–£5 style shows through, and above £5 the wines have individuality, regional character and finesse. Getting the more expensive wines on to UK shelves and persuading consumers to try them is the next big challenge for South Africa.

South Africa: the state of play

Annual South African wine sales in the UK have risen from almost nothing to 7.6 million cases, making it the fifth largest sector of the market, ahead of Spain, Chile and Argentina. This growth is set to continue, especially since an agreement was signed with the EU allowing the country to export a proportion of wine free of custom duty, which has enabled the South African industry to fund promotional marketing and Ethical Trading Initiatives.

The established regions of Stellenbosch, Paarl, Franschhoek and Constantia continue to form the heartland of the wine industry, but in the search for quality and better micro-climates, new areas have been discovered: Elim and the coastline around Darling and Groenekloof for bright, zingy Sauvignons; Wellington for new plantings of big-hearted Shiraz; and cool-climate Langkloof on the Western Cape for late-ripening Shiraz and Cabernet.

Chenin Blanc, which used to occupy a third of the whole vineyard area, is shrinking in hectarage, but what South Africa is losing in quantity it is gaining in quality, as growers use old vines and lower yields to really show what this grape is capable of. Sauvignon Blanc and Shiraz are the varieties now sweeping into the vineyards. They are being planted on carefully selected sites to make the most of their particular flavour characteristics. The 'Cape Blend' is a new category based on Pinotage blended with other grapes – usually Cabernet Sauvignon, Cabernet Franc, Merlot or Shiraz. There's even talk of planting Tinta Barocca, Petit

New this year

- cool-climate Sauvignons from Elgin, Darling, Elim and Constantia
- Andrew Gunn, Iona Sauvignon Blanc 2003 (Elgin) £12
- Warwick, Three Cape Ladies 2001 (Stellenbosch) £12
- Charles Back, Spice Route, Malabar 2002 (Swartland) £25

Verdot and Malbec in the search to add in better flavours.

Not everything in South Africa's wine industry is rosy. On the downside, there have been accusations of producers cheating: adding flavouring compounds to some Sauvignon Blancs to give them the bright, lively characteristics demanded by the international market. The industry has reacted with indignant denial, and at the time of writing no hard evidence of tampering exists. In many other countries such rumours would have been swept under the carpet but in the new South Africa there is a tendency towards open soul-searching, and the rumours are likely to persist until the industry comes out with a clear condemnation.

Problems with vineyard viruses continue despite all new plantings being certified virus-free. Care is needed by growers to reduce cropping levels, select the right clones and to ensure ripeness.

Top red wines

- Niels Verburg, Luddite Shiraz 2002 (Walker Bay) £15
- Remhoogte Estate, Bonne Nouvelle 2002 (Stellenbosch) £20+
- Condé, Cabernet Sauvignon 2001 (Stellenbosch) £20
- Hamilton Russell, Pinot Noir 2002 (Walker Bay) £23
- Boekenhoutskloof, Syrah 2000 (Franschhoek) £24
- Rustenberg, Peter Barlow 2001 (Stellenbosch) £24
- Vergelegen, Red 2001 (Stellenbosch) £26

Top white wines

- Iona, Sauvignon Blanc 2003 (Elgin) £10
- Jordan, Chardonnay 2002 (Stellenbosch) £10
- Klein Constantia Sauvignon Blanc 2003 (Constantia) £11
- Raats, Chenin Blanc 2003 (Stellenbosch) £13
- Vergelegen, White 2003 (Stellenbosch) £22

Top grape varieties

Cabernet Sauvignon

South African Cabernet grows well almost everywhere and gives deep-flavoured, almost minty styles. It is being planted across the Cape with increasing speed.

Shiraz

This variety might just become the signature grape of South Africa. It is rapidly increasing in hectarage, particularly around Wellington, Swartland and warmer corners of Franschhoek. The style is concentrated with ripe fruit and peppery spice with a good balance of alcohol and flavour, and some ageing potential.

Pinotage

This 1920s cross between Pinot Noir and Cinsaut, seen as South Africa's variety, has now shed its old-tarry taste and is full of ripe, plummy fruit. Critics say it lacks star quality but the new 'Cape Blend' category, blending Pinotage with Cabernets Sauvignon and Franc, Merlot and Shiraz, is showing good form.

Merlot

Merlot does particularly well in Stellenbosch and Paarl, where it develops ripe, plummy, chocolate flavours. Thirty per cent of recent plantings are less than four years old.

Chenin Blanc

Chenin Blanc has a long, unglamorous history in South Africa. Today, much is being uprooted and replaced with more characterful varieties. However, a new wave of conscientious producers, which keeps yields low and achieves full ripeness, is making glorious examples, with citrus and tropical-fruit flavours.

Sauvignon Blanc

Newly fashionable, this variety is now taking root in Constantia, Durbanville, Cape Point and Elim. The style is vibrant, crisp and lively with herbaceous and mineral characters.

Chardonnay

Chardonnay, gaining ground in South Africa, is now showing good regional character. Elgin and Walker Bay versions tend to be citrus-fresh, while fatter, creamier flavours come from the Stellenbosch. Oak is being used more judiciously of late to let the fruit shine through.

Semillon

Two hundred years ago this variety occupied 93 per cent of all vineyards; now it has shrunk to a tiny (but significant) one per cent. Following excellent results from producers such as Boekenhoutskloof, who make a dry, concentrated, lime-scented style, it deserves more attention.

Wine regions

Cape Point
This new, cool-climate coastal region on the western ridge of the Cape peninsula looks promising for Sauvignon Blanc.

Constantia
This quality wine-producing region is based on 300-year-old plantings on the eastern slopes of the Cape Peninsula. It is particularly good for lively Sauvignon Blancs and velvety Merlots.

Durbanville
Formerly a bulk wine-producing region, this area north of Cape Town close to the Atlantic Ocean is developing a reputation for fine Sauvignon Blanc and Merlot.

Elim
A tiny but important vineyard area around Cape Agulhas, Elim is Africa's most southerly point. Sauvignon Blanc is the variety to watch.

Oliphants River
Known for massive co-operatives turning out bulk everyday reds and fortified wines, this hot, dry region 300 kilometres north of Cape Town depends on cooling Atlantic breezes. There has been a move towards better-quality wines by reducing yields.

Northern Cape
This hot, dry region essentially produces bulk white and fortified wines, but is showing clear indications of improvement.

Paarl
With its wide range of soils and climates, Paarl is slightly warmer than Stellenbosch and notable for warm, spicy Shiraz and deep-flavoured Cabernet. Significant smaller areas are beautiful **Franschhoek**, which produces excellent Semillon plus fine Cabernet Sauvignon and Shiraz; hot **Wellington**, gaining a following for its big-flavoured Shiraz; and **Simonsberg-Paarl** with a reputation for deep-flavoured Cabernets and soft, rounded Merlots.

Robertson
This warm, inland area, irrigated by the River Breede, is cooled by south-easterly breezes in the late afternoon. This factor, combined with a limestone soil, make it a surprisingly suitable for white grapes, particularly Chardonnay and Sauvignon Blanc. However, Shiraz is the developing star to watch for.

Stellenbosch
Taking in **Jonkershoek Valley**, **Simonsberg-Stellenbosch**, **Bottelary Hills**, **Devon Hills** and **Papegaaiberg**, this district – which spreads out around the town of Stellenbosch – has a huge variety of soils, slopes and climates. Extensively planted with Cabernet Sauvignon, Shiraz and Merlot, it is the powerhouse of quality red-wine production, although Sauvignon Blanc has increased dramatically recently. Each ward is striving to establish a regional style, and a new generation of winemakers is moving up the slopes to get better flavours and establish regional styles.

Swartland
These warm, dry, rolling hillsides are known for big, powerful reds; now the region is showing that it can do quality too. Cooler coastal areas around **Darling**, especially its sub-region **Groenkloof**, produce startlingly good Sauvignons, while hotter inland areas provide exciting new Shiraz wines on dry-farmed vines. **Tulbach**, north-east of Swartland, is moving steadily towards red-wine production.

Walker Bay
This maritime region, famous for its Pinot Noirs, has suddenly sprouted new properties and fresh enthusiasm. Pinot Noir is still the best variety around **Hermanus**, but higher in the **Hemel-en-Aarde Valley** and at **Bot River**, Cabernet Sauvignon, Shiraz and Pinotage are doing well. **Elgin** has the advantage of altitude and a coastal effect, and is developing elegant Cabernet Sauvignons and soft Pinot Noirs.

Pick of the producers
Boekenhoutskloof Franschhoek winery making fabulous dry, lime-scented Semillon and Shiraz. Its more affordable Porcupine Ridge label comes from regional grapes, while Wolf Trap and Chocolate Block are from dry-farmed Swartland Grenache and Cinsaut.

Fairview It is goats with everything at this Paarl estate: Goats do Roam, Goat Rotie and the new Goats do Roam in Villages. Winemaker Charles Back ardently supports Rhône varieties, such as Viognier. Spice Route is a Swartland offshoot producing powerful, deep-flavoured wines.

Flagstone Dynamic company using grapes from across the Cape for a huge range of wines. Watch out for super-ripe reds such as Writer's Block Pinotage and clear whites such as The Berrio Sauvignon Blanc.

Hamilton Russell The first estate to see the potential of Walker Bay for making cool-climate Pinot Noir and Chardonnay. Heading towards organic cultivation in all but certification.

Iona Harvests can be two months later than the rest of the Cape at this new high-altitude, coastal vineyard near Elgin where Sauvignon Blanc is the main focus.

Jordan The soil changes with every step in the Bottelary Hills but Kathy and Gary Jordan get the best out of each vineyard. Cobbler's Hill Bordeaux blend and Nine Yards Chardonnay excel.

Raats Dedicated winemaker Bruwer Raats makes fantastic Chenin Blanc and Cabernet Franc in the Bottelary Hills and Simonsberg.

Remhoogte Estate Stellenbosch estate part-owned by French wine guru Michel Rolland. The first vintage of Cape Blend Bonne Nouvelle has dense, ripe fruit and glorious complexity.

Rustenberg Renovated Stellenbosch estate where vines are moving up on to the slopes. Most notable among the resulting quality wines are Peter Barlow Cabernet and John X Merriman Bordeaux blend.

Starke-Conde A new small winery, based in the cool Jonskershoek Valley, making spectacular Cabernets.

Vergelegen Perfectionist winemaking by Andre van Rensburg makes this state-of-the-art winery a star. Flagship blends, known as Vergelegen red and white, accompany varietal wines.

Warwick The acclaimed Bordeaux-blend Trilogy looks set to be matched by Three Cape Ladies, an equal Pinotage/Merlot/Cabernet Sauvignon blend.

Vintage guide

When to drink
- **reds** – fruit character is at its best in young wines (keep 2–3 years); complexity develops well in many top-end wines over 5–10 years
- **whites** – most Sauvignons, Chardonnays and Chenins are ready when released; top-end wines can develop over a year or so

2003 An outstanding year across the board

2002 Mixed results with good wines from top producers

2001 Excellent reds

2000 Concentrated, flavourful reds

Top UK merchants for South African wine

- Fortnum & Mason
- Handford Wines
- Harrogate Fine Wine Company
- The Nobody Inn
- The Oxford Wine Company
- Swig

Spain

From crisp, fresh whites to rich, noble reds, Spanish wines are showing more innovative flavours than ever before

What's hot ✔ Toro and Cigales: characterful, quality reds in the mould of Ribera del Duero at a fraction of the price ✔ Monastrell: Spain's last great hidden red variety, now getting proper winemaking attention ✔ Tarragona – cheaper reds than Priorat but with the same power ✔ Costers del Segre: not so much up-and-coming as fully arrived ✔ Aragon: finally realising its potential and at great prices

What's not ✘ overpriced Rioja and Ribera del Duero ✘ over-extracted 'boutique' wines which collapse after a few years ✘ under-appreciation by most UK wine buyers ✘ cheap (in every sense) Cava

New this year

- Cellers Anima, Anima Negra, 2001 (Balearic Islands)
- La Legua, Capricho 1999 (DO Cigales)
- Celler de Cantonella, Cervoles, Negre 1999/Blanc 2002 (Costers del Segre)
- Celler de Roure, Maduresa 2001 (DO Valencia)
- Hermanos de Villar, Oro de Castilla (barrel ferment) 2003 (DO Rueda)

Why buy Spanish wine?

Spain has it all. Sunshine. Ripe fruit. Attractive flavours. Rich reds, juicy rosés and crisp whites. The wines simply slip down a treat and are generally easy on the pocket.

Spain: the state of play

Pundits have tipped Spain to be the wine world's Next Big Thing for at least the last 15 years, yet it has never quite fully delivered – until now. The eternal bridesmaid has at last got its act together, and is now making superb wines at all prices and from all regions.

The country's international reputation has been mostly based on the wines of three star regions: Rioja, Ribera del Duero and, more recently, Priorat (plus a few isolated top performers dotted around this huge, vine-filled nation). Today, although the Big Three remain the most talked-about areas, the most exciting developments are taking place

Spanish classifications

Spain's equivalent of France's *appellation contrôlée* is the **denominación de origen (DO)**. It controls the grapes, yields and alcohol levels of the wines it governs. In 1991 a higher category, **DOCa**, was introduced. Only Rioja qualifies so far, but Priorat may join it soon. Below DO comes **VdlT** (*vino de la tierra*), equivalent to France's *vin de pays*.

Spanish wine is also graded according to its age: *joven* is for young wines; *sin crianza* means without oak; *crianza* wines spend at least six months in oak and are only released after two years of ageing; and *reserva* wines are aged for three years, of which at least one is in oak. To be **gran reserva**, a wine is aged for a full five years, at least two in oak.

elsewhere. Winemaking is more assured, fruit flavours are given greater prominence, and old-style over-reliance on oak is on the wane. Spain is no longer just providing plonk at the bottom end of the market, but showing it can be the equal of any country in the middle and upper echelons as well.

Ironically, part of this revolution has arisen because of the cult status enjoyed by the trio of star regions. The price of land has risen astronomically in all three with the result that winemakers have been forced to look elsewhere to establish new ventures. This has resulted in a rise in the number of excellent-quality (and well-priced) reds from previously obscure regions such as Toro,

Cigales, Tarragona, Costers del Segre, Utiel-Requena and Jumilla.

The price tags of wines from the Big Three have been soaring upwards. While the best-quality wines can justify equalising the prices of their rivals from Italy, France and California, there are plenty of bandwagon-jumpers who have hiked prices, upped yields and not paid sufficient attention to quality. When buying from these regions go by producer and not by DO – see box opposite.

The rise of top-end boutique wines has resulted in a winemaking shift towards ripe-fruited reds with lashings of new oak. They have instant appeal, but their lack of structure leaves drinkers with a hole in the middle of the wine after a few years and an even bigger hole in the wallet. Once again, stick to the top names.

Though more characterful whites are appearing than ever before, the picture is less rosy for Cava, which has become the bargain-level fizz in UK supermarkets – not surprisingly, as prices have been slashed so its quality (and image) has dipped. Life cannot be easy for serious Spanish sparkling producers when they are up against Cava wines with the same DO designation being sold cheaply in bulk deals.

And thereby lies Spain's greatest problem. Few UK retailers appear to have woken up to the new Spanish revolution, and the majority continue to view the country as capable of producing only low-priced, generic wines. For Spain's true colours to be seen, this blinkered attitude needs to change.

Top grape varieties

🍇 Tempranillo
Spain's top-quality varietal goes under a number of aliases (Ull de Llebre, Cencibel, Tinto Fino and Tinto de Toro). It gives the strawberry accents to classic Rioja as well as the rich, structured black fruit of Ribera del Duero and Toro. It blends well with Cabernet and is equally at home with vanillary American oak and French.

🍇 Garnacha
The most widely planted red variety in Spain, for years Garnacha has been pigeonholed as nothing more than the variety behind fresh, fruity *rosados* (rosés) and the junior partner in Riojan and Navarran blends. In recent years, however, it has been revealed as the driving force behind the blockbuster wines from Priorat, Tarragona and Calatayud. The secret? Low yields, no

---

Top red wines

- Castel de Remei, Gotim Bru 2002 (Costers del Segre) £8
- Bodegas Guelbenzu, Evo 2001 (Navarra) £15
- Bodegas Montecillo, Rioja Gran Reserva 1995 (Rioja) £18
- Vina del Olivo, Contino 1997 (Rioja) £25
- Cellers Scala Dei, Cartoixa Tinto 1996 (Priorat) £27
- Allende, Calvario 1999 (Rioja) £35
- Alvaro Palacios, Finca Dofi Tinto 1996 (Priorat) £40
- Vega Sicilia, Valbuena 1998 (Ribera del Duero) £52
- Dominio de Pingus, Pingus 2001 (Ribera del Duero) £275

Top white wines

- Bodegas Tobia, Alma de Tobia Blanco 2002 (Rioja) £10
- Bodegas Palacio de Fefinanes, Albariño 1583 2001 (R Baixas) £20
- Clua Cellars, Vindemia Blanco 1998 (Terra Alta) £20

---

water … and out comes sweet and spicy fruitiness.

🍇 Monastrell
Only now emerging as a quality grape in its own right. Known as Mourvèdre in France it makes gutsy, slightly earthy, black-fruited wines in Alicante, Jumilla and Valencia. Though increasingly seen as a single varietal it is probably at its best when blended with Garnacha (and Tempranillo).

🍇 Albariño
Long-regarded as Spain's premier white variety, this native of Galicia remains ever-so-slightly frustrating. In good years it confirms its reputation, producing elegant, balanced wines filled with soft, pear-like fruits, but in poor vintages it just lacks guts. The key to its success is choosing the best sites, keeping yields low and avoiding oak.

🍇 Verdejo
The indigenous white variety most likely to blaze a trail, Verdejo is a native of the high, dry region of Rueda. Intense, with good acidity and an aroma that brings to mind grapefruit, bison grass and white fruits, it is equally good as an unoaked single varietal,

blended with Sauvignon or for making pretty serious barrel-fermented wine.

Wine regions

North-west

Investment continues to pour into **Galicia**, particularly **Rías Baixas**, but the wines remain a mixed bag. The best are among the finest whites in Spain, but the white revolution remains frustratingly distant.

North-east

Penedès and the expanded **Catalunya** region have long tipped their hat at 'French' varieties such as Cabernet. The best examples are genuinely Spanish interpretations, the poorest rather bad copies of French wines. South and inland from Barcelona, **Priorat**'s cult status for full-bodied, black-hearted reds continues, while neighbouring **Tarragona** has taken the lead and is producing similarly styled, lower-priced but excellently made reds. Further inland, **Costers del Segre** is finally living up to its reputation for concentrated, fruit-forward wines – mainly thanks to Castel de Remei and a revitalised Raimat estate.

Duero Valley

Toro has recently emerged as Spain's hottest region. The wines are big and black-fruited with great class. The same is happening in **Cigales**, the new DO of **Arribes del Duero**, and, to a lesser extent, **Bierzo**. All are regions to watch. Good whites continue to come from **Rueda** – though a sameness is beginning to creep in. **Ribera del Duero** remains achingly hip – and achingly pricy. Its best wines are undoubtedly among Spain's finest. **Rioja**, like any large region, has a wide spread and while it cannot compete in price and quality at the bottom end, in the mid- and top-end brackets it continues to shine.

South of Madrid

Evidence that the Spanish revolution is truly national is shown by dramatic improvements in the **La Mancha**, **Valencia**, **Utiel-Requena** and **Jumilla**. The stewed prunes of old are now replaced by clean, pure fruit.

Pick of the producers

Finca Allende Miguel Angel Gregorio is the guru of new-style Rioja, producing richly fruited, densely structured examples.

Julian Chivite Massive Navarran producer, making top-quality wine at every price point. Chardonnay is Spain's finest.

Carlos Falco The wines of the Marqués de Griñon – innovator, scientist and pioneer – hail from Toledo, Rioja and the new region of Arribes del Duero. They remain at the top.

Guelbenzu Native international varieties from Ribera del Quiles are used for top-end elegant reds with great ageing potential.

Hacienda Monasterio The boom in small Ribera estates started here. Monasterio (and its sister wine Pingus) remains streets ahead.

Montecillo For true Rioja, look no further: the finest traditional producer in Rioja Alta.

Alvaro Palacios Top boutique producer in Priorat for fine Garnacha-based wines.

Puig Roca The Augustus range includes quite simply the finest Chardonnay and Cabernet from Penedès.

Castel de Remei Consistent, characterful reds have elevated this producer (and the Costers del Segre DO) into the top league.

Vega Sicilia Spain's legendary Ribera del Duero estate seems incapable of making a poor wine. All wine lovers should try Unico.

Vintage guide

When to drink

- **reds** – drink lighter reds (*jovens*, *crianzas*) within a few years. Older Rioja *reservas* and big-structured Riberas, Priorats, Toros etc. will last 10, 15, 20 years or even longer
- **whites** – drink Albariño within 3 years, White Rioja at 10–15

2003 Drought conditions, followed by torrential rain. Choose carefully
2002 Rainy conditions; variable wine
2001 High quality across the board
2000 Better in the south than north
1999 Decent vintage overall
1998 High quality across the country

Top UK merchants for Spanish Wine

- D Byrne & Co
- The Halifax Wine Company
- Moreno Wine Merchants
- Sommelier Wine Company

Spain: sherry

Classic and much-maligned fortified wine, with many complex styles: from dry and tangy to raisiny and sweet

What's hot ✔ dry fino and manzanilla sherry (with olives, almonds or shellfish on a summer day) ✔ rich, syrupy, black Pedro Ximénez sherry, made from sun-dried grapes ✔ *almacenista* (individually matured) sherries, especially from Lustau

What's not ✗ cream and pale cream sherries (sweet – the vicar's favourite)

New this year

- Age-dated sherries: **VORS** (Very Old Rare Sherry) for 30-year old wines; **VOS** for 20-year old wines. 12-, 15-year-old and single vintage wines can now be labelled.

Why buy sherry?

At the fino end of the style spectrum, sherry is one of the most refreshing, tangy, aperitifs there is. Richer, nuttier manifestations (amontillado, oloroso) are fascinating post-prandial (and cheese-matching) wines; Pedro Ximénez sherry is denser and sweeter than chocolate. Unfortunately, most people buy the sickly export versions (e.g. Harvey's Bristol Cream) that have no similarity to the traditional wine at all.

Sherry styles

Dry, pale **fino** and **manzanilla** are made from first-pressed (finest-quality) Palomino grapes; the basic wines are fortified and then barrel-aged under the influence of the local yeast *flor*. Flor is the magic ingredient: it covers the wine, protecting it from oxidation, and meanwhile imparts a tangy ripeness. Dry fino is typically nutty, salty tasting and very elegant – particularly chilled.

Amontillado is a rich, nutty dry sherry that starts as a fino but is aged until it becomes a deeper amber colour. **Pasada** (and **manzanilla pasada**) is paler and more delicately complex – in between fino and amontillado styles. **Oloroso** is one step richer than amontillado; it can be dry (resonant of spice and nuts) or sweet (rich, walnuty). **Palo cortado** is a style close to oloroso but with some of the finesse of

amontillado. Real sweet sherry contains either oloroso or **Pedro Ximénez** wine (made from dried grapes, with a black-treacle and raisin character).

Sherry vintages

Sherry is made using an elaborate system of barrel-maturation known as the *solera* system. Each year's sherry is used to top up older, maturing barrels, in order to create a consistent style that is eventually bottled, when mature, from the oldest barrel. No one vintage, until recently, has been bottled alone.

Pick of the producers

Barbadillo, Domecq, González Byass, Hidalgo, Lustau, Osborne, Williams & Humbert.

Top sherries

- Domecq, La Ina Fino £9
- González Byass, Tío Pepe Fino £10
- Lustau, Viejo de Jerez Almacenista Viuda, Dry Oloroso £11
- González Byass, Rich Oloroso Matusalem, half bottle £13
- Obispo Gascon Palo Cortado, Barbadillo £18
- González Byass, Palo Cortado Apostoles £25
- Solera Especial Pedro Ximénez, Williams & Humbert £25

Top UK merchants

- D Byrne & Co
- Fortnum & Mason
- Sommelier Wine Company
- Tanners Wines

USA: California

Heart-warming New World wines with a serious edge – Napa Cabernet Sauvignons are among many Californian wines competing for world superiority

What's hot ✔ Cabernet Sauvignon from the Napa Valley ✔ Sonoma Coast Pinot Noir and Chardonnay ✔ California sparkling wine: superb quality yet terrifically unfashionable, so great prices ✔ Petite Sirah: rich, blueberryish wines from old vines

What's not ✘ overcropped Merlot and Chardonnay: cheap but dull, even bitter-tasting ✘ wines from the too-hot Central Valley ✘ over-oaked Chardonnay (there's still a lot of it about) ✘ poor-quality 1998 wines, rained on by El Niño ✘ pink Zinfandel: sweet, frothy mouthwash

What's new

- Anderson Valley Pinot Noir: new ventures into this cool-climate northern region are generating interesting new wines; good sparkling too
- anti-GMO vineyards in Mendocino
- Ridge Vineyards, York Creek, Petite Sirah 2000 (Santa Cruz) £17

Why buy California wine?

Full of fruit, in reliable vintages California wines have every reason to be as appealing as Australia's, but for one thing: availability. The thirsty American market drinks most of what's produced, so anything reaching the UK is expensive and relatively rare. Californians are making an effort to combat this by introducing a number of entry-level ranges (at around the £4 mark), and these have plenty of ripe-fruit appeal, but the prices rise significantly when customers begin to trade up. Mid-quality wines tend to come in at around £12. For those prepared to spend this amount there's plenty of variety on offer: ripe, cherry-fruited Pinot Noirs from Carneros and the Russian River Valley; rich, powerful Cabernet Sauvignon from Napa; Chardonnays from Sonoma; ripe, spicy Italian and Rhône varietals from the Sierra Foothills; and California's signature Zinfandel: full of jammy rich, black fruits and powerful enough to knock your

socks off. At celebratory prices, Napa Cabernets are California's (even America's) cult wines. Since beating a handful of Médoc *crus classés* at an important blind tasting in Paris in 1976, these classy, black-fruited wines, full of inky concentration, have set a cracking lead.

California: the state of play

America's faltering economy means that it at last sees the need to export its wines to the UK. But while there are now more California wines available here, they tend to be concentrated at the bottom end of the market. Gulpable, fruity big brands (such as anything Gallo) are so widespread that they are obscuring the real picture – Diageo's bland Blossom Hill, for example, is now an even bigger seller than Australia's Jacob's Creek. The 'real wines' are those in the mid-quality bracket, from interesting regions and California's innovative producers.

This year's region to watch (particularly for fabulous Pinot Noir and Syrah) is Mendocino, an AVA (American Viticultural Area) that may well be at the centre of an interesting clash. In March 2004 growers in Mendocino, long a stronghold of organic viticulture, voted in favour of 'Measure H', banning the propagation or cultivation of genetically modified (GM) crops in the county (backed up by major local company Fetzer, home of the organic brand Bonterra). Since this commendable action was taken in the north of the state, Pierce's Disease (a travelling vine killer) has continued to take hold from the south. The only defence against Pierce's currently looks to be the planting of suitably modified GM vines (a development some 15 years away). With neighbouring counties (like Sonoma) following Mendocino's lead, it's to be hoped that the northerners win the political battle, while an alternative defence is found in the south.

In terms of 'this year's grape', look to Petite Sirah. Until recently very much in the background as a 'jug wine' blending grape – and maligned for being a poor cousin of Syrah – 'PS' is now hot property. Old-vine vineyards are being rediscovered for the rich,

dark berryish wines they produce, which should be snapped up as soon as spotted.

Top grape varieties

❦ Cabernet Sauvignon

It was Napa Cabernet that really put California on the world wine map, and it's this region that still grows the top-quality fruit. Some wines have a similar blackcurranty character to Bordeaux, but many are now made in rich, super-concentrated 'blockbuster' styles that sell at astronomical prices. The shame is, the latter are so dense and strong, that it's hard to drink more than a mouthful at a time. Cabernet is widely planted throughout the state, giving generous cassis and plum fruit in its everyday versions.

❦ Merlot

The best Merlots (from Napa, Alexander Valley and Monterey) can be as good as anything from Pomerol, but unfortunately Californians have over-capitalised on their success with this grape, and the current wines show a tendency to dilution. Only by paying £10 a bottle or more can you be assured of the chunky cherry and plum flavours that show what Merlot is truly capable of.

❦ Zinfandel

Weighing in as anything from 'White Zinfandel' (pale rosé) to black-fruited 'blockbuster' wine, and even port-like fortified styles, the average bottle of Zin is usually full of gutsy berry and jam fruit. Beware the high alcohol levels: Zinfandel grapes can easily reach 16 per cent alcohol in an average California summer. Sonoma (Dry Creek Valley) and the Sierra Foothills make the benchmark wines. Zinfandel is thought to be closely related to Italy's Primitivo.

❦ Pinot Noir

Californians might like to challenge red Burgundy, but the truth is they have their own fine Pinot Noir style. Ripe, appealing cherry-and-plum Pinots are emerging, and from the best cool-climate regions (Carneros, Russian River Valley, Sonoma Coast and Santa Barbara) the wines take on an extra level of spicy sophistication.

❦ Syrah

Syrah has great potential in California – up in the Sierras and in Sonoma there are powerful, spicy-fruited versions (like Australian

---

Top red wines

- Bonny Doon, Ancient Vignes Carignane 2000 (Santa Cruz) £11
- Pedroncelli, Mother Clone Zinfandel 2000 (Dry Creek Valley) £11
- Saintsbury, Pinot Noir 2001 (Carneros) £18
- Ridge Vineyards, Geyserville Zinfandel 2000 (Sonoma) £23
- Au Bon Climat, Knox Alexander Pinot Noir 2000 (Santa Barbara) £35
- Seghesio, Omaggio 1999 (Sonoma) £35
- Robert Mondavi, Reserve Cabernet Sauvignon 1995 (Napa Valley) £58
- Joseph Phelps 'Insignia' 1999 (Napa Valley) £100
- Far Niente, Cabernet Sauvignon 2000 (Napa Valley) £100+
- Stag's Leap Vineyards, Cask 23 Cabernet Sauvignon 2000 (Napa) £135

Top white wines

- Bonterra Vineyards, Viognier 2002 (Mendocino) £10
- Frog's Leap, Sauvignon Blanc 2003 (Napa Valley) £14
- Roederer Estate, NV Quartet sparkling (Mendocino) £17
- Alban Vineyards, Roussanne 2000 (Edna Valley) £28
- Flowers, Chardonnay 2001 (Sonoma Coast) £28
- Marcassin, Chardonnay 2000 (Sonoma Coast) £100+

Shiraz) and minerally, austere wines (more akin to Hermitage from the Rhône) to be found. But Syrah risks being an Australian 'wannabe': it must find a definitive California style in order to get the attention and location it deserves. (Many of the 'right' vineyard sites are already full of Cabernet Sauvignon.)

Chardonnay

The Californian taste seems to favour strapping, rich, vanilla-flavoured Chardonnays that swamp the palate with oak. This is a shame because from cooler wine regions (Sonoma Coast, Russian River and parts of Carneros) this grape can show real minerally charm and complexity – even a potential to mature with age. A recent drive for more acidity and less 'soupiness' in the wines has been a good thing.

Sauvignon Blanc

California seems determined to get Sauvignon right – even from warmer regions (Napa Valley) where growers might sensibly leave this cool-climate variety well alone. Avoid the over-oaked versions but otherwise expect plenty of crisp, tangy, lime-fruited varietal definition from today's wines. They are best from cooler coastal or northern regions like Lake County.

Wine regions

Napa Valley

California's most famous region is renowned for its award-winning red wines. Big, powerful Cabernet Sauvignon is the speciality (though not always worth its hefty price tag), together with good-quality wines from the other Bordeaux varietals. From the valley floor AVAs **Stag's Leap**, **Oakville** and **Rutherford**, expect complexity, longevity and elegance; from hillside vineyards (**Howell Mountain**, **Mount Veeder**, **Atlas Peak** and **Diamond Mountain**) you will find the brawniest Napa wines of the lot. Napa Chardonnays tend to be bold and even clumsy, but Sauvignons can be surprisingly tangy.

Sonoma County

Just over the Mayacamas mountains from Napa lies sprawling Sonoma County, which, due to its widely varying sub-appellations, can be a tricky region to get to know. Warmer **Dry Creek Valley** produces top-notch Zinfandels. Cooler **Russian River** and the remote, windswept **Sonoma Coast** are each looked upon as the 'new Burgundy' for their classy Pinot Noirs and

Chardonnays. **Alexander Valley** has a whole spectrum of soil types, grapes and wine styles. Sonoma doesn't have Napa's slick image – but nor does it (as a rule) generate such sky-high prices.

Carneros

At the southern end of Napa and Sonoma, Carneros is cooler (foggier) and the ideal territory for growing ripe, complex Pinot Noir, smooth, fruited Chardonnays and elegant sparkling wines.

Mendocino and Lake County

Mendocino has the highest acreage of organic vineyards in California (if not the world), and many growers are enthusiastically converting to biodynamics too. Mendocino is turning out particularly fine Syrah at the moment, while its sub-region **Anderson Valley** is gaining a reputation for refined Pinot Noir, Gewurztraminer and Chardonnay. **Lake County** is the place to watch for zesty California Sauvignon Blanc.

Central Coast

Stretching from San Francisco in the north to Los Angeles in the south, this vast area incorporates cool-climate coastal regions such as **Monterey** and southern **Santa Barbara** with its sub-regions **Santa Maria** and **Santa Ynez Valley**, which are especially good for Chardonnay and Pinot Noir. The more mountainous inland **Santa Cruz** region, just south of San Francisco, is home to off-beat wineries experimenting with Rhône, Italian and Bordeaux varieties. **Edna Valley**, further south in San Luis Obispo, makes some of the state's most refined Chardonnay. The sweltering inland Central Valley – including Lodi, the Sacramento Valley and San Joaquin Valley – is too hot to grow decent-quality wine, but is home to many of the state's everyday juicy 'jug' wines.

Sierra Foothills

Some of California's oldest (and most undervalued) vineyard territory, these Gold Rush hills are home to fabulous Zinfandels, Syrahs and Rhône varietals, plus some impressive Sangiovese bottlings. Look out for sub-regions **El Dorado**, **Calaveras** and **Amador** county.

Pick of the producers

Au Bon Climat (Santa Barbara) Classy Pinot Noir and Chardonnay in the Burgundian mould from bohemian Jim Clendenen. Also a range of Italian-style wines.

Beringer (Napa) A vast empire (recently merged with Australian Mildara-Blass), still turning out ripe, fruit-forward, appealing wines, particularly Howell Mountain reds.

Bonny Doon (Santa Cruz) Anything offbeat and eccentric suits Randall Grahm: his collection of Rhône-style wines is one of his best (especially Le Cigare Volant and 'Ancient Vines' Carignane), and Italian varietals feature highly too.

Duckhorn (Napa) Cabernets and Merlots (particularly from Howell Mountain) top the Duckhorn range; Paraduxx is a separate brand for strapping Zinfandels, and Goldeneye a newer label for elegant (and fashionable) Anderson Valley Pinot Noir.

Fetzer (Mendocino) Large northern winery with an affordable and highly drinkable portfolio. The Bonterra label (Syrah, Sangiovese, Roussanne, etc.) is now organic and GM-free.

Frog's Leap (Napa) Ripe, rich, juicy Cabernet and Zinfandel and tangy Sauvignon come from this organic, slightly offbeat estate.

Marcassin (Sonoma Coast) Opulent, expensive, virtually unobtainable Sonoma Coast Chardonnay and Pinot Noir from Helen Turley – one of the state's most sought-after wine consultants.

Mondavi (Napa) This leading light and (1960s) pioneer of the Napa Valley wine industry still leads the field today with top Napa Cabernet and Chardonnay, plus a host of other varietals. Look out for impressive joint-venture wines: 'Seña' (from Chile), 'Luce' (from Tuscany), 'Opus One' (in Napa, with the Rothschilds of Bordeaux), and 'Arrowood' (Sonoma).

Joseph Phelps (Napa) Upmarket grower with classic, single-vineyard Cabernet and Bordeaux blend 'Insignia' heading its list. Rhône varietals (Syrah, Viognier) and an exciting new Sonoma Coast Pinot Noir venture are not far behind.

Ridge (Santa Cruz) Paul Draper makes some of the state's most prized, complex (yet not unaffordable) Zinfandels and Cabernets; look out for black-fruited Petite Sirah too.

Saintsbury (Carneros) Dick Ward and David Graves are renowned for making the finest expressions of Carneros Chardonnay and Pinot Noir.

Seghesio (Sonoma) Italian origins show through in superb, concentrated Sangiovese. Watch out for Zinfandel and the Sangiovese-Bordeaux blend too.

Stag's Leap Wine Cellars (Napa) Home of Cask 23, SLV and Fay, three of Napa's most impressive long-ageing, complex red wines. Cask 23 made its name beating Bordeaux's finest in the blind 'Paris Tasting' of 1976.

Willams Selyem (Sonoma) Top-class Pinot Noirs in the Burgundian mould, proving that the foggy Sonoma Coast has the potential to produce deeply complex wines.

Vintage guide

When to drink
- **reds** – drink young except top reds, which need up to 10 years' ageing (maybe even more)
- **whites** – drink the youngest available; only top Chardonnays will age (for 2–3 years)

2003 Rollercoaster rainy, then hot-and-cold vintage. Wines of variable quality

2002 Long, mild growing season with wines of very good to excellent quality

2001 Wines of uneven quality, better in south than north. Seek out top producers

2000 Mild season: wines of consistent good quality

1999 Small but intensely flavoured crop. Top-quality reds and whites

1998 Record rainfall in this El Niño year led to underripe, dilute wines. Avoid

1997 Quality vintage: some of the best Cabernets of the decade

Top UK merchants for California wine

- Adnams Wine Merchants
- Harrods
- Liberty Wines
- Uncorked
- The Winery
- Villeneuve Wines

USA: Washington, Oregon and New York State

Washington

Although Washington State has a reputation for being wet and windy, this applies only to the coastal regions. Further inland, over the dividing range of the Cascade Mountains, most grapes are grown in the American Viticultural Areas (AVAs) of Columbia River, Yakima Valley, Walla Walla and Red Mountain, where hot, dry conditions prevail. This is ideal growing country for red grapes in particular: Cabernet Sauvignon has long held sway at the premium end of the market, and Bordeaux-style Meritage blends are popular. Many producers, however, are beginning to recognise that Syrah may turn out to be the region's strong point, and there has been growing investment in the variety.

White wines can disappoint. Chardonnay is often oaky and dull, and Sauvignon Blanc can lack the necessary acidity. Semillon and Riesling are the high points. The best wines cost over £10 a bottle and can be hard to find in the UK.

Pick of the producers: *Bookwalter, DeLille Chaleur Estate, L'Ecole, Eroica, McCrea.*

Oregon

In terms of both volume of wine produced and global recognition, Oregon runs a fairly poor third to the other West Coast states of California and Washington. This is a shame, because its cool climate is ideally suited to the production of classy, aromatic white wines (Pinot Gris and Riesling, for example) and Pinot Noir that can verge on the Burgundian ideal of elegance.

Most of the planting is located in the Willamette Valley, with more vineyards to the south. Pinot Gris is the most widely planted white grape, with Chardonnay and Riesling next, but growers are also producing some decent Pinot Blanc. As far

as red grapes are concerned, this is Pinot Noir country, although the area has had some success with Gamay and Tempranillo.

As with Washington, price is not the region's strong point. It can be hard to find these wines in the UK, particularly for under £10 a bottle.

Pick of the producers: *Abacela, Argyle, Bergström, Brick House, Chehalem, Domaine Drouhin, Firesteed, King Estate.*

New York State

Today New York State has 150 wineries (25 years ago there were 19). It precedes Oregon on the list of the USA's top wine producers – and, like Oregon, concentrates on quality rather than quantity. As winemaking in cool climates like this becomes increasingly understood, these wines are improving in leaps and bounds. Riesling, Gewurztraminer and Chardonnay fare well among top whites; Cabernet Franc, Pinot Noir and Merlot among the reds. The state's other forte is Icewine.

The best regions lie in the warmest (and most populated) areas: the Hudson River Valley and Long Island both benefit from warm maritime air, and succeed even with robust Cabernet reds. Long Island also produces impressively fruity Chardonnay and Merlot. The Finger Lake region is the largest wine-producing area, with Icewine and sparkling wine taking precedence, along with Riesling that's good enough to bottle age. Central New York – running north to south from Lake Ontario – is an area to watch. Very few wines can be found in the UK, as they are consumed by thirsty New Yorkers.

Pick of the producers: *Bedell Cellars, Dr Konstantin Frank, Château LaFayette Reneau, Lenz Winery, Palmer Vineyards, Paumanok Vineyards, Standing Stone Vineyards, Wölffer Estate.*

Other wine-producing countries

Bulgaria

This Black Sea country's hearty, medium- to full-bodied reds are not the stars they once were in the 1980s. Bulgaria's fortunes have waned since the indigenous and delicious Mavrud and Melnik grapes were celebrated alongside recognisable Cabernet Sauvignon and Merlot: instability due to post-Communist land redistribution is only just settling down. Domaine Boyar (contributing 70 per cent of UK sales), backed by French and Australian dollars, has made a significant niche for itself in supermarkets, but quality remains an issue. Many bottlings offer juicy, fruity value for money (watch out for the company's Blueridge range) but lack consistency and premium character. The Damianitza winery shows a little of what Bulgaria *should* be achieving given its resources, with its worthwhile Uniqato, ReDark and No Man's Land reds.

Pick of the producers: *Domaine Boyar, Damianitza, Rousse Ridge, Vinprom.*

Brazil

Brazilian wines were virtually absent on UK shelves until recently; now there are six wineries exporting to this country. Ninety per cent of the wine comes from the south, where Italian immigrants landed in the 1870s. Their grape plantings were not a success, nor were the American hybrids planted in the 1960s and '70s; but today's crop of international grape varieties seems to have helped Brazil turn a corner. It is still faced with something of a challenge: heavy rainfall means that growers often have to harvest grapes before full ripeness is achieved, when acidity is still high. Fortunately, these are great attributes for making sparkling wine, as Champagne house Moët & Chandon's presence can attest. We're unlikely to see sparkling Brazilian wine in the UK yet as our fizz shelves are already groaning with Cava, etc. at around the same price. But still wine production is on the increase, and ever-improving – winemaking consultant/guru Michel Rolland has spotted the country's potential and spends time making rich, concentrated reds here.

Pick of the producers: *Aurora Cooperative, Baron de Lantier, Miolo (with Michel Rolland as consultant), Salton, Casa Valduga.*

China

Despite having almost as many vineyards as Australia, China's wine industry is still relatively youthful. Most of its vines produce table grapes, and the as-yet-fairly-mediocre wines are consumed on home turf. But the best vineyards (in the coastal provinces of Shandong, Hebei and Tianjin) have real potential. Huadong winery (Shandong) was the first to focus on European grapes such as Chardonnay, Riesling and Cabernet. (Its Tsingtao Chardonnay is one of the best Chinese exports.) Huaxia Winery in Changli (Hebei) is responsible for Great Wall Red, gaining a reputation outside China. State wineries Chang Yu and Qingdao (Shandong) also show promise, but it is Spain's Miguel Torres who looks to be tapping into the true potential of this country: his Great Wall Torres Wine Company is busy supplying the restaurants of Beijing, Shanghai et al with Cabernet Sauvignon and other successful grapes. The *Guide* will be curious to see these wines when they eventually reach UK shores.

Pick of the producers: *Great Wall Torres Wine Company, Huadong Winery, Huaxia Winery.*

Croatia

The limestone karst soils of the Dalmatian Coast (whose temperate maritime climate is popular with holidaymakers to Adriatic islands) are ideal for making red wines – particularly from Merlot, Cabernet Sauvignon and local Plavac Mali (full-bodied and robust). Most of Croatia's wine, however, is produced inland, along the Drava River: white wines from Riesling, Malvasia, Posip and Grasevina (Welschrielsing) predominate. In 1996, Croatian Mike Grgich, founder of California's Grgich Hills Cellar, and his nephew, winemaker Ivo Jeramaz, opened Grgich Vina winery. In 2002, the previously murky origins of California's famed Zinfandel grape were unravelled by grapevine geneticist Carole Meredith, who discovered that Zinfandel and the indigenous Croatian grape Crljenak are one and the same.

Pick of the producers: *Grgich Vina, Miljenko Grgiè, PPK Kutjevo, Zlatan Otok.*

Georgia

This former Soviet state is sandwiched between the Black Sea in the west, where a sub-tropical climate prevails, and a mountainous interior, where continental weather patterns predominate. Georgia has been credited as the cradle of a winemaking culture that goes back eight millennia (Lebanon claims to be an ancient vinous transit point between Georgia and Western Europe). But with less than 40 hectolitres sold in the UK in 2003, Georgian wine represents a drop in our wine barrel. Out of 100 wineries, only the produce of the large GWS winery is available in the UK (via importer Pernod Ricard). Its 'Old Tbilisi' white, a blend from the indigenous Rkatsiteli and Mtsvane grapes, and the 100 per cent Saperavi 'Tamada' red are pleasant, concentrated wines from vines planted at least 30 years ago.

Pick of the producers: *GWS.*

India

India has been growing grapes since 300 BC, and makes quality wines even though the climate in most parts of the country is not predisposed to this. Most crops (and there are often two per vine) become table grapes or raisins. But wine grapes have real potential too, as involvement from leading lights consultant Michel Rolland and Champagne house Veuve Clicquot testifies. India has nearly 20 wineries; Maharashtra, Karnataka and Andhra Pradesh are the most important wine-producing states. Styles vary from spicy *blanc de blancs* sparkling wine (particularly Omar Khayyam from Château Indage) to crisp whites (Sauvignon Blanc and Chenin Blanc from Sula Vineyards), cherry-smooth rosé, and full-on Cabernets and Syrahs (especially from Grover Vineyards).

Pick of the producers: *Grover Vineyards, Château Indage, Sula Vineyards.*

Israel

The bad old days of semi-sweet, pasteurised kosher wines are nearly over. The dominant Carmel group (controlling 50 per cent of Israeli production) has got the message and is beginning to turn out quality-driven wine from boutique producers. It now has a rigorous yield-reduction programme and uses less irrigation – initiatives proving successful both in export markets and at home. Galilee and Shomron submit most of Israel's wine: the sub-regions to watch out for are the Judean Hills and the Golan Heights. Bordeaux grape varieties dominate, with patches of Syrah, Gewurztraminer and others. Israel enjoys little vintage variation, so quality is relatively consistent. Several wineries, led by foreign-trained young winemakers using new techniques, are working to promote a united front and are releasing wines under the banner 'Handcrafted Wines of Israel'.

Pick of the producers: *Castel, Flam, Galil Mountain, Clos de Gat, Margalit, Yarden.*

Lebanon

Lebanon has 12 commercial wineries, most of them built within the past eight years. Only châteaux Musar and Ksara have been around for over half a century (Ksara dates back to the mid-1800s). In 1996 Musar, Ksara, and rising star Château Kefraya banded together to set standards and promote quality in Lebanese wines. Others soon joined. The Bekaa Valley, where over 90 per cent of Lebanon's wine grapes are grown, possesses an iron-rich, gravel- and limestone-based soil. Its frost- and disease-free climate, with long, mild summers, rainy winters and an average daytime temperature of 25°C, is ideal for grape-growing, and there is little vintage variation. The southern French grapes Grenache, Cinsaut, Carignan and Syrah predominate, offering wines of surprising quality and ageability. Newer wineries are planting rather less of these (except Syrah), and more of Cabernet Sauvignon, Merlot, Sauvignon Blanc and Viognier. Chardonnay and Semillon were almost certainly brought from France during the Crusades.

Pick of the producers: *Châteaux Kefraya Ksara, Musar; Massaya; Maison Nakad, Clos St Thomas, Domaine Wardy.*

Mexico

More and more Mexican wine is coming into the UK. Much of the country is too hot for vines, but proximity to the sea provides conditions that are cool enough. Baja California is the best location, about

15 kilometres from the Pacific Ocean, and wines from here are improving with each vintage. Cabernet and Chardonnay are widespread. Tempranillo, Nebbiolo, Zinfandel and Petite Syrah (especially from LA Cetto) can create vibrantly fruity, rich, rewarding red wines; Chenin Blanc and Viognier make some quaffable whites. Mexico is successfully feeding off neighbouring California's success, and with such favourable growing conditions, very little vintage variation, and tremendous quality for the price, it should go from strength to strength.

Pick of the producers: *Château Camou, LA Cetto, Casa Madera, Monte Xanic, Casa de Piedra, Santo Tomás.*

Moldova

Moldova suffered greatly under former premier Gorbachev's uprooting scheme of the 1990s, when it lost many of its old vines. There are seven major wine regions. Rucari is known primarily for red wines, based on the indigenous Saperavi and Bordeaux interlopers Cabernet Sauvignon and Merlot. Whites are made there too, but are more prevalent in Balti, Stauceni and Ialoventi regions. Romanesti boasts nearly equal levels of white from Aligoté and Rkatsiteli, and red from Bordeaux varietals and Pinot Noir. But it is Cricova that's home to most of the 405 hectolitres of Moldovan wine ending up on UK shores. This intensive winegrowing zone sports a massive underground cellar 80 metres deep, with 65 kilometres of roads and a supposed 120 square kilometres of storage space. Though two-thirds of Moldovan wine is red, sparkling wines can be good. Wine production is overwhelmingly destined for Russia, Belarus, the domestic market and Ukraine, however UK importers Hayman Barwell Jones under Master of Wine Angela Muir have begun importing Firebird brand wines at £3.99–£5.49.

Pick of the producers: *Firebird.*

Romania

Romania is littered with unique indigenous varieties such as Feteasca Alba and Grasa. One, Tamaioasa, is described as the 'frankincense grape' for its perfumed, long-lived qualities. Others are more familiar: Merlot, Pinot Gris and Pinot Noir can achieve lovely purity and ripeness in the Dealul Mare region. The change from state control to private wine production hasn't gone smoothly in Romania. While vineyard practices are sound, the technology for winemaking, bottling and packaging has lagged behind. Eight viticultural regions range from the mild and relatively damp Black Sea area to the mountainous interior with its dramatic changes of altitude and weather. German investment, flying Australian winemakers and, lately, a South African consultant, are doing much to improve the quality of Romanian wine, but there is still a long way to go.

Pick of the producers: *Cotnari S.A, Cramele (Prahova Wine Cellars), SERVE.*

Slovakia

Winegrowing is broadly divided into the south-west (home to varieties such as Grüner Veltliner, Wälschriesling, Pinot Gris, Muscat, and Blafränkisch that would be recognisable in nearby Austria), the south (the warmest region, along the Danube River), and the south-east (comprising the Slovak Tokay area, just across the border from its more famous Hungarian neighbour). Foreign capital has only very recently begun flowing into this small country. The most noteworthy results are from the Kastiel Béla joint venture between Baron Ullmann and Egon Müller (of Germany's Müller-Scharzhof fame): early bottlings have been erratic and unusually sweet – counter to the goal of top-quality dry Riesling – but its future looks bright.

Pick of the producers: *Château Béla, Vladimír Sodona, Château Topolcianky, Vinicky.*

Slovenia

Not to be confused with Slovakia, this northernmost and most modern of the former Yugoslavian states possesses four major wine regions – the Coastal Adriatic, Collio (along the Italian border), the north-east (bordering Austria) and south-east (bordering former Yugo-partner Croatia). Slovenians claim that their portion of the Collio region is better than that on the Italian side, determined as it was by the bureaucrats of the formerly ruling Austrian Empire. Slovenia's winemaking history stretches back to Roman times, but current viticultural influences upon this EU newcomer are felt from the countries that border it – Hungary, Italy, Austria and Croatia. Winemakers are slowly beginning to make wines more deserving of international attention. Styles vary from light and dry whites to full-bodied reds and full-throttle stickies.

Pick of the producers: *Borko, Cotar, Kristancic, Vinag Maribor, Marjan & Salko, Movia, Simcic.*

Switzerland

Switzerland's difficult terrain, steep slopes and expensive labour don't deter vineyard plantings on every square metre of feasible space. An eager-to-drink domestic market sees to it that everything the country produces is thirstily consumed. This means there's not much Swiss wine left for us in the UK, but what there is has its own unique stamp. Switzerland's top white grape, Fendent (aka Chasselas), is maligned for its bland, waxy texture but this is actually a great asset when it comes to matching Thai or Indian spicy food, and the best versions are earthy, honeyed and delicious, showing every nuance of Swiss *terroir*. Petite Arvine, Amigne and Aligoté are equally individual Swiss white grapes. Gamay, Cornalin and Humagne Rouge represent the red camp. Familiar varieties Pinot Noir and Pinot Blanc also excel. Swiss wines are becoming more affordable, at around the £6–£7 mark, and although some remain bland, from better producers they are a great alternative to heavy New World palate-swampers.

Pick of the producers: *Luc Massy, Mauler, Caves Orsat, Les Perrières, Jean-Paul Ruedin, J&P Testuz, Frédéric Varone, Zweifel.*

Uruguay

Tannat is the grape which makes Uruguayan wines stand out from the rest. As tannic as its name suggests, it is Uruguay's most widely planted quality variety and makes thick, dark, tough wines. Improving techniques in the most progressive wineries have gone some way to make tannins taste softer, while blending Tannat with Cabernet Sauvignon, Merlot and Tempranillo adds another dimension to the deep, mulberry-like fruit. Viognier, Chardonnay and Sauvignon Blanc are also showing potential, while Albariño has been planted at a cool site just outside Montevideo. Most of the vineyards are concentrated in the south and south-west of the country, close to the River Plate which separates Uruguay from Argentina. Canalones, near Montevideo, is the most densely planted area. These coastal vineyards have a maritime climate and see around 1,000mm of rain each year. This apparent disadvantage means that irrigation is not required, and the country's extended ripening season has the potential to produce elegant flavours.

Pick of the producers: *Bouza, Castelo Pujol, Castillo Viejo, Irurtia, Juanicó, Pisano.*

Where to buy wine

Explanation of symbols

 The merchant operates mixed case sales only

 The merchant operates unmixed case sales only

 Mail-order only

 Online sales only

 The merchant has elected to participate in *The Which? Wine Guide*'s £5 voucher scheme. For more information on this voucher scheme see page 4

 Generally low prices and/or a large range of modestly priced wines

 Exceptionally good service

 High-quality wines across the range

 A wide range of wines from around the world

Criteria for inclusion

The criteria for the 'Highly recommended' merchants are as follows.

- Wide-ranging wine choices from the majority of wine regions covered.
- Over 30 wines to choose from.
- Quality: not everything listed has to be top rank, but there must be good opportunity to trade up from the basic, everyday level.
- A wide range of price points and value for money.
- A certain percentage of trade must be with the public.
- Good customer service and/or detailed information in-store.
- Innovation: the ability to reflect trends and source new and inspiring wines.

We also strongly urge you to take very seriously the merchants in the 'Also recommended' listing. These too have been carefully assessed (the criteria for this section are similar to the above, but with slightly lower thresholds).

Highly recommended

Supermarkets and chains

Asda Stores

Head office: Asda House, Great Wilson Street, Leeds LS11 5AD
(265 branches nationwide)
Tel: 0113-243 5435   Fax: 0113-241 7766   Website: www.asda.com

Closed 25 Dec, 1 Jan, Easter Sun   **Cards** Yes   **Discount** 5% on 6 bottles; 3 bottles for £10, 3 bottles for £12 (on selected wines)   **Order online** Yes   **Delivery** Available through asda.com home shopping, free in selected stores for orders of £99+   **Glass hire** Free with order   **Tastings and talks** In-store customer tastings and larger evening events   **Newsletter** No   **Special promotions** Regular, phone for details

🍇 *Wide choice of branded wines, plus some interesting regional offerings from Bordeaux* 🍇 *Quirky grape varieties from Australia (one of the few supermarkets to supply wines with individual character)* 🍇 *Cut-price offers and discounts for bargain hunters*

Like most other supermarkets' price lists, Asda's starts with a tidal wave of branded wines, fitting snugly under the £4 and £5 marks. The Australian section is neatly divided up by grape variety (Cabernet, Chardonnay, Merlot), and Italy and Spain have the merest of nods towards their wide ranges of wines. There's also a lot of budget own-brand wine, as well as Piat d'Or/Black Tower-type offerings, plus some rather untrustworthy bottlings from Romania and Bulgaria.

So things do not, at first, look good. But peer a bit closer and you'll now find tempting wines that could (and should) encourage buyers to experiment a bit more. Tucked at the back of the Australian wine section are red wines from Grenache, Tarrango, Sangiovese, Durif, Barbera and even Graciano grapes. On offer too are wines showing the character and interesting flavours of the main Bordeaux communes (Pauillac, St-Julien and St-Estèphe among others) – though these cost a little more; it's a shame the same is not true for Burgundy and the Rhône. The self-proclaimed strong points of South and North America don't bring in the surprises they could, but the South Africa list's high points include Danie de Wet Limestone Chardonnay. So Asda *can* make things interesting when it tries – which is more than can be said for some supermarkets.

Best Buys

- Inycon, Sicilian Cabernet Rosé 2002 (Sicily) £4.94
- Sirocco, Cabernet Shiraz 2000 (Tunisia) £4.98
- Rutherglen Estates, Sangiovese 2003 (Australia) £5.02
- Louis Bernard, Gigondas 2001 (Southern Rhône) £8.97
- Neil Ellis, Cabernet Sauvignon 2001 (South Africa) £10.03
- Château Lacoste-Borie 2000 (Bordeaux) £14.98

Booths Supermarkets

Head office: 4 Fishergate, Preston PR1 3LJ
(Branches throughout Lancashire, Yorkshire, Cumbria, Cheshire)
Tel: (01772) 251701   Fax: (01772) 255642
Email: admin@booths-supermarkets.co.uk   Website: www.booths-wine.co.uk

Closed 25 & 26 Dec, 1 Jan, Easter Sun   **Cards** Yes   **Discount** 5% on 6+ bottles   **Order online**
Yes   **Delivery** Nationwide service (min. 12 bottles)   **Glass hire** Free with orders of £25+, £10
deposit   **Tastings and talks** Available in selected stores, phone for details   **Newsletter** No
Special promotions Price promotions, generic tastings

🍷 *One of the most imaginative supermarket ranges in the country* 🍷 *Wide choice*
of 'glugging' wines at sub-£5 prices 🍷 *Plenty of trade-up options, for example top*
Bordeaux châteaux and fine Italian wine 🍷 *Helpful wine list*

This is a truly comprehensive list – buyer
Sally Holloway and the Booths team manage
to provide not only near-global coverage, but
wines in just about every price bracket too.

The list starts with an impressive array of
sub-£10 sparklers (Chapel Down Brut from
the UK and Chandon fizz from Argentina
among them). Champagne itself begins at a
generous £11.99, but the nice thing about
Booths is that you can trade up (even up to
£89.99-a-bottle Roederer Cristal if you wish).
Everyday still wines begin at under £4,

with plenty of cut-price offers to lure the
punters in, but adventurous wine lovers need
not despair. Things get more interesting
around £5, and better still from around £6
to £7. It's hard to pick out strengths and
weaknesses here, as Booths – as ever – has
worked hard on every aspect of its range.
With about 26 stores to supply, it keeps
things manageable: wines from smaller (more
conscientious producers) can feature highly,
and as many as 50 per cent of the shops can
supply the full wine selection.

Best Buys	£4.99
• Peter Lehmann, BV Grenache 2001 (Australia) £4.99	• New Wave Wines, Curious Grape Bacchus 2002 (England) £5.99
• Bodegas Ochoa, Ochoa Tempranillo/Garnacha, Navarra 2001 (Spain) £4.99	• Bonterra, Chardonnay/Sauvignon/ Muscat Organic 2002 (California) £6.99
• Aliante, Rosso del Salento 2001 (Italy)	• Shaw & Smith, Sauvignon Blanc, Adelaide Hills 2002 (Australia) £7.99

Bottoms Up

See Thresher Group, page 124

Majestic Wine Warehouses

Head office: Majestic House, Otterspool Way, Watford,
Hertfordshire WD25 8WW
(115 branches in UK, 3 in France)
Tel: (01923) 298200   Fax: (01923) 819105
Email: info@majestic.co.uk   Website: www.majestic.co.uk

Closed 25–27 Dec, 1 Jan   **Cards** Yes   **Discount** Available, phone for details   **Order online** Yes
Delivery Nationwide service, free in mainland UK (min. 12 bottles)   **Glass hire** Free with 1 mixed case
Tastings and talks Available, phone for details   **Newsletter** 5 times per year to regular customers
Special promotions Regional promotions (**£5**)

The Which? Wine Guide 2005
voucher scheme

£5

Valid at participating merchants,
as listed in
The Which? Wine Guide 2005,
until 30 October 2005

See terms and conditions overleaf

The Which? Wine Guide 2005
voucher scheme

£5

Valid at participating merchants,
as listed in
The Which? Wine Guide 2005,
until 30 October 2005

See terms and conditions overleaf

The Which? Wine Guide 2005
voucher scheme

£5

Valid at participating merchants,
as listed in
The Which? Wine Guide 2005,
until 30 October 2005

See terms and conditions overleaf

Terms and Conditions

- The vouchers in *The Which? Wine Guide 2005* are valid from 30 October 2004 until 30 October 2005. Each £5 voucher can be used against a wine purchase of £50 or more. No photocopies or any other kind of reproduction of vouchers will be accepted. The vouchers may not be used in conjunction with any other discount, offer or promotional scheme.

- The vouchers are redeemable against a £50 wine purchase. For a voucher to be redeemable, the customer must mention at the time of buying his or her intent to use a *Which? Wine Guide* voucher. The £5 is to be deducted from the bill inclusive of VAT, with the participating merchant bearing the cost of the £5 discount.

- Participating establishments are highlighted in the pages of *The Which? Wine Guide 2005* by the (£5) symbol in the merchant's entry.

Terms and Conditions

- The vouchers in *The Which? Wine Guide 2005* are valid from 30 October 2004 until 30 October 2005. Each £5 voucher can be used against a wine purchase of £50 or more. No photocopies or any other kind of reproduction of vouchers will be accepted. The vouchers may not be used in conjunction with any other discount, offer or promotional scheme.

- The vouchers are redeemable against a £50 wine purchase. For a voucher to be redeemable, the customer must mention at the time of buying his or her intent to use a *Which? Wine Guide* voucher. The £5 is to be deducted from the bill inclusive of VAT, with the participating merchant bearing the cost of the £5 discount.

- Participating establishments are highlighted in the pages of *The Which? Wine Guide 2005* by the (£5) symbol in the merchant's entry.

Terms and Conditions

- The vouchers in *The Which? Wine Guide 2005* are valid from 30 October 2004 until 30 October 2005. Each £5 voucher can be used against a wine purchase of £50 or more. No photocopies or any other kind of reproduction of vouchers will be accepted. The vouchers may not be used in conjunction with any other discount, offer or promotional scheme.

- The vouchers are redeemable against a £50 wine purchase. For a voucher to be redeemable, the customer must mention at the time of buying his or her intent to use a *Which? Wine Guide* voucher. The £5 is to be deducted from the bill inclusive of VAT, with the participating merchant bearing the cost of the £5 discount.

- Participating establishments are highlighted in the pages of *The Which? Wine Guide 2005* by the (£5) symbol in the merchant's entry.

🍷 *Cheery 'New World' upbeat image belies a dedication to classic wines, particularly Bordeaux* 🍷 *Quality wines below the £10 mark (at least two-thirds from each wine region)* 🍷 *Good all-round global range*

Majestic has been upping its image over the last few years: customers can now even print off an up-to-date wine list in-store via the Majestic Intranet. In 2003 a Fine Wine Centre was opened in St John's Wood, London, complete with oak floor and wine racks, and a plasma screen providing audiovisual info on wines, winemakers, and so on – plus all the efficient service and fine wine you'd expect from a top London wine merchant.

The shelves of Majestic's shops present some stunning claret, top Burgundy and prestige champagne, and the rest of the range is broader than ever. The bijou pockets of Burgundy from Fontaine-Gagnard (Chassagne-Montrachet) and Robert

Chevillon (Nuits-St-Georges) are well worth looking out for, and although the Italian, Rhône and Spanish choices could do with more depth, there are some stunning wines from southern France.

The New World selection is expanding, with interesting offerings from California and regional South Africa. New-wave icon wines from Chile are making good hunting ground, and Aussie wines bring in plenty of alternative grape varieties (that is, more than mere Chardonnay, but Marsanne, Verdelho, Petit Verdot and Zinfandel). And fans will be pleased to know that Majestic's multi-buy offers on champagne (for example, buy three, save 33.3 per cent) are still as tempting as ever.

Best Buys

- Marc Ducournau, Vin de Pays des Côtes de Gascogne 2003 (South-west France) £4.49
- Curious Grape Empire Zest 2002 (England) £4.99
- Château Pech-Redon Sélection La

Clape 1999 (Languedoc) £7.99
- Fournier Père et Fils, Menetou-Salon 2002 (Loire) £8.99
- Montes Alpha Syrah, Apalta Valley 2001 (Chile) £11.99
- Kanonkop, Pinotage, Stellenbosch 2001 (South Africa) £12.74

Oddbins

Head office: 31–33 Weir Road, Wimbledon, London SW19 8UG
(227 branches in UK, Calais and Dublin)
Tel: 020-8944 4400   Fax: 020-8944 4411
Email: customer.services@oddbinsmail.com   Website: www.oddbins.com

Closed Varies between branches   **Cards** Yes   **Discount** Available, phone for details   **Order online** Yes
Delivery Nationwide service, free for orders of £100+   **Glass hire** Free with order, deposit required
Tastings and talks Regular in-store tastings   **Newsletter** 3 per month by email, regularly by post
Special promotions Regular monthly in-store

🍷 *Appears to be aiming for a wealthier clientele than in its student-loving past, but doesn't yet have the quality wines to support this move* 🍷 *Wines show less individual character than previously* 🍷 *Appealing champagne offers still entice at every price point*

With fewer wines, and less of the funky, spit-and-sawdust about it, Oddbins seems a lot more restrained and a little too tasteful these days: its old irreverence and sense of fun have gone. The takeover by multinational Castel group in January 2002 seems to have dulled things down – just as many Oddbins fans feared it would. Even the in-your-face

window displays have been replaced by colour schemes akin to those of another well-known high-street merchant.

The wines themselves seem to have lost their rock 'n' roll too. Champagnes make a good start to the list, with a mix of prestige wines and affordable bubblies such as Italian Prosecco and sparkling Shiraz at under £10.

But Argentina – prime territory for old-style Oddbins exploration – is bland. The same goes for the Rhône, Southern France and Languedoc-Roussillon: what's on offer comes from bulk producers rather than characterful ones. And in Australia – traditional Oddbins territory – even though the coverage of the regions (Limestone Coast, Clare Valley, Langhorne Creek) is commendably wide, the estates representing them are an uninspiring lot; bulk producers mainly. Even more alarming are the cut-price two-for-£10 and £3.99 offers, all too reminiscent of the supermarkets.

Oddbins says that it is now 'championing premium-quality wines'. But where are they? The 'Oddbins Classics' is an okay selection, but doesn't (yet) have the breadth to rival Burgundy and Bordeaux specialists. Perhaps the group would be better sticking to its previous core territory: young customers looking for a bargain but willing to trade up. Similarly, expanding into wholesale sales doesn't look like a good idea either. This is spreading Oddbins far too thinly.

On the plus side, Oddbins Direct (the mail-order/online service) looks to be a success. Much of the literature is still as colourful and zany as ever (thank goodness). Wines are now almost universally listed by region, to highlight their origins and the way they should taste. Chile and South Africa still have extensive listings. And there's still a bit of trail-blazing going on (in true Oddbins style), with the wines of Morocco providing a splash of interest, a few new-wave wines from the Italian south, and Greece's top growers (Gerovassiliou, Gaia, Kir-Yianni) getting a worthy mention.

Best Buys

- Beni M'Tir, L'Excellence de Bonassia, Cabernet/Merlot 2000 (Morocco) £5
- Viña Leyda, Las Brisas, Maipo 2002 (Chile) £8.99
- Bonterra Vineyards, Sangiovese, Mendocino 1998 (California) £9
- Delas, Vacqueyras 2000 (Southern Rhône) £10.99
- Vergelegen, Merlot, Helderberg 2000 (South Africa) £13.99
- Gaia Estate Aghiorghitiko, Nemea 2000 (Greece) £16.29

Somerfield Stores

Head office: Somerfield House, Whitchurch Lane, Bristol BS14 0TJ
(590 branches nationwide)
Tel: 0117-935 9359   Fax: 0117-307 0003
Email: customer.service@somerfield.co.uk   Website: www.somerfield.co.uk

Closed 25 Dec **Cards** Yes **Discount** 5% on orders of 6+ bottles **Order online** No **Delivery** Free within 5-mile radius or for orders of £25+ **Glass hire** No **Tastings and talks** Monthly in-store tastings in some stores **Newsletter** No **Special promotions** Regular offers across the range

❦ *Bargain bottles from around the globe – particularly good choices from the New World* ❦ *Range of wines in synthetic closures and screwcaps, to ensure reliability*

The cheapest bottle of fizz at Somerfield (excluding buck's fizz) is an amazing £3.99. This, at the start of the wine list, bodes well for a lot of thirst-quenching bargain fun. Same goes for the Australian list of cheapies (starting sub-£3), which begins with rather pedestrian brands but gently builds up to more interesting bottlings around £5–£6. Indeed, Angela Mount, Somerfield wine buyer and creator of this expansive and top-value range, has been working hard to tempt the public into spending a few pounds more.

She's also determined that the wines over-deliver on quality, to prove that a slightly higher price really makes all the difference.

Dipping into the South America, South Africa and Italian sections (Somerfield's strong points), there are some definite treasures among the target £5–£7 range: Cono Sur's Chilean Pinot Noir, Goats do Roam red and white from South Africa, and fashionable Italian wines from Sicily and Puglia. But you have to peer closely to spot them among the own-brand bargains.

Only a few wines here hint at the full wealth of flavours and regional differences available today, which is a shame. But for day-to-day affordable drinking, plenty of choice is on offer.

Best Buys

- L A Cetto, Petite Sirah, Baja Peninsula 2000 (Mexico) £4.99
- Familia Zuccardi, Terra Organica, Bonarda/Sangiovese, Mendoza 2003 (Argentina) £4.99
- Viña Casablanca, Joseba Alluna, Casablanca Sauvignon Blanc 2003 (Chile) £5.03
- Vignerons de Beaumes de Venise, Vacqueyras 2002 (Southern Rhône) £5.49
- Calatrasi, Accademia de Sole Nero d'Avola/Cabernet Sauvignon 2001 (Sicily) £5.99
- Champagne Pol Rivière NV (Champagne) £10.99

Tesco Stores

Head office: New Tesco House, Delamare Road, Cheshunt, Hertfordshire EN8 9SL
(550 branches nationwide)
Tel: (0800) 505555   Email: customer.service@tesco.co.uk   Website: www.tesco.com

Closed 25 & 26 Dec   **Cards** Yes   **Discount** 5% on 6+ bottles   **Order online** Yes   **Delivery** Nationwide service (min. order 12 bottles of wine or 6 of champagne), free for orders of £99+   **Glass hire** Yes   **Tastings and talks** In-store tastings in selected stores, phone for details   **Newsletter** 4 times per year   **Special promotions** Available, phone for details

❦ *Attractive Australian wines, including some interesting smaller parcels*
❦ *Ditto for New Zealand* ❦ *Excellent champagnes, from own-label to big names*
❦ *Good-value South African range* ❦ *Many wines under screwcap*

'Tesco is the laregest wine retailer in the UK – one in four bottles of wine sold is from Tesco,' says Helen McGinn, PR manager for Tesco's wine range. But that doesn't necessarily mean the wines are any good. A lot of consumers find it hugely convenient to buy their wines at the same time as they buy their food. That Tesco is selling an ocean of wine is no surprise, but could it do even better?

Well, the Spring 2004 tasting revealed some delicious bottles – an own-label blanc de blancs champagne, for example (Tesco's own-label champagnes have long been a strength); a lovely peachy Gavi in the Tesco 'Finest' range; some good-value South African in the form of Graham Beck Waterside White and Leopard's Leap The Lookout Red; some smashing Australian varietals from Tim Adams; excellent Alsace Gewurztraminer; and richly impressive; southern French reds.

The store also has some low points: for example, from the hit-and-miss 'Finest' range, a Pinot Grigio that tasted somewhat bitter, a weedy Côtes du Rhône-Villages Reserve and a very odd, minty-mocha-flavoured Touriga Nacional.

That said, the Antipodean wines remain a very strong suit at Tesco, the fizz is fab, and the cheaper reds, on the whole, show well against the competition. The screwcap initiative reported on in the last *Guide* is proving a great success – at the end of 2003 Tesco had over 80 screwcap wines and it plans to launch at least the same number again. Helen says none has been converted back into cork, which speaks volumes.

And there appears to be dynamic team at work here and a happy willingness to keep interesting flavours, grapes and regions on the shelves – hence the Gavi, the small parcels of Down Under Semillons and Rieslings, the decent aromatic Alsace wines, the English wines and so on. Not everything on Tesco's shelves meets with the *Guide's* approval, but an awful lot does, including the general attitude of the team – and that's not bad going for such a huge operation.

Best Buys

- Tesco Picajuan Peak, Chardonnay 2003 (Argentina) £3.23
- Leopard's Leap, The Lookout Red, Western Cape 2002 (South Africa) £5.03
- Errázuriz, Shiraz, Aconcagua 2000 (Chile) £5.99
- Sharpham Estate Reserve, Devon 1999 (England) £6.53

- Goats do Roam in Villages Red, Western Cape 2002 (South Africa) £7.03
- Ravenswood, Vintners Blend, Zinfandel 2001 (California) £7.03
- Tim Adams, Clare Valley Riesling, Clare Valley 2003 (Australia) £8.03
- Tesco Blanc de Blancs Champagne NV (Champagne) £16.99

Thresher Group

Head office: Enjoyment Hall, Bessemer Road, Welwyn Garden City, Hertfordshire AL7 1BL
(2,000 branches nationwide)
Tel: (01707) 387200   Website: www.threshergroup.com

Closed 25 Dec **Cards** Yes **Discount** 10% on 6 bottles, 15% on 12 bottles **Order online** No
Delivery Free within 10-mile radius for large orders **Glass hire** No **Tastings and talks** Bespoke
tastings in-store **Newsletter** No **Special promotions** Nectar promotions, seasonal deals

❦ *Not the most inspirational of ranges, with the main focus being on sub-£5 and sub-£10 glugging wine (with rather a lot of branded wine thrown in)*
❦ *Some interesting bottles, particularly from Italy and South Africa*

The Thresher Group includes Victoria Wine, Wine Rack, Bottoms Up and Thresher. Now, after the mergers, makeovers and shake-ups of the last few years, there are 2,000 outlets in all. That's a lot of wine to supply.

The aim of the group is to 'break down the traditional barriers to wine buying' by demystifying European classic wines – basically a company move towards easy-to-understand global brands, including the house brand Radcliffe's. It's the global brands that can supply enough wines to feed so many stores, but unfortunately these brands are also uninspiring – approachable, affordable and drinkable, yes, but exciting, no.

The *Guide's* last Thresher Group review revealed much rationalisation: the Rhône and Loire sections had some appetising glugging wines (if nothing sophisticated) but areas such as Bordeaux were being cut back. The formula's pretty much the same today, but the news is not all bad. There are some imaginative, flavourful wines for customers to trade up to – such as Canaletto Nero d'Avola from Sicily, L'Avenir Sauvignon Blanc from South Africa, and Bonterra organic Viognier and Chardonnay from California in the £5–£10 price bracket. There are higher fliers too (especially champagnes) for those in celebratory mode. All in all this isn't a quirky range, but it makes a good introduction to the subject.

Best Buys

- Beyerskloof, Pinotage 2003 (South Africa) £5.99
- Canaletto, Nero d'Avola/Syrah 2002 (Italy) £5.99
- Pic St-Loup Réserve 2002 (southern France) £5.99

- Turckheim, Tokay Pinot Gris 2002 (Alsace) £6.99
- Cono Sur, Vision Riesling 2002 (Chile) £8.99
- Bonterra, Cabernet Sauvignon 2001 (California) £9.99

Unwins

Head office: Birchwood House, Victoria Road, Dartford, Kent DA1 5AJ
(389 branches throughout southern England)
Tel: (01322) 272711　Fax: (01322) 294469　Email: info@unwins.co.uk　Website: www.unwins.co.uk

Closed 25 Dec　**Cards** Yes　**Discount** Available, see in-store for details　**Order online** Yes　**Delivery** Free locally　**Glass hire** Available, see in-store for details　**Tastings and talks** Available, phone local store for details　**Newsletter** No　**Special promotions** Weekly and monthly

❦ *Dependable, affordable wines with one or two real quality bottlings thrown in* ❦ *New-wave Rhône wines to try* ❦ *But champagne and claret selections weaker than in previous years*

'Safe' these wines may be, but this list isn't all bland brands. Unwins isn't afraid to tempt customers up into the £7–£10 ranges where there's a little more quality: witness the Hugel Riesling and Gewurztraminer from Alsace (£9.99 apiece) and new-wave Coteaux du Tricastin Rhônes from top growers Chapoutier and Delas (£5.55 and £5.99). Plus there's a spectacular wine or two for celebrations from almost every country. This is what makes Unwins a better all-round merchant than many other high-street stores.

But there's not as much daring as could be hoped from a company trading since 1843.

The champagne list – praised previously in the *Guide* – has nothing like the range it used to: gone are the big bottles and there are only a few vintage wines. Nor are the clarets anything like as good as they have been.

Unwins is the largest off-trade drinks retailer in the south-east of England and, with nearly 400 stores to supply, keeping things interesting on this scale is something of a challenge. It has done well with the Rhône, Burgundy and Italy, so maybe the more 'customer-centric' changes promised for the near future will include bolstering the rest of the list.

Best Buys

- Angoves, Petit Verdot/Malbec, South Australia (Australia) £4.99
- Marqués de Griñon, Tempranillo/Berberana, Rioja (Spain) £5.99
- Bodegas Ochoa, Graciano/Garnacha, Navarra (Spain) £6.49
- Villa Caffagio, Chianti Classico, Tuscany (Italy) £9.99
- Marchesi Antinori, Castello della Sala Chardonnay (Italy) £10.99
- Château Megyer, Tokaji Aszú 5 Puttonyos (Hungary) £15.99

Victoria Wine

See Thresher Group, opposite

To find a wine merchant with a particular strength in wines from a certain country or region, see the regional chapters in the 'Best wine-producing countries' section.

Waitrose

Head office: Doncaster Road, Southern Industrial Area,
Bracknell, Berkshire RG12 8YA
(145 branches nationwide)
Tel: (01344) 424680   Fax: (01344) 825255
Email: nathalie_winder@waitrose.co.uk   Website: www.waitrose.com

Closed Public holidays (selected branches may be open) **Cards** Yes **Discount** 5% on 6+ bottles, excl. multi-values **Order online** Yes **Delivery** Nationwide service (Waitrose Direct), free for orders of £100+ **Glass hire** Free, charge for breakages **Tastings and talks** Ongoing programme of tastings across 75 branches **Newsletter** Fine Wine Newsletter quarterly **Special promotions** Monthly programme of discounts & themed promotions

❦ *A supermarket ruling out bulk-made brands and sticking to adventurous wine choices* ❦ *Fabulous selection of top-quality wines from the 'Inner Cellar'* ❦ *Over 20 organic wines to choose from* ❦ *Plenty of choice beyond the usual Cabernets and Chardonnays*

This *is* a supermarket, but from the quality of wines you might be forgiven for thinking otherwise. Even high-street merchants fall short of offering over 20 different grape varieties from Australia, a choice of 23 Bordeaux at under £20 a bottle, 32 different ripe-and-reliable Rhône and Southern French wines at under £5 a bottle, *and* quirky oddities such as Mexican Petite Sirah and Hungarian Pinot Grigio (both delicious).

The Waitrose team has always worked very hard to ensure even its cheapest wines (starting at £2.49 for own-brand Côtes du Rhône, and claret in half bottles) are interesting. Mid-range wines are as enticing as ever – with encouragement to try them out at in-store tastings and food-and-wine

workshops; and wines from Australia, Chile and New Zealand highlight the different regional characters.

At the top of the range is a concise but very worthwhile *en primeur* Bordeaux range including châteaux Léoville-Barton and Cos d'Estournel, plus top-notch Vieux Château Certan (Pomerol) and châteaux Margaux, Latour, Angélus and Mouton-Rothschild. Then turn to the Inner Cellar listings (special wines available in 55 Waitrose stores), which offer astonishing quality (price being no object here) with bottles such as La Tâche from Domaine de la Romanée-Conti, Penfold's Yattarna and Super-Tuscan Ornellaia. Astounding, really, considering this is a supermarket.

Best Buys

- Cono Sur, Pinot Noir, Colchagua Valley 2003 (Chile) £4.99
- Wild Cat Catarratto, Firriato 2002 (Sicily) £4.99
- New Wave Wines, Curious Grape Flint Dry 2001 (England) £5.99
- Cave de Turckheim, Gewurztraminer

2002 (Alsace) £6.49
- Château Reynella, Basket Pressed Shiraz, McLaren Vale 2001 (South Australia) £13.99
- Réserve de la Comtesse (second wine of Château Pichon-Lalande), Pauillac 1999 (Bordeaux) £17.99

Wine Rack

See Thresher Group, page 124

Mail-order and online only

The Cellar Masters Wine Company

Maycroft, 93 West Lane, Sharlston, Wakefield, West Yorkshire WF4 1EP
Tel: (01924) 862229   Fax: (01924) 860331   Email: otto@hinderer.freeserve.co.uk

Open Daily **Cards** No **Discount** No **Order online** No **Delivery** Nationwide service (min. 3 cases), free within Yorkshire **Glass hire** Yes **Tastings and talks** Annual tasting for clients, others by request **Newsletter** Incorporated in annual list **Special promotions** Various

❦ *Impressive global range* ❦ *Young merchant concerned with good quality and accessibility in its wines* ❦ *Separate list of organic wines* ❦ *Very fine champagnes*

Otto Hinderer set up Cellar Masters in 1998. He is a trained, experienced sommelier so knows the importance of quality wines for restaurants, and much of his trade is carried out therewith.

Specialities here are Burgundy, New Zealand, Champagne, Spain and organic wines. Champagne starts at a highly reasonable £13.35 a bottle (Bauget-Jouette Carte Blanche) and ventures up to Taittinger's Comtes de Champagne Rosé 1995 and Krug Clos du Mesnil 1990 (£63 and £255 respectively). The separate list of organic wines includes a diverse selection from the Rhône, the Oc, Friuli (Italy) and Napa Valley in California. And Burgundy covers some curious Givry from Domaine Joblot but gets classy with the Vougeots of Domaine de la Vougeraie.

Prices start at around the (very reasonable) £6 mark and reach the upper echelons with some classy 'celebratory' wines topping £50 a bottle – the latter crop up particularly in the classic regions of France, Italy and Spain.

Otto lists his wines by producer rather than region, but, as in so many cases, it's the maker that generates the quality, so his allegiances are no bad thing.

Best Buys

- Cave de Turckheim, Pinot Blanc 2002 (Alsace) £4.88
- Marqués de Penamonte, Crianza, Toro 1999 (Spain) £6.46
- Clos Malverne, Basket Press Pinotage, Stellenbosch 2000 (South Africa) £6.51
- Saint Clair Estate, Doctor's Creek Pinot Noir, Marlborough 2001 (New Zealand) £9.98
- Mont Redon, Châteauneuf-du-Pape Blanc 2002 (Southern Rhône) £12.19
- Newton, Unfiltered Merlot, Napa Valley 1999 (California) £16.22

Domaine Direct

6–9 Cynthia Street, London N1 9JF
Tel: 020-7837 1142   Fax: 020-7837 8605
Email: info@domainedirect.co.uk   Website: www.domainedirect.co.uk

Closed Sat, Sun **Cards** Yes **Discount** Available on some wines, for 10+ cases only **Order online** Yes **Delivery** Nationwide service (min. 1 mixed case), free for 3+ cases & within M25 **Glass hire** No **Tastings and talks** Biannual themed tastings, charged at cost; regular private tastings, free to customers **Newsletter** No **Special promotions** Occasional bin-end lists, special seasonal offers

❦ *Specialists in quality Burgundy straight from the producer* ❦ *Detailed vintage reports* ❦ *Five top Napa Valley estates represented* ❦ *Wide range of half bottles*

Burgundy is the speciality at this esteemed merchant, and has been since it set up in business in 1981. The team, led by buyers and

Domaine Direct pioneers Hilary Gibbs and Simon Taylor-Gill, make it their mission to seek out the most reliable of Burgundy growers – not an easy task in this region, which is renowned for its mixed offerings. Reliability, they feel, is gained through trade with the smaller houses (or domaines) whose quality is good throughout their range of wines, not just (as with some top *négociants*) at the top of the spectrum. And if the level of detail on the list is anything to go by, their search for top-quality wine must be as rigorous as any Burgundy fanatic could wish for.

The detailed vintage notes are particularly helpful, with enough information to provide a thorough knowledge of the harvest and assist with buying decisions. At first sight there appears to be less information on the producers than in previous years, but details satisfying 'who are they?' 'what's their history?' 'what are their best communes?' now appear at the back of the list in the 'domaine directory'. This is an alphabetical listing of the main Burgundy growers that makes great browsing – leaving the actual

price lists at the front clear and concise, allowing the easiest possible cost comparisons to be made.

The mark of many a good merchant is the quality of extra services on offer, and Domaine Direct works hard in this department. Aside from its add-on speciality wines from Western Australia and California, the company has recently expanded to cover Bordeaux, the south of France and South Africa too. Another nice touch is the interesting Sommelier Selection: 'wines with the balance and flavour profile to work with, rather than against, food' (such as St-Bris Sauvignon from Chablis, now a full-on AOC wine rather than a wannabe VDQS).

Domaine Direct not only (still) does a very fine job of making Burgundy understandable at not insurmountable prices, but has a list and a newly revamped website that are testament to its high ideals.

Best Buys

- Jean-Hugues Goisot, St-Bris Sauvignon 2002 (Burgundy) £6.25
- Horrocks Wines, Jumbuk Semillon/ Chardonnay, Clare Valley 2002 (South Australia) £7.25
- Domaine de la Croix Senaillet, La Grande Bruyère, St-Véran 2001 (Burgundy) £7.95
- Tollot-Beaut, Chorey-lès-Beaune 2000 (Burgundy) £11.25

- Anne Gros, Bourgogne Hautes Côtes de Nuits 2000 (Burgundy) £11.50
- Bernard Morey, Santenay Vieilles Vignes 2001 (Burgundy) £12.50
- Hubert et Olivier Lamy, St-Aubin *premier cru* Les Frionnes 2000 (Burgundy) £12.95
- Jean-Marc Pavelot, Savigny-lès-Beaune *premier cru* Narbantons 2000 (Burgundy) £14.50

Fine & Rare Wines

Pall Mall Deposit, 124–128 Barlby Road, North Kensington, London W10 6BL
Tel: 020-8960 1995   Fax: 020-8960 1911   Email: fine_wine@frw.co.uk   Website: www.frw.co.uk

Closed Sat, Sun, public holidays, 25 Dec–1 Jan **Cards** Yes **Discount** No **Order online** No
Delivery Nationwide service (min. order £200) **Glass hire** No **Tastings and talks** Available on request, phone for details **Newsletter** No **Special promotions** Online, 1–3 times per week

---

❦ *Impressive stocks (some of the largest in the UK) of genuinely fine and rare wines* ❦ *Beware – elevated prices to match* ❦ *Old World classics predominate, but New World blockbusters also offered* ❦ *Lesser-known fine wines available*

No newsletters, no unwieldy descriptions next to the wines (although this year there's the pithy addition of some buyers' notes), no customer tastings in-store, no club, no special discounts, no clutter at all. Fine & Rare clients know exactly what they're looking for so there's no point in over-

embellishing things.

F&R started out in 1994, and the wines speak as loudly for themselves now as they did then. The wine list amounts to over 100 pages of very big names indeed: Leroy, Bonneau du Martray and Domaine de la Romanée-Conti from Burgundy; top châteaux Lafite-Rothschild, Margaux, Cheval Blanc and Le Pin from Bordeaux; plus Gaja (Sperss and Sori Tildin), Conterno and Scavino (top Barolo) and Antinori (Tignanello, Solaia, Solengo) among the pages of Italian treasures. All, of course, at eye-watering prices: £944 for one bottle of claret (Le Pin, no less), £300 for a bottle of Harlan Estate California wine.

Customers can't purchase entirely online, but you can contact F&R through the website and the transaction is completed and confirmed by phone. Email promotions are sent out as often as three times a week. And the company also buys fine wine from the general public – so if you have any rare Burgundy that you just don't fancy, you can bet that F&R will.

Best Buys

- Château Fourcas Dupré, Listrac 1990 (Bordeaux) £14.41
- Tim Adams, Aberfeldy Shiraz 2000 (Australia) £16.50
- Chapoutier, Côte Rôtie Les Becasses,
- 2000 (Northern Rhône) £17
- Marquis d'Angerville, Volnay Champans 2000 (Burgundy) £19.60
- Graham, Port 1975 (Portugal) £19.75
- Caparzo, Brunello di Montalcino 1997 (Italy) £20

Howard Ripley

25 Dingwall Road, London SW18 3AZ
Tel: 020-8877 3065   Fax: 020-8877 0029
Email: info@howardripley.com   Website: www.howardripley.com

Closed Sun, public holidays, 25 & 26 Dec, 1 Jan **Cards** Yes **Discount** No **Order online** Yes **Delivery** Nationwide service (min. 1 case) **Glass hire** No **Tastings and talks** By arrangement, wine dinners with growers 2–3 times a year **Newsletter** No **Special promotions** Occasional email offers

❦ The very finest domaines from Burgundy ❦ Similarly spectacular selection of fine German wine ❦ Detailed tasting notes to help choices

Nothing's changed at Howard Ripley: this is still one of the UK's very best sources of fine Burgundy. Approach it from whatever angle you wish - whether you're seeking out top growers, top vintages, top villages, affordable estates, or a full range of vineyard expressions from each grower - few, if any, other merchants will match this breadth. It's a good place for moneyed aficionados as well as anyone wanting to discover Burgundy. From Frédéric Esmonin, for example, you can compare and contrast all the great wines of Gevrey – Gevrey-Chambertin, Mazis-Chambertin, Griottes-Chambertin, Chambertin Clos de Bèze and Chambertin

itself – and so appreciate the nuances these great *terroirs* give their wines. In terms of white Burgundy, there are Meursaults to be tried from Darviot-Perrin, Lafarge and Morey, showing how the different growers express this region. And if you want to sample the big names first, look no further: Leflaive, Leroy and Dominique Laurent (among others) are all here.

Expect a similarly thorough approach with the impressive German wines on offer. And at long last the team have added VAT to the list prices; so although the bill for one mixed case might still be a shock, it will be less of a shock than in the past.

Best Buys

- Geantet-Pansiot, Marsannay 2000 (Burgundy) £15.25
- Guy Amiot, Les Chaumes, Chassagne-Montrachet Rouge 2000 (Burgundy) £16.25
- Didier Darviot-Perrin, Les Blanches, Volnay 2002 (Burgundy) £17.50
- René Lequin-Colin, Les Charrières, Chassagne-Montrachet 1999 (Burgundy) £17.75
- Hudelot-Noëllat, Chambolle-Musigny 2002 (Burgundy) £19
- Gérard Chavy, Les Charmes, Puligny-Montrachet 2001 (Burgundy) £19.25

Mayfair Cellars

Unit 3B, Farm Lane Trading Centre, 101 Farm Lane, London SW6 1QJ
Tel: 020-7386 7999   Fax: 020-7386 0202
Email: sales@mayfaircellars.co.uk   Website: www.mayfaircellars.co.uk

Closed Sat, Sun, public holidays, 25 Dec–1 Jan   **Cards** Yes   **Discount** Available, phone for details
Order online Yes   **Delivery** Nationwide service, free for orders of £100+   **Glass hire** No   **Tastings and
talks** Yes, phone for details   **Newsletter** No   **Special promotions** Regular offers; *en primeur* Bordeaux,
Burgundy **(£5)**

🍇 *'Small' and 'upmarket' summarise this merchant* 🍇 *Succinct but classy list*
🍇 *Top-notch Burgundy estates available from recent vintages*

Mayfair Cellars started out in 1989 as a fine wine specialist selling to private clients, but has since opened its doors (or rather, its mailing list) to the general public – and also has a nice line in selling to top restaurants (the Fat Duck in Bray, Gordon Ramsay and the Glasshouse among them).

Burgundy is the real passion, with Anne-Françoise Gros, Darviot-Perrin and Gérard Chavy listed among the offerings of 2002 *en primeur* wines. Bordeaux, apparently, is less popular with clients (and the Mayfair team). But California, southern French and Italian wines appear to tick over quite nicely.

Mayfair has been more open-minded about what it sells in recent years, illustrated by less conventional (less pricy) wines from Cahors and Austria's Wachau region. But this company still has a penchant for the elite: 'Of the 3,000 wines we taste each year, less than 1 per cent get listed. We would rather have a gap than list a dull wine,' says buyer Alex Hunt. It is an agent for just a few top growers per region rather than bringing in a wider spread (Jacquesson, for instance, is the only champagne; JosMeyer the only Alsace grower). It's a shame the kind of buying power that brings in these classy wines couldn't be put to good use broadening this luxurious range even further.

Best Buys

- Viré-Clessé Tradition 2000, René Michel (Burgundy) £9.50
- Château Viranel 1998, St-Chinian (southern France) £8.50
- Clos du Val Carneros Chardonnay 2000 (California) £15.50
- Chassagne-Montrachet *premier cru* Les Bondues 2000 (Burgundy) £19.95
- Vosne-Romanée Les Damodes 2000 (Burgundy) £19.95
- Dow's Crusted Port, bottled 1997 (Portugal) £16.50

Montrachet Fine Wine Merchants

59 Kennington Road, Waterloo, London SE1 7PZ
Tel: 020-7928 1990   Fax: 020-7928 3415
Email: charles@montrachetwine.com   Website: www.montrachetwine.com

Closed Sat, Sun, public holidays   **Cards** Yes   **Discount** No   **Order online** No   **Delivery** Nationwide
service (min. 1 case), free for 3+ cases   **Glass hire** No   **Tastings and talks** Frequent tastings and talks,
mainly *en primeur* wines   **Newsletter** No   **Special promotions** No

🍇 *Specialist in small Burgundy growers* 🍇 *Helpful, knowledgeable staff*
🍇 *French classics, vintage port and top German bottlings, including small reliable producers*

Very much a family-sized, family-focused wine merchant this, specialising in top-quality Burgundy from small, family domaines. Charles Taylor MW and fellow director Louisa de Faye Perkins founded the company in 1995, and have built a reputation for dealing in first-class wines, not only from Burgundy but also from Bordeaux and the Rhône, plus impressive allocations of top German wines, more from Alsace, the Loire and Champagne, and port from Portugal. Their years of trading experience mean that they have developed loyal partnerships with the growers they work with, and receive excellent allocations as a result: the 2002

Burgundy offer, with Meursault and four *premiers crus* of Volnay from Domaine Marquis d'Angerville, and five *premiers crus* of Nuits St-Georges from Henri Gouges, says it all. There's also Chassagne-Montrachet from Jean-Marc Pillot and Puligny-Montrachet from Louis Carillon – well, at a merchant with *this* name, there had to be some.

Much Montrachet wine is sold for laying down, and good advice is available as to how, where and for what length of time you should do this. The team are well-versed in the Burgundies (and so on), as all the staff are taken to France and Germany to meet producers and taste extensively.

Best Buys

- Bertrand Ambroise, St-Romain Blanc 2002 (Burgundy) £11.75
- Domaine Chandon de Briailles, Savigny-lès-Beaune, Premier Cru Fourneaux 2002 (Burgundy) £14.50
- Domaine Jacques Cacheux et Fils, Vosne Romanée 2002 £18

- Vincent Girardin, Puligny-Montrachet, Vieilles Vignes 2002 (Burgundy) £19.50
- Domaine Yves Boyer-Martenot, Meursault Les Narvaux 2002 (Burgundy) £19.50
- Domaine Henri Gouges, Nuits St-Georges 2002 (Burgundy) £19.75

O W Loeb & Company

3 Archie Street, London SE1 3JT
Tel: 020-7234 0385   Fax: 020-7357 0440
Email: finewine@owloeb.com   Website: www.owloeb.com

Closed Sat, Sun **Cards** Yes **Discount** Available on 5+ cases **Order online** No **Delivery** Nationwide service, free for 2+ cases **Glass hire** No **Tastings and talks** Annual & regular tastings **Newsletter** Yes **Special promotions** Regular offers

---

❦ *Smart merchant, celebrated for its fine stocks of Rhône, Burgundy, Alsace and German wines* ❦ *Prices aren't as intimidating as they might be – many come in at around the £5 mark* ❦ *Plenty of choice from which to compile a mixed case*

Loeb wasn't able to send a full wine list to the *Guide* this year, so a complete review hasn't been possible. However, judging from the stellar Burgundies and Rhône wines in its 2002 and 2001 offers (released in 2004) this merchant is still on fine form and worthy of its place among the country's top merchants.

Loeb is really into its Burgundies: over 20 here come from the famous commune of Chassagne-Montrachet alone, including *grands* and plenty of *premiers crus*. Not all are from big-star growers, but there's enough detail and tasting information on the printed list for customers to get to know the wines in all but flavour. For label hunters, the

Volnays of Marquis d'Angerville, the Vosne-Romanée of Confuron-Cotetidot and the Chambolle-Musigny of Domaine Dujac are well worth looking out for.

The quality of the Spanish wines, newly on offer at Loeb this year, is also praiseworthy. This small but dedicated range includes some classy bottlings from the fashionable Priorat region. But on Germany, the Loire, New Zealand and South Africa – collections for which this company is also celebrated – it's impossible to report. Suffice to say that Loeb has been trading since 1874 and still retains its extremely smart reputation.

Best Buys

- La Planta, Ribera del Duero 2002 (Spain) £7.95
- Domaine Marius Delarche, Pernand-Vergelesses 2002 (Burgundy) £10.70
- Vincent Girardin, Santenay Premier Cru Maladière 2002 (Burgundy) £11.97

- Domaine Tollot-Beaut, Chorey-lès-Beaune 2002 (Burgundy) £12.76
- Domaine Dujac, Gevrey-Chambertin 2002 (Burgundy) £17.55
- Domaine Patrick Javillier, Pommard 2002 (Burgundy) £19.51

Peter Wylie Fine Wines

Plymtree Manor, Plymtree, Cullompton, Devon EX15 2LE
Tel: (01884) 277555   Fax: (01884) 277557
Email: peter@wylie-fine-wines.demon.co.uk   Website: www.wyliefinewines.co.uk

Closed Sat, Sun, public holidays **Cards** No **Discount** Available, phone for details **Order online** Yes **Delivery** Nationwide service **Glass hire** No **Tastings and talks** No **Newsletter** No **Special promotions** New arrivals and promotions by mailouts & email

---

❦ *Fascinating speciality range, featuring Bordeaux from the early 1800s*
❦ *Madeira, vintage port, fine and rare old wines in plentiful supply* ❦ *Yquem vintages spanning the twentieth century* ❦ *2000 Bordeaux from many top châteaux*

Peter Wylie says of himself that he is 'a wonderful person to buy wine from'. Certainly the scope and quality of his list are pretty wonderful. Château-bottled clarets begin with 'pre-1860' Château Belair and continue into 1900 Tertre Daugay, 1904 Léoville Lascases and wartime wines from Mouton-Rothschild (1914) and Lafite (1918). Just about every vintage of the 1940s, 1950s and glorious 1960s is highlighted in truly spectacular (*cru classé*) form: for example, nearly 100 wines from the fabulous 1961 vintage, and 60 from the impeccable 1966 - all still drinking very well.

Just as generously stocked are the 1970s, 1980s and 1990s bins but, as has been said before in this *Guide*, Peter prefers the wines to be in outsize bottles to add interest (magnums, double-magnums, impérials and jeroboams are all available).

In short, there's plenty of birthday and special-occasion treats on offer – even going as far back as 1812 (though this particular white Bordeaux will set you back £9,750). Burgundy, Rhône, California wines, champagne, cognac and armagnac do get a look in too, but it's claret that's really the main event here. You can peruse, be amazed, and purchase via the website.

Best Buys

- Château d'Armailhac 2000 (Bordeaux) £32
- Château Suduiraut 1989 (Sauternes) £38
- Heitz, Napa Cabernet Sauvignon 1978 (California) £40

- Jaboulet Aîné, Hermitage La Chapelle 1986 (Northern Rhône) £50
- González Byass port, vintage 1963 (Portugal) £65
- Dom Pérignon champagne 1990 (Champagne) £75

The Sunday Times Wine Club ✉

See Laithwaites (South England), page 155

Swig

188 Sutton Court Road, London W4 3NY
Tel: (08000) 272272   Fax: 020-8995 7069
Email: imbibe@swig.co.uk   Website: www.swig.co.uk

Closed Sat, Sun **Cards** Yes **Discount** No **Order online** Yes **Delivery** Nationwide service (min. 1 mixed case) **Glass hire** No **Tastings and talks** 6 tastings per year incl. large annual South African tasting in May & Italian tasting in Autumn **Newsletter** No **Special promotions** By email £5

❦ *Top Italian producers, especially from Piedmont* ❦ *Very classy selection from the Cape, with many top producers represented* ❦ *Helpful advice by phone or online*

Swig (Serious Wine Imbibers Group) stocks wines from various quarters of the vinous map, but Italy and South Africa are the main passions here – followed closely by New Zealand's Pinot Noir. Owner Robin Davis used to be a buyer for an all-Italian wine importer so it's hardly surprising that Swig's Italian range includes many of the top producers from Piedmont and Tuscany, such as Gaja, Roberto Voerzio, Giacomo Ascheri, Isole e Olena and Piero Antinori. There's plenty of back-up from Sardinia, Sicily and Lombardy, among other Italian regions.

The South African list is, if anything, even more exciting. It features a stellar cast of the best Cape winemakers, among them Boekenhoutskloof, De Toren, Jordan, Kanonkop, Springfield and Steenberg. It's hard to imagine a South African selection that could top it in the UK. The range is well presented in brochure form and comes with decent tasting notes. Elsewhere, look out for a few treasures from France, New Zealand and Australia. It should be easy to put together the minimum one mixed case, as this is a very stylish and classy collection of wines, if a little short on cheap-and-cheerful bottles. Refreshingly, it comes from a young, dynamic and very unstuffy team, who are happy to provide a personal service and discuss customers' preferences.

Best Buys

- Pieropan, Soave Classico Superiore, Veneto 2002 (Italy) £8.95
- Springfield, Life from Stone, Sauvignon Blanc, Robertson 2003 (South Africa), £9.50
- Brolio, Chianti Classico, Tuscany 2001

(Italy) £12.50
- De Toren, Fusion V, Stellenbosch 2001/2 (South Africa) £20
- Sitorey, Moresco, Gaja, Piedmont 1998 (Italy) £21.50
- Boekenhoutskloof, Syrah, Franschhoek 2001/2 (South Africa) £25

Vin du Van Wine Merchants

Colthups, The Street, Appledore, Kent TN26 2BX
Tel: (01233) 758727   Fax: (01233) 758389

Closed Sat, Sun, public holidays **Cards** Yes **Discount** No **Order online** No **Delivery** Nationwide service (min. 1 case), free within 10-mile radius **Glass hire** No **Tastings and talks** No **Newsletter** No **Special promotions** No

❦ *Virtually unmatched selection of boutique Australian wines* ❦ *Unusual older Australian vintages available* ❦ *Eccentric, upbeat, lively wine brochure* ❦ *Down Under sticky and sparkling wines* ❦ *24-hour delivery, UK-wide*

Don't look for boring blends and brands from Australia here. Look out for alternative, offbeat wines from the regions – the type of wine that Australian winemakers really like making.

Ex-art director Ian Brown has just about the most eccentric take on the business of any merchant in this *Guide*. Browsers of his list will notice a rather unusual form of note-taking ('... if the surface of your tongue appears smooth & shiny it's probable that your buds have been stolen by pixies ...'), but be not deterred. He has put together one of the best ranges of Australian wines in the UK, and for this wine lovers should breathe a grateful sigh of relief.

For starters (and it's worth repeating, because it is such a rare achievement), there's more than just Chardonnay ('Big oaky Chardonnay no longer sells', says Ian) – Viognier, Roussanne, Verdelho, Chenin Blanc and Pinot Gris are all on offer. And more than Merlot is available, notably Tempranillo ('quirky for Oz!'), Zinfandel, Petit Verdot and Pinot Noir. Fizz features too (ranging from Ashton Hills Salmon Brut to Hollick sparkling

Coonawarra Merlot), and don't forget the famous Australian sticky wines – the ones they'd rather we didn't get our hands on, but, thanks to Vin du Van, we most certainly do.

The list – decorated with parsnips and toy reindeer would you believe – is rather randomly presented, and the notes might jar the sensibilities of anyone not in the most humorous of moods. But there's no shortage of really good regional wine here, including the likes of Heathcote (very fashionable!), Clare and Limestone Coast, not to mention back vintages of icon wines such as Grange, Bin 707, Henschke and Mount Mary. For those looking to escape the boredom that can be Australian brands this is a great place to seek adventure.

Best Buys

- Shaw & Smith, Sauvignon, Adelaide Hills 2003 (South Australia) £9.95
- Pierro, Sauvignon/Semillon, Margaret River 2002 (Western Australia) £9.95
- Mount Horrocks, Watervale Riesling 2002 (South Australia) £11.95
- Henschke, Louis Semillon 1998 (South Australia) £11.95
- Turkey Flat, Barossa Valley Grenache Noir 2001 (South Australia) £11.95
- Veritas Heysen, Vineyard Shiraz 1999 (South Australia) £13.95
- Dromana Estate, Pinot Noir 2001 (Victoria) £10.50

Virgin Wines

The Loft, St James's Mill, Whitefriars, Norwich NR3 1TN
Tel: (01603) 886688   Call centre Tel: (0870) 164 9593   Fax: (01603) 619277
Email: help@virginwines.com   Website: www.virginwines.com

Closed 25 & 26 Dec, 1 Jan, Easter Sun **Cards** Yes **Discount** No **Order online** Yes **Delivery** Nationwide service (min. 12 bottles) **Glass hire** No **Tastings and talks** Various, based on new listings, phone for details **Newsletter** No **Special promotions** Regular promotional discounts, phone for details

❧ *Plenty of pre-chosen mixed cases, plus a helpful by-style guide to selecting your own* ❧ *Good-value range, focusing mostly on sub-£10 options* ❧ *Free £20 voucher for all newcomers* ❧ *Personal wine advisers (new) will help you with your choices*

Virgin aims to offer its customers greater wine diversity: though the wines are not exactly an exciting bunch, they fit the bill for everyday drinking – and there are no bulk-made brands. The easy-to-use website guides browsers through a series of options: the Wine Wizard – 'if you like that, then you'll love this' – links together favourite wines and new ones; wines are grouped by style, such as 'Fragrant Dry Whites', 'Rioja-style Reds', 'Huge Reds' and 'Kiwi Sauvignon'; and you can browse through and hit the 'Mix me a case' button. Or

follow your tastebuds by price, buy by the pre-selected mixed case, or try the quarterly Globetrotters First Class mixed case, following the team's latest buying excursion.

A multitude of helpful codes (covering dryness, elegance, oakiness, body, price) guide you, but if you make a mistake, Virgin offers a risk-free process: 'if you don't like a wine, you don't pay'. The *Guide's* main criticism previously still stands, however: regional information is not always listed, which is a major shortfall. Customers need the option to search by country and region to get a real feel for a wine. Still, it's light-hearted, breezy, non-intimidating formula has made Virgin Wines Europe's largest online wine retailer.

Best Buys

- Calatrasi d'Istinto, Catarratto, Chardonnay 2004 (Italy) £5.99
- Villa Maria, Private Bin Lightly Oaked Chardonnay 2001 (New Zealand) £6.99
- Michel Torino, Don David Torrontés, Salta 2003 (Argentina) £7.99

- Domaine Henri Pelle, Menetou-Salon 2002 (Loire) £8.99
- Cline Cellars, Ancient Vines Mourvèdre 2002 (California) £13.49
- Domaine du Vieux Lazaret, Châteauneuf-du-Pape Blanc 2003 (Southern Rhône) £13.99

The Wine Company

See The Nobody Inn (South-west England), page 171

The Wine Society

Gunnels Wood Road, Stevenage, Hertfordshire SG1 2BG
Tel: (01438) 741177   Fax: (01438) 761167
Email: memberservices@thewinesociety.com   Website: www.thewinesociety.com

Closed Sun   **Cards** Yes   **Discount** Available, phone for details   **Order online** Yes   **Delivery** Nationwide service, free for 12+ bottles & for orders of £175+   **Glass hire** Free   **Tastings and talks** Large nationwide programme of wine events with growers, phone for details   **Newsletter** 8 times a year **Special promotions** Offers on specific regions & wine styles

🍇 *Extensive wine listings spanning all price ranges, styles and regions* 🍇 *Superb range of Bordeaux from affordable petits châteaux to treasured crus classés* 🍇 *Exemplary customer service, from next-day delivery to an efficient export service*

With 80,000 members, The Wine Society still ranks as one of the UK's highest-achieving merchants. Offering an upbeat, adventurous set of wines to so many patrons is quite a task. It says something for the efficiency of buyer Sebastian Payne MW and his team, and the track record of the company (established in 1874), that it is providing more than ever this year. The Wine Society is all about making things easier for the consumer. One of its nicest touches is a handy and very clear-cut quarterly list.

The Wine Society is run as a co-operative. For a £40 fee you become a member for life, and benefit from the pleasures of over 1,500 available wines (up to 400 of them new each year), over 80 wine events and 15 regional offers a year (including Bordeaux, Burgundy, Rhône, port and *en-primeur*), themed pre-chosen mixed cases – ideal for gifts – and detailed cellar

planning services. In short, you get a lot for your money. And if you want to buy wines to keep (while they appreciate in value and/or drinking quality) The Wine Society charges only a nominal fee, to keep your wines in perfect condition over the years, at its air-conditioned warehouse space in Stevenage.

The most adventurous of the wines chosen are undoubtedly from Bordeaux and Australia on a big scale, but other surprises come in from France's Jura, Greece, Uruguay and Austria, showing that the Wine Society team aren't afraid to buy at boutique level too – even though there'd be no hope of all 80,000 members trying out a bottle. But whereas elsewhere the range is broad, there seems to be a dearth of real Burgundy (if anything, the Beaujolais collection outshines this). However, the Spain and Italy selections, of questionable breadth previously, appear to be fleshing out this year.

In all, the Wine Society keeps its loyal patrons in both easy-going (easy-priced) wines and aspirational wines, with real aplomb, and we doubt that for devotees there's ever really a need to look beyond this list. Unless you're a Burgundy fan that is.

Best Buys

- The Society's Claret (Bordeaux) £4.75
- Cave de Turckheim, Pinot Blanc 2002 (Alsace) £4.95
- Pisano Viña Barrancal, Tannat 2002 (Uruguay) £5.75
- Tselepos, Nemea 2001 (Greece) £8.50

- Ducorneau, Chapelle l'Enclos, Madiran 1999 (South-west France) £9.95
- Château Caronne-Ste-Gemme, Haut-Médoc 1996 (Bordeaux) £12.50
- Jules Camuset, Non-Vintage Brut (Champagne) £12.95
- Perrin, Gigondas 1998 (southern Rhône) £13.50

Wrightson & Co Wine Merchants

Manfield Grange, Manfield, Darlington, North Yorkshire DL2 2RE
Tel: (01325) 374134   Fax: (01325) 374135
Email: simon@wrightsonwines.co.uk   Website: www.wrightsonwines.co.uk

Closed Sat, Sun, Christmas, Easter, public holidays **Cards** Yes **Discount** Negotiable, minimum 5%
Order online Yes **Delivery** Nationwide service (min. 3 cases), free within 40-mile radius (min. 2 cases)
Glass hire Free with order **Tastings and talks** Customer tastings Mar, Jun, Dec; quarterly tutored tastings for certain clients **Newsletter** Available **Special promotions** via the website

❦ *Bordeaux is the speciality, with bottles from all price ranges* ❦ *Old and rare Bordeaux vintages available* ❦ *Extensive sub-£10 listings, offering great value for bargain hunters* ❦ *Interesting sherry, port and dessert wine choices*

Order from Wrightson for Bordeaux, above all else. Simon Wrightson is nothing if not passionate about his wines, and invites equal enthusiasm from his customers, tempting them with enticing investment figures for 1982 Bordeaux: Château Gruaud-Larose, he says, has appreciated by 1,600 per cent, increasing from £84 to £1,450 per case.

Other châteaux and vintages are available on which to take a risk, but there are wines for drinking too. Mature wines such as 1982 Château Pétrus and 1986 Talbot come at a price (£19,000 and £780 a case respectively), but Simon is only too happy to help out with a cheaper selection: he prides himself on an extensive sub-£10 listing, and even brings in sub-£6 cheapies to please the budget buyers – and all are interesting individual choices.

It's easy enough to imagine filling a mixed case of wine from this selection, especially with some supremely good-value wines to balance out the more expensive bottlings. But given that this list is entirely mail-order, more descriptive notes covering Spain, Portugal and Australia might be useful, for a start. South Africa, a speciality here in the past, appears to have dwindled, which is a shame.

Best Buys

- Stonecross Rosé, Worcester 2002 (South Africa) £5.22
- Château Hauterive, Cahors 1998 (Languedoc) £5.60
- Château de Lariveau, Canon-Fronsac 2000 (Bordeaux) £10.80

- Domaine Mittnacht Klack, Gewurztraminer Grand Cru Rosacker 2000 (Alsace) £11.42
- Château Cameron, Sauternes 1998 (Bordeaux) £11.78
- Pierre Courtois Brut NV (Champagne) £14.25

London

Berry Bros & Rudd

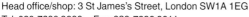

Head office/shop: 3 St James's Street, London SW1A 1EG
Tel: 020-7396 9600   Fax: 020-7396 9611

Duty Free Shops, Terminal 3, Departures Lounge, Heathrow Airport TW6 1JH
Tel: 020-8564 8361   Fax: 020-8564 8379

Terminal 4, Departures Lounge, Heathrow Airport TW6 3XA
Tel: 020-8754 1961   Fax: 020-8754 1984

Berry's Wine & Fine Food Shop
Hamilton Close, Houndmills, Basingstoke, Hampshire RG21 6YB
Tel: (01256) 323566   Fax: (01256) 340144
Email: londonshop@bbr.com   Website: www.bbr.com

Closed Sun, public holidays (exc. Heathrow) **Cards** Yes **Discount** 5% on 1 mixed case **Order online** Yes **Delivery** Nationwide service, free for orders of £150+ **Glass hire** £9.90 for 30 glasses, subject to sale or return conditions **Tastings and talks** Full programme of tastings & dinners **Newsletter** Via email **Special promotions** Regular offers through mailouts & online **(£5)**

❦ *Still one of the finest merchants in the UK* ❦ *Tempting wines at all price points* ❦ *Shows the best of what New World wines (particularly from Australia) can achieve* ❦ *Extensive range of Burgundy* ❦ *Characterful wines from outside 'classic' territories: Canadian Icewine, Oregon Pinot Gris, and more* ❦ *Madeiras, sherries and ports aplenty* ❦ *A stunning range of Rhône wines*

In the 300 years since it was established Berry Bros has built up such a wide range of wines that you might find it easier to use the search engine of its website, rather than the wine list, to peruse them. The pages and pages of elegant literature make great reading for those with plenty of browsing time, but don't expect to get to grips with this lot in a hurry.

It'll surprise no one that traditional Bordeaux, Burgundy and Northern Rhône wines feature so highly here. French classics for cellaring have always been the speciality, but today there's a modern slant. You can buy them by the bottle, by the mixed case, *en primeur*, or you can read about them on the website and then buy them over the counter in the St James's Street shop. (Those search engines are available in the shop for those who find rows and rows of bottles too daunting to take in.)

Burgundy listings are solid, lengthy, and go back through the 1990s vintages with renowned and reliable growers – Chandon de Briailles, Faiveley, Gérard Chavy, Etienne Sauzet and Domaine Leflaive, for example.

The full spectrum of communes, from ground level to glorious, gets a showing. Bordeaux receives similar thorough treatment. Underperforming countries and regions get representatively fewer entries, so there's more space for the Australian, Alsace or upbeat Southern Rhône wines (for example) that the team feel are genuinely worth it. The 'Wines with Personality' range is a recent invention for showing just the characters a wine *should* have, and it's very handy. But there are more wines on the full BBR list with the necessary credentials than are spotlighted in this little collection, particularly from the Languedoc-Roussillon and Italy.

All the added extras that mark out the best merchants are here – wine courses, cellar dinners, and wine tastings with interesting themes (such as 'Aristocratic Italians', '2000 Bordeaux, the best vintage ever?' and 'Perfect Pessac'). And any mixed case Alun Griffiths MW et al put together for the Customer Club will certainly match, or beat, expectations – such is the ability and integrity of his team.

Best Buys

- Château de Pennautier, Cabardès 2001 (Languedoc) £5.75
- Montes, Malbec Reserve, Colchagua Valley 2001 (Chile) £6.95
- Domaine du Petit Métris, Coteaux du Layon-Chaume 2001 (Loire) £10.25
- King Estate, Pinot Gris 2001 (Oregon) £11.25

- Château du Trignon, Gigondas 2001 (Southern Rhône) £11.95
- Trimbach, Riesling Réserve 2000 (Alsace) £14.95
- Fattoria Le Terraze, Sassi Neri, Rosso Conero, Marche 2000 (Italy) £19.95
- Pierro, Chardonnay, Margaret River 2000 (Western Australia) £22.95

Bordeaux Index

6th Floor, 159–173 St John Street, London EC1V 4QJ
Tel: 020-7253 2110   Fax: 020-7490 1955
Email: sales@bordeauxindex.com   Website: www.bordeauxindex.com

Closed Sat, Sun, public holidays **Cards** Yes **Discount** No **Order online** No **Delivery** Nationwide Service, free for orders of £2,000+ **Glass hire** No **Tastings and talks** Occasional, phone for details **Newsletter** No **Special promotions** Email offers available daily

---

🍇 *Bordeaux en primeurs* 🍇 *Vintages dating back to 1928* 🍇 *Investment Bordeaux from the very top properties* 🍇 *White Bordeaux (Sauternes) in halves, bottles and magnums* 🍇 *Fine Burgundies and Rhônes from the 1980s, 1990s and 2000s* 🍇 *Samples of precious wines from around the world*

This is a very smart merchant indeed. As its name implies, it focuses mainly on Bordeaux: old vintages and new, Right Bank and Left, and both red and white guises. The wine here (whether Bordeaux or not) is primarily on sale for investment purposes, so expect wine from the most fashionable properties *only*, and top vintages. And expect it to be expensive.

The minimum spend here is £500, be it for one bottle (say, a unit of Château d'Yquem from 1967 or Pétrus from 1975) or for an unmixed case (say, from Gruaud-Larose 2000 or Clos de Vougeot 2002 from J Prieur). Customers spend an average £50 a bottle.

Investment services include tailor-made portfolio management (with monthly price reports) 'to suit your risk appetite', plus plenty of guidance notes (and recommendations) from top journalists Robert Parker, Hugh Johnson and the like, as well as the experienced Bordeaux Index team – who have close links with the financial markets and the wine producers.

Although Bordeaux (and particularly St-Emilion) features very highly, look out also for top Burgundy, Rhônes, Super-Tuscans, champagnes and California collectibles. And don't forget, you *can* drink them: these wines are not just for storing and selling on.

Best Buys (exc. VAT)

- Château Haut-Batailley, Pauillac 1997 (Bordeaux) £10
- Château La Fleur de Jaugue 2000 (Bordeaux) £10
- Mont de Milieu, Chablis 2002 (Burgundy) £11.66

- Banfi, Brunello di Montalcino, Tuscany 1999 (Italy) £18.75
- Domaine de Perdrix, Vosne-Romanée 2002 (Burgundy) £20
- Château Troplong-Mondot, St-Emilion 2001 (Bordeaux) £20.83

Corney & Barrow

Head office: 1 Thomas More Street, London E1W 1YZ
Tel: 020-7265 2400   Fax: 020-7265 2539

8 Academy Street, South Ayrshire KA7 1HT
Tel: (01292) 267000   Fax: (01292) 265903

Oxenfoord Castle, by Pathhead, Midlothian EH37 5UB
Tel: (01875) 321921   Fax: (01875) 321922

Belvoir House, High Street, Newmarket, Suffolk CB8 8DH
Tel: (01638) 600000   Fax: (01638) 600860

194 Kensington Park Road, London W11 2ES
Tel: 020-7221 5122   Fax: 020-7221 9371
Email: wine@corbar.co.uk   Website: www.corneyandbarrow.com

Closed Sun, public holidays **Cards** Yes **Discount** Available, phone for details **Order online** Yes **Delivery** Nationwide service, free for 3+ cases, 2+ cases within M25, or for orders of £200+ **Glass hire** Varies, phone for details **Tastings and talks** Winemaker dinners, annual & regional tastings **Newsletter** No **Special promotions** Available, phone for details

---

❦ *Burgundy and Bordeaux choices of stratospheric quality* ❦ *Blue-chip service offering both investment wines and venerable vintages dating back to the early 1900s* ❦ *Good selection of sub-£7 wines – and no dull brands* ❦ *One-to-one service tailored to your individual tastes* ❦ *Plenty of informative reading matter to browse*

The days of selling just port, sherry and Bordeaux, so popular when this merchant set up in business in 1780, are long gone – these wines (of course) still provide the hub of what's here, but they're now supported by a far wider cast … although not, perhaps, as wide as would be expected from a merchant of this stature.

The blue-chip, royal-warrant image is of great importance to this company, and much store is set by offering the greatest of the great, in wine terms. Among the most fantastic wines here are Salon 1990 champagne (£112 a bottle), Château Pétrus, Pomerol 2000 (£186) and Château l'Angélus St-Emilion 2000 (£151); Château d'Yquem 1993 and Echézeaux from Domaine de la Romanée-Conti 1996 are price-on-application; and for much more Bordeaux you can turn to the broking list on www.corneyandbarrow.com.

It's no surprise that the Burgundies and Bordeaux are an illustrious lot, but the true quality of this merchant shines through in the top-class Loire wines (such as Savennières from Nicolas Joly), Spanish wines from Dominio de Pingus and Alvaro Palacios, Schloss Schönborn from Germany, and fabulous Cakebread and Dominus wines from California's Napa Valley.

The surprise is that, despite the enormous tome of an elegant and book-bound wine list, the range of wines available is startlingly limited. Where are the fashionable southern Italian wines, the cool-climate Australian stars, the new-wave Chilean icon wines, for example? Perhaps it's because C&B concentrates on the growers for which it is the main agent in the UK. Perhaps, and more likely, it's because C&B supplies its range across four shops and 11 wine bars – and to maintain the full range in each it can't be as broad-ranging as many other fine wine merchants.

Notwithstanding the range, the quality of both service and wines is unquestionably good. Being sole agent may mean some wine names won't be that familiar but, be assured, nothing less than the best would ever enter this merchant's illustrious cellars. And, what's more, the same member of staff will talk you through each of your purchases, with the kind of old-fashioned service at which the company really excels.

(Best Buys overleaf)

Best Buys

- Bodegas Lurton, Bonarda, Mendoza 2002 (Argentina) £6.29
- Die Kranz, Touriga Nacional, Calitzdorp 2001 (South Africa) £8.58
- Alvaro Palacios, Les Terrasses, Priorato 2001 (Spain) £12.93
- Quinta do Vale, Dona Maria, Douro 2000 (Portugal) £13.28

- Olivier Leflaive, Chablis Premier Cru Fourchaume 2001 (Burgundy) £17.92
- Tardieu Laurent, Vacqueyras Vieilles Vignes 2001 (Southern Rhône) £19.09
- Domaine Taupenot Merme, Chambolle-Musigny 2000 (Burgundy) £21.97
- Château Prieuré Lichine, Margaux 2000 (Bordeaux) £24.97

Fortnum & Mason

181 Piccadilly, London W1A 1ER
Tel: 020-7734 8040   Fax: 020-7437 3278   Website: www.fortnumandmason.co.uk

Closed 25 Dec, 1 Jan **Cards** Yes **Discount** Available on case sales only **Order online** Yes
Delivery Nationwide service **Glass hire** No **Tastings and talks** Regular in-store tastings, private events also available **Newsletter** No **Special promotions** No

🍇 *One of London's top merchants, whose sheer range and class are as impressive as ever* 🍇 *Stocks of every wine style imaginable, from Austrian Grüner Veltliner to Italian Super-Tuscan* 🍇 *Delicious range of sweet wines from around the world* 🍇 *Stellar own-label range from top-quality growers*

As would be expected from this grand establishment, Fortnums stocks some of the most esteemed and sought-after names in the world of wine. All the famous champagnes are here (at not over-inflated prices), as are *cru classé* Médocs (Margaux, Pichon-Longueville, Palmer and the like, from Bordeaux vintages going back to the vibrant 1982s); top-class wines from Burgundy's smaller, finer estates, such as Méo-Camuzet, Comtes Lafon and de Vogüé; suitably stunning Rhône from Chave, Clape and Graillot; top Italian estates from the Veneto (Guerrieri-Rizzardi, Allegrini, Inama are all represented); and the illustrious Screaming Eagle Cabernet Sauvignon from Napa, California – on sale at an unfeasibly high price.

But this is not just a shop for traditional wine buffs: it's a source for those keen to investigate any wine that's different, imaginatively made or made only in small parcels. Buyer Tim French and his team are looking for *terroir*-driven, interesting wines: they're proud of their smaller, less-known ranges, such as Austria's nutty Grüner Veltliners, English wines from spicy, quirky grape varieties, and Greek wines from leading estates Biblia Chora and Kir Yianni. Rare New Zealand reds also make an appearance, and there's a particularly broad selection of German wines.

And Fortnums is especially proud of its range of sweet wines, which includes Sauternes, Tokaji, Austrian stickies, Canadian Icewine, Greek and Californian dessert wine, 10- to 20-year-old malmsey madeira, oloroso sherries and a selection of vintage port dating back to Taylor's 1963.

Best Buys

- Château Haut Rian, White Bordeaux 2002 (Bordeaux) £6.75
- Domaine Santa Duc, Les Blovac, Rasteau-Villages 2000 (southern Rhône) £8.50
- Sartarelli, Verdicchio dei Castelli di Jesi

Tralivio, Marches 2002 (Italy) £11.50
- Quinta de la Rosa, Douro Tinto, Douro Valley 2001 (Portugal) £15
- Yalumba, Tricentenary Vines Grenache, Barossa Valley 1999 (Australia) £17.75
- Aldo Conterno, Printanie, Chardonnay, Piedmont 2001 (Italy) £17.90

Handford Wines

12 Portland Road, Holland Park, London W11 4LE   Tel: 020-7221 9614
105 Old Brompton Road, South Kensington, London SW7 3LE
Tel: 020-7589 6113   Fax: 020-7581 2983
Email: wine@handford.net   Website: www.handford.net

Closed Public holidays **Cards** Yes **Discount** 5% on 1 case **Order online** Yes **Delivery** Nationwide service, free locally (SW1, SW3) and for orders of £120+ **Glass hire** Free for local customers **Tastings and talks** Weekly tastings, see 'events' link on website **Newsletter** Quarterly **Special promotions** Pre-shipment, limited release, *en primeur* **£5**

❦ *Best source of South African and Spanish wines in London* ❦ *Top-notch French listings* ❦ *Plenty of exciting wine choices in the £10–£20 range* ❦ *New shop in South Kensington (stocking suitably glamorous wines to match)*

After 14 years of increasingly successful business, Handford has at last opened another shop, in another smart location, in South Kensington. This will be good news for Handford customers – who enjoy a distinctively upper-crust selection of wines from this merchant – but disappointing for fans of the much-loved Vigneronne, now closed, whose site Handford has taken over.

Handford is concerned that supermarket sales now stand at 72 per cent of all UK wine trade, and is determined to fill the gap and offer what the major outlets don't. With plentiful supplies of individually crafted wines, it certainly achieves its goal. It has a

good supply of sub-£10 options, with the list really hitting its stride in the £10–£20 group, so browsers can trade up gradually.

The Bordeaux and Burgundy shelves are richly stocked, as are the Loire and Alsace sections – the latter range being one of the broadest in the UK, with as many as six top producers (Trimbach, Kreydenweiss and Zind-Humbrecht among them). From outside France, the spectacular selection of South African wines is of particular interest (including top growers such as Thelema, Hamilton Russell, Veenwouden, Vergelegen and Boekenhoutskloof), as are those from Spain and Portugal.

Best Buys

- Guelbenzu, Azul, Navarra 2001 (Spain) £9.49
- Bouchard Finlayson, Sans Barrique, Chardonnay, Walker Bay 2001 (South Africa) £9.99
- Pazo de Señorans, Albariño, Rías Baixas 2002 (Spain) £14.99
- Pernand-Vergelesses, *premier cru* Blanc Ile des Hautes Vergelesses 1998 (Burgundy) £18.99
- Domaine de Courbis, Cornas Champelrose 2000 (N Rhône) £18.99
- Thelema, Cabernet Sauvignon, Stellenbosch 2000 (South Africa) £18.99

Harrods

Brompton Road, Knightsbridge, London SW1X 7XL
Tel: 020-7730 1234   Fax: 020-7225 5823   Email: alistair.viner@harrods.com

Closed Sun (exc. Nov–Jan), 25–27 Dec **Cards** Yes **Order online** Yes **Discount** Case discounts for wines under £30 per bottle **Delivery** Nationwide service, free for orders of £100+ **Glass hire** No **Tastings and talks** Available most Sat, special late-opening evenings & monthly promotional evenings **Newsletter** Monthly   **Special promotions** Monthly region- & country-specific offers

❦ *All-star selection of Burgundy from the smartest and smallest domaines* ❦ *Champagne of the Month, featuring discounted top brands* ❦ *The finest California wines, by region* ❦ *Wide choice of affordable sub-£10 bottles*

The Harrods wine department isn't nearly as intimidating as it might be: there's a relaxed atmosphere in the special enclave of the shop devoted to wine, and there are still plenty of bottles under £10 to choose from – although customers do pay a premium for upper-echelon stuff. For those not feeling quite so Knightsbridge, there's an excellent mail-order set-up and lots of literature to browse at home, but that would be missing out: Saturday morning promotional tastings, featuring such treasures as South American wines from Viña Leyda and Cousiño-Macul (Chile) and Catena-Zapata (Argentina), change their theme each month, and there are late-evening tastings in-store too.

Harrods, of course, has access to a great many *great* wines. Bordeaux *crus classés* are plentifully supplied, as would be expected (but vintages date back to 1949, which perhaps isn't so expected). And smart Burgundies, while beginning at a mere £13.50 for a bottle of red (£9.50 for white) climb to a swingeing £3,100 (yes, this is for *one* bottle: Domaine de la Romanée-Conti 1989). Most wines, though, hover around the £30 mark.

Harrods is proud of its obscurer wines, notably those of Israel, England and Austria. And it's also justifiably confident about its smart own-label range, including wines from leading producers Willi Opitz, Maison Sichel, Châteaux Léoville-Barton, Climens and Pichon-Lalande. Two other high points are the 11 Alsace growers to choose from (many merchants just stick with one to represent this region) and the incisive California collection, although more than a handful of these wines come in at (well) over £50 a bottle.

Where the range falls down, however, is in the surprisingly neat, short selections from the Loire and Rhône (perhaps understandable with the Loire, as it is less fashionable, but there should be more to say about the Rhône, surely?). Germany gets quite a curt nod too, and although Spain has plenty of Rioja and Ribera, and Italy includes Super-Tuscans and Amarone (no surprise there), the rest of these countries' wines are covered with little more than competence. Where's the passion in the second half of the list?

Best Buys

- Ostertag, Sylvaner Vieilles Vignes 2002 (Alsace) £8.95
- Mont Tauch, Les Quatres, Fitou 2000 (Languedoc) £9.95
- Thelema, Sauvignon, Stellenbosch 2001 (South Africa) £11.95
- Turkey Flat Vineyards, Grenache, Barossa Valley 1999 (Australia) £12.50
- Rippon Vineyard, Pinot Noir, Otago 1999 (New Zealand) £16.95
- Willi Opitz, Pinot Gris Trocken Spätlese 2000 (Austria) £17.95
- Domaine Leflaive, Bourgogne Blanc 1997 (Burgundy) £21.50
- Réserve du Général, second wine of Château Palmer, Margaux 1997 (Bordeaux) £24.50

Haynes Hanson and Clark

See listing in Midlands section, page 175

Jeroboams

Head office: 43 Portland Road, London W11 4LJ (7 branches in London)
Tel: 020-7985 1560   Fax: 020-7229 1085

3 The Market Place, Cirencester GL7 2PE
Tel: (01285) 655842   Email: sales@jeroboams.co.uk   Website: www.jeroboams.co.uk

Closed Sun (some branches), public holidays **Cards** Yes **Order online** Yes **Discount** Available, phone for details **Delivery** Nationwide service (min. 1 case), free for orders of £200+ **Glass hire** Free **Tastings and talks** Tastings and tutored tastings **Newsletter** No **Special promotions** Ongoing

❦ *Highly traditional merchant, renowned for its champagnes, Bordeaux and Burgundy* ❦ *Adventurous listings of southern French wines do justice to the favoured wine country here* ❦ *Well-chosen varietal wines from Western Australia*

Jeroboams' pleasing glossy-mag list makes a good sit-down read for an hour or so. How very suited to the 'gentlemanly' ambience of this merchant! Jeroboams has always been ultra-traditional – with plenty of claret and Burgundy, plus pre- and post-prandials to whet and wind down the palate (champagne aplenty, plus port, madeira, liqueurs and fine sherry) – and it still is.

Châteaux Fombrauge, Teyssier and Citran are readily available from Bordeaux (plus some of the excellent well-priced second labels from the top *crus classés*: La Dame de Montrose, Réserve de la Comtesse, Connetable Talbot). Burgundy listings hit all

the right communes and, although the producer names don't rank as highly as some of the prices would suggest, all that is made up for on reaching the eminently affordable Rhône and Loire choices. The aim for buyers Mike Hall and Neil Sommerfelt MW is to be the sole agency for a producer's wines, so they are exclusive to Jeroboams. This could be why some of the growers are less well known, and also why they are often allowed to be sole representatives of their region – although it might be nice to have a few more producer options for the thriving collection of Western Australian wines (which outshines anything else from that country).

Best Buys

- Conca de Barberà, Castillo de Montblanc, Viura/Chardonnay, 2002 (Spain) £4.65
- Rosé XL Les Grès, Coteaux du Languedoc 2002 (Languedoc-Roussillon) £4.95
- Jean Rijckaert, Chardonnay Vieilles

- Vignes, Arbois, 2000 (France) £9.65
- Domaine le Clos de Cazaux, Cuvée des Clefs d'Or, Vacqueyras Blanc, 2000 (Southern Rhône, France) £8.80
- Moss Wood Semillon, Margaret River, 2001 (Western Australia) £10.35
- Château Teyssier, *grand cru* St-Emilion (Bordeaux) £14.95

John Armit Wines

5 Royalty Studios, 105 Lancaster Road, London W11 1QF
Tel: 020-7908 0600   Fax: 020-7908 0601
Email: info@armit.co.uk   Website: www.armit.co.uk

Closed Sat, Sun, public holidays   **Cards** Yes   **Discount** Available, phone for details   **Order online** Yes
Delivery Nationwide service (min. 1 case), free for orders of £180+   **Glass hire** No   **Tastings and talks** Regular tastings and events, phone for details   **Newsletter** No   **Special promotions** Available, phone for details

❦ *High-class producers from New World countries* ❦ *Excellent French wines, especially from Burgundy and the Rhône* ❦ *Italy taken very seriously, with superb reds* ❦ *Fine German whites from top producers* ❦ *Excellent 'bespoke' service*

'Our wines can be enjoyed at the following hotels and restaurants …' it says at the end of the John Armit brochure, and there follows six pages of closely typed names, many of them famous establishments. John Armit is very big in the trade, and many of this *Guide*'s readers will have unknowingly already selected bottles from this company when out for dinner.

But its mail-order business is thriving too,

and marketing manager Sarah Maclean reckons 70 per cent of sales are now direct to the public. The brochure is certainly one of the best-looking ones around, laid out clearly and with plenty of tasting notes and other annotations to aid your choice. And the website - launched in Spring 2004 – is well worth checking out too.

One thing this company is strong on is the high number of bespoke services -

such as the personal advice offered for those buying presents, or the 'Collector's plan', working to a set budget, or, indeed, the Cellar Service, by which the Armit team put together an entire range for those equipping a new collection (you'll need a hefty outlay for this one). Then there's the wedding list, the investment advice and numerous fashionable dinners and tastings events. Other merchants offer some of these services; this one has the lot.

But that's typical of this operation, which is smart, upmarket and somehow rather urbane. And that goes for the wines too: generally a stylish and sophisticated range – the likes of California's Dominus, New Zealand's Seresin,

Italy's Angelo Gaja and Ornellaia – which is at its best in France, Spain, Italy (check out the Super-Tuscans) and California. This year the German section is looking particularly enticing too, featuring Carl Loewen, Dr Loosen, Müller Catoir and Selbach-Oster.

If such a glittering array of labels sounds expensive, remember that not everything here is top-drawer. Most John Armit wines are in the 'premium' category, but look out for some worthwhile special offers in the summer or winter sales, with plenty of easy-drinking wines at around £7 a bottle. One minor drawback to the list as a whole, though, is that there's a distinct lack of mature bottles.

Best Buys (12-bottle prices)

- Bodegas Capcanes, Mas Domis, Montsant 2001 (Priorat, Spain) £89
- Seresin, Pinot Gris, Marlborough 2003 (New Zealand) £93
- Steenberg, Sauvignon Blanc, Constantia 2003 (South Africa) £98
- Château Petit Védrines, Sauternes 2001 half bottles (Bordeaux) £135
- Paul Blanck, Tokay Pinot Gris Patergarten 2001 (Alsace) £162
- Yarra Yarra, Syrah, Victoria 2000 (Australia) £230
- Beaumont des Crayères, Nostalgie 1999 (Champagne) £265
- Dominus, Napanook, Napa 1999 (California) £290

Lea and Sandeman

Head office: 170 Fulham Road, London SW10 9PR
Tel: 020-7244 0522   Fax: 020-7244 0533

211 Kensington Church Street, London W8 7LX
Tel: 020-7221 1982   Fax: 020-7221 1985

51 High Street, Barnes, London SW13 9LN
Tel: 020-8878 8643   Fax: 020-8878 6522
Email: sales@leaandsandeman.co.uk   Website: www.londonfinewine.co.uk

Closed Sun, public holidays **Cards** Yes **Discount** Available on orders of 12+ bottles **Order online** Yes **Delivery** Nationwide service, free for orders of £250+ or 1+ cases within London **Glass hire** Free with case order, must return clean **Tastings and talks** In-store tastings every 3–4 months **Newsletter** No **Special promotions** Primeur and Christmas offers, including champagne **£5**

🌻 *Smart Burgundy, Italian and Rhône wines, with annual en primeur offers*
🌻 *Carefully chosen second-label wines from the top Bordeaux châteaux* 🌻 *Superb collection of southern French choices from Languedoc-Roussillon*

Lea and Sandeman is a small enough firm not to be under any obligations to its growers/suppliers: if it no longer likes a wine, or thinks it's too expensive, it can delist it. And it's always bringing in new and interesting bottlings to add to, or replace any duds in the range – these

include names that you might not find elsewhere.

For especially refreshing fare look to the good-value *petits châteaux* from Bordeaux, premium Italian producers, exciting Languedoc choices or well-priced champagnes from smaller producers. From

Bordeaux, a good selection of bigger players is in evidence, but Lea and Sandeman has cleverly chosen to feature its more affordable second-label wines (for example, Dame de Montrose from Château Montrose, Baron de Milon from Château Duhart-Milon). The New World adds in a few individual bottles, but the Old World is definitely the main event.

Customers here are obviously a discerning bunch, as apparently they're now buying into a new and exciting range of grape varieties (New Zealand Pinot Gris, Austrian Grüner Veltliner, and Italian Greco and Falanghina look like good choices), and moving away from glossy over-extracted wines. All credit to Lea and Sandeman for giving them enough options.

Best Buys

- Abbazia Santa Anastasia, Nero d'Avola di Sicilia 2001 (Italy) £6.94
- Bergerie de l'Hortus, Cuvée Classique, Pic St-Loup 2001 (Languedoc-Roussillon) £7.50
- Domaine de la Mordorée, Tavel Rosé La Dame Rousse 2002 (Loire) £9.95
- Domaine François Lumpp, Givry Premier Cru Clos Jus 2000 (Burgundy) £13.50
- Château Haut Lariveau, Fronsac 1998 (Bordeaux) £13.95
- Domaine Cordier Père et Fils, St-Véran en Faux 2001 (Burgundy) £13.95

Moreno Wine Merchants

11 Marylands Road, London W9 2DU
Tel: 020-7286 0678   Fax: 020-7286 0513
Email: merchant@moreno-wines.co.uk   Website: www.morenowinedirect.com

Closed Sun **Cards** Yes **Discount** Available on orders of 12+ bottles **Delivery** Nationwide service, free within Central London **Glass hire** No **Tastings and talks** Available, externally by customer request **Order online** No **Newsletter** No **Special promotions** Bimonthly offers through mailouts **£5**

🍇 *Mouth-watering fine and rare Spanish wines dating back to 1878* 🍇 *Wide range of different Riojas* 🍇 *Fascinating modern Spanish collection including all the small-and-intriguing wine regions* 🍇 *Argentina and Chile also covered*

Moreno has for many years been justifiably renowned for its superb collection of fine and rare Spanish wine: most twentieth-century vintages are represented, should you want a mature older Rioja – even white Rioja (1878 is the oldest bottle, from Marqués de Murrieta) – and stunning Vega Sicilia dates from 1959 (at £310 a bottle).

Modern-day Spain is well covered too. Along with wines from all the smaller regions – those just starting to show their winemaking class – there are bottlings from the fashionable enclaves Ribera del Duero and Priorat. Good descriptions of these in the wine list, should you not have met them before.

One criticism of Moreno is that surely it could better illustrate the less-known parts of Spain by stocking a broader selection of producers and wines. And the same goes for its second-specialities, Chile and Argentina. Few UK merchants really take South America seriously and, given the strong Spanish connection here, it would be a good area for this merchant to embrace.

Moreno is Spain's middleman: many Spanish wines on sale in the UK will have arrived on these shores via this merchant. And because it imports the wines direct, its list prices are very reasonable.

(Best Buys overleaf)

Best Buys

- Bodegas Navajas, Rosado Sin Crianza, Rioja 2002 (Spain) £4.99
- Viña Casablanca, White Label Sauvignon Blanc 2003 (Chile) £5.49
- Bodegas Biurko Gorri, Tempranillo, organic Rioja 2002 (Spain) £6.99
- Bodegas Palacio de Fefinanes, Albariño, Rías Baixas 2002 (Spain) £10.99
- Bodegas Masia Barril, Tinto Clasico, Priorat 1995 (Spain) £13.49
- Bodegas Pago de Carraovejas, Tinto Crianza, Ribera del Duero 2001 (Spain) £14.99

The Oxford Wine Company

See listing in South England section, page 156

Philglas & Swiggot

21 Northcote Road, Battersea, London SW11 1NG
Tel: 020-7924 4494   Fax: 020-7642 1576

64 Hill Rise, Richmond, Surrey TW10 6UB
Tel: 020-8332 6031   Email: karen@philglas-swiggot.co.uk   Website: www.philglas-swiggot.co.uk

Closed Mon (Richmond only) **Cards** Yes **Discount** Available on orders of 1+ mixed cases **Order online**
No **Delivery** Nationwide service (min. 1 case), free within 3-mile radius **Glass hire** Free with order
Tastings and talks Occasional in-store tastings, winemaker dinners planned **Newsletter** Occasional
regional offers on rare wines **Special promotions** Regular offers on still wines & champagnes **£5**

❦ *One of the best Australian ranges around* ❦ *A Burgundy list to suit most pockets*
❦ *Fine wines from Italy* ❦ *High-class New Zealand bottles* ❦ *Fashionable names*
from the USA ❦ *Subscribers' Club for pre-selected mixed cases*

Karen and Mike Rogers' first shop was opened 12 years ago and the last edition of the *Guide* predicted that there could be a second branch soon. Sure enough, in February 2003, another Philglas & Swiggot (geddit?) was launched in Richmond Hill – and, Mike reports, a third is under consideration, also in London.

This success seems to ride on two factors – helpful personal service (several readers have commented on this) and a characterful range of wines that focuses on the more interesting and high-quality end of each area. Don't bother coming here if you want to bulk buy cheap Liebfraumilch or if you're after bland cross-regional Australian bargains though – this merchant deals in more premium, exciting stuff and as such offers a nice contrast to many of London's wine retailers.

P&S originally focused on Australia (it has since broadened its range considerably), and Down Under wines remain something of a speciality – indeed, the list opens with

several pages of bottles, grouped by grape variety, offering such goodies as Suckfizzle Sauvignon/Semillon, Jim Barry Shiraz, Rockford Grenache and Grosset Gaia Cabernet Sauvignon. Prices look eminently fair. Business now includes much from France (check out the myriad fine Burgundies and Rhônes in particular) and Italy (a classy slate all round). It's good to see Germany and Austria grabbing decent chunks of the range, and the set from the United States is enticing too, including wines from Ridge, Andrew Will, Joseph Phelps and Newton. The Argentina and Chile sections could do with filling out (there are only half-a-dozen wines from each country), but South Africa has better representation from the likes of Thelema, Vergelegen and De Toren; New Zealand contains many highly reputed names such as Mudhouse, Isabel, Neudorf and Mount Difficulty; while the fizz positively sparkles. Indeed, the range of just 13 sparkling wines is one of the best short sets we've seen, with

Nyetimber (UK), Graham Beck (South Africa), Juvé y Camps (Spain) and Pelorus (New Zealand).

A young, dynamic and enthusiastic independent merchant that deserves its current success.

Best Buys

- Evans & Tate, Cabernet/Merlot, Margaret River 2001 (Australia) £8.99
- Pieropan, Soave Classico, Veneto 2003 (Italy) £9.99
- Leeuwin Estate, Riesling, Mount Barker 2001 (Australia) £12.99
- Grant Burge, The Holy Trinity, Grenache, Barossa Valley 1999 (Australia) £15.99

- Ridge, Geyserville, Santa Cruz 2000 (California) £22.85
- Schloss Gobelsburg, Grüner Veltliner Ried Lamm, Kremstal 2002 (Austria) £22.99
- Patrick Javillier, Clos du Cromin, Meursault 2000 (Burgundy) £27.99
- Augustus Clape, Cornas 2000 (Rhône) £37.50

La Réserve

Head office: 7 Grant Road, London SW11 2NU
Tel: 020-7978 5601   Fax: 020-7978 4934

56 Walton Street, Knightsbridge, London SW3 1RB
Tel: 020-7589 2020   Fax: 020-7581 0250

29 Heath Street, Hampstead, London NW3 6TR
Tel: 020-7435 6845   Fax: 020-7431 9301

Milroys of Soho, 3 Greek Street, London W1V 6NX
Tel: 020-7437 9311   Fax: 020-7437 1345

203 Munster Road, Fulham, London SW6 6BX
Tel: 020-7381 6930   Fax: 020-7385 5513
Email: realwine@la-reserve.co.uk   Website: www.la-reserve.co.uk

---

Closed Sun (Knightsbridge, Soho), public holidays (all stores) **Cards** Yes **Discount** No **Order online** Yes **Delivery** Nationwide service, free within M25 (min. 1 case) and for orders of £200+ **Glass hire** Free (min. 12) **Tastings and talks** Set wine courses throughout the year, bespoke tastings & courses, periodic customer tastings **Newsletter** No **Special promotions** Seasonal offers, phone for details

---

❧ *Classy merchant balancing affordability with a wide range of premium and collectable wines* ❧ *Characterful reds from southern France* ❧ *Top-notch Burgundy, Bordeaux and champagne* ❧ *Fascinating Italian wine range* ❧ *Stylish line-up of Australian Shiraz*

Author William Boyd has a few words to say at the start of La Réserve's very beautiful list: 'Trust your vintner' is the essence of it. This isn't a bad way to approach wine as you'll be nurtured through vinous experiences that reflect the buying trips, tastings and vintage launches your merchant has learned from. And La Réserve isn't a bad place to start either, given the spectrum and quality of the wines it brings in.

Back to the list – which is like an upmarket travel brochure, or a glossy magazine, with lots of colour photos. There are profiles and opinions to read, and easy-reference wine lists clearly showing regions, vintages and relevant prices.

It comes as quite a surprise then to see a host of sub-£5 wines in the French wine section, though other starter wines come in nearer £12, involving such luxuries as Etienne Sauzet's Burgundies, Pieropan's Soave Classico from Italy, Shaw & Smith's Australian Sauvignon and New Zealand Chardonnay from Isabel Estate. La Réserve's main stock costs between £30 and £50 a bottle, with superb offerings particularly from Italy, the Rhône, Burgundy, Bordeaux and Australia – and one or two nifty champagnes thrown in.

(Best Buys overleaf)

147

Best Buys

- Picpoul de Pinet St-Peyre 2002 (Languedoc) £4.95
- Languedoc Rouge Murviel les Montpellier (Languedoc) £4.95
- A Mano, Primitivo di Puglia 2002 (Italy) £6.95
- Muga, Muga Blanco 2002 (Spain) £7.95
- Ellen Bussell, Cullen Wines, Red 2002 (Western Australia) £10.95
- Lirac Blanc, Reine des Bois, Mordorée 2002 (Southern Rhône) £14.95

Roberson Wine Merchant

348 Kensington High Street, London W14 8NS
Tel: 020-7371 2121   Fax: 020-7371 4010
Email: retail@roberson.co.uk   Website: www.robersonwinemerchant.co.uk

Closed Sun **Cards** Yes **Discount** 10% on 1+ cases **Order online** Yes **Delivery** Nationwide service, free within Central London **Glass hire** Yes **Tastings and talks** Tastings every Saturday for customers & regular events throughout the year **Newsletter** Yes **Special promotions** Regular offers throughout the year

🍇 *Glittering array of champagnes, including older bottles from top houses*
🍇 *Top-notch selection from Bordeaux* 🍇 *Many of the Loire's most highly reputed producers* 🍇 *Serious Super-Tuscan collection* 🍇 *Wide range of fine spirits*

It's very Kensington, Roberson, from the dramatic and stylish 'Gaudíesque' design of the shop to the opening stages of the list, which focus firmly on an impressive selection of champagne. In fact, there were more than 60 champagnes on the latest list, including the odd magnum and jeroboam, naturally. Billecart-Salmon is well represented, but there's Bollinger, Pol Roger, Veuve Clicquot, Moët and Krug among the illustrious names here too.

Bordeaux is another range to linger over, and Roberson's is one of the largest collections in London. Ditto Burgundy, with plenty of top names sprinkled throughout. The Rhône features several vintages of

Châteauneuf-du-Pape from Château de Beaucastel, while the Loire looks to Henri Bourgeois, Saget, Dagueneau and Vacheron. Star names – so little is under £10. Some cheaper fare appears under the French country wines and Italian headings (although Italy soon soars off into the stratosphere with the Super-Tuscan reds). There are ten vintages of Château Musar from the Lebanon.

Many regions and countries are similarly treated – with a particular focus on one individual producer, and shorter ranges from other luminaries of the area. Spirits are dealt with well, and there are ranges of grappas, eaux de vie, malts and calvados.

Best Buys

- Coudoulet de Beaucastel 1999 (Rhône) £11.95
- Vasse Felix, Cabernet Sauvignon, Margaret River 1999 (Australia) £15.25
- Vacheron, Sancerre Rouge 2000
- (Loire) £17.50
- Château Filhot, Sauternes 1996 (Bordeaux) £26.95
- Joseph Perrier, Brut magnums (Champagne) £35.95
- Bollinger RD 1979 (Champagne) £105

Selfridges & Co

400 Oxford Street, London W1A 1AB   Tel: 020-7318 2375
1 Exchange Square, Manchester M13 1BD
Tel: 0161-838 0608

1 The Dome, Trafford Centre, Manchester M17 8DA
Tel: 0161-629 1220

Upper Mall East, Bullring, Birmingham B5 4BP
Tel: 0121-600 6842/6703
Email: andrew.willy@selfridges.co.uk   Website: www.selfridges.co.uk

Closed 25 Dec, Easter Sun   **Cards** Yes   **Discount** 8.5% on 1 case, 10% for Selfridges Card holders   **Order online** No   **Delivery** Nationwide service   **Glass hire** No   **Tastings and talks** Regular in-store tastings & bespoke tastings for customers   **Newsletter** No   **Special promotions** Regular in-store offers (£5)

🍇 *A firm emphasis on top-quality wines* 🍇 *Delightful champagnes, some from smaller growers* 🍇 *Admirable Italian wines* 🍇 *Australia dealt with in some depth* 🍇 *Older wines and large-format bottles*

Selfridges offers exactly what you would expect: a stylish and upmarket wine list, put together by the highly knowledgeable buyer Andrew Willy. Its main fortes are Bordeaux, Burgundy, Italy, Spain, Australia and the USA.

As the *Guide* has pointed out before, this is not the place to come for cheap and cheerful wine – there's very little here under £7 a bottle, nor under £10 for that matter. If, however, you are looking for a special bottle, this may be just the retailer you want. Andrew has some truly exciting, world-class wines – be it Jean-Louis Chave's Hermitage 1999 (£250 in magnums), Vega Sicilia Unico 1989 (£145), Château d'Yquem Sauternes 1976 (£525) or Napa Valley's Screaming Eagle 1997 (£2,300 for just one bottle). The champagnes are especially tempting and include an admirable range from smaller producers.

These examples are taken from the 'ordinary' list. A supplementary fine-and-rare wine list highlights older Bordeaux vintages, Sauternes and some venerable vintage port and madeira, among others. A very classy collection all round, which carries no extra padding in the form of sub-standard bottles filling out the range.

Best Buys

- I Frati Lugana, Ca dei Frati 2000 Trentino (Italy) £9.99
- John Armit, St-Emilion 1998 (Bordeaux) £10.99
- Trimbach, Reserve Riesling 1999 (Alsace) £13.25
- Alain Graillot, Crozes-Hermitage 2001 (Rhône) £14.50
- Patrick Javillier, Meursault Clos du Cromin 2000 (Burgundy) £31.50
- Stag's Leap Fay Vineyard, Cabernet Sauvignon, Napa Valley 1998 (California) £55

Uncorked

Exchange Arcade, Broadgate, London EC2M 3WA
Tel: 020-7638 5998   Fax: 020-7638 6028
Email: drink@uncorked.co.uk   Website: www.uncorked.co.uk

Closed Sat, Sun, public holidays   **Cards** Yes   **Discount** 10% on 1 case   **Order online** No   **Delivery** Nationwide service, free for orders of £200+   **Glass hire** Free with order   **Tastings and talks** Dedicated tastings & occasional shop tastings   **Newsletter** 3 general lists per year   **Special promotions** Printed new release/*en primeur* & email offers

🍇 *Convenient City location and wines to suit a City budget* 🍇 *Illustrious, 'cherry-picked' wines from around the world* 🍇 *Wide range of en primeur Bordeaux, from the affordable upwards* 🍇 *Niche Cabernet Sauvignon producers from the Napa Valley* 🍇 *Older vintages available*

Andrew Rae and Jim Griffen have been trading their impressive set of wines to City folk for ten years now, whether ex-VAT for investment (that is, for laying down), or for drinking. There's no shortage of illustrious, prize-winning wine here, at extremely competitive prices: classics from France, Italy and Port(ugal); seriously complex wines from independent Australian producers; and fabulously impressive, though not cheap, California listings from small but near-perfect Napa producers Abreu, Araujo, Dalla Valle and Harlan – all difficult to find elsewhere in the UK. Shafer and Ridge (also from California) are less uncommon, but just as welcome here. Alongside a wide range of champagnes and Rhône wines are some interesting one-offs such as Huët's 1962 Vouvray Clos du Bourg Moelleux and Niepoort's Redoma Tinto from the Douro Valley, Portugal.

A solid range of Burgundy *en primeurs* comes from good mid-ranking producers, and a wider-ranging Bordeaux selection takes in top-notch Le Pin and châteaux Angélus, Valandraud and l'Evangile from the Right Bank; Palmer, Gruaud-Larose and Ducru-Beaucaillou from the Left. The ex-VAT list also includes an impressive smattering of other by-the-case goodies.

Uncorked, supplying unquestionably superior vinous wares, is renowned for its unstuffy attitude, and the team is still as unintimidating as ever.

Best Buys

- Muga, Rioja Blanco 2002 (Spain) £7.49
- Giuseppe Inama, Soave Classico Superiore 2001 (Italy) £8.49
- Daniel Brusset, Grand Montmirail, Gigondas 2001 (southern Rhône) £13.95
- Stefano Lubiana, Pinot Noir, Tasmania 2000 (Australia) £16.95
- Château Lagrange, St-Julien 1997 (Bordeaux) £19.95
- Pavillon Blanc de Château Margaux (Bordeaux) £21

The Winery

4 Clifton Road, London W9 1SS
Tel: 020-7286 6475   Fax: 020-7286 2733
Email: info@thewinery.com   Website: www.thewinery.com

Closed 25 & 26 Dec, 1 Jan **Cards** Yes **Discount** 5% on 1 mixed case **Order online** No **Delivery** Nationwide service, free locally **Glass hire** Free with order **Tastings and talks** In-store tastings Sat pm, larger ones every 6 weeks **Newsletter** No **Special promotions** No (£5)

🍇 *Merchant with a new spin on Burgundy, the Rhône and South-west France*
🍇 *New-wave German growers, some never seen in the UK before*

A flick through this wine list won't bring much comfort to those looking for familiar producers and familiar wine names: Pangua Sodupe, Uccelliera and Zum Krug might at first seem utterly confusing. This isn't at all a place for name-droppers to shop; instead, it's a haven for wine lovers with more exploratory tendencies.

The Winery is the brainchild of David Motion, whose creative zeal, in vinous terms, is mostly tuned towards the lesser-known wines of French regions, particularly the Southern Rhône, South-west France, Languedoc and Burgundy. And the Winery team actually go to these places and choose the wines themselves;

everything is imported direct, which bodes well for good-value prices.

Almost all The Winery's wines are exclusivities, not found elsewhere in the UK; the extensive producer profiles in the wine list highlight why the wines are so special. Apart from France, strong features at the moment are Spain, California and Germany. Plus, there's a quirky Piedmont selection from Italy.

For those uneasy about buying unknowns, there are free tastings every six weeks at the shop (sometimes with a regional theme, sometimes not). And one or two tried-and-trusted Burgundy names can be enjoyed, too, from reassuringly illustrious sites such as Bonnes Mares, Echézeaux and Corton Bressandes.

Best Buys

- Navarrsotillo, Noemus Blanco, Rioja Baja 2003 (Spain) £6.50
- Noëllat, Bourgogne Aligoté 2000 (Burgundy) £9.50
- Eldredge, Mourvèdre/Shiraz/Grenache, Clare Valley 2000 (Australia) £11.99

- Rebenhof Joannes Schmitz, Urziger Würzgarten Spätlese Trocken 1999 (Germany) £12.50
- Domaine de la Tour du Bon, Bandol Rouge 2001 (Provence) £15.99
- Robert Sinskey, Merlot Los Carneros, Napa Valley 1997 (California) £19.99

For an explanation of the symbols used at the top of some of the merchant entries, see page 118.

South England

Alexander Hadleigh Wine Merchants

19 Centre Way, Locksheath, Southampton SO31 6DX
Tel: (01489) 564563   Fax: (01489) 885960
Email: info@ahadleigh-wine.com   Website: www.ahadleigh-wine.com

Closed Sun, public holidays **Cards** Yes **Discount** 7.5% on 1 mixed case **Order online** Yes **Delivery** Nationwide service, free within 20-mile radius & for orders of £110+ **Glass hire** Yes **Tastings and talks** Available every Sat in-store; wine club tasting evenings, evening events for local groups **Newsletter** In-store 3 times per year **Special promotions** Introductory offers, good bin-end selections **£5**

🍇 *Excellent choice of big-format bottles* 🍇 *Bordeaux in admirable depth, including fine and mature wines* 🍇 *Super estate Rieslings from Germany* 🍇 *New Zealand taken seriously* 🍇 *High-standard Australia range* 🍇 *Champagnes of great finesse, including older bottles*

A top-notch list, this, and one that shows a happy bent towards larger bottles. The company's managing director, New Zealander Del Taylor, claims its portfolio provides that all-elusive 'wow' factor – and when you come across two densely typed pages of 'large format' bottles, you have to agree. There's everything here from magnums of Sauternes to jeroboams of California Cabernet and a balthazar of champagne; many from top names and at decent prices. Larger bottles are sadly under-used outside corporate hospitality, and they certainly make impressive presents, especially for weddings. (There's an equally impressive list of half bottles here for the more cautious.)

Size isn't everything, of course, and plenty of ordinary-format bins here excite: from Bordeaux, Germany and New Zealand, as well as great dessert and sparkling wines. The 'Fine Wine Collection' includes more famous names, with Australia's Henschke and Penfold's Grange among the New World 'cult' favourites. Fine single malt whiskies stand out too. Some prices can be steep, unfortunately, if you compare the same wines with the supermarket lists, but how many supermarkets have a 'wow' factor (or, say, a sparkling Icewine from Canada)?

Best Buys

- Chiarlo, Nivole Moscato d'Asti DOCG (half bottle) Piedmont (Italy) £6.75
- Simon Hackett, Old Vine Grenache, McLaren Vale 1999 (Australia) £9.15
- Guy Saget, Pouilly-Fumé Les Logères 2002 (Loire) £10.98
- Willi Brundlmayer, Riesling Ried Steinmassel Trocken (Austria) £15.25
- Neudorf Estate, Nelson Chardonnay 2002 (New Zealand) £16.58
- Jacquart, Brut Mosaïque NV Magnum (Champagne) £52.98

Arthur Rackham emporia

216 London Road, Guildford, Surrey GU4 7JS
Tel: (0870) 870 1110   Fax: (0870) 870 1120
Email: cellars@ar-emporia.com   Website: www.ar-emporia.com

Closed 25 Dec, Good Fri **Cards** Yes **Discount** 10% on 12 bottles wine/champagne **Order online** Yes **Delivery** Nationwide service, free for orders of £100+ **Glass hire** Free with order **Tastings and talks** Weekend tastings in-store, tutored tastings & food-and-wine pairing **Newsletter** Online **Special promotions** Wine of the week, *en primeur* & exotic, fine wines **£5**

🍇 *Interesting, original website* 🍇 *Fine champagne selection* 🍇 *Strong on South African wines* 🍇 *Upmarket range from New Zealand*

James Rackham, proprietor of this 'emporia', sent us a huge tome of information, mostly print-outs of the rather good website. 'Our mission is to enhance food with a well-chosen wine', the site announces. If you're interested in food and wine matching, this website could well become a favourite, as there are loads of detailed, mouth-watering tips. Those who prefer to pop into the shop will usually find bottles open for tasting, especially at weekends. The range available reveals a high level of quality producers from many areas of the world. The emphasis is on class rather than cheap bargains. The Champagne and southern French sections of the list look impressive, as do those from South Africa and Australia. New Zealand features excellent, food-friendly whites from Isabel Estate, Lawson's Dry Hills and Milton Vineyard, among others, and the California set is a classy bunch. It would be nice to see a couple of areas (Portugal and Argentina) filled out a bit more, but perhaps this will happen as part of the 'ten-year plan' James says he is embarking upon as he aims to move from being a regional merchant to a national wine-agency business.

Best Buys

- Klein, Sauvignon Blanc, Constantia 2003 (South Africa) £8.99
- Juvé y Camps, Vintage Cava, Penedès 2001 (Spain) £9.95
- Bonny Doon, Ca' Del Solo Big House Red 2001 (California) £9.99
- Marc Bredif, Vouvray 2001 (Loire) £12.45
- Sileni, Chardonnay, Hawke's Bay 1999 (New Zealand) £12.50
- Heggies, Eden Valley Merlot 1999 (South Australia) £14.49

Bacchus Wine

Warrington House Farm Barn, Olney, Buckinghamshire MK46 4HN
Tel: (01234) 711140   Email: wine@bacchus.co.uk   Website: www.bacchus.co.uk

Closed Sun **Cards** Yes **Discount** Available on orders of £100+ **Order online** Yes **Delivery** Nationwide service (min. 12 bottles), free within 10-mile radius **Glass hire** Free with order **Tastings and talks** Occasional winemaker tastings, phone for details **Newsletter** No **Special promotions** Various, phone for details **£5**

🍇 *Great source of good-value wines, plenty for under £10* 🍇 *Wide selection from Austria and Italy* 🍇 *Modestly priced Bordeaux features highly* 🍇 *Unusual wines from quirky producers*

Bacchus owner Russell Heap doesn't pander to rave reviews about wine, and has no time for brands and cut-price bargains. But he does believe in diversity and individuality, often at more than fair prices. Russell and his fellow wine buyer, Margit Dabernig-Kent, work hard to seek out the best examples of a given style per region, focusing on wines between £5 and £10 a bottle, and a delve into the price list shows immediately how successful they are – the average bottle spend at Bacchus is £6.

As far as diversity goes, the speciality areas are typically varied: Bordeaux, Burgundy, Alsace, the Loire, Austria and Italy (the Italian selection is particularly strong). Oddities such as white Rioja, Australian Pinot Noir and Portuguese Dão also feature. Not to mention that most refreshing of summer wines, rosé - 'They love rosé now!' says Russell of his customers.

All credit for the determinedly good-value, unusual wines stocked here. Perhaps next year Bacchus will tell us all a bit more about them? A few extra tasting notes and producer details would help.

(Best Buys overleaf)

Berry Bros & Rudd

See listing in London section, page 137

Helen Verdcourt Wines

Spring Cottage, Kimbers Lane, Maidenhead, Berkshire SL6 2QP
Tel: (01628) 625577

Open Daily **Cards** No **Discount** Available on orders of 12+ cases **Delivery** Free within 20-mile radius **Glass hire** Free with order **Tastings and talks** Monthly through 3 local wine clubs **Newsletter** No **Special promotions** No (£5)

🍇 *'Small but perfectly formed' merchant, supplying a range of prestige wines from around the world* 🍇 *Top names from the Rhône* 🍇 *Extensive Chilean listings* 🍇 *The best bottles from South Africa*

Helen Verdcourt continues to create this near-perfect microcosm of the wine world, selling quality wines direct from Spring Cottage in Maidenhead. Sounds idyllic? Well, juggling with (and occasionally sipping) names such as Mas la Plana, Muga and Martínez Bujanda (Spain); Ridge (California); and Finca El Retiro and Weinert (Argentina) must make for fun times not only for Helen but for her customers too.

The Rhône and Chile are this year's favourites with Helen (think Guigal, Jaboulet, Graillot for the former; Montes, Casa Lapostolle and Carmen for the latter). And although it's unusual for a top merchant not to stock more Bordeaux and Burgundy than this (are they being phased out? too expensive?), Château Angélus makes a welcome, glamorous appearance from St-Emilion. From everywhere else there'll be something to make even the most demanding taste buds drool – although perhaps there are not as many of these luxurious wines as previously.

While there's not a lot below the £5-a-bottle mark, there's plenty between £5 and £10, with prices rising to the upper echelons. Joining one of the three tasting clubs that meet every month could be a good way of getting a sneak preview of the more expensive bottles.

Laithwaites

Head office/shop: New Aquitaine House, Exeter Way, Theale,
Reading, Berkshire RG7 4PL
Tel: (0870) 444 8383   Fax: (0870) 444 8182

3 Holtspur Parade, Holtspur, Beaconsfield, Buckinghamshire HP9 1DA
Tel: (01494) 677564

121 Arthur Road, Windsor, Berkshire SL4 1RU
Tel: (01753) 866192

417 Brighton Road, South Croydon, Surrey CR1 6EU
Tel: 020-8760 9191
Email: orders@laithwaites.co.uk   Website: www.laithwaites.co.uk

Closed 25 Dec **Cards** Yes **Discount** Available on orders of 6- & 12-bottle cases **Order online** Yes
Delivery Nationwide service **Glass hire** No **Tastings and talks** Over 50 events per year nationwide;
customers can meet winemakers & taste their wines with them **Newsletter** No **Special promotions**
Through mailings & online

❦ *UK's biggest source of mail-order wine (also through the Sunday Times Wine Club)* ❦ *Mid-priced wines (above £6) are where the real quality begins* ❦ *Full gamut of Australian choices* ❦ *Sweeping range of Bordeaux châteaux*

The vast number of its customers testifies to Laithwaites' great service, enthusiastic and informative marketing campaigns and impressive range of wines. With the ebullient Tony Laithwaite (who founded the company in 1969) still at the helm, and leading wine authority Hugh Johnson fronting the *Sunday Times Wine Club*, there's every reason for wine lovers to be tempted into this club. It offers access to prestigious winemaker dinners and tastings, 16 new lists a year, four shops in which to see-and-buy, food-and-wine matching courses, tours and cruises.

Sometimes the enthusiastic marketing (promoting easy-choice, pre-selected mixed cases) might obscure some of the 2,500 or so wines you get to choose from here. Although it's a dauntingly hefty read, perusal of the extensive list shows up the full breadth of choice available, particularly since it's the higher price level (£6–£12) that sees a true onset of quality. Try Grosset's Riesling from Australia, the wide range of *premier cru, grand cru* and *villages* Chablis, Mas de Daumas Gassac's range from the Languedoc, and cool-climate wines from Central Otago (New Zealand), and you won't fail to be impressed.

Best Buys

- Mount Athos Vineyards, Oak-aged red 1998 (Greece) £8.15
- De Bortoli, Family Reserve Durif 2003 (Australia) £8.55
- Domaine Mas du Bouquet, Vacqueyras 2002 (Rhône) £9.69

- Thelema, Chardonnay, Stellenbosch 2001 (South Africa) £13.50
- Grosset, Polish Hill Riesling, Clare Valley 2003 (Australia) £14.99
- Familia Martínez, Bujanda Gran Reserva, Rioja 1998 (Spain) £14.99

To find a wine merchant with a particular strength in wines from a certain country or region, see the regional chapters in the 'Best wine-producing countries' section.

The Oxford Wine Company

Head office: The Wine Warehouse, Witney Road, Standlake,
Witney, Oxfordshire OX29 7PR
Tel: (01865) 301144   Fax: (01865) 301155

Millets Farm, Frilford Heath, Abingdon, Oxfordshire OX13 5HB
Tel: (01865) 392200

44 Peel Street, Kensington, London W8 7PD
Tel: 020-7727 0780   Fax: 020-7229 4955
Email: info@oxfordwine.co.uk   Website: www.oxfordwine.co.uk

Closed 25 & 26 Dec **Cards** Yes **Discount** 5% on 1 case, other by negotiation **Order online** Yes **Delivery** Nationwide service (min. 1 case), free within 35-mile radius **Glass hire** Yes **Tastings and talks** Yes, phone for details **Newsletter** Quarterly **Special promotions** Regular offers **(£5)**

❦ *Good solid range, in all price brackets* ❦ *Over 1,500 wines, mainly shipped direct from the producer* ❦ *Spectacular selection of champagnes and dessert wines* ❦ *Top-quality wines available as well as sub-£5 cheap brands*

Much Oxford Wine Company business is carried out with the wine trade (local restaurants and hotels), hence the wide choice on this list. A particularly impressive range of dessert wines (nearly 60, including Canadian Icewine), and nearly 30 half bottles, are accompanied by a commendable selection of champagnes and sparkling wines: big bottles (methusalahs, salmanazars and nebuchadnezzars), Krug and sparkling Shiraz to boot.

There's a good spectrum of Bordeaux, including *cru classé* Médocs (Calon-Ségur, Pichon-Baron, Gruaud-Larose, Lynch Bages); classy Alsace from domaine Hugel; and things get adventurous with Portugal, Italy and South Africa, where choices even widen out to include Oregon and Washington State, along with Uruguay and Mexico. But the promised wine from Idaho seems to have been delisted – a shame.

Burgundy listings are well thought out, with all the major regions covered, but seem to lack real class. And though the impressive stack of over 80 Australian wines unfortunately begins with some cheap, dull brands, quality improves immeasurably with Shiraz from all the main regions, right up to the esteemed Penfold's Grange.

Fortunately for non-Oxfordshire/London residents, this range is available for delivery nationwide, and the company's website allows long-distance perusal of this impressive bunch of wines.

Best Buys
- Verdicchio dei Castelli di Jesi Classico, Rione 2002 (Italy) £4.99
- Hugel, Blanc de Blancs, Pinot Blanc 2002 (Alsace) £7.99
- Les Dentelles de Cézanne, Gigondas 2001 (Southern Rhône) £9.99
- Mumm Cuvée Napa NV (California) £11.55
- Guelbenzu, Evo, Navarra 2001 (Spain) £14.95
- Thelema, Cabernet Sauvignon, Stellenbosch 2001 (South Africa) £18.99

Specialist Award winners are listed on pages 17 and 18.

S H Jones

Head office/shop: The Cellar Shop, 2 Riverside, Tramway Road,
Banbury, Oxfordshire OX16 5TU
Tel: (01295) 251177   Fax: (01295) 259560

27 High Street, Banbury, Oxfordshire OX16 5EW
Tel: (01295) 251179   Fax: (01295) 272352

9 Market Square, Bicester, Oxfordshire OX26 6AA
Tel: (01869) 322448   Fax: (01869) 353907

121 Regent Street, Leamington Spa, Warwickshire CV32 4NU
Tel: (01926) 315609   Fax: (01926) 315609
Email: retail@shjones.com   Website: www.shjones.com

Closed Sun, public holidays exc Good Fri **Cards** Yes **Discount** Available on 1 mixed case **Order online** Yes **Delivery** Nationwide service, free within 40-mile radius of Banbury (min. 12 bottles) **Glass hire** Free with order **Tastings and talks** 2 sets of tutored tastings each year plus talks for wine clubs/in villages **Special promotions** Monthly ⑤

🍇 *An excellent all-round range of wines, focusing on quality and good value*
🍇 *Fabulous collection of vintage and wood ports* 🍇 *over 50 half-bottle choices*
🍇 *Lengthy champagne and sparkling wine listings*

Things have changes at this merchant over the past couple of years: it's opened up a new 'cellar shop' (in November 2003) in Banbury for a start, with easy parking and daily tastings for passing customers. The wine selection is a thoroughly good, near-comprehensive round-up of the 'best of the rest' (nothing flashy or overly expensive), with S H Jones taking great care to supply wines that reflect local character – even if it only offers a few bottles from each region – ranging from Spain's Priorat to California's Sierra Foothills and France's Plc St-Loup.

The Burgundy selection doesn't look as lustrous as it once did, but from Bordeaux there's an excellent choice of *petits châteaux*, good-value wines from among the *crus classés*

and a precious collection of second wines from the top-of-the-heap châteaux such as Gruaud-Larose, Palmer and Beaucaillou, which are well worth their (cheaper price).

Value for money, and keeping things interesting, appear to be the rules of thumb here: prices (starting at around £3 and £4) only top £20 when absolutely necessary – though Vidal-Fleury's 1999 Côte-Rôtie and Allegrini's 1999 Amarone della Valpolicella provide good excuses. Alternative Aussie grape varieties (Petit Verdot, Barbera, Sangiovese, Nebbiolo) are welcome, a treasure-trove is on offer from the Languedoc and South-west France, and there's an ongoing dynamic programme of tastings.

Best Buys

- Château Laurent, Les Coteaux du Pic, Pic St-Loup 2001 (Languedoc) £6.75
- Chapel Down Brut NV sparkling (England) £8.99
- Domaine Alquier, Faugères 2000 (Languedoc) £9.09
- Bodegas O'Fournier, B-Crux

Tempranillo-Merlot-Malbec, Uco Valley 2001 (Argentina) £12.99
- Jean-Pierre et Martine Meffre, Domaine St-Gayan, Gigondas 2000 (Southern Rhône) £14.59
- Seghesio Zinfandel, Sonoma 2001 (California) £14.59

Sommelier Wine Company

The Grapevine, 23 St George's Esplanade, St Peter Port,
Guernsey, Channel Islands GY1 2BG
Tel: (01481) 721677   Fax: (01481) 716818

Closed Sun, public holidays   **Cards** Yes   **Discount** Available on 12+ bottles   **Order online** No
Delivery Free within Guernsey (min. 6 bottles)   **Glass hire** Free   **Tastings and talks** Private tastings
for groups, 2 annual public tastings   **Special promotions** Fortnightly mixed-case offers, annual sale **£5**

❦ *Some of the world's finest wines brought to Guernsey* ❦ *Extensive collection of
characterful white wines from Alsace, Italy and Australia* ❦ *Chart-topping reds,
from Burgundy to the Barossa* ❦ *Fortified wines from around the world*

In 1986, Richard Matthews saw a gap in the
market on the island of Guernsey – and set up
the Sommelier Wine Company. To begin with
it was a bit of a hobby, but then things got a lot
more serious. Today, Sommelier's weighty
brochure is a real pleasure to read, and there
aren't enough superlatives to describe the
depth, breadth and detail of this selection.
Those lucky enough to be able to partake of
its contents should allow at least an hour to
peruse and digest the well-written, informative
list before committing to a purchase.

The choice on offer ranges through some
luxurious fine wines (Corton-Charlemagne

Burgundy from Simon Bize, Hermitage La
Chapelle from Paul Jaboulet-Aîné in the
Rhône, and clarets from châteaux Léoville-
Barton, Gruaud-Larose and Margaux) to
affordable-but-interesting choices from the
Rhône, Australia … just about everywhere
really. Sensibly, though, it avoids the very big
brands. The company doesn't need to delve
too far into the cheap-and-cheerful as
Channel Island prices are duty-free, so
anyone shopping here starts with a healthy
financial advantage. But there's no website,
nor can Richard deliver to the mainland, so
it's only locals who get to benefit.

Best Buys

- Bruno Sorg, Pinot Blanc 1999 (Alsace)
£4.95
- Florent Baumard, Savennières Trie
Speciale Sec 1997 (Loire) £10.95

- Aldo Conterno, Barbera d'Alba 1994
(Italy) £12.10
- Kanonkop Pinotage, Stellenbosch 2002
(South Africa) £11.75
- Rockford, Basket Press Shiraz,
Barossa 1999 (Australia) £14.25

Stone, Vine & Sun

13 Humphrey Farms, Hazeley Road, Twyford, Winchester, Hampshire SO21 1QA
Tel: (01962) 712351   Fax: (01962) 717545
Email: sales@stonevine.co.uk   Website: www.stonevine.co.uk

Closed Sun, public holidays   **Cards** Yes   **Discount** 5% on 12+ bottles   **Order online** Yes   **Delivery**
Nationwide service, free within 30-mile radius   **Glass hire** No   **Tastings and talks** Tutored tastings and
regular, large customer tastings in south of England   **Newsletter** Quarterly   **Special promotions** One-off
shipments, email offers, magazine clubs **£5**

❦ *New company with an exciting range of wines* ❦ *In-depth choices from
Burgundy, the Rhône, Austria, South Africa and the Loire* ❦ *Strong focus on the
£6–£12 bracket, with plenty of quality at higher price points too* ❦ *Lively website
invites direct sales countrywide*

Stone, Vine & Sun opened its warehouse
doors only recently, but the enthusiastic

team, who like to think of themselves as
'diverse but not too oddball', have already

built up a strong portfolio of wines, covering every major wine region. They have even started developing a compelling set of speciality areas too (South Africa, Austria and Germany among them).

Diversity stems from trying to catch as much of the stone, vine and sun about the wines as possible: in other words, the wines have to capture their setting as precisely as can be done. The Languedoc selection manages this very well – while also keeping to the company's core £6–£12 price range – as do choices from South

Africa, notably the Walker Bay, Malmesbury, Paarl, Robertson, Franschhoek and Olifants River regions. SVS ships many of its wines itself, and though some producers may be unfamiliar, they are well worth trying.

There are offerings at the quality end of the vinous spectrum, too: Quarts de Chaume and Bonnezeaux sweet wines from the Loire, 1996 Vouvray from Domaine Huët, a broad and confident selection of Burgundies (helpfully listed by commune), and also some classy Rhône wines.

Best Buys

- Château de Caseneuve, Les Calcaires, Pic St-Loup 2000 (Languedoc) £7.65
- Domaine Philippe Portier, Quincy 2002 (Loire) £6.95
- St-Urbans-Hof, Wiltinger Schlangengraben Riesling Spätlese, Saar 1999 (Germany) £11.50
- Domaine Tollot-Beaut, Chorey-lès-Beaune 2000 (Burgundy) £12.50
- Kracher, Beerenauslese half bottle 1999 (Austria) £16.50
- Rustenberg, Peter Barlow, Stellenbosch 2001 (South Africa) £20

Victor Hugo Wines

Head office: Longueville Road, St Saviour, Jersey JE2 7SA
Tel: (01534) 507977   Fax: (01534) 767770

Cash & Carry, Longueville Road, St Saviour, Jersey JE2 7SA
Tel: (01534) 507978   Fax: (01534) 507978

Wine Saver, 15 Weighbridge Place, St Helier, Jersey JE2 3NF
Tel: (01534) 507991   Fax: (01534) 507991
Email: sales@victor-hugo-wines.com   Website: www.victor-hugo-wines.com

Closed Sun, public holidays   **Cards** Yes   **Discount** Available on 1+ case   **Order online** Yes   **Delivery** Free within Jersey (min. 1 case)   **Glass hire** Free with order   **Tastings and talks** Regular tutored tastings for private customers, dinners, wine clubs   **Newsletter** Monthly   **Special promotions** Regular offers   **£5**

🍷 *Excellent choice of top-name champagnes* 🍷 *Bordeaux taken seriously* 🍷 *New Zealand's classiest producers* 🍷 *Big names from Italy* 🍷 *Local wines from Jersey*

Last year Victor Hugo Wines merged with Orange & Co to become, according to managing director Martin Flageul, the largest wine merchant in the Channel Islands. He points towards Australia, Chile, New Zealand and Spain as major strengths of the list, as well the classic French regions Bordeaux, Burgundy and Champagne. His brochure bears this out, opening with some very tempting champagnes – including welcome ranges from Laurent-Perrier, Taittinger, Veuve Clicquot and Jacquesson – and moving on to a thoroughly decent collection from Bordeaux in particular, and a fairly concise but very classy choice from

New Zealand. Prices run the gamut from a reasonable selection of bottles under £6 to the likes of Penfold's Grange 1998 at £102.50.

Of the areas Martin doesn't highlight, the Rhône stands out, with producers Guigal, Vidal-Fleury and Ogier well represented; as does the Italian set, arranged by region and taking in Tedeschi, Masi, Fontanafredda and Umani Ronchi among other good growers. All in all, this merchant seems to have matured nicely since the last *Guide*, and now has a good, all-round selection to keep the Channel Islanders happy, including a couple of wines actually produced there.

Best Buys

- Château Meaume, Bordeaux Supérieur 2000 (Bordeaux) £5.95
- Oyster Bay, Chardonnay, Marlborough 2003 (New Zealand) £6.59
- Nepenthe, The Rogue, Merlot/ Cabernet, Adelaide Hills 2002 (Australia) £7.95
- Château Caronne, Ste-Gemme 2000 (Bordeaux) £9.65
- J Vidal-Fleury, St-Joseph 1999/2000 (Northern Rhône) £10.95
- Jacquesson, Brut Perfection NV (Champagne) £18.25

Vintage Roots

Bridge Farm, Reading Road, Arborfield, Berkshire RG2 9HT
Tel: 0118-976 1999   Fax: 0118-976 1998
Email: info@vintageroots.co.uk   Website: www.vintageroots.co.uk

Closed Sat, Sun, public holidays **Cards** Yes **Discount** 5% on 5+ cases **Order online** Yes **Delivery** Nationwide service, free within 30-mile radius **Glass hire** Deposit required, charge for breakages **Tastings and talks** By request, 2 annual mail-order tastings (summer & Christmas) **Newsletter** 6 times a year **Special promotions** 6 times a year **(£5)**

🍇 *Global range of organic and biodynamic wines* 🍇 *Organic champagne, Bordeaux and Burgundy on offer* 🍇 *Opportunities for cork recycling*

After a slowish start for this company back in 1986, much more organic wine is available in the world today and is of better quality than ever before. Growers are continuing to sign up for the organic/ biodynamic way of life, and more and more consumers demand to drink its produce.

Visit Vintage Roots at its Reading shop, or via its busy website or colourful list (which clearly outlines what it takes to be organic, biodynamic or GMO-free) and you'll find one of the best and most comprehensive organic wine lists in the country. For a start, the fruits of the champagne industry's move to organics are beginning to show this year; organic wines from Germany, England, Greece, Australia and New Zealand are all present; and there are particularly strong selections from southern France, Spain and Argentina. And, impressively, there are even a few more organic Burgundies and Bordeaux creeping in – and from some of the classy communes – but the top biodynamic Burgundies are too expensive for Vintage Roots' price range.

Director Neil Palmer and his team focus on wines at around the £5 mark but with plenty of scope to trade up to mid-range prices. Look out also for organic tastings twice a year, mixed pre-chosen cases, and new own-label brand Touchstone wines (from Argentina), of which Neil is particularly proud.

Best Buys

- Terre Cortesi Moncaro, DOC Verdicchio dei Castelli di Jesi 2003 (Italy) £4.99
- Domaine de Soulié, AOC St-Chinian 2002 (Languedoc-Roussillon) £4.99
- Millton Vineyards, Gisborne Chardonnay 2002 (New Zealand) £6.99
- Fetzer Vineyards, Mendocino Bonterra, Zinfandel 2000 (California) £9.25
- Champagne Carte d'Or, Serge Faust NV (Champagne) £14.95
- Clos Plince, AOC Pomerol 2000 (Bordeaux) £18.50

East England

Adnams Wine Merchants

Head office: Sole Bay Brewery, Southwold, Suffolk IP18 6JW
Tel: (01502) 727222   Fax: (01502) 727223

Main shop: Adnams Wine Cellar and Kitchen Store, Victoria Street,
Southwold, Suffolk IP18 6JF
Tel: (01502) 727200   Fax: (01502) 727223

The Wine Shop, Pinkneys Lane, Southwold, Suffolk IP18 6EW
Tel: (01502) 722138
Email: wines@adnams.co.uk   Website: www.adnamswines.co.uk

Closed 25 & 26 Dec, 1 Jan, Good Fri, Easter Sun **Cards** Yes **Discount** 5% on 5+ cases **Order online** Yes **Delivery** Nationwide service, free for 1+ cases **Glass hire** Free within local delivery area, min. order 1 case **Tastings and talks** Regular events programme, including winemaker lunches/dinners **Newsletter** Monthly **Special promotions** Once a month

❧ *Wines from the world's quirkier, more 'hands-on' producers* ❧ *Enticing range of pre-chosen mixed cases (from £57 upwards)* ❧ *Top-quality biodynamic and organic listings* ❧ *Classic wines (Bordeaux, Burgundy, Rhône) from old vintages*

The wine list at this extra-specially good wine merchant bombards you with vinous opportunity the moment you open it. (In fact, as you do so, a flutter of leaflets present mixed-case ideas and seasonal offers – ignore these at your cost, they're packed with great-value wines and lead the way to some of the typically quirky Adnams bottles that you might never have tried before. But back to the list …) Alongside the wine listings you'll see tasting notes, photographs and pithy anecdotes about the producers and their wines. And a flurry of green-leaf symbols (denoting organic or biodynamic wine) will guide those looking for holistically produced bottlings.

The French Country Wines list ('The Flavours of Provence', 'Whites and Reds from the Warm South') kicks things off with tempting bottles such as fashionable Picpoul de Pinet from the Côteaux du Languedoc; the Loire listings bring in honeyed Vouvray from Domaine Huët; and the Rhône offers up organic wines from Vignes du Roy, Perrin and Coudoulet de Beaucastel. And five different Alsace growers (most merchants stock only one or two) show just what this region is capable of. Burgundy and Bordeaux don't disappoint in the sub-£20 price region, but sidetrack to the Fine Wine List for the really good stuff (châteaux Léoville-Barton, Haut-Bailly, Pichon-Baron, and the most high-profile back-to-earth Burgundian of the lot, Domaine Leflaive). And expect no less from the New World: Ridge Zinfandel, Saintsbury Pinot Noir and Murphy Goode 'Fumé Blanc' all grace the California pages with their illustrious presence.

Nowadays, there's a bit more of a cosy, user-friendly feel to this list – possibly due to the pervasive presence of bearded, avuncular-looking Alastair Marshall (senior wine buyer), or owing to the fact that the £4–£10 range (with help from a new, ex-Wine Society, general manager) is now burgeoning. Either way, the underpinning zeal with which Adnams has always chosen its wines appears still to be there. Let's hope supplying the whole country so generously (free delivery for 12 or more bottles) hasn't undermined this team's uncompromising veto on bulk-made wines.

(Best Buys overleaf)

161

Best Buys

- La Grange Rouge, Grenache/
  Chardonnay, Vin de Pays d'Oc 2002
  (Languedoc-Roussillon) £4.99
- Château Lacroix, Merlot Rosé 2002
  (Bordeaux) £6.99
- Domaine de l'Harmonie, J M Brocard,
  Pinot Noir de St-Bris 2002 (Burgundy)
  £7.99

- Tim Gramp, Grenache, McLaren Vale
  2001 (Australia) £8.99
- Delaire Estate, Sauvignon Blanc,
  Stellenbosch 2002 (South Africa) £9.99
- Martinborough Vineyard, Pinot Noir,
  Wairarapa 2000 (New Zealand) £15.99
- Domaine Rossignol-Trappet, Gevrey-
  Chambertin 2000 (Burgundy) £18.99
- Les Pagodes de Cos, St Estèphe 1998
  (Bordeaux) £19.99

The Colchester Wine Centre

See Lay & Wheeler, opposite

Corney & Barrow

See listing in London section, page 139

Hedley Wright Wine Merchants

The Twyford Centre, London Road, Bishop's Stortford, Hertfordshire CM23 3YT
Tel: (01279) 465818   Fax: (01279) 465819
Email: sales@hedleywright.co.uk   Website: www.hedleywright.co.uk

Closed Sun (Jan–Nov) **Cards** Yes **Discount** Available, phone for details **Order online** Yes
Delivery Nationwide service, free within 15-mile radius **Glass hire** Free **Tastings and talks** Tastings
in-store, winemaker evenings and cellar suppers **Newsletter** No **Special promotions** Occasional
(£5)

🍷 *Versatile merchant bringing in something from every region and at every price*
🍷 *Rhône wines from Guigal, Burgundy from Marquis d'Angerville* 🍷 *Impressive*
German and Australian wines 🍷 *Keen prices across the board*

This is a tremendously good something-of-everything merchant: one that keeps an eye firmly on price and individuality, with many a grape and region to pick from. It wouldn't be hard to select a mixed case (the minimum purchase) from this collection, whether you are after South American, Mediterranean, classic Bordeaux or Burgundy, or oddities such as English, Uruguayan or Lebanese wine. There may be only 13 California wines to choose from, for example, but these come from a broad spectrum of regions, nine different grapes and nine different growers. Across the board, there's plenty of variety to keep things interesting.

Of particular merit at Hedley Wright is the enthusiastic collection of German wines, covering (again) every major region and style: fine Rieslings from the Mosel; bolder, fuller wines from the Rheingau and Nahe; Pinot Gris from the Pfalz; Silvaner from Franken; and more. The Australian collection is also impressive (Grosset and Cullen are two top growers), and a tantalising array of sweet wines (Australian, Austrian, Hungarian and French) brings the list to a close.

And good news: the bimonthly mixed case of 12 different bottles *still* only costs £73: taken from this collection, that has to be good value.

Best Buys	£7.99
• Alenya, Viura/Chardonnay, Conca de Barberà 2001 (Spain) £4.49	• Ruggeri, Prosecco Santa Stefano NV, Veneto (Italy) £9.99
• Brumont, Madiran Torus 2000 (South-west France) £7.99	• Seghesio, Zinfandel, Sonoma County 2000 (California) £13.95
• Domaine Les Grands Bois, Cairanne Cuvée Eloise 2000 (Southern Rhône)	• Pierro, Cabernet Sauvignon, Margaret River 1996 (Australia) £18.95

Lay & Wheeler

Head office: Holton Park, Holton St Mary, Suffolk CO7 6NN
Tel: (0845) 330 1855   Fax: (0845) 330 4095

The Colchester Wine Centre, Gosbecks Park, 117 Gosbecks Road,
Colchester, Essex CO2 9JT
Tel: (01206) 713560   Fax: (01206) 769552
Email: sales@laywheeler.com or wine.centre@laywheeler.com   Website: www.laywheeler.com

Closed Sun, public holidays **Cards** Yes **Discount** No **Order online** Yes **Delivery** Nationwide service, free local (Colchester) delivery and for orders of £150+ **Glass hire** £1 per dozen with order **Tastings and talks** Events held in Colchester, London & Edinburgh, to suit all levels **Newsletter** No **Special promotions** At least 18 wines on promotion at any one time **£5**

❦ *Traditional but classy East Anglian wine merchant* ❦ *Good-quality wines, from everyday to ultra-premium (with high prices to match)* ❦ *Helpful cellar plan arrangements* ❦ *Tempting pre-selected cases for delivery*

Celebrating 150 years of family business in 2004, Lay & Wheeler has a lot to congratulate itself about. Right from the expansive wine listings from the Languedoc at the front of its price list, to the classy Burgundies and Bordeaux on offer, the team are working as hard as ever to provide a top-quality range of wines – and wine services – that take in every possible vinous need.

But are they spreading themselves too thinly; is the list as richly varied as it has been in the past? Some of the wines can be found more cheaply elsewhere, and though many wines are in the £8 to £15 bracket, there's not all that many to choose from below. These are signs that seem to be reflected in the packaging, too: more pages of glossy brochure are devoted to setting the scene than to the wines themselves.

Fortunately all this highly effective marketing isn't totally without substance to back it up. Henschke, Veritas and Moss Wood wines from Australia show this country at its absolute best in wine terms; other New World countries are represented by their finest available, rather than their fullest range of wines. The in-bond selection from top Italian house Gaja similarly shows the cream of Italy. Classic wines (Bordeaux, Burgundy) are chosen to show the breadth of their regions – and their depth, too, with examples from across a number of vintages.

Mixed in with the well-known wine producers are more obscure names whose wines are equally good, but have yet to reach full stardom. The exacting buying skills of David Roberts MW mean that whether a wine is known or not – or whether it's cheap, or not – you can take a hefty bet that it will be more than drinkable. Reliability is a real watchword here.

L&W extras include the Wine Discovery Club: with four excellent mixed cases for beginners, the Bin Club, which provides an efficient cellar-planning service, and the Colchester Wine Centre (L&W's new retail outlet), which hosts the famous wine-themed dinners ('New Zealand Pinot Noir', 'Bordeaux across the Spectrum') with delicious menus designed to complement the wine.

(Best Buys overleaf)

Best Buys

- Château Moulin de Ciffre, Faugères 2001 (Languedoc) £8.45
- Olivier Leflaive, Montagny Premier Cru, Côte Chalonnaise 2001 (Burgundy) £9.95
- Mas de La Dame, La Stèle Blanc, Coteaux d'Aix en Provence 2003 (Provence) £10.95
- Lawson's Dry Hills Marlborough Pinot Noir 2002 (New Zealand) £11.95

- Veritas, Cuvée Stephanie Shiraz/Mataro/Viognier, Barossa Valley 2002 (Australia) £12.61
- Alain Graillot, St-Joseph 2001 (Northern Rhône) £13.95
- Meyer-Fonné, Riesling Grand Cru Wineck-Schlossberg 2002 (Alsace) £14.95
- Réserve de la Comtesse, Pauillac 1999 (Bordeaux) £16.95

Noel Young Wines

56 High Street, Trumpington, Cambridge CB2 2LS
Tel: (01223) 844744   Fax: (01223) 844736
Email: admin@nywines.co.uk   Website: www.nywines.co.uk

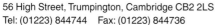

Closed Public holidays, Sun (Jan only) **Cards** Yes **Discount** 5% on 1 case **Order online** Yes **Delivery** Nationwide service, free within 20-mile radius (min. order £75) **Glass hire** Free with order if returned clean/unbroken **Tastings and talks** Evening tastings, details published on website **Newsletter** 5–6 issues per year **Special promotions** Discounted mixed case, *en primeur*, pre-release (£5)

❦ *Great range of fine Australian reds* ❦ *Serious passion for Syrah/Shiraz* ❦ *Unrivalled Austrian selection* ❦ *Fine Burgundies galore* ❦ *Germany given rare attention* ❦ *Wide choice of New Zealand whites* ❦ *Fine bottles from America, including Washington State*

Noel Young continues to build up his company, offering one of the most impressive, exciting ranges of wine around. Australia is his first love – indeed, he makes wines there himself under the Magpie Estate label – so expect a wide choice of top-notch producers from Down Under, including Shaw & Smith, Veritas, Charles Melton, Balnaves and Cullen. A passion for big and powerful Syrah/Shiraz stands out, but there are enough elegant bottles here too, and plenty of aromatic whites throughout.

This year Noel reports a gradual shift back to traditional wines, 'although Australia has built up a big loyalty'. A recent fine wine mailing included plenty of goodies from

Burgundy and the Rhône, and an exceptional collection of Alsace whites from the likes of Hugel and Albert Mann. Back in the New World, the list of serious wines from New Zealand and California seems to grow stronger all the time.

Perhaps most welcome are the less fashionable whites of Germany and Austria – where else would you find over 60 wines from Austria, including the fabulous dessert wines of Kracher, and the subtle, racy dry whites of Brundlmayer and Schloss Gobelsburg? But then that's typical of this merchant. Once Noel seizes on something he likes, he deals with it in admirable depth.

Best Buys

- Domaine des Forges, Chaume, Coteaux du Layon 2000 (Loire) £9.99
- Schloss Gobelsburg, Grüner Veltliner Renner 2002 (Austria) £12.49
- Charles Melton, Cabernet Sauvignon, Barossa Valley 1999 (Australia) £20.99

- Cullen Estate, Diana Madelaine, Cabernet Sauvignon, Margaret River 2001 (Australia) £29.95
- Billecart-Salmon, Blanc de Blancs NV (Champagne) £33.99
- Hugel, Gewurztraminer, Vendange Tardive magnum 1989 (Alsace) £70

Peter Graham Wines

Europa House, Martineau Lane, Norwich NR1 2EN
Tel: (01603) 598910   Fax: (01603) 598919
Email: louisa@petergrahamwines.com   Website: www.petergrahamwines.com

Closed Sat, Sun **Cards** Yes **Discount** Available on 12+ bottles **Order online** No **Delivery** Nationwide service (min. 1 mixed case), free within Norfolk & Suffolk **Glass hire** Free **Tastings and talks** 150–200 talks/tastings per year, including visiting producers **Newsletter** 6 mailshots per year **Special promotions** No (£5)

🍷 *Good-value selection of bottles under £6* 🍷 *Solid, strong ranges from Burgundy and the Rhône* 🍷 *Plenty of exciting dessert wines* 🍷 *Excellent Australian wines* 🍷 *Numerous wine talks and tastings through the year*

Directors Louisa Turner and Graham Donaldson preside over a six-year-old, highly successful and expanding Norfolk business which has now left its original 'medieval' shop and moved to new premises on the outskirts of the city – they call it a 'consolidated showroom, warehouse, office complex on the Norwich bypass'.

The list opens with an admirable bunch of wines (Graham's top 20) that certainly represents good value for money – they are 'crowd-pleasers', as the company puts it, and all under £6 a bottle. (You must buy them by the case, as with all the wines here, but that brings a 10 per cent discount.) Then the list crosses the Channel to take in much of interest from France, including some

excellent Burgundy and Rhône. Italy gets a decent showing, but it's Australia, South Africa and Chile that impress the most, especially Australia, which numbers Jim Barry, Simon Hackett, Vasse Felix, Charles Melton and Wirra Wirra among its producers. The New Zealand wines are carefully selected too, and include the fine reds of Sileni and Esk Valley. Other parts of the globe receive less attention, and look as though they could be expanded in time, but there are certainly enough good dessert wines, ports and sherries to keep customers happy.

Graham Donaldson teams up with TV chef Delia Smith to present 15 food and wine workshops in 2004.

Best Buys

- Grenache Rosé 2002, Owens Estate, Geoff Merrill (Australia) £6.50
- Chandon, Brut NV (Argentina) £8.99
- Sileni, Cellar Selection, Merlot/Cabernet Franc, Hawke's Bay 2000 (New Zealand) £9.95

- Mercurey La Framboisière, Faiveley 1998 (Burgundy) £13.95
- Crozes-Hermitage, Domaine de Thalabert, Jaboulet 1999 (Southern Rhône) £14.75
- Jim Barry, The McRae Wood Shiraz, Clare Valley 1999 (Australia) £16.50

T & W Wines

5 Station Way, Brandon, Suffolk IP27 0BH
Tel: (01842) 814414   Fax: (01842) 819967
Email: contact@tw-wines.com   Website: www.tw-wines.com

Closed Sat, Sun, public holidays **Cards** Yes **Discount** No **Order online** Yes **Delivery** Nationwide service, free for 2+ cases **Glass hire** Free with order **Tastings and talks** No **Newsletter** No **Special promotions** No (£5)

🍷 *Huge set of half bottles* 🍷 *Loads of larger bottles* 🍷 *Mature wines galore* 🍷 *Fine Burgundy, Loire and Alsace collections* 🍷 *Long list of biodynamic wines* 🍷 *Serious German and Austrian ranges* 🍷 *Good Australian choices*

What is it about East Anglia? There seems to be an unusually high number of excellent wine merchants there, and many of them have a very idiosyncratic, passionate approach to the subject. This particular enthusiastic East Anglian retailer is now working from spacious new premises at Brandon, Suffolk. Managing director Trevor Hughes certainly needs a lot of space – his latest list holds over 3,200 wines, including 240 half bottles; one of the largest selections in the UK.

Mature wines are another strength here: a quick flick through the big, glossy brochure reveals plenty of older vintages, some in halves or larger-format bottles. Many come from France, which is the main preoccupation here. The Burgundies, in particular, are dazzling and include such luminaries as Domaine Dujac, Olivier Leflaive, Domaine Rossignol-Trapet and Jean Thevenet. Older vintages abound, right back to the 1970s and 1960s, and there are suggestions for younger wines 'for laying down'. Of the other French sections, the Loire is outstanding, with wines from Huët,

Domaine des Baumard and Didier Dagueneau among others, along with plenty of sweeties, and Alsace offers comprehensive ranges from both Trimbach and Hugel, including many mature wines.

Away from France, Trevor is the UK agent for Austria's Willi Opitz, and this list has lots of his delightful dessert wines from Neusiedlersee. Germany rarely gets such detailed attention - look for wines from JJ Prüm, Reichsrat Von Buhl and Bürklin Wolf at prices that range from around a fiver to nearer £200. Italy and California turn up more treasures at T&W, as do biodynamic wines – there's a separate list for the latter.

This really is a fascinating selection, and a list that makes for happy browsing again and again, with barely one bottle that could be described as mundane. Three words of warning – the list is in a slightly strange order (the Rhône suddenly pops up in between New World countries); there's little that could be described as cheap; and prices are ex-VAT, something to bear in mind when adding up the cost of a mixed case.

Best Buys

- Trimbach, Riesling 2000 half bottles (Alsace) £6.45
- De Bortoli, Pinot Noir, Victoria 2002 (Australia) £7.95
- Taltarni, Brut Rosé, Victoria 2000 (Australia) £10.95
- JJ Prüm, Graacher Himmelreich Riesling Kabinett, Mosel 1992 (Germany) £13.95

- Domaine Huët, Vouvray Le Clos de Bourg 1996 (Loire) £14.50
- Willi Opitz, Welschriesling Eiswein, Neusiedlersee 1999 half bottles (Austria) £25.80
- Domaine Dujac, Echëzeaux 2001 (Burgundy) £67.50
- Bollinger, Grande Année magnum 1989 (Champagne) £122

Thos Peatling Fine Wines

Head office: Westgate House, Westgate Street, Bury St Edmunds, Suffolk IP33 1QS
Tel: (01284) 755948   Fax: (01284) 714483

37–39 Little London, Long Sutton, Lincolnshire PE12 9LE
Tel: (01406) 363233   Fax: (01406) 365654
Email: sales@thospeatling.co.uk   Website: www.thospeatling.co.uk

Closed Sun, public holidays **Cards** Yes **Discount** 5% on 12+ bottles **Order online** Yes **Delivery** Nationwide service **Glass hire** Free with order **Tastings and talks** Regular in-store tastings held in Bury St Edmunds **Newsletter** No **Special promotions** Various in-store reductions and offers

🍇 *Plenty of cheaper-priced wines to entice new buyers* 🍇 *Good-value wines in the mid-price ranges* 🍇 *Smart selection of en primeur Bordeaux*

A lot of work has been done since last year in upgrading this rather dry, uninspiring list (it tells you what the wine is, but nothing about it, sometimes not even the country it's from) into something with a bit more flair, with a wealth of interesting bottles. Delve into the rows of black-and-white print and you'll find wines from some of the world's quirkier wine regions, Switzerland and Israel among them, plus such intriguing offerings as Guigal's Tavel Rosé, and better still his 2000 Hermitage. Old vintages of claret (including Lafite 1961), and top Australian bottlings (Jim Barry's Armagh and Yalumba's Octavius) also make their mark.

Now there are Austrian wines, English wines (from the Ickworth estate, just nearby), Swiss Petite Arvine and Pinot Gris, top-notch Chilean wines such as Almaviva and Casa Lapostolle, trendy southern Italian choices, and more – as well as the jolly good Burgundy and Bordeaux listings.

In short, Thos Peatling now gives buyers scope to trade up into the middle price brackets and is a more rounded, interesting merchant as a result. But a hearty plea for more description here. Who are the small producers from which you so proudly import directly? Why have you chosen them?

Best Buys

- Tyrell's Old Winery, Cabernet/Merlot 2000 (Australia) £4.29
- Torrelongares, Garnacha, Cariñeña 2002 (Spain) £4.75
- Domaine de la Commandière, Quincy 2001 (Loire) £8.49

- Jansz, Premium Brut Cuvée sparkling (Australia) £9.99
- Domaine Berthet Rayne, Châteauneuf-du-Pape Blanc 2001 (Southern Rhône) £13.99
- Quady's Starboard Dessert Wine, Madera 1990 (California) £14.99

Veritas Wines

103 Cherry Hinton Road, Cambridge CB1 7BS
Tel: (01223) 212500   Email: info@veritaswines.co.uk   Website: www.veritaswines.co.uk

Closed Sun, public holidays   **Cards** Yes   **Discount** 5% on 6+ bottles   **Order online** No   **Delivery** Nationwide service   **Glass hire** Free with order   **Tastings and talks** Free tastings Fri & Sat, ticketed wine events at least monthly   **Newsletter** Weekly by email   **Special promotions** Available **£5**

🍇 *Quality Rhône bottlings spanning the price ranges* 🍇 *Wide choice of Italian wines* 🍇 *Luscious dessert wines from Hungary, Canada, Australia and France* 🍇 *Lively website* 🍇 *Australian choices from across the regions*

Veritas buying director Charlie Stephenson says that there's been an increased demand for Mediterranean wines this year. And, despite its mere two years of age, VW seems to have responded to its customers' requirements with alacrity. Italy, Spain and Southern France are all strongly represented here.

The whole list has a rather haphazard feel to it, but it's worth noting the eclectic though short list from North America, which includes Stag's Leap (California) and Hedges from Washington, mixed in with Inniskillin (from Ontario, Canada). And it would be shame to miss out on anything French: claret involves a delve back into

Bordeaux' history (Gruaud-Larose 1975, Grand Puy Lacoste 1983), a wider, more up-to-date range from Burgundy and Chablis, plus Rhône choices (where things really hit their stride) with five different Gigondas bottlings (bargain-value territory this) and quality *cuvées* from Delas and Domaine Cuilleron (both for Condrieu).

Jolly email bulletins and appealing banter greet visitors to the website or those signing on to the mailing list, as Charlie notifies his customers weekly of news, offers and general winey gossip. And look out for the enticing bin-end wines in the 'Fine and Rare' section at the end of the list.

(Best Buys overleaf)

Best Buys

- Falasco, Garganega, Veneto 2002 (Italy) £6.49
- Duca di Castelmonte, Nero d'Avola, IGT di Sicilia 1999 (Italy) £6.99
- René Mure, Riesling d'Alsace 2001 (Alsace) £9.99

- Domaine Amadieu, Gigondas Grand Romane 2000 (Southern Rhône) £11.49
- Crown Estates, Tokaji Aszú 5 Puttonyos 1993 (Hungary) £12.49
- Grosset, Semillon/Sauvignon Blanc, Clare Valley 2001 (Australia) £13.49

Wines of Interest

46 Burlington Road, Ipswich, Suffolk IP1 2HS
Tel: (0870) 224 5640   Fax: (0870) 224 5641
Email sales@winesofinterest.co.uk   Website: www.winesofinterest.co.uk

Closed Sun, public holidays **Cards** Yes **Discount** Available on 1 unmixed case **Order online** Yes
Delivery Nationwide service, free delivery available, phone for details **Glass hire** Free with order
Tastings and talks Weekday evenings, for groups, wine clubs & professional bodies; advanced bookings recommended **Newsletter** No **Special promotions** Various, includes seasonal case offers **£5**

❦ *Thoughtfully chosen selection of quality wines* ❦ *Plenty of choices around £5 and £10* ❦ *Well-researched New World collection, including excellent choices from Mexico and Argentina* ❦ *Characterful whites from Austria, Alsace and Germany*

The two Jonathans, Williamson and Hare, get twitchy about any wine that's bland and boring. They stock no brands: their aim is to offer only wines that growers are passionate about. Ringing a change this year, the 2000 vintage in Bordeaux has been met with enthusiasm. But they still don't let prices rise too high: most regions provide plenty of wines at around the £10 and £20 marks, with a few £50 bottles for treats – Riesling Grand Cru Goldert 1999 from Clos Saint Imer, Alsace, for example, or unusual Chardonnay Trockenbeerenauslese 1998 from Jurtschitsch Sonnh of Austria.

But it's quality, not fancy names, that counts here. Mystery six-packs, offering savings of 15 to 20 per cent, could be anything from red, white or rosé to fizz or even fortified wine, and are a nice way for customers to try wines that they normally wouldn't. The Sampling Club costs £24 a year to join, for which you receive wines of the month at half price, plus whole cases of the same at 5 per cent discount. Wines of Interest also helps in the learning process by offering wine and quiz tastings, and useful factsheets giving guidance on storing wine, wine faults, cork versus plastic tops, organic and biodynamic wines, and much more.

Best Buys

- Aliante, Negroamaro di Puglia 2001 (Italy) £5.50
- Alain Brumont, Gros Manseng, Vin de Pays de Gascogne 2002 (south-west France) £5.55
- Michel Torino, Don David Malbec,

Cafayate 2001 (Argentina) £7.95
- Château Patache d'Aux, Médoc 1999 (Bordeaux) £9.95
- L A Cetto, Nebbiolo Reserve, Baja California 1996 (Mexico) £10.70
- Campbells, Rutherglen Muscat NV, Victoria, half bottle (Australia) £7.95

South-west England

Averys Wine Merchants

Head office: 4 High Street, Nailsea, Bristol BS48 1BT
Tel: (01275) 811100   Fax: (01275) 811101

9 Culver Street, Bristol BS1 5LD
Tel: 0117-921 4146   Fax: 0117-922 6318
Email: sales@averys.com   Website: www.averys.com

Open Daily **Cards** Yes **Discount** No **Order online** Yes **Delivery** Nationwide service **Glass hire** No **Tastings and talks** Regular tastings and talks in-store **Newsletter** Yes **Special promotions** Bin-end sales, regular offers

🍇 *Wide range of well-priced, good-value bottles* 🍇 *Long list of wines from Bordeaux and Burgundy* 🍇 *Fine and rare wines at the Bristol shop* 🍇 *Good mail-order service* 🍇 *Excellent Italian range* 🍇 *Germany taken seriously*

The 2003/4 glossy brochure from Averys is a joy to read: it is easy to negotiate, gives all crucial information needed and has useful, short-but-precise tasting notes. It opens with a vintage chart and a selection of 17 wines under £5 before heading into some special mixed-case selections (from £49.95 for 12 bottles) and a range of Avery's own-label wines.

So far, so organised. Averys was founded over 200 years ago, and doesn't shirk the traditional side of the business, listing page after page of Bordeaux and Burgundies, champagnes, sherries, ports and madeiras. Happily, these sections mainly run the gamut from easy-drinking, affordable bottles to illustrious stars. Of the other classic areas of France, the Rhône section stands out, with wines from Yves Gras, and plenty of very good-value bottles, and the Loire range has been filled out with new producers from Reuilly, Quincy, Sancerre and Pouilly.

Outside France, it is well worth stopping off in Italy and Germany. The former carries everything from a Chardonnay/Garganega blend for £3.95 to fine Amarone and Barolo for around £30; the latter reveals an above-average set, with plenty from the prestigious Mosel region.

Although venerable, Averys appears to have moved with the times, and now has a neat set of wines from most New World countries; South Africa looks tempting this year, and includes wines from Vergelegen, Hamilton Russell, Nitida and Weltevrede.

The *Guide* has heard good things about the efficiency of the mail-order service here. Mail-order director Richard Davis reports a growing interest in Spanish reds, rosé and Sauvignon Blanc. If you can, do try to visit the atmospheric wine shop in central Bristol, where there are many more rare and fine wines for sale (kept under lock and key in what the company calls 'The Cage'). Some of these are available by mail order too but it's best to go and peruse the rarer wines in person. All in all, a reliable, good-value, modern-meets-traditional list.

Best Buys

- Dr L Riesling, Mosel 2002 (Germany) £6.95
- Santa Duc Sélections, Côtes du Rhône Villages Rasteau 2000 (Rhône) £7.95
- Tedeschi Capitel San Rocco, Vino di Ripasso, Verona 1999 (Italy) £8.50
- Averys Fine Chablis 2002 (Burgundy) £9.50
- Roberto Stucchi, Badia a Coltibuono, Chianti Classico, Tuscany 2000 (Italy) £10.95
- Le Haut Médoc de Prieuré Lichine 2000 (Bordeaux) £12.95
- Averys Special Cuvée NV magnums (Champagne) £32.95
- Wynns, Michael Shiraz, Coonawarra 1998 (South Australia) £37

Bennetts Wines

High Street, Chipping Campden, Gloucestershire GL55 6AG
Tel: (01386) 840392   Fax: (01386) 840974
Email: enquiries@bennettsfinewines.com   Website: www.bennettsfinewines.com

Closed Sun, public holidays, 5 days over Christmas **Cards** Yes **Order online** No **Discount** Available on orders of 12+ bottles **Delivery** Nationwide service, free within 20-mile radius, min. 12 bottles **Glass hire** Free with order of 12+ bottles **Tastings and talks** 2 large public tastings per year, regular winemaker dinners at local restaurants **Newsletter** Bimonthly **Special promotions** Regular pre-shipment offers, phone for details

🍷 *Tempting fine and rare wine list* 🍷 *Real focus on quality wines* 🍷 *Plenty of extras, including en primeur Burgundy offers*

Bennetts opts for a quality-first approach to wine, so don't expect a cheap deal, though a good browse through its extensive wine list will let you know exactly how very tempted you're going to be!

Names such as Bonneau du Martray, Comtes Lafon and de Vogüé are there to lure you from Burgundy; plus Allegrini, Aldo Conterno, Gaja and Avignonesi from Italy; and châteaux Lynch-Bages, Léoville-Poyferré, Latour and Pichon-Baron from Bordeaux. (The vintages of many wines in the fine and rare list go back as far as 1945.) Away from the classics, expect great wines from California, Australia, Alsace, Germany,

Spain and regional France too. But be aware that if partner Charlie Bennett doesn't like a region, he doesn't stock it – so fans of South Africa and South America won't find themselves so well provided for.

There are plenty of lesser-known producer names here as well. And they're certainly to be trusted, as wines here are de-listed immediately if the quality drops. 'Nothing is ever stocked without tasting first, and no bottle is stocked for padding,' says Charlie, who reports that this year his customers have moved towards more food-friendly subtle wine styles (for example, from Italy and Burgundy).

Best Buys

- Pieropan, Soave Classico Superiore 2003 (Italy) £9.35
- JosMeyer, Mise du Printemps, Pinot Blanc 2003 (Alsace) £10.65
- Domaine Huët, Vouvray Le Mont Demi-Sec 1998 (Loire) £14.25
- Domaine de la Mordorée, Lirac Cuvée de la Reine des Bois 2003 (Southern Rhône) £15.99
- Vasse Felix, Cabernet Sauvignon 2000 (Western Australia) £13.99
- Quinta de la Rosa, Douro Reserve 2000 (Portugal) £17.95

Great Western Wine Company

The Wine Warehouse, Wells Road, Bath BA2 3AP
Tel: (01225) 322800   Fax: (01225) 442139
Email: retail@greatwesternwine.co.uk   Website: www.greatwesternwine.co.uk

Closed Sun, public holidays **Cards** Yes **Discount** No **Order online** No **Delivery** Nationwide service, free within 20-mile radius & for orders of £150+ **Glass hire** Yes **Tastings and talks** Free in-store tastings, regular tutored events, wine courses & talks **Newsletter** 2–3 times per year **Special promotions** Various offers, details by newsletter **£5**

🍷 *Good-value wines with plenty of individual character* 🍷 *Inspired choices from the Languedoc and southern France* 🍷 *Helpful staff provide guidance through the more eclectic wines listed* 🍷 *Watch out for winemaker dinners*

Managing director Philip Addis favours direct shipment when it comes to buying wines. This way he doesn't have to pass on the middleman's costs to his customers, and he can ensure the presence of wines guaranteed to have plenty of individual character. A flick through the (expensive-looking) pages of this list reveals – even from the illustrious regions of Bordeaux, Burgundy, Italy and California – very little over £15. Many cost wines are under £10, but are chosen only if they're interesting.

The list begins with an eclectic selection from the south of France: six different types of Jurançon (ranging from £7.50 to a steamy anomaly at £40.50), Madiran, Cahors, plus still and sparkling wines from Limoux. Then a carefully picked sub-£15 selection of Bordeaux (Château Siran, in Margaux, being Philip's only visit to the upper echelons). A similar group of well-priced Burgundies follows (Philippe Brenot's Bâtard-Montrachets is the one luxury, at over £60).

France gets the best coverage here, with the Loire and Rhône still among the strongest regions. Among others, Philip dips into Austria, England and Argentina with one grower apiece, and South Africa (topped by Fairview and Charles Back) makes a succinct but excellent appearance too.

Best Buys

- Fitou Domaine de Roudene Fûts de Chêne, 2001 (Southern France) £6.95
- Fermoy Estate Semillon, Margaret River 2001 (Western Australia) £9.95
- Boeger Barbera, El Dorado, 1999 (California) £11.50
- Sancerre, Vincent Pinard, Cuvée Nuance 2002 (Loire) £12.95
- St-Joseph Les Côteaux, Domaine Durand, 2001 (Northern Rhône) £12.95

The Nobody Inn

Doddiscombsleigh, nr Exeter, Devon EX6 7PS
Tel: (01647) 252394   Fax: (01647) 252978
Email: info@nobodyinn.co.uk   Website: www.nobodyinn.co.uk

Closed 25 & 26 Dec, 1 Jan   **Cards** Yes   **Discount** 5% on 1 case   **Order online** No   **Delivery** Nationwide service, free wihin 10-mile radius   **Glass hire** Free with 2+ cases   **Tastings and talks** Monthly, phone for details   **Newsletter** Quarterly   **Special promotions** Yes, phone for details   **(£5)**

❦ *Fabulous range of sweet Loire wines* ❦ *Top wines from California and Australia – interesting regions, producers and grape varieties* ❦ *Sixty half bottles to choose from* ❦ *New mail-order branch, The Wine Company*

The sweet Bordeaux and Loire wines at the start of this list are definitely worth getting excited about – Nicolas Joly's Savennières and Gaston Huët's Vouvray Cuvée Contance aren't seen nearly often enough, nor are the fabulous Bonnezeaux and Quarts de Chaumes from the amazing 1997 vintage. Not everyone's interested in Loire wines, but this gives an idea of the sort of passion with which this list is put together. When The Nobody Inn team like a wine, they make sure it's available in all its vintages and from all its different winemakers.

This isn't the place to come for a wide range from the classic regions, but from the least-expected of sources (Loire, Spanish, Italian and Portuguese white wines,

Jurançon and Pacherenc du Vic Bilh from Southern France) there are some terrific surprises. Likewise, at the top of the quality tree, Italian reds such as Barolo Sperss from Gaja, Sassicaia and Ornellaia make a splash. As do Australian wines in the form of Penfold's Grange and Henschke's Hill of Grace. California and Australian wines are listed by varietal, and within these ranges hide some fabulous regional wines from the countries' best producers.

The newly launched mail-order arm of The Nobody Inn, The Wine Company, is set to send this diverse range countrywide. It puts more emphasis on £5–£8 wines, and includes a range of pre-chosen mixed cases as well as wines from the Inn's usual list.

Best Buys

- Umani Ronchi, Verdicchio dei Castelli di Jesi Classico 2000 (Italy) £4.66
- I Gary Crittenden Sangiovese, Mornington Peninsula 1999 (Australia) £9.34
- Ducournau, Pacherenc du Vic-Bilh, Chapelle l'Enclos 1999 (South-west France) £10.16
- Thelema Merlot, Stellenbosch 1998 (South Africa) £11.60
- Seghesio Zinfandel, Sonoma 1999 (California) £14.25
- J J Prüm, Wehlener-Sonnenuhr Riesling Kabinett, Mosel 1997 (Germany) £14.63

Yapp Brothers

The Old Brewery, Mere, Wiltshire BA12 6DY
Tel: (01747) 860423   Fax: (01747) 860929
Email: sales@yapp.co.uk   Website: www.yapp.co.uk

Closed Sun, public holidays **Cards** Yes **Discount** No **Order online** Yes **Delivery** Nationwide service, free within 20-mile radius or for orders of 2+ cases **Glass hire** Yes **Tastings and talks** Available for wine groups/societies **Newsletter** 5–6 per year **Special promotions** In-store & online wines of the month/mailouts

🍷 *Rhône wines from Côte-Rôtie, Cornas and beyond* 🍷 *Stunning white, rosé, red and sparkling wines from forgotten corners of the Loire* 🍷 *New and hearty wine styles from the Languedoc-Roussillon* 🍷 *Unmissable oddities from south-west France*

It's business as usual at Yapp Brothers. This merchant sells wines from small-but-top-quality family domaines – many stocked for years, others new – and bases its business on friendship rather than formal contracts. While that might seem strange in these times of globe-spanning trade agreements, it's probably because the Yapp team have found a formula that works. These growers are chosen because they respect tradition and the *terroir*, and are exacting in every detail of winemaking, which comes through in great-tasting wines. You can read about them in the wine list, plus how the Yapps found the wines, why they like them and why customers might like them too.

The Loire, Rhône and Languedoc-Roussillon are the specialities – exciting, upcoming appellations such as Gigondas, Vacqueyras, and Lirac from the Rhône are featured; Bouches de Rhône, Bellet and Bandol come in from further south; and Jasnières, Savennières, Reuilly and Quincy make appearances among the better-known Loire appellations. Star growers such as Gérard and Jean-Louis Chave, Alain Graillot, Auguste Clape, Nicolas Joly and Jean-Pierre Meffre line up next to lesser-known names.

Look out, too, for the wines the Yapps can't resist bringing in from Chablis, Alsace, Champagne, Jurançon and Irouléguy, plus the occasional Australian Shiraz. Remember, it's quality rather than comprehensive supply that tempts this team.

Best Buys

- Jean-Jacques Teiller, Menetou-Salon 2003 (Loire) £9.75
- Denis Chéron, Vacqueyras Cuvée Spéciale 1999 (Southern Rhône) £9.75
- Cave de St-Désirat, St-Joseph Blanc 2000 (Northern Rhône) £9.95
- Michel & Laurent Berger, Montlouis Vendange Tardive 1997 (Loire) £12.95
- Jacques Dalmasso, Domaine de la Source, Bellet 2000 (Provence) £16.95
- Auguste & Pierre Clape, Cornas Cuvée Renaissance 2000 (Northern Rhône) £19.75

Midlands

Ceci Paolo

The New Cooks Emporium, 21 High Street, Ledbury, Herefordshire HR8 1DS
Tel: (01531) 632976   Fax: (01531) 631011
Email: patriciaharrison@cecipaolo.com   Website: www.cecipaolo.com

Closed Sun, public holidays **Cards** Yes **Discount** Available, phone for details **Order online** No
Delivery Nationwide service **Glass hire** No **Tastings and talks** Tutored and other tastings,
winemaker dinners **Newsletter** 4–6 per year **Special promotions** Various in-store **£5**

❦ Specialist in Italian and Australian wine, newly embarked on an impressive
food-and-wine matching venture ❦ A succinct selection but oozing with quality
❦ Each bottle is chosen as a true reflection of its place of origin

First and foremost Ceci Paolo is a cooks' emporium, but as well as oils, vinegars, a deli with Italian/Mediterranean and Asian influences, food paraphernalia and glasses, a number of truly delicious Italian and Australian wines are on sale: the wine side has more than doubled over the last couple of years.

Being a confirmed 'foodie', it's no surprise that owner Patricia Harrison has settled on Italy as a speciality, this country's wines being such elegant food-matchers – whether light-bodied aromatic whites (such as the Garganega, modern Soave and Lugana) from the north of the country,

powerful tangy reds (beloved Chianti, Brunello or Barolo), or warm-hearted animally wines from the deep south made from Primitivo and Negroamaro grapes. Patricia was born in Sydney, so her Australian choices come as no surprise either – from some of the very best Down-Under producers: Mount Horrocks, Mount Langi Ghiran, Shaw & Smith for starters.

This is also a good way of accessing the marvellous collection of wines from Liberty Wines, one of the UK's finest Italian wine stockists, which supplies Ceci Paolo. Best of all, visit the revitalised sixteenth-century timbered Herefordshire outlet.

Best Buys

- Alpha Zeta, G, Garganega, Veneto 2002 (Italy) £5.29
- A Mano, Primitivo di Puglia 2001 (Italy) £6.49
- Allegrini, Valpolicella Classico, Veneto 2002 (Italy) £7.49

- Shaw & Smith, Sauvignon Blanc, Adelaide Hills 2001 (Australia) £9.99
- Mount Horrocks, Watervale Riesling, Clare Valley 2002 (Australia) £12.49
- Vin Santo di Capezzanna Riserva, Tuscany 1997 (Italy) £15.99

Croque-en-Bouche

221 Wells Road, Malvern Wells, Worcester WR14 4HF
Tel: (01684) 565612   Fax: (0870) 706 6282
Email: mail@croque-en-bouche.co.uk   Website: www.croque-en-bouche.co.uk

Open Any time by arrangement **Cards** Yes **Discount** 1.5% on orders under £500, 3% on orders of
£500+ **Order online** Yes **Delivery** Nationwide service (min. 1 case), free within 10-mile radius **Glass
hire** No **Tastings and talks** No **Newsletter** No **Special promotions** No

❦ Multi-talented merchant: lots of upbeat choice, including bottles at £5–£10
❦ Old vintages of Australian reds ❦ Geared up to Internet trading
❦ Top Bordeaux and Italian offerings, plus Spanish and California bottles

Now that he can concentrate solely on the wine-merchanting side of his business (the Croque-en-Bouche restaurant sadly closed in 2002), Robin Jones continues to do great things with his wine listings from Australia, the Rhône and New Zealand. Best of all is his amazing treasure trove of old Australian vintages – Shiraz ages spectacularly: try Robin's 1970 Lindeman's Hunter Shiraz (Bin 4110) or 1974 McWilliams Philip Hermitage to be convinced.

As well as covering the wine world pretty comprehensively, Robin likes to focus on anything 'weird and different', which can mean Petite Syrah from Mexico, Canadian Pinot Noir or sweet Israeli wine. At a heftier price tag are a few old vintages of Bordeaux and Burgundy (Château Brane-Cantenac 1929 or 1978 Pommard).

If you're looking for more familiar great names, you won't be disappointed by Château de Beaucastel from the Rhône, Veuve Clicquot champagne, or châteaux d'Yquem and Nairac Sauternes. And if you want to have just one special bottle and keep the rest of the case price down, this will be no trouble either: the average bottle spend at C-en-B is a respectable £8. Expect lots of tips and tasting notes to aid choices along the way.

Best Buys

- Frescobaldi, Chianti Castiglione 2002 (Italy) £8
- Trimbach, Riesling 2000 (Alsace) £9.50
- Norton, Reserve Malbec 2002 (Argentina) £9.50
- Torbreck, The Steading 2000 (Australia) £16.50
- St-Joseph Les Royes, Courbis 1998 (Northern Rhône) £18.50
- Château de Fuissé, Pouilly-Fuissé Les Clos 1998 (Burgundy) £19

Gauntleys of Nottingham

4 High Street, Exchange Arcade, Nottingham NG1 2ET
Tel: 0115-911 0555   Fax: 0115-911 0557
Email: rhone@gauntleywine.com   Website: www.gauntleywine.com

Closed Sun (exc. Dec), public holidays **Cards** Yes **Discount** Available on 12+ bottles **Order online** No **Delivery** Nationwide service, free for 12+ bottles within Nottingham **Glass hire** No **Tastings and talks** By appointment **Newsletter** No **Special promotions** En primeur Rhône, Burgundy, Alsace, Loire, Spain (£5)

🍇 *Small-scale merchant with impressive stocks of Rhône, Alsace and southern French wine* 🍇 *Not cheap wines, but high quality across the board*
🍇 *Stocks of fine Havana cigars (similarly expensive)*

Gauntleys has been supplying Nottingham since 1880, which ought to be long enough to develop an enviable rapport with the prestigious French properties listed here … except, that is, that the speciality in those days was tobacco, not wine. It is, instead, sheer charm, determined effort and persistence that (since the late 1980s) have helped buyer John Gauntley to build up this impressive list from Alsace and southern France – including JosMeyer, Clos St-Landelin and Zind-Humbrecht. Similarly, châteaux Fortia and de Beaucastel, and domaines Chapoutier, Chave and Jamet, have to be virtually fought for from the Rhône. Prices are reasonable for these fine wines, but be aware that the average spend here is £25 to £30 a bottle. For the quality, they're worth it.

John Gauntley and fellow buyers Chris Goodrum and Victoria Ross still travel to the French wine regions to top up their list, and venture into Italy, Spain and Germany. But, apart from a few other one-offs, that's basically it. These are the wines they're passionate about, and they're content to supply only what they like and are confident in. Would that more merchants were the same. It means we can really trust their choices.

Best Buys

- Domaine Boxler, Pinot Blanc 2000 (Alsace) £8.12
- Domaine Michel Lafarge, Bourgogne Passetoutgrain 1998 (Burgundy) £7.00
- Domaine des Bosquets, Gigondas 1999 (Southern Rhône) £10.50

- Pascal Jamet, St-Joseph Côte Sud 1999 (Northern Rhône) £9.58
- Chapoutier, Coteaux d'Aix, Beautes Domaine Beates 1998 (Provence) £10.50
- Domaine de la Rectorie, Côte de Vermile Argile Blanc 1997 (Southern France) £8.92

Haynes Hanson & Clark

Head office: Sheep Street, Stow-on-the-Wold, Gloucestershire GL54 1AA
Tel: (01451) 870808   Fax: (01451) 870508

25 Eccleston Street, London SW1W 9NP
Tel: 020-7259 0102   Fax: 020-7259 0103
Email: london@hhandc.co.uk/stow@hhandc.co.uk

Closed Sat, Sun (London); Sun (Stow); public holidays, 25–28 Dec **Cards** Yes **Discount** 10% on 1 case, also available on 5+ cases house champagne (Pierre Vaudon) **Order online** No **Delivery** Nationwide service, free within Stow, Central London & for orders of £650+ **Glass hire** £4 per tray of 24 **Tastings and talks** Approx. 15 tastings held annually for account customers in London, Stow, Cheshire, Derbyshire, Hampshire **Newsletter** Monthly offers **Special promotions** Wide range throughout the year

❧ *Burgundy specialist now expanding its list to cover the rest of the world's wine regions* ❧ *Two outlets: in London and Gloucestershire* ❧ *Wines of character and class across the board* ❧ *Plenty of quality sub-£10 choices*

As long as a wine shows real regional character and top, top quality, then, in Haynes Hanson and Clark's book, it doesn't have to be fashionable at all. In fact, the team love anything that's less fashionable, especially if it's made in precious quantities from small parcels of land. This is probably why they love Burgundy, and niche wines such as dry white Bordeaux and Portuguese Dão.

HH&C's list covers more of the world than many might imagine, given its reputation for Burgundy; in fact, only a handful of countries aren't featured (Austria, Argentina and Uruguay, for example). The Rhône, Loire, Alsace and Bordeaux all loom

large, as do one or two (uniquely elegant) wines from the New World. A recent Italian addition, Sassicaia, might be an ultra-fashionable outsider, but here is sourced direct from the estate, so prices are about the best you'll find (£75 a bottle or so).

But it's really the Burgundy listings that keep regular customers returning here – Chandon de Briailles, Domaine Roumier, Comte de Vogüé, Faiveley, Mugneret, Clos du Tart and many other producers, from all the top *grands* and *premiers crus*, and from all the best vintages. Those on the customer mailing lists are invited to the company's sumptuous Burgundy tastings, and *en primeur* and other tempting offers are available.

Best Buys

- Domaine des Forges, Coteaux du Layon St-Aubin la Ligne 2002 (Loire) £8.15
- Charles Koehly et Fils, Pinot Gris St-Hippolyte 2002 (Alsace) £9.90
- Château de Trignon, Gigondas 2001 (Southern Rhône) £12.65

- Isole e Olena, Chianti Classico 2000 (Tuscany) £14.25
- Réserve de Léoville-Barton 1997 (Bordeaux) £17.15
- Domaine Chandon de Briailles, Les Lavières, Savigny-lès-Beaune *premier cru* 2000 (Burgundy) £17.20

Jeroboams

See listing in London section, page 142

Nickolls & Perks Fine Wines

37 Lower High Street, Stourbridge, West Midlands DY8 1TA
Tel: (01384) 394518   Fax: (01384) 440786
Email: sales@nickollsandperks.co.uk   Website: www.nickollsandperks.co.uk

Closed 25 & 26 Dec, 1 Jan **Cards** Yes **Discount** 5% on 1 unmixed case **Order online** Yes
Delivery Nationwide service, free within 10-mile radius **Glass hire** Free with order **Tastings and talks**
Monthly malt whisky tastings **Newsletter** No **Special promotions** Bin-ends by email, annual sale **£5**

❦ *Specialists in wines from older vintages (almost every twentieth-century vintage is represented)* ❦ *Fine stocks of cellarable Bordeaux, ports, Rhônes and Burgundies* ❦ *Quality across the board* ❦ *'Modern' wines from the New World's top producers* ❦ *Mature vintage champagne dating back to Dom Pérignon 1962*

What's nice about Nickolls & Perks is that the proprietors know the wines first-hand: whatever the quality, they taste a bottle (not yours) before it goes on sale, and provide extensive tasting notes and a recommended drinking time. Even the most illustrious wines on the Bordeaux *en primeur* list have a note by them, right from châteaux Angélus and Ausone to Rauzan-Ségla, Teyssier and Talbot.

Prices only rarely dip below £10 a bottle – and more often hover around the £20 or £30 mark – because quality always comes first if a wine is to develop with age. That's the point about this list: the wines have to be of cellarable quality. And N&P has the ideal site for storage, too, if required: its fifteenth-century, vaulted maturation cellars.

This company has been operating since 1797, and houses stocks of ancient vintages: Bordeaux back to 1940, ports to 1934, Rhône to 1959 and madeira (a virtually indestructable wine) from as early as 1845, as well as one-off bottlings and cases to mark the vintages along the way. Plus there are collectable New World wines, such as Penfold's Grange, Almaviva and Hess Collection, from Australia, Chile and California respectively.

Best Buys

- Château Fourcas-Duprés, Listrac, Médoc 1997 (Bordeaux) £9
- Thelema Estate, Cabernet Sauvignon, Stellenbosch 2000 (South Africa) £15
- Château Nairac, Barsac 1989 (Bordeaux) £15
- Château Frombrauge, St-Emilion 1985 (Bordeaux) £23
- Château de Mont Redon, Châteauneuf-du-Pape 1990 (Southern Rhône) £25
- Jacques Prieur, Clos de Vougeot 1985 (Burgundy) £30

For an explanation of the symbols used at the top of some of the merchant entries, see page 118.

Tanners Wines

Head office: 26 Wyle Cop, Shrewsbury, Shropshire SY1 1XD
Tel: (01743) 234500   Fax: (01743) 234501

4 St Peter's Square, Hereford HR1 2PG
Tel: (01432) 272044   Fax: (01432) 263316

36 High Street, Bridgnorth, Shropshire WV16 4DB
Tel: (01746) 763148   Fax: (01746) 763973

Warehouse Shop: Severn Farm Enterprise Park, Welshpool, Powys SY21 7DF
Tel: (01938) 552542   Fax: (01938) 556565
Email: sales@tanners-wines.co.uk   Website: www.tanners-wines.co.uk

Closed Sun (exc. Dec), public holidays **Cards** Yes **Order online** Yes **Discount** 2.5% on 3+ cases, 5% on 5+ cases, 7.5% on 10+ cases **Delivery** Nationwide service (min. 12 bottles), free for orders of £80+ **Glass hire** Free with order of party drinks **Tastings and talks** Spring, Autumn, corporate & tutored producer tastings **Newsletter** 'Tanners News' published 4 times a year **Special promotions** In-store every 6 weeks

❦ *Wide choice of classic claret vintages and top-of-the range Burgundies*
❦ *Imaginatively chosen wines from even the most unusual regions, including Switzerland, Mexico and Greece* ❦ *Award-winning website* ❦ *Listings from the world's top organic vineyards* ❦ *Extensive selection of vintage port*

France has always been the mainstay of Tanners' wine choices, and the broad spectrum of wines on its list today is all judged against French benchmarks – which, given the top-class Burgundies and Bordeaux on offer, is a pretty good sign for quality (Bonneau du Martray, Méo-Camuzet, Chandon de Briailles, Domaine Leflaive and Etienne Sauzet all make appearances among the Burgundy growers).

This is after all a highly traditional merchant, dating back through four generations of the Tanner family, inhabiting its Dickensian premises in Shrewsbury since 1872, so it's no surprise to see such an emphasis on the likes of claret and port. But the good thing about Tanners is its modern take on doing business.

Claret is made easy by dividing it into 'earlier-drinking châteaux', 'châteaux for long-term ageing' and 'older vintages' (back to 1966 Latour, with 1988 Léoville-Las-Cases and 1982 Mouton-Rothschild along the way). As well as the traditional stuff,

Tanners has a real yen for organic wines – look out for the environmentally friendly wines symbol in the list – and anything else that's different and good. 'Oddments' come in small batches.

The wine list is one of the best-presented, handy little booklets out there, this year more colourful than ever before, with all the helpful codes and useful information you could wish for. There are enticing mixed cases, quarterly newsletters, tastings, winemaker events, and a lively staff who combine youth and enthusiasm and the experience of many decades of family merchanting.

Quality means these wines don't come cheaply (you can't get many for under £5) but there's plenty between £5 and £10, and choices change and evolve continually. Wine buyer James Tanner says that rosé wines and Sauvignon Blanc are showing the most popularity at the moment, but there's plenty else, so why not visit the newly revamped showroom in Shrewsbury to have a look?

(Best Buys overleaf)

Best Buys

- Patrick Ducournau, Domaine Mouréou, Organic Madiran 1999 (South-west France) £6.99
- Jean-Max Roger, Morogues, Le Petit Clos, Menetou-Salon 2002 (Loire) £8.95
- Beerenauslese, Neusiedlersee, Kracher 2002, half bottle (Austria) £9.99

- Eden Valley, Yalumba Viognier 2002 (Australia) £10.40
- Churchill's White Port (Portugal) £10.99
- Paul Jaboulet Aîné, Crozes-Hermitage Blanc, La Mule Blanche 2001 (Northern Rhône) £12
- Turkey Flat Shiraz, Barossa Valley 2000 (Australia) £13.60
- H. Germain, Chassagne-Montrachet Rouge 2000 (Burgundy) £14.80

Weavers of Nottingham

Vintner House, 1 Castle Gate, Nottingham NG1 7AQ
Tel: 0115-958 0922   Fax: 0115-950 8076
Email: weavers@weaverswines.com   Website: www.weaverswines.com

Closed Sun (exc. last 2 before Christmas)   **Cards** Yes   **Order online** Yes   **Discount** 5% on 5–9 cases, 10% on 10+ cases   **Delivery** Nationwide service; free within 40-mile radius of Nottingham, Lincoln, Leicester, Derby, Grantham, Newark (min. 6 bottles)   **Glass hire** 20p per dozen   **Tastings and talks** Various, private or corporate, winemaker & gourmet evenings   **Newsletter** Weekly, online, by post as required   **Special promotions** In-store promotions, bin-end lists & sales   **(£5)**

🍷 *Neat range of interesting wines from around the world* 🍷 *Enthusiastic family business, with helpful staff providing good advice* 🍷 *Sizeable list of half bottles* 🍷 *Range of whiskies and spirits available*

The Trease family is now in its fifth generation here at Weavers. In the past this *Guide* has opined that the trimmings (website, wine list, popular tastings held at the family's Georgian town house) are all shipshape and ready to roll at this merchant, but the wines behind them could do with a bit more 'zest'. At the last review things had improved at Weavers, and this year the same has happened again. Australia, Rhône and New Zealand's wines are now real favourites with the Trease family (with some not-unfashionable wines among them). With these offerings, and those from other regions, they try to run the gamut from affordable house wines (beginning, unfortunately, with some rather dull bottlings) right up to stars such as Opus One (from California – premium New World wines are just as popular as traditional Old World names) and Antinori's Tignanello from Italy. The Treases also like to get hold of different wines such as Banyuls, unusual madeiras and Greek Nemea.

This isn't an enormous selection of wines but it's one that takes in a variety of interests. Customers apparently travel considerable distances to visit Weavers, and now it's easy to see why.

Best Buys

- Three Choirs, Premium Estate 2001 (England) £5.82
- Château Pech Celeyran La Clape, Coteaux du Languedoc 2001 (Languedoc) £5.64
- Boschendal, Cabernet Sauvignon, Coastal Region 2002 (South Africa) £7.41

- Frog's Leap, Sauvignon Blanc, Napa Valley 2002 (California) £13.98
- Jean Marc Brocard, Chablis Premier Cru, Montmains 2000 (Burgundy) £13.04
- Domaine Font de Michelle, Châteauneuf-du-Pape 2000 (Rhône) £14.93

North England

Corkscrew Wines

Arch No. 5, Viaduct Estate, Carlisle, Cumbria CA2 5BN
Tel: (01228) 543033   Fax: (01228) 543033   Email: Corkscrewwines@aol.com

Closed Sun, public holidays   **Cards** Yes   **Discount** Available on 12+ bottles   **Order online** No
Delivery Nationwide service, free within 25-mile radius or for orders of 2+ cases   **Glass hire** Free
Tastings and talks 4 tastings per year plus wine societies   **Newsletter** Yes   **Special promotions** Wines
of the month and special offers £5

🍇 *Extremely well-priced range proving that wines can be adventurous and cheap
at the same time* 🍇 *Growing list covering every major wine region* 🍇 *Especially
fine Spanish collection* 🍇 *Focus on smaller, more interesting producers*

The good (and unusual) thing about
Corkscrew is that it lists plenty of sub-£5
bottles, without stooping to bolster the
collection with brands; some good-value
finds from California are real proof of
intrepid research. Each wine is described
with a handy tasting note, and everything
here – mainly from the world's smaller
producers – is chosen for its 'high ratio of
value for money'.

In the past, Corkscrew hasn't had good
things to say about French wine, but there's
now a small collection of trustworthy (and
noteworthy) Bordeaux producers, and an
adventurous leap into the Mediterranean
parts of the country has resulted in some
imaginatively chosen, well-priced choices.
Burgundy and the Rhône are tackled with
still more confidence, focusing on growers
with quality and tradition at heart. Spain has
also become a bit of a passion.

Enthusiastic proprietor Laurie Turner says
that he's looking to make Portugal and Italy
the next big things, though the latter shows
pretty well already, with a wide selection of
regions, price ranges and styles. Watch out
for good-value wines of the month, and
tempting six-for-£25 offers.

Best Buys

- Negro Amara II Meridione, Puglia 2002 (Italy) £4.99
- Château St-Elizabeth, Grenache/Syrah, Costières de Nîmes 2001 (Languedoc) £4.99
- Cave de Chusclan, Seigneurie de Gicon, Côtes du Rhône-Villages 2002

(Southern Rhône) £5.99
- Clos dels Codols Montsant, nr Priorat 2001 (Spain) £7.99
- Cossart Gordon, five-year-old malmsey (Madeira) £13.99
- Castell del Falset, Tarragona 1998 (Spain) £14.99

D Byrne & Co

Victoria Buildings, 12 King Street, Clitheroe, Lancashire BB7 2EP
Tel: (01200) 423152   Fax: (01200) 423152

Closed Sun, 25 & 26 Dec, Good Fri, Easter Sun & Mon   **Cards** Yes   **Discount** £2 per case   **Delivery**
Nationwide service, free within 50-mile radius (min. 1 case)   **Glass hire** Free with order   **Tastings and
talks** Annual week-long in-store tasting; small in-store private tastings   **Newsletter** No   **Special
promotions** Region-specific mixed case & monthly shop displays £5

🍇 *Amazing selection from both Spain and Portugal* 🍇 *Rare wide choice of
German wines* 🍇 *French wines galore – many at good prices* 🍇 *Top estate wines
from California and Oregon* 🍇 *Beautiful old shop!*

If you had to choose just two or three wine shops to visit in person, this would have to be one of them. In over 125 years of trading this Lancashire family firm has built up a fabulous collection of wines, and it really is something to see such venerable bottles in the shop, which is still kitted out in the original fixtures and fittings. Apart from the wines, there are also weird and wonderful (their description) liqueurs, whiskies, vodkas, brandies and beers.

There's another good reason to get over to Clitheroe, rather than pick up the phone to order. D Byrne does not send out mail-order lists. Customers are welcome to request a specific wine to be delivered by mail, but there is no brochure. You need to know what you want, in other words.

Where to start with such an enormous range? First up is a great and lengthy Iberian collection, from the wines of famous top *bodegas* Muga, La Rioja Alta, Cune and Torres to lesser-known bottles from the regions of Toro, Tarragona, Rías Baixas and Priorat. A particularly comprehensive range from Ribera del Duero includes bottles from star estates Vega Sicilia, Pesquera and Pago de Carraovejas, among others. Portugal receives similar treatment, with plenty of table reds from the Douro, and a host of different grape varieties adding to the appeal.

The French wines are fabulous too, with some very tempting prices. Australia, New Zealand and Chile get a more than fair showing, serious German whites abound, and Italy is stuffed full of gems from producers such as Ca'Dei Frati, Masi, Prunotto and Planeta. The United States section reveals bottles from such reputable and stylish producers as Broadley and Firesteed (Oregon), Clos du Val, Duxoup, Frog's Leap, Qupé and Ridge (California).

Add to all this a wide variety in half bottles, a vast array of single malts and other spirits, one of the best selections of sherry around, and eminently fair pricing.

Best Buys

- Brampton, Sauvignon Blanc, Stellenbosch 2003 (South Africa) £5.89
- Mas Collet Cellar de Capcanes, Tarragona 2000 (Spain), £6.29
- Emilio Lustau, Solera Reserva Los Arcos Dry Amontillado sherry (Spain) £8.89
- Rapaura Road, Craggy Range, Riesling, Marlborough 2003 (New Zealand) £9.99
- Jolivet, Sancerre, Caillottes 2001 (Loire) £11.79
- Quinta do Crasto Reserva, Douro 2001 (Portugal) £13.69
- Pago de Carraovejas, Tinto Reserva, Ribera del Duero 1999 (Spain) £24.19
- Tim Adams, Fergus magnums, Clare Valley 1997 (Australia) £24.99

EWGA

Head office: Challan Hall, Silverdale, Lancashire LA5 0UH
Tel: (01524) 701723   Fax: (01524) 701189

Wine Time, 37 Beetham Road, Milnthorpe, Cumbria LA7 7QN
Tel: (015395) 62030

Wine Time, 95 Causeway Lane, Rufford, Ormskirk, Lancashire L40 1SL
Tel: (01704) 821151
Email: deryn@ewga.net

Closed Sun, 25 Dec, 1 Jan **Cards** Yes **Discount** No **Order online** No **Delivery** Nationwide service (min. 1 case), free within Lancashire North & Cumbria **Glass hire** Free **Tastings and talks** Tutored tastings & in-store tastings **Newsletter** bimonthly **Special promotions** Ongoing £5

🍷 *Long list of half bottles and of dessert wines* 🍷 *Handy everyday wines alongside famous-name clarets and top champagnes* 🍷 *Full range of prices, but special emphasis on sub-£10 wines*

EWGA's list does not, as a rule, offer an adventurous range, nor a very extensive one, but the wines stocked are from reliable producers. Newcomers should visit one of the two Wine Time shops in order to really get a grip on this collection. The wine list might serve as a handy reminder, but lacks enough meaty description. You'd want to know more, for a start, about the Vergelegen and Hamilton Russell wines from South Africa or the Oregon Pinot Noirs and the Austrian Grüner Veltliners. The illustrious list of Bordeaux merits more discussion – especially because some of the wines come from classic old vintages.

Apart from the dull presentation of the wine list, the other snag here is that countries listed by Adrian Moeckell and team as specialities (Australia, Burgundy and the Rhône) come up with wines that are special enough at the top level (Grange from Australia, Chapoutier's wines from the Rhône, for example), but offer most bottles from centres of mass production. Where are the intrepid producers who make fewer, but more interesting, wines in the middle ranges?

One good point though: EWGA has added a bonded storage warehouse to its services – the only one in the north-west to be specially set up for wines and spirits.

Best Buys

- Louis Perdrier Brut, Sparkling Burgundy NV (Burgundy) £3.85
- Casa Lapostolle Sauvignon Blanc, 2002 (Chile) £4.75
- Vasse Felix, Cabernet/Merlot 2001 (Western Australia) £7.75

- Meerlust, Chardonnay, Stellenbosch 1998 (South Africa) £9.50
- Tokaji Aszú 4 Puttonyos, 1993 (Hungary) £11.95
- Viña Real Gran Reserva, Alavesa, Rioja 1994 (Spain) £13.95

Great Northern Wine

The Warehouse, Blossomgate, Ripon, North Yorkshire HG4 2AJ
Tel: (01765) 606767   Fax: (01765) 609151
Email: info@greatnorthernwine.com

Closed Sun, public holidays, 25 & 26 Dec **Cards** Yes **Order online** No **Discount** 10% on 12+ bottles **Delivery** Nationwide service, free within 25-mile radius **Glass hire** No **Tastings and talks** Tastings with meal, fun events, general talks on various wines **Newsletter** No

🍇 *Wide selection of well-priced wines from Italy, Burgundy and Spain* 🍇 *Good Australian and South African choices* 🍇 *Unusually good Portugese selection*

Wine buyer Mark Ryan and his team do a great job of sourcing sensibly priced wines, with all the world's major wine regions covered. Careful Australian choices bring in a variety of different grapes (Verdelho, Malbec, Tempranillo and Chambourcin being some less-usual ones) and regions (including Orange and Langhorne Creek), but Mark reports that his customers are showing a big swing in preference back to Old World wines because of their perceived quality and value for money. So the wide range of Portuguese wines (notably the regions of the Douro, Bairrada, Dão and

Alentejo), although an unusual focus, will undoubtedly prove very popular.

Great Northern Wine underwent a management buyout in the Summer of 2003, so the wine list may yet see a further shake-up. If so, it would be good to see some of the other regions tackled with the same enthusiasm as Portugal, including a few smaller, more quality-conscious producers. What would also be encouraging is a little more detail and description brought into the wine list, so customers could see exactly why Mark chooses the wines he does.

(Best Buys overleaf)

Best Buys

- Santa Rosa, Sangiovese/Bonarda 2001 (Argentina) £4.99
- Somerbosch, Cinsaut/Cabernet 2002 (South Africa) £4.99
- Niepoort, Redoma Rosé 2001 (Portugal) £9.35

- Ruggeri, Prosecco Brut sparkling wine (Italy) £9.59
- Château de Lastours, La Signature de Terroir, country wine 2000 (France) £12.65
- Vaudoisey-Crueusefond, Volnay 1999 (Burgundy) £14.99

The Halifax Wine Company

18 Prescott Street, Halifax, West Yorkshire HX1 2LG
Tel: (01422) 256333
Email: andy@halifaxwinecompany.com   Website: www.halifaxwinecompany.com

Closed Sun, Mon, Tue after bank holiday Mon, 1st week Jan and Aug **Cards** Yes **Discount** Available on 1 case **Order online** Yes **Delivery** Nationwide service, free within Calderdale **Glass hire** Free with order **Tastings and talks** In-store tastings, annual pre-Christmas tasting **Newsletter** Quarterly **Special promotions** Various £5

❦ Fabulously wide array of wines from around the world ❦ Particularly good collections from Spain, New Zealand, Argentina and Chile ❦ Many sumptuous sweet wines ❦ Plenty of unusual grape varieties and regions ❦ Classic Bordeaux, Burgundy, Rioja and Chianti in the upper price brackets

Andy Paterson and his wife Karen opened the doors of the Halifax Wine Company for business in August 2001, and have already built up one of the most amazingly wide-ranging collections of wine in the country, with the list expanding from 400 to 700 wines over the past year.

The Australian collection includes some zesty Rieslings, and Shiraz in a range of prices and styles from across the country; Italy has plenty of newly prestigious wines from the south (and more besides). The Chile and Argentina options are wider-ranging than most; there are big, gutsy Rhônes; fine Burgundies (many stunning 1996s); Bordeaux from the affordable to wish-list bottlings; a wide selection of

Alsace; and an unusually substantial collection from Spain. This hedonists' list is filled with classic wine, prize vintages and collectable oddities, and a fantastic assortment of sweet wines focuses on some particularly fine Hungarian Tokajis.

Andy reports that Chardonnay sales have dropped by 90 per cent over the last year and that 'customers are looking for something different and stimulating'. His offbeat collection of Austrian and Greek wines, Jurançon, and Portugese Bairrada and Dão probably help here.

Just one quibble: the California and sparkling wine sections of the list could be filled out a little to balance the breadth of the rest of the collection.

Best Buys

- Nieto y Senetiner, Reserva, Merlot, Mendoza 2001 (Argentina) £5.95
- Stanton & Killeen, Rutherglen Muscat NV half bottles (Australia) £9.95
- Sepp Moser, Grüner Veltliner Breiter Rain, Kremstal 2002 (Austria) £12.95

- Kuentz-Bas, Riesling Grand Cru Pfersigberg 1998 (Alsace) £13.95
- Mills Reef, Elspeth Single Vineyard Syrah, Hawke's Bay 2000 (New Zealand) £13.95
- Marqués de Villamagna, Iverus Gran Reserva, Rioja 1995 (Spain) £15.45

Hoults Wine Merchants

10 Viaduct Street, Huddersfield, West Yorkshire HD1 6AJ
Tel: (01484) 510700   Fax: (01484) 510712

5 Cherry Tree Walk, The Calls, Leeds LS2 7EB
Tel: 0113-245 3393   Fax: 0113-246 7173
Email: rob@hoults-winemerchants.co.uk

Closed Sun, public holidays (exc. May day) **Cards** Yes **Discount** 10% on 1 mixed case **Order online** No **Delivery** Locally only, free service **Glass hire** Free **Tastings and talks** No **Newsletter** By email only, includes exclusive offers **Special promotions** Ongoing **£5**

🍷 *Well-priced French country wines* 🍷 *Some gems from the Loire and Rhône*
🍷 *Solid Spanish red range* 🍷 *Top New Zealand whites* 🍷 *Fine set of sparklers*

Rob Hoult's retail 'experiments' are at an end, he says, and he is now concentrating on 'what we do best', which is to sell wines that he believes in and that he can hold in volume and offer at good case price – which translates into a wide range of bottles mainly costing between £5 and £10 that are stocked in quantity. 'Our range is aimed squarely at the consumer and not at other merchants or wine critics, and as such it probably looks less star-studded than most lists, but our wines are for selling and drinking, not looking at and dusting,' he says, firmly.

Quality wines from such reliable sources of delicious drinking as Alsace's Turckheim, New Zealand's Villa Maria, Chile's Montes and Concha y Toro, and Australia's Brown Brothers and Penfold's bear witness to Rob's aims. And despite his protests, it's still possible to spot some highly fashionable (and desirable) labels here – Cloudy Bay, Bonny Doon, La Rioja Alta, Guigal's Condrieu, Krug champagne, and seven vintages of Château Musar for starters. All in all, it should certainly be possible to start off buying fairly humble wine from most quarters, and build up steadily towards those more costly cult labels. Something you certainly can't say about every wine merchant. If you can't find time to pop into the Huddersfield shop, there's a customer club by email.

Best Buys
- Lazy Lizard, Sauvignon Blanc 2003 (France) £4.49
- Alasia Langhe, Nebbiolo Piedmont, 2001 (Italy) £5.99
- Quady, Elysium Black Muscat half bottle 2000 (California) £7.49
- Trinity Hill, Chardonnay, Hawke's Bay 2000 (New Zealand) £8.99
- Château de Tracy, Pouilly-Fumé 2002 (Loire) £16.99
- La Rioja Alta, Gran Reserva Rioja, 1994 (Spain) £25.65

Martinez Fine Wine

35 The Grove, Ilkley, West Yorkshire LS29 9NJ
Tel: (01943) 603241   Fax: (0870) 922 3940
Email: editor@martinez.co.uk   Website: www.martinez.co.uk

Closed Sun, 25 & 26 Dec **Cards** Yes **Discount** 5% on 6 bottles, 10% on orders of £150+ **Order online** Yes **Delivery** Nationwide service, free within 20-mile radius (min. 1 case) **Glass hire** Free with order **Tastings and talks** Tutored tastings for clubs & societies & 'call my bluff' evenings **Newsletter** 4–6 times per year **Special promotions** Regular through newsletter & local paper **£5**

🍷 *Hoards of bargain wines overlooked by supermarkets* 🍷 *No brands, just regional wines of real quality* 🍷 *Plenty of trade-up options from Bordeaux, top-class Australian estates, California and the Rhône* 🍷 *Excellent website*

Martinez determinedly stocks 'anything but brands' – but also achieves the near-impossible feat of starting its range at a ridiculously low £3.25 a bottle and keeping it there long enough to quench the thirsts of local bargain hunters. There's no need to buy supermarket wines when you can shop at Martinez: browse through this merchant's excellent website (search by country and region, by grape variety, by price, or by A–Z of producers) and put together a case for delivery, or mug up on prices, or read the Noble Rot newsletter. Not only are there, for example, at least 18 French wines on sale at under £5 a bottle, but there are pages of

wines at under £15 too. The interesting Australian selection is well supplied in this respect, with Shaw & Smith, Mount Horrocks, Shadowfax, Turkey Flat and many other quality estates represented.

Most of the Martinez wines are selected with an eye for value rather than luxury – although Château Mouton-Rothschild's 2001 vintage, priced at £159, might disprove this – but there are also plenty of carefully chosen oddity wines here.

Things have changed a bit at Martinez; there is now only one main branch open, in Ilkley, but this still remains everything that a small independent merchant should be.

Best Buys

- Bodegas Olarra, Otoñal Blanco, White Rioja 2003 (Spain) £4.75
- Pierre Boniface, Roussette de Savoies 2003 (France) £7.99
- Mas de Fournel, Cuvée Classique, Pic St-Loup 2002 (Languedoc) £8.75

- Mount Langi Ghiran, Organic Riesling, Victoria 2003 (Australia) £9.99
- Miranda, Sparkling Shiraz, Barossa Valley 1994 (Australia) £12.99
- Château Léoville-Barton, Médoc 1998 (Bordeaux) £18.99

Portland Wine Company

Head office: 16 North Parade, Sale M33 3JS
Tel: 0161-962 8752   Fax: 0161-905 1291

152a Ashley Road, Hale, Altrincham, Cheshire WA15 9SA   Tel: 0161-928 0357

82 Chester Road, Macclesfield, Cheshire SK11 8DL   Tel: (01625) 616147

45–47 Compstall Road, Marplebridge, Stockport, Cheshire SK6 5HG
Tel: 0161-426 0155
Email: enquiries@portlandwine.co.uk   Website: www.portlandwine.co.uk

Closed 25 & 26 Dec, 1 Jan **Cards** Yes **Discount** 5% on 6 bottles, 10% on 12 bottles **Order online** Yes **Delivery** Nationwide service, free within 10-mile radius **Glass hire** Free with order **Tastings and talks** Sat in-store and tutored tastings at Hale **Newsletter** 4 per year **Special promotions** Various, via newsletter **(£5)**

🍇 *Good, all-round merchant accessible through regular bulletins and an easy-to-handle website* 🍇 *One of the best Chilean wine ranges in the country* 🍇 *Spain's new-wave red-wine regions all represented*

The Portland team are as determined as ever that their wines should be a gamut-running lot, covering cheap starter-point wines right up to top-end bottlings – the best the appellation can provide. Most regions include good, solid examples from different *terroirs*, without anything too adventurous (Australia, Burgundy, South Africa). Others get a little more daring: champagne begins with £14

Baron de Beaupré NV and builds up to 1959 vintage Drappier Carte d'Or – a vintage to invite curiosity. Chilean choices include quality wines from Montes, Seña and Casa Lapostolle, and cool-climate bottles from the of-the-moment Casablanca region. The extensive Spanish range covers just about everywhere, taking in fashionable Costers del Segre, Priorat, Ribera del Duero and Rías

Baixas. And Bordeaux, impressively, runs from the modest to the majestic without inundating the visitor with choice but picking out some interesting clarets from the 1980s and 1990s along the way, with some barely affordable wish-list options at the end.

Portland's increasing Internet presence will help those wanting to mail-order, as there's no specific wine list to browse through by page. And Mancunians should watch out for the tutored tastings and wine courses: if they're set up with the same clarity as the wine selection, they'll be a good learning ground for sure.

Best Buys

- Muscadet Sèvre-et-Maine 'Fief de la Brie' 2001, Bonhomme (Loire) £4.99
- Concha y Toro, Sauvignon Blanc 2003 (Chile) £4.99
- Vida Nova, Algarve 2002 (Portugal) £8.75

- Lustau, Solera Reserva Puerto Fino sherry (Spain) £8.75
- Gregoletto, Prosecco Brut sparkling (Italy) £9.49
- Seghesio, Zinfandel, Sonoma 2000 (California) £13.99

Vinceremos Wines & Spirits

74 Kirkgate, Leeds LS2 7DJ
Tel: 0113-244 0002   Fax: 0113-288 4566
Email: info@vinceremos.co.uk   Website: www.vinceremos.co.uk

Closed Sat (exc. Nov/Dec), Sun, public holidays **Cards** Yes **Discount** 5% on 5+ cases, 10% on 10+ cases **Order online** Yes **Delivery** Nationwide service (min. 1 case), free within central Leeds **Glass hire** Free **Tastings and talks** Available, phone for details **Newsletter** Occasional **Special promotions** Occasional (£5)

🏆 *Specialist in organic and biodynamic wines* 🏆 *Full array of organic grape varieties from Bonterra, California* 🏆 *Increasing global choice – more this year from Italy and the quality French appellations* 🏆 *Most wines between £5 and £10* 🏆 *Plenty of popular choices from Mediterranean France*

Vinceremos now has 20 years' experience of trading organic wines, and this shows in the scope and quality throughout its selection. That the range has increased is not only testimony to the team's intrepid investigation into all things organic, but to the number of growers around the world who are adopting holistic techniques for the long-term health of their vineyards – and the long-term flavour of their wines.

As mentioned in previous reviews, every wine listed here is either organic, biodynamic or made with holistic vineyard management in mind. The name of the company, Vinceremos, comes from the Spanish *venceremos* 'we shall overcome': and so far it has been totally successful in overcoming any prejudice and, more recently, any quality blips. The Organic Wine Club listings for 2004 show a dramatic increase in quality. (Vinceremos administers the Club on behalf

of HDRA, the UK organic organisation.) Not only is this a wider and broader list than ever before, but the wines come from an increasing number of exciting appellations (Gigondas, Vacqueyras in the Rhône, Saumur-Champigny and Chinon from the Loire, St-Emilion in Bordeaux for a start). Even England (with two vineyards) makes an appearance, as does Morroccan wine.

It is the Italian section, however, that is growing fastest of all, with exciting wines from the south (the 'new-wave' old grapes Nero d'Avola, Primitivo, Montepulciano and Aglianico are all in there), plus Chianti choices and even Barolo and Amarone from the misty north. Spain is following fast, with no less than seven Riojas on offer, and more from the newer Spanish DOs. In short, filling a mixed case from this tasty selection is now not only a responsible thing to do, but it is easy too.

Best Buys

- Era, Nero d'Avola 2003 (Italy) £4.49
- La Nature, La Riojana, Torrontés 2003 (Argentina) £4.69
- Muscat (sweet wine), Bonterra, half bottles 2000 (California) £4.99
- Achard Vincent, Clairette de Die Brut NV (Languedoc) £8.59

- Clos Montirius, biodynamic Vacqueyras 2000 (Southern Rhône) £9.99
- Château Barrail des Graves, Cuvée des Deux Milles 2000 (Bordeaux) £12.49
- Chianti Classico Riserva, San Michele DOCG 1999 (Italy) £12.99
- José Ardinat, Carte d'Or, Brut sparkling NV (Champagne) £14.99

The Wright Wine Company

The Old Smithy, Raikes Road, Skipton, North Yorkshire BD23 1NP
Tel: (01756) 700886   Fax: (01756) 798580
Email: bob@wineandwhisky.co.uk   Website: www.wineandwhisky.co.uk

Closed Sun (exc. Dec) **Cards** Yes **Discount** 5% on 1 mixed case, 8–10% on 1 unmixed case **Order online** No **Delivery** Locally only (35-mile radius) for wine, free service; nationwide service for whisky only, max. 6 bottles **Glass hire** Free with reasonable order **Tastings and talks** No **Newsletter** No **Special promotions** Various, some promoting regions **(£5)**

🍇 *A wonderful array of premium Australian red and white wines* 🍇 *Alsace taken seriously with a fuller range than most* 🍇 *Chilean section keeps up with the times* 🍇 *Wide range of large-format and half bottles*

This is a long list, and in places it really excels. Take Australia, for example – one of buyers Bob Wright and Julian Kaye's greatest strengths. There are so many top labels from Down Under here that it is hard to know where to start: listed under 'Reds' are, among others, Heggies, Mount Langi Ghiran, Charles Melton, Jim Barry and Yarra Yering, while 'Whites' draw in the likes of Shaw & Smith, Giaconda, Vasse Felix and Plantagenet. It's certainly refreshing (in more ways than one) to see such a broad range of names after scanning doz   of lists that feature the same old big brands.

So, Wright Wine is good at Australia, but it also shines in New Zealand, Chile, Spain, Alsace (where you will find JosMeyer, Mann, Trimbach and Ostertag) and for fizz, in the shape of sparklers (some from England), champagnes and top names in

Cava. Bob and Julian are keen on large-format bottles too - there are plenty of magnums, jeroboams and even bigger bottles – and for those who prefer smaller packages, their range includes an astonishing 120 wines available in half bottles too, one of the best collections around. Among the more obscure sections, it is heartening to see Greece getting a look-in, Canada's dessert wines making an appearance and several Tokajis from Hungary. Malt whisky is taken very seriously indeed here, with 10 pages of the list devoted to it.

All in all, this is a list to linger over. Even for those who want a bargain, there's plenty at around £5 as well. The list is not annotated, but Bob says that tasting notes on display in the shop, plus regular wine samplings in-store, have helped improve sales. With wines like these, it's hardly surprising.

Best Buys

- Domaine Albert Mann, Riesling 1999 (Alsace) £8.15
- Casa Lapostolle, Merlot, Casablanca Valley 2002 (Chile) £9.15
- Jackson Estate, Sauvignon Blanc, Marlborough 2003 (New Zealand) £9.75

- Rockford, Riesling, Eden Valley 2000 (Australia) £10.50
- Nyetimber, Classic Blend Brut 1994 (England) £16.95
- Lenswood Vineyards, Knappstein Pinot Noir, Adelaide Hills 2002 (Australia) £19.50

Scotland

Cockburns of Leith

7 Devon Place, Haymarket, Edinburgh EH12 5HJ
Tel: 0131-346 1113   Fax: 0131-313 2607

382 Morningside Road, Edinburgh EH10 5HX
Tel: 0131-446 0700
Email: sales@winelist.co.uk   Website: www.winelist.co.uk

Closed Sun **Cards** Yes **Discount** Not available **Order online** Yes **Delivery** Nationwide service, free in and around Edinburgh (min. 3 cases) or for 3+ cases **Glass hire** Free **Tastings and talks** Small groups & for businesses on a corporate level **Newsletter** No **Special promotions** Available, phone for details **£5**

🍷 *Good-value selection from around the world* 🍷 *Exciting range of well-priced sparklers* 🍷 *Australia list worth a serious browse* 🍷 *New Zealand represented well* 🍷 *Good choice of sherries and madeiras*

Despite a very recent management buyout, it's business as usual at Cockburns, which this *Guide* has recommended before now for its 'reliable, well-priced wines from just about everywhere'. This 200-year-old merchant has particular strengths in ranges from Bordeaux, Burgundy and Australia, but this is a long list, and there's something from all major wine-producing regions of the world.

Or perhaps that should be 'business looks better than usual'. The outstanding wide variety of inexpensive bottles, many under £5, is a rare commodity for an independent merchant. Among these 'cheapies' that give you change for a fiver are a Prosecco, an Australian Gewurz-Verdelho, Spanish *rosado*, plenty of South African, Chilean and Australian reds, and more reds from the southern parts of both France and Italy. These are usually exactly the styles of wine that perform well at the cheaper end of the price spectrum, so it's encouraging to see so many listed. Incidentally, there is a New

Zealand Sauvignon Blanc from the reputable producer St Clair at just over £5.80 which must be worth a try. If you join the company's free wine club, there's an extra 10 per cent off most bottles and a chance to find out about tasting events.

Finer wines creep in here and there, especially in the classic French sections of the list. The sweet wines look interesting, and include California, French, Australian, German and Hungarian options. Sherry is well represented, with bottles from González Byass, Williams & Humbert, Domecq and Barbadillo, and there are 12 madeiras. Spirits too are well worth a good browse, not only for the outstanding malt whiskies (naturally, in this neck of the woods), but also for the eaux de vie and the liqueurs.

It would be good to see some parts of the list extended, and this is now highly likely, as Cockburns is clearly in the throes of some dynamic changes. A merchant to keep a close eye on as it moves into a new phase.

Best Buys

- Spago NV, Prosecco di Conegliano Frizzante, Veneto (Italy) £4.63
- Echeverria, Merlot Reserve 2001 (Chile) £5.61
- Tuatara Bay, Sauvignon Blanc, Marlborough 2003 (New Zealand) £5.82
- Kuentz Bas, Riesling Cuvée Tradition 2001 (Alsace) £6.32
- Ironstone, Zinfandel 1999 (Western Australia), £6.89
- Hamilton Russell, Chardonnay, Walker Bay 2002 (South Africa) £11.71
- JP Robert, Blanc de Blanc (Champagne) £12.99
- Tokaji, Aszú 5 Puttonyos 1993 (Hungary) £16.17

Corney & Barrow

See listing in London section, page 139

Raeburn Fine Wines

Head office: 21–23 Comely Bank Road, Edinburgh EH4 1DS
Tel: 0131-343 1159   Fax: 0131-332 5166

Tastings only: The Vaults, 4 Giles Street, Leith, Edinburgh EH6 6DJ
Tel: 0131-343 1159
Email: sales@raeburnfinewines.com   Website: www.raeburnfinewines.com

Closed 25 Dec, 1 & 2 Jan **Cards** Yes **Discount** 5% on 1 unmixed case, 2.5% on 1 mixed case
Order online No **Delivery** Nationwide service, free within city of Edinburgh (min. 12 mixed bottles) or for
4+ cases **Glass hire** Free with order **Tastings and talks** By request and with visiting winemakers
Newsletter No **Special promotions** En-primeur & special offers, phone for details **(£5)**

🍇 *Extensive Burgundy collection* 🍇 *No shortage of top Bordeaux available*
en primeur 🍇 *Impressive collection of Austrian wines* 🍇 *Edinburgh wine vaults*
well worth a visit (or try the website)

Ask for a Raeburn wine list and all you'll get
is a temporary snapshot, downloaded from the
website – do this yourself and it'll be more up
to date. The best way to get to know these
wines, as has always been the case, is to attend
a tasting at Raeburn's Edinburgh vaults.
Wherever you travel from, you won't regret it.

'We look for the best, and like to take on
young producers who are on the way up,'
advises self-taught Kenyan wine lover Zubair
Mohamed. But with that, he also takes some
pride in stocking sensationally good (and
eminently recognisable) names such as Henri
Gouges, Domaine Clos du Tart and de

Vogüé, among the Burgundies, and is strong
in domaine-bottled Rhône and Italian
wines. There's no doubt that Zubair
certainly knows what he's doing when it
comes to supplying top-class classic wines.

Apart from the obvious, Austria is a
confident speciality here; the Languedoc,
California and New Zealand (this isn't just
Old World territory) are also available in
strong selections.

Much of the stock costs more than £20 a
bottle (no surprise there, given the quality)
but there are plenty of interesting finds for
under a tenner too.

Best Buys

- Jean Orliac, Domaine de l'Hortus, Pic
  St-Loup 1996 (Coteaux du Languedoc)
  £6.99
- Bodega Infinitus, Malbec/Syrah 1999
  (Argentina) £8.99
- Luigi Dessilani e Figlio, Roero Arneis,
  Vino Bianco da Tavola 1996 (Italy)
  £9.75

- Emmanuel Reynaud, Château des
  Tours, Vacqueyras 2001 (Southern
  Rhône) £10.80
- Weingut Fritz Haag, Brauneberger
  Juffer Sonnenuhr Riesling Auslese
  1992 (Germany) £13.99
- Pelorus Brut sparkling, Cloudy Bay,
  Marlborough 1995 (New Zealand)
  £14.99

Specialist Award winners are listed on pages 17 and 18.

Valvona & Crolla

19 Elm Row, Edinburgh EH7 4AA
Tel: 0131-556 6066   Fax: 0131-556 1668

VinCaffè, The Walk, Edinburgh EH7 4AA
Tel: 0131-556 6066
Email: wine@valvonacrolla.co.uk   Website: www.valvonacrolla.com

Closed 25 & 26 Dec, 1 & 2 Jan **Cards** Yes **Discount** Available on collected orders only; 7% on 12+ bottles, 10% on 36+ bottles **Order online** Yes **Delivery** Nationwide service, free for orders of £125+ or of £50+ within Edinbrugh **Glass hire** Free with collected orders **Tastings and talks** Free tastings every Sat, tutored producer & themed tastings **Newsletter** Annual events list **Special promotions** Selected seasonal 6- & 12-bottle case offers

🍇 *Great range from smaller Italian wineries* 🍇 *Top Tuscan reds including many Super-Tuscans* 🍇 *Comprehensive trawl through Piedmont's best estates* 🍇 *Sweet and sparkling Italian bottles* 🍇 *Distinguished choices from other countries, especially Australia*

It must be great to live close to this lovely, characterful deli, piled high as it is with wonderful foodstuffs and wine. The business was founded in Edinburgh in the 1860s, and has been on the same premises since 1934. The current managers, John Ritchie and Philip Contini (a grandson of one of the founders), have strived hard to maintain an old-fashioned, authentic appeal while introducing new ideas and keeping the range of fine wines up to date. The latest launch is a new wine bar and café called VinCaffè, opening in Edinburgh in autumn 2004.

Back to the vintner's side of things. The focus is on Italy here, and the range is notable for the comprehensive number of smaller estates represented – from Abruzzo and Basilicata through to Umbria and Veneto. Wines from Piedmont are particularly impressive. Italian dessert wines, sparklers both sweet and dry, and grappa feature too.

The bottles are not exclusively Italian at V&C. There are wines from many sectors of the globe, notably distinguished selections from Australia, New Zealand and Spain, a worthy choice from South America, and fine malt whiskies. And some more surprising entries appear on the list – such as Austrian whites, Canadian Icewine and Hungarian Tokaji. Or rather, that would be surprising for many Italian delis, but perhaps not here.

Best Buys

- A Mano, Primitivo di Puglia 2002 (Italy) £6.99
- Planeta, La Segreta Bianco 2002 (Sicily) £7.99
- Cape Mentelle, Shiraz, Margaret River 2000 (Australia) £10.95
- Aldo Vajra, Dolcetto d'Alba, Piedmont 2002 (Italy) £11.95
- Isole e Olena, Vin Santo half bottle, Tuscany 1997 (Italy) £27.95
- Aldo Conterno, Barolo Bussia Soprana, Piedmont 1998 (Italy) £45

To find a wine merchant with a particular strength in wines from a certain country or region, see the regional chapters in the 'Best wine-producing countries' section.

Villeneuve Wines

1 Venlaw Court, Peebles EH45 8AE
Tel: (01721) 722500   Fax: (01721) 729922

82 High Street, Haddington EH41 3ET
Tel: (01620) 822224   Fax: (01620) 822279

49A Broughton Street, Edinburgh EH1 3RJ
Tel: 0131-558 8441   Fax: 0131-558 8442
Email: wines@villeneuvewines.com   Website: www.villeneuvewines.com

Closed 25 & 26 Dec, 1 & 2 Jan **Cards** Yes **Discount** 5% on 1 case **Order online** Yes **Delivery** Nationwide service, free within Peebles/Haddington/Edinburgh & for orders of £100+ **Glass hire** Free **Tastings and talks** Large annual tasting in November, occasionally others **Newsletter** Occasional **Special promotions** Various, phone for details **£5**

🍇 *Stunning range of Italian bottlings* 🍇 *Quality wine choices from across the world, even at basic price levels* 🍇 *Proudly listing individual, more unusual wines* 🍇 *Imaginative options from Australia, California and South Africa* 🍇 *Spirits, liqueurs and whiskies on offer*

This ambitious young wine merchant is determined to outshine its competitors by providing a more interesting, more adventurous and more widely sourced list of wines that gets better every year. Flicking through the many pages of its hefty brochure, it's easy to see how wine buyer Kenneth Vannan and his team are going from strength to strength.

This range will appeal both to drinkers of fine wine and to those scouting for something more out of the ordinary but at an everyday price. Take the southern French selection, for example. Not only are there fascinating Jurançons to be had for less than £10, but Villeneuve also explores the realms of fashionable Château Puech-Haut and Château de Beck from the Coteaux du Languedoc (up to £20 and £30 a bottle). Everyday Bordeaux start at £3 a bottle and climb to over £50 for classed-growth clarets such as St Estèphe's Calon-Ségur. And champagne comes in for as little as £15 (for Champagne Victor, still the real thing!), running the gamut up to £300 for a bottle of Krug Collection Vintage 1981 – and no, that's not a jeroboam or Methuselah, but an everyday 75-cl bottle!

Italian choices are some of the most mind-blowing of all. Again, starting at around the £5/£6 mark for Tedeschi Soave and Bardolino, options take in Allegrini's Amarone della Valpolicella (£35), Aldo Conterno's spectacular Barolo Granbussia (£100), Super-Tuscans Sassicaia (£100) and Suolo (£80), and fashionable Aglianico del Vulture from Basilicata in the deep south (£32). The California choices are equally illustrious, including Duckhorn, Stag's Leap Wine Cellars, Atlas Peak, Darioush, and (hard-to-get-hold-of) Joseph Phelps' wines from the Napa Valley. Plus the best from Australia and South Africa too.

In short, Kenneth is happy to depart from the norm with this list (a rare enough trait in a wine merchant these days) because he is confident that he will spot good winemaking when he sees it. His ever-more adventurous customers obviously trust his judgement too.

Sherry, port and madeira, as well as other liqueurs, are interwoven through the list. And (this is Scotland after all) there's a fine selection of malt whisky to finish off with.

Best Buys

- Château Ksara, La Reserve de Couvent, Bekaa Valley 1997 (Lebanon) £8
- Quinta do Portal Tinta, Douro red, 2000 (Portugal) £9
- Thelema Sauvignon Blanc, Stellenbosch 2003 (South Africa) £12
- Seghesio Arneis, Healdsburg, Sonoma, 2001 (California) £14
- Cloudy Bay, Pelorus sparkling, Marlborough 1999 (New Zealand) £16
- Carmignano Villa di Capezzana, Tuscany 1999 (Italy) £17
- Henriques & Henriques, 10-year-old Malmsey (Madeira) £18
- Mount Langi Ghiran, Cabernet Sauvignon/Merlot, Victoria 1997 (Australia) £18

Wine Raks

21 Springfield Road, Aberdeen AB15 7RJ
Tel: (01224) 311460   Fax: (01224) 312186
Email: enq@wineraks.com   Website: www.wineraks.com

Closed Sun, 25 & 26 Dec, 1 & 2 Jan **Cards** Yes **Discount** 5% on 1 mixed case **Order online** Yes **Delivery** Nationwide service, free within Aberdeen for 1+ case **Glass hire** Free with order **Tastings and talks** 2 large, ticketed tastings per year (May and Nov), group tastings on request **Newsletter** No **Special promotions** Quarterly seasonal selection cases

🍷 *Plenty of interesting sub-£5 wines* 🍷 *Wide range of Bordeaux châteaux from 1990s vintages* 🍷 *Individual Australian estates and quirky sparkling red wines* 🍷 *Oddities like Canadian Icewine and Indian sparkling*

This talented Aberdeen merchant offers three different approaches to wine: first up are budget bottles, with plenty of appealing sub-£5 wines, particularly from southern France. Second, it takes a top-down approach, bringing in the elite châteaux of Bordeaux for real buffs (and those with big budgets), notably the spectacular 1990s selection from the likes of châteaux Beychevelle, Angélus, Troplong-Mondot and Chasse-Spleen. And thirdly, it lists anything odd, quirky or a little bit different, to keep its customers guessing. Red sparkling wines (Australian mostly), traditional sherries from Spain, niche wines from South-west France, and Indian Omar Khayyam Brut sparkling are examples from this latter camp – and at

prices that reach into the 'budget' ranges too.

So hats off to Wine Raks for keeping things so lively and affordable. This merchant may have honed its speciality areas (Australia, Bordeaux) rather than keeping things consistently fabulous, but there are plenty of first-class surprises here: witness a handful of top-quality German bottles, Huët's magnificent Loire wines, unusual Burgundy growers to try out, champagne varying from nice-and-affordable (£12.66 a bottle) L Aubry et Fils Brut Classic up to Krug Rosé at £126.06, broad-ranging Italian choices, port going back to 1955, and individual Australian labels Charles Melton, Ninth Island, Gary Crittenden, Mount Langi Ghiran and Penfold's Grange.

Best Buys

- Cave Les Vignerons de Castelnau de Guers, Picpoul de Pinet Terres Cotières 2001 (Languedoc) £4
- Casa Filgueira, Vinedos y Bodega Filgueira, Tannat 1999 (Uruguay) £4.78
- Lustau, Puerto Fino Solera Reserva, dry sherry (Spain) £7.78
- Taltarni, Brut Tache, Victoria & Tasmania 2000 (Australia) £7.93
- La Dame de Montrose (second wine of Château Montrose), St-Estèphe 1998 (Bordeaux) 13.09
- Heathcote, Curagee Shiraz, Victoria 1998 (Australia) £13.88

191

Wales

Ballantynes Wine Merchants

3 Westgate, Cowbridge, Vale of Glamorgan CF71 7AQ
Tel: (01446) 774840   Fax: (01446) 775253

211–217 Cathedral Road, Cardiff CF11 9PP
Tel: 029-2022 2202   Fax: 029-2022 2112
Email: enq@ballantynes.co.uk   Website: www.ballantynes.co.uk

Closed Sun, public holidays   **Cards** Yes   **Discount** 8% on 1 case   **Order online** No   **Delivery** Nationwide service, free for 1+ cases within Cardiff, Cowbridge, Bridgford   **Glass hire** Free with orders of 12+ bottles   **Tastings and talks** Regular in-store tastings every 4 weeks, occasional tutored tastings with producers   **Newsletter** Every other month   **Special promotions** Regular fine wine offers, case of the month, etc. **£5**

🍇 *Wales's top wine merchant* 🍇 *Wide selection of Bordeaux* 🍇 *Extensive Burgundy listings* 🍇 *Carefully chosen Australian selection* 🍇 *Good all-round choices covering all regions*

Ballantynes's beautifully presented list shows the sort of pride it takes in its wines. It's a shame, though, it doesn't impart more detail and tasting notes. The reason is probably that the list is bimonthly, and this popular merchant's high turnover means there just isn't time to collate such reading matter. Be not deterred, however – six 'Fine Wine' lists are also released a year, and these really get down to the nitty gritty.

As for the specifics, the team take most pride in their Burgundian and Italian selections. Some Burgundian growers have been supplying the company for over 20 years so there's a great deal of loyalty and some fine wine involved – not to mention old, rare and rather expensive bottles too. This is far and away the best wine merchant in Wales, so it's hardly surprising that many of the wines here are exclusivities – top producers, on seeing such a good all-round list, will readily choose this as an outlet for their wines.

Look out for the generously reduced prices on the tempting annual bin-end list and get involved with the regular in-store tastings.

Best Buys
- Mittnacht Frères, Gewurztraminer 2001 (Alsace) £8.99
- Cline, Zinfandel 2000 (California) £9.49
- Domaine des Espiers, Gigondas Tradition 2001 (Southern Rhône) £12.49
- Shiraz Reserve Vergelegen 1999 (South Africa) £12.50
- Vouvray Le Haut Lieu Sec 2001 (Loire) £12.99
- Villa Cafaggio, Chianti Classico Riserva 1999 (Tuscany) £14.99

For an explanation of the symbols used at the top of some of the merchant entries, see page 118.

Irma Fingal-Rock

64 Monnow Street, Monmouth NP25 3EN
Tel: (01600) 712372   Fax: (01600) 712372
Email: tom@pinotnoir.co.uk   Website: www.pinotnoir.co.uk

Closed Tue, Wed, Sun & Jan   **Cards** Yes   **Discount** 5% on 1 case when collected   **Order online** No
Delivery Nationwide service, free within 30-mile radius, London and for orders of £100+   **Glass hire**
Free   **Tastings and talks** Annual tasting in London, local tastings on request   **Newsletter** Annual
Special promotions Occasional, wine of the month (£5)

🍇 *Affordable, interesting Burgundy collection, enthusiastically pieced together by a one-man merchant* 🍇 *Also a small collection of favourites from the Loire, Rhône, the Americas and the rest of the world (including Wales)*

Ex-barrister Tom Innes runs a one-man Burgundy show here in south Wales. He has occasional part-time assistance, and 'help' from his children, but otherwise this smart business is the kind of small merchant that keeps the UK wine trade lively – it's only small companies such as this that can ferret out unusual properties and really make new discoveries.

Tom stocks around 100 Burgundies, dozens of them coming in at under £10 a bottle – showing, as he puts it, 'that it *is* possible to find interesting domaine-bottled Burgundy at accessible prices' (possible, yes, but not many merchants achieve this feat).

You may not have heard of many of these producers before (domaines Gachot-Monot, Heimbourger and Poulleau don't make many appearances elsewhere in the UK), but don't let that put you off. Tom is an exacting taster, and has many loyal customers. All the main communes are here (smarter wines coming in from Morey St-Denis, Vosne-Romanée and Puligny-Montrachet), plus some that are otherwise difficult to come by – Irancy for a start. Added to eclectic wines and a very personal service, there's also the annual tasting held in Middle Temple, London, for a low-down on the wines if you think Monmouth is too far away.

Best Buys

- Domaine de la Fuye, organic Saumur, 2001 (Loire) £6.95
- Clos Toulmin Pinot Noir, AC Bourgogne Ordinaire 2000 (Burgundy) £8.55
- Rolf Binder, Christa-Rolf Shiraz/Grenache 1999 (Australia) £8.95
- Domaine Denis Pommier, Chablis *premier cru* Beauroy 1999 (Burgundy) £9.98
- Domaine Pascal Prunier, Auxey-Duresses Vieilles Vignes 1999 (Burgundy) £13.70
- Domaine Bruno Fèvre, Monthelie *premier cru* Sur la Velle 1999 (Burgundy) £14.35

Northern Ireland

Direct Wine Shipments

5–7 Corporation Square, Belfast, Northern Ireland BT1 3AJ
Tel: 028-9050 8000   Fax: 028-9050 8004
Email: enquiry@directwine.co.uk   Website: www.directwine.co.uk

Closed Sun (exc. Dec), Easter Mon & Tues, 1 May, 25 & 26 Dec **Cards** Yes **Discount** 10% on 1 case, discretion on larger orders **Order online** No **Delivery** Nationwide service, free for orders of 1+ case within Northern Ireland **Glass hire** Free with bulk order **Tastings and talks** Tastings, dinners and courses, phone for details **Newsletter** Weekly online, mailings twice per year **Special promotions** Monthly (£5)

🍇 *Belfast company that battled the odds to become the successful business it is today* 🍇 *Plenty of customer opportunities to learn about wine* 🍇 *Wide range of Spanish bottles* 🍇 *Top Rhône wines from the Chapoutier estate* 🍇 *Sales, offers and promotions for bargain hunters*

Direct Wine is seeing a move away from New World wines in favour of Italy, Spain and France. This comes as little surprise when you look at its wine list. The Spanish selection brings in a plethora of different wine styles and regions: from Priorat big, beefy Tempranillo and Garnacha reds; from Rías Baixas fine Albariño whites; and from Ribera del Duero stunning reds from Vega Sicilia and Pingus. Italy, too, has a fair smattering of regional wines, and from France there's a crop of top-quality producers. In contrast, the far-from-short Australian selection includes wines from a handful of bulk-producing growers only. DWS's standard approach is to pick a good grower and stick with them – for example, of the 20 or so Rhône wines on offer, 12 come from Chapoutier. No bad thing in terms of quality, but this merchant would do well to add more depth to the range by bringing in a few more growers. Especially since Peter McAlindon and his team put so much effort into increasing customer awareness and confidence with tastings, a free customer club (a free bottle with a case) and a strong focus on £5 and £10 wines. Fortunately, this year they have targeted over 100 new wines for the list.

Best Buys

- Vinos Sanz Rueda, Blanco 2002 (Spain) £4.99
- Hugel, Gentil 2002 (Alsace) £6.99
- Masi Renzo Fattoria di Basciano, Chianti Rufina, Tuscany 2001 (Italy) £6.99
- Deakin Estate, Select Sparkling Shiraz (Australia) £7.99
- Martin Codax, Albariño, Burgans 2002 (Spain) £8.59
- Marqués de Caceres, Rioja Reserva 1995 (Spain) £11.99

Specialist Award winners are listed on pages 17 and 18.

James Nicholson Wine Merchant

27A Killyleagh Street, Crossgar, Co. Down, Northern Ireland BT30 9DQ
Tel: 028-4483 0091   Fax: 028-4483 0028
Email: info@jnwine.com   Website: www.jnwine.com

Closed 25 & 26 Dec, 1 Jan, Easter Mon   **Cards** Yes   **Discount** 10% on 12+ bottles   **Order online** Yes
Delivery Nationwide delivery service (min. 1 case), free throughout Northern Ireland   **Glass hire** Free
(min. order 1 case)   **Tastings and talks** Regular Sat in-store tastings, tutored tastings, winemaker
dinners   **Newsletter** Every 6 weeks   **Special promotions** Wines of the month, regular case offers (£5)

🍇 *A fair number of cheaper, good-value bottles* 🍇 *Serious, lengthy Bordeaux section*
🍇 *Appealing range of smaller growers* 🍇 *Top Iberian producers*
🍇 *Fine Antipodean wines* 🍇 *Interesting 'new release' members' club*

This is undoubtedly one of Northern Ireland's best merchants, and it is flourishing as the fine-dining lifestyle in Belfast and surrounds has really taken off in recent years. James and his team have spent nearly 30 years building up an impressive range of growers, teasing out many labels well before they became famous.

The brochure starts with a selection of bottles for around a fiver, and a jolly good set it is too, including an Australian Riesling, French Chenin Blanc and a Pic St-Loup. A decent party selection for bulk purchasing follows, with the emphasis on sub-£4.50 prices, and then it's straight into champagnes and sparkling wines, with a strange sherry hiccup in the middle (Hidalgo, so we'll forgive the running order).

Overall, the strongest parts of the Nicholson range appear to be Bordeaux, the Rhône, Spain and Australia, and praise should also be extended to the New Zealand and Italian sections and the enticing dessert wines and ports. James Nicholson aficionados can join the 'JN Club', which offers a pre-release tasting of certain wines bimonthly, free of delivery charge.

Best Buys

- Borja, Viña Borgia 2001 (Spain) £4.75
- Best's Victoria Riesling, Victoria 2002 (Australia) £5.99
- Hidalgo, Manzanilla La Gitana sherry (Spain) £7.75
- Quinta de la Rosa Tinto, Douro 2001 (Portugal) £8.95
- Cloudy Bay, Pelorus Blanc de Blancs NV (New Zealand) £12.95
- Drappier, Carte d'Or NV (Champagne) £14.99

Also recommended

Supermarkets and chains

Morrisons

Head office: Hilmore House, Thornton Road, Bradford, West Yorkshire BD8 9AX
(over 500 branches nationwide)
Tel: (01274) 494166   Fax: (01274) 494831
Website: www.morereasons.co.uk

Newly combined with fellow supermarket giant Safeways, Morrisons is set to keep the wine side of its business simple. It's sticking with its own set of 500 or so wines, rather than incorporating the Safeways range (which would have totalled over 1,300 wines). The emphasis on value for money (a Morrisons' speciality) remains steady, though the wines could be a bit more exciting, and a few more trade-up options would be welcome. Maybe that's a project for the future – as the *Guide* went to press, a shake-up was still in progress. As it is, for as little as £2.69 a bottle you can pick up an Argentinian red, and for under £5 there's something from almost everywhere in the world – and from one or two quirky grape varieties too.

> **Best Buys**
> - Castellani, Verdicchio Classico 2003 (Italy) £3.99
> - Cono Sur, Pinot Noir 2002 (Chile) £4.99
> - Urziger Würzgarten Auslese, Mosel 2002 (Germany) £7.99

Nicolas

Head office: 31–33 Weir Road, Wimbledon, London SW19 8UG
(20 branches in Greater London)
Tel: 020-8944 7514   Fax: 020-8944 3019

The cheerful French greeting from behind the till as you enter a Nicolas shop might lift your spirits (and your expectations), but over the last few years it hasn't been enough to lift the quality of the wines on the shelves. Fortunately, things are improving. Nicolas is once again enhancing the image of French wine by bringing in tasty oddities from less-usual regions (such as Jurançon, Savoie, Bandol, Limoux and Cassis), showing the full range of flavours France can achieve. It doesn't just focus on sub-£5 bottles (something it's been guilty of recently) but presents plenty of trade-up options: Bordeaux choices run from the affordable to classy, and the champagne list is as extensive as it was in the good old days. Let's hope this change for the better continues.

> **Best Buys**
> - Château Gentilhommière, Abymes 2002 (Savoie) £7.75
> - Les Hauts Clochers, Chardonnay, Limoux 2000 (Languedoc) £9.95
> - Château de Tiregard, Pecharmant 2001 (Languedoc) £10.50

Safeways

See Morrisons, left

Sainsbury's Supermarkets

Head office: 33 Holborn, London EC1N 2HT
(525 branches nationwide)
Tel: (0800) 636262   Fax: 020-7695 7610
Website: www.sainsburys.co.uk

Sainsbury's starts its list with some singularly unexciting low-price Burgundy and Bordeaux listings, and the Loire, Rhône, South of France and Germany show a similar approach: plenty of Sainsbury's own-brand wines offering excellent reliability and cheap prices, but nothing that shouts out personality.

From Italy things get a little more exciting: many wines are sub-£5 a bottle (many own-brand) and there's a real regional focus here. But Australian offerings slump back into brand territory again, with, disappointingly, not one single region mentioned; California choices are equally poor. Things don't improve for the New Zealand and Argentina selections either, but wines from South Africa and Chile seem to inspire the Sainsbury's team a little more – the selection is good rather than great, but there's a wider choice available, and one or two quality estates listed.

Best Buys

- Sainsbury's Moroccan Cabernet Sauvignon 2002 (Morocco) £3.99
- Fairview, Goats do Roam 2002 (South Africa) £4.99
- Inama, Soave Classico Superiore, Signature Collection, Veneto 2002 (Italy) £7.99

Mail-order and online only

A & B Vintners

Little Tawsden, Spout Lane, Brenchley, Kent TN12 7AS
Tel: (01892) 724977   Fax: (01892) 722673
Email: info@abvintners.co.uk
Website: www.abvintners.co.uk

Ken Brook and John Arnold continue to specialise in three dynamic and exciting regions of France: Burgundy, the Rhône Valley and the deep south (Languedoc-Roussillon, Bandol, Provence). The two directors spend a lot of time across the Channel, delving into the best from these areas, and specialising seems to have paid off – A&B reckons it takes on new wines from around 6–10 extra growers every year. Some wines are available only in small allocations and may run out, so get on the mailing list and contact the company directly if you want to order something in advance from a specific domaine. Look out especially for Mas de Libion, Domaine de Lavabre, Yves Cuilleron, Michel Lafarge and Pierre-Yves Colin-Morey – but there are plenty of other gems to keep Francophiles well and truly happy. **£5**

Best Buys

- Fourrier, Adagio des Terroirs Rouge, Faugères 2001 (Languedoc) £8.25
- Domaine Christophe, Chablis 2002 (Burgundy) £8.74
- Mas de Libian, Côtes du Rhône-Villages Rouge 2001 (Southern Rhône) £8.74

Albany Vintners

113 Mount View Road, London N4 4JH
Tel: (0845) 330 8858   Fax: (0870) 460 1547
Email: sales@albanyvintners.com
Website: www.albanyvintners.com

This is a blue-chip broker, specialising in Bordeaux but with a lively interest in the top offerings of other regions and countries. Only the greatest and best (and hardest to get hold of) names make it on to the list here – Harlan Estate in California, Clarendon Hills in Australia and Pingus in Spain stand alongside Pétrus, Yquem and Romanée-Conti, and Italy and the Rhône don't look exactly rustic. The stock list is updated daily, and if this is your wine-buying territory (the average price per bottle here is £40; minimum spend is £200) it's worth signing up to receive special offers by email. Prices are quoted exclusive of duty and VAT, so be sure to calculate the final price before taking the plunge on a case of Château Lafite 2000. **£5**

Best Buys (exc. VAT)

- Guigal, Côtes du Rhône 2001 (Southern Rhône) £5.87
- Bernard Ambroise, Nuits-St-Georges Vieilles Vignes 2001 (Burgundy) £22
- Château Lafite, Pauillac 1986 (Bordeaux) £172

Arriba Kettle & Co

Buckle Street, Honeybourne, nr Evesham, Worcestershire WR11 7QE
Tel: (01386) 833024   Fax: (01386) 833541
Email: arribakettle@btopenworld.com

Barry Kettle's range of wines hits an impressively high standard, and displays admirable enthusiasm for particular countries and regions – France, Jerez and South Africa in particular. Among the top-notch producers listed are Barbadillo (sherry), Grahams (port), Wither Hills (New Zealand) and Henry Pelle (Loire), and there are some appealing small domaines from France here. But the best collection is from the Cape, where rich pickings can be had from top estates De Wetshof, Kanonkop and Neil Ellis, among others. Most bottles are priced between £5 and £10, and it should be easy to put together the minimum mixed case required to suit most pockets. This is a short but well chosen list, and features recipes, musings and decent tasting notes. Look out for special-offer leaflets, and annual tastings in November. **(£5)**

Best Buys (exc. VAT)

- Barbadillo, Manzanilla Pasada, Solear sherry (Spain) £7
- Neil Ellis, Sauvignon Blanc, Groenekloof 2003 (South Africa) £8.45
- Wither Hills, Pinot Noir, Marlborough 2002 (New Zealand) £13.95

Ashley Scott

PO Box 28, The Highway, Hawarden, Flintshire CH5 3RY
Tel: (01244) 520655   Fax: (01244) 520655

A neat, family-run operation, with a succinct range from around the world, Ashley Scott reports a steady increase in New World wines at the expense of France. Highlights of the list include Joseph Perrier champagne, Willm from Alsace and Humberto Canale from Argentina. Australia appears particularly strong, with offerings from Geoff Merrill, Palandri, Dromana and Grant Burge among others. Otherwise, it's the fortified selection that catches the eye, with madeiras from Henriques & Henriques and some Barossa Valley 'tawny port' that looks particularly tempting. This merchant is also big on tastings – the main one in November, a Spring one in April, and other tastings and talks for charity fund-raising.

Best Buys

- Humberto Canale, Black River Malbec (Argentina) £4.99
- Willm, Pinot Blanc d'Alsace 2001 (Alsace) £5.95
- Henriques & Henriques, ten-year-old malmsey (Madeira) £16.95

The Australian Wine Club

PO Box 3079, Datchet SL3 9ZL
Tel: (0800) 856 2004   Fax: (0800) 856 2114
Email: orders@australianwine.co.uk
Website: www.australianwine.co.uk

The exploration of 'real Australian wine' is set to begin its ventures anew. After its acquisition by Cellarmasters (a division of Fosters), the company didn't thrive as was hoped: cheap and cheerless wines began to sneak into the list, and there was a sad trend away from the usual high-quality Australian estates. Now, however, this merchant is back in the safe (but zany) hands of its original creators, Craig Smith and Frank Luff (the cat). The small-scale producers are returning, characterful wine regions have returned, and quality is once again available to all. Top of the tree are Penfold's Grange (of course), Pierro from Margaret River, Grosset and Mount Horrocks from Clare Valley. With luck more such stars will return to the fold very soon. Not cheap, but well worth it.

Best Buys

- De Bortoli, Gulf Station, Pinot Noir, Yarra Valley 2001 (Australia) £8.99
- Petaluma, Bridgewater Mill, Cabernet Sauvignon, South Australia 1998 (Australia) £10.99
- Pierro, Chardonnay, Margaret River 2001 (Australia) £19.99

Benson Fine Wines

96 Ramsden Road, London SW12 8QZ
Tel: 020-8673 4439   Fax: 020-8675 5543
Email: bensonwines@connectingbusiness.co.uk
Website: www.bensonfinewines.co.uk

If a special bottle of old claret takes your fancy, this is the merchant to come to. Clare Benson has been specialising in fine and rare wines for 25 years now and has a treasure trove of classic old vintages. She offers advice on handling, further cellaring and decanting, and also knows the provenance of her wines (how they've been stored before they reach her). Apart from rare, wartime Bordeaux and spectacular clarets from the 1982 vintage, you'll find red Burgundy dating back to 1865, Rhône wines from the 1960s, and nineteenth-century port and madeira. For £10 a year, join the Benson Wine & Dine Society (see website for details), and enjoy some spectacular tastings and intriguing fine-wine-and-supper evenings. Prices are fair, but not cheap.

Best Buys (exc. VAT)

- Fretelli, Barolo 1970 (Italy) £50
- Château Clos de l'Oratoire,
  St-Emilion 1982 (Bordeaux) £50
- Blandy's, Malmsey, believed 1792
  (Madeira) £1,000

Colombier Vins Fins

Colombier House, Cadley Hill, Ryder Close,
Swadlincote, Derbyshire DE11 9EU
Tel: (01283) 552552   Fax: (01283) 550675
Email: colombier@colombierwines.co.uk
Website: www.colombierwines.co.uk

Jehu Attias is a qualified winemaker from Bordeaux who also runs a Burgundy *négociant* business. Quite what he and his French wife Micheline are doing in the middle of Derbyshire the *Guide* hasn't quite fathomed, but there's no doubt this is a smart little business. Colombier has expanded beyond its usual French and Italian shores this year, and developed a strong global

coverage. Throughout, there's a good balance between unknowns (as from Burgundy and the Bordeaux *petits châteaux*) and superstars (top Bordeaux châteaux, champagne, Brunello di Montalcino). Jehu likes to give customers the opportunity to buy wines at cost price, particularly with his cheaper wines, to encourage experimentation. To this end the new Argentinian and South African listings offer plenty of bargain surprises.

Best Buys (exc. VAT)

- Prieuré de Château Ksara, Bekaa
  Valley 2001 (Lebanon) £4.55
- Vergelegen, Sauvignon Blanc,
  Stellenbosch 2003 (South Africa)
  £5.99
- Domaine de la Solitude,
  Châteauneuf-du-Pape Blanc 2001
  (Southern Rhône) £11.75

dodici

PO Box 428, Harpenden, Herts ALS 3ZT
Tel: (01582) 713004   Fax: (01582) 767991
Email: sales@dodici.co.uk
Website: www.dodici.co.uk

This is a brand-new business brimming with enthusiasm for all things Italian and Spanish. In fact so new is it that only the Italian list was available for review before the *Guide* went to press. Founder Angus Mitchell has worked in both countries and fills the monthly newsletter with tourist tips based on his first-hand knowledge, alongside wines from some of the best modern producers – Planeta in Sicily, Brolio in Chianti, Allegrini in Veneto and Franz Haas up north in the Alto Adige – plus lots of background information on the estates themselves. Special-offer mixed cases give a good idea of what you can buy and all sorts of tastings are promised in the Harpenden area. Order by phone, fax or email.   **£5**

Best Buys

- Leonardo, Chianti, Tuscany 2003
  (Italy) £6.50
- Planeta, La Segreta Rosso 2003
  (Sicily) £8.75
- Anselmi, San Vincenzo, Veneto 2003
  (Italy) £9.25

Farr Vintners

220 Queenstown Road, Battersea, London
SW8 4LP
Tel: 020-7821 2000   Fax: 020-7821 2020
Email: sales@farrvintners.com
Website: www.farrvintners.com

If you're looking for an absolutely top wine, money no object, this is the place to come. Much of the wine trade stocks up here too, so wine lovers need to be quick off the mark, which is where the website and email bulletins come in handy.

Bordeaux makes up 80 per cent of what's on offer (Farr owns the largest stocks of Bordeaux in the country; fine vintages, new vintages, all appellations), Burgundy accounts for 10 per cent, the Rhône 5 per cent, and Italy follows, while there seem to be more rarities and fine vintages making up the remainder here than ever before: Michel Rolland's Argentinian wine, for example, and 1988 Penfold's Grange from Australia. Bordeaux *en primeur* is a Farr speciality, and listings have plenty of helpful description and tasting notes from reputable journalists. Some good prices are to be had, but note the minimum spend, £500.

Best Buys
- Guigal, Châteauneuf-du-Pape 2001 (Southern Rhône) £13.75
- Réserve de Léoville-Barton, second wine of Château Léoville-Barton, St-Julien 2000 (Bordeaux) £15.27
- Château d'Angludet, Margaux 1989 (Bordeaux) £22.00

Fine Wines of New Zealand

95 Camden Mews, London NW1 9BU
Tel: 020-7482 0093   Fax: 020-7267 8400
Email: sales@fwnz.co.uk
Website: www.fwnz.co.uk

Margaret Harvey MW was waving the banner for the wines of her homeland long before they became the sought-after items they are today. Her short list of top-quality wines takes in long-established producers such as Cloudy Bay and Hunters, alongside newer finds Mills Reef and Redmetal. Margaret is always on the lookout for 'more exciting wines', so you will find bottles from the Gimblett Gravels and Awatere regions, and Bordeaux-style reds and Pinot Gris from Ata Rangi, as well as her own Aotea label. Lists published in April, September and November include mixed-case offers in addition to the latest news on New Zealand wines. More regular updates appear on the website.

Best Buys
- Aotea, Sauvignon Blanc 2003 (New Zealand) £8.95
- Riesling, Waipara West 2003 (New Zealand) £10.50
- Palliser Estate, Pinot Noir, Martinborough 2001 (New Zealand) £14.50

Four Walls Wine Co

The Old Forge, Chilgrove, nr Chichester, West Sussex PO18 9HX
Tel: (01243) 535360   Fax: (01243) 535418
Email: fourwallswine@aol.com

Four Walls; two approaches. On an everyday basis you can shop here for good-value, respectable names from the short house selection (even better value if you collect a case yourself, as you will receive a free bottle). For more special occasions, settle down to browse the densely packed pages of fine wines on the main list.

Burgundy and Bordeaux make up the bulk of the offerings, but here also are the best of Alsace, the Rhône, the sweet wines of the Loire, rare German whites and red wines from Italy, Spain, the United States and Australia. Four Walls counsels calm when it comes to purchasing fine wines – why panic-buy the latest vintage and then wonder where to store it, when you can cooly pick up a few nicely matured bottles from this list? **£5**

Best Buys

- Alpha Zeta, Soave RST, Veneto 2002 (Italy) £4.95
- Enate, Tempranillo/Cabernet Sauvignon, Crianza, Somontano 2000 (Spain) £8.45
- Château Rocher-Corbin, Montagne-St-Emilion 1999 (Bordeaux) £8.95

High Breck Vintners

11 Nelson Road, London N8 9RX
Tel: 020-8340 1848   Fax: 020-8340 5162
Email: hbv@richanl.freeserve.co.uk

Andrew and Linda Richardson, the newish owners of High Breck, have merrily adopted the company's tradition of seeking out interesting producers to set alongside the core business of premium claret and other fine wines. The result is a real goodie-bag of a list including both traditional Rioja and trendy Priorat from Spain, the full range of Madirans from the excellent Alain Brumont, and Australian brutes from Grant Burge. Affordable mature vintage ports are a bonus. This is a good source of *en primeur* Bordeaux and the chatty newsletter adds unusual one-off offers, often with an intriguing tale behind them. If you are questing for a particular rare bottle, High Breck will undertake to track it down for you, possibly from unlisted stock in its own cellar.

Best Buys

- Château de la Colline, Bergerac Rouge 2000 (South-west France) £6.90
- Alain Brumont, Pacherenc de Vic-Bilh, Jardin de Bouscassé 1998 (south-west France) £6.90
- Château de Belle-Coste, Costières de Nîmes, Cuvée St-Marc 1999 (Languedoc) £7.15

i-love-wine.co.uk

4 Beaver Close, Buckingham, Buckinghamshire MK18 7EA
Tel: (01280) 822500   Fax: (01280) 823833
Email: sales@i-love-wine.co.uk
Website: www.i-love-wine.co.uk

The internet-only arm of enthusiastic wholesale operation For the Love of Wine, i-love-wine specialises in Italy and, possibly uniquely in the UK, the wines of Switzerland. Two bottles are inexplicably priced at £999 but otherwise there are loads of affordable wines to explore, mostly from estates that are not well known in the UK but which 'produce wine from the heart' according to director Robert Steel. The buyers have scoured Italy and turned up interesting oddities such as sweet Frascati and Nuragus from Sicily alongside the mainstream regions and a huge selection from the south. Watch out for regular offers and discounts as well as espresso coffee and Italian olive oil.   **(£5)**

Best Buys

- Les Perrières, Gamay de Peissy 2002 (Switzerland) £7.50
- Falanghina Campi Flegrei, Cantina Farro, 2002 (Italy) £8.25
- Casa Emma, Chianti Classico, Tuscany 1999 (Italy) £10

Indigo Wine

7 Beverstone Road, London SW2 5AL
Tel: 020-7733 8391   Fax: 020-7733 8391
Email: info@indigowine.com
Website: www.indigowine.com

Director Ben Henshaw's family owns the Domaine St-Hilaire in the Languedoc, which produces a wide range of varietal *vins de pays*. From this starting point he has built a slickly presented list of some of the most exciting small-scale producers throughout the south of France, including Gros Noré, Château Grès St-Paul and Domaine Fontanel, plus a number of producers in the southern Rhône 'discovered' by US wine critic Robert Parker. These wines are excellent value for their quality, and a mixed case will quickly synchronise you with the pulse beat of wine fashion. Sign up for the email newsletter to keep abreast of offers and tastings. **£5**

Best Buys

- Domaine St-Hilaire, Vermentino, Vin de Pays d'Oc 2002 (Languedoc) £4.75
- Château St-Martin de la Garrigue, Bronzinelle, Coteaux du Languedoc 2001 (Languedoc) £7.25
- Château Grès St-Paul, Antonin, Coteaux du Languedoc 2000 (Languedoc) £9.75

Liberty Wines

Unit D18, The Food Market, New Covent Garden, Vauxhall, London SW8 5LL
Tel: 020-7720 5350   Fax: 020-7720 6158
Email: info@libertywine.co.uk

The Italian range here is something special, from Franz Haas in the north down to Morgante in Sicily via some of the finest estates in Piedmont and Tuscany. Australia too has a glossy portfolio and Liberty has picked out bright stars in many other regions, the latest venture being into Austrian Grüner Veltliner from Loimer. The Liberty team is excellent at unearthing really drinkable wines that offer both quality and value. Indeed, smaller operations come here when they want to source their 'latest great-value finds' – Chianti Leonardo and Quincy from Domaine des Ballandors being two notable recent hits. Primarily a supplier to the trade, Liberty caters well for private customers with a mail-order list on which prices include VAT and delivery.

Best Buys

- Alpha Zeta, 'C' Corvina 2002 (Italy) £4.95
- Domaine des Ballandors, Quincy 2002 (Loire) £7.99
- Loimer, Langenlois Grüner Veltliner, Kamptal 2002 (Austria) £8.99

Roger Harris Wines

Loke Farm, Weston Longville, Norwich, Norfolk NR9 5LG
Tel: (01603) 880171   Fax: (01603) 880291
Email: sales@rogerharriswines.co.uk
Website: www.rogerharriswines.co.uk

The original bottle of Beaujolais shipped by this specialist merchant was sent by Roger Harris to himself, in Nairobi, in 1974. Now, having presumably got to know every nook and cranny of Beaujolais over the last 30 years, Roger is venturing back into Africa to bring home wines from the Cape. This is indeed an exciting move, as the dedication with which he's provided the UK with Beaujolais – importing flavoursome, reliable wines from each of the 10 *crus*, plus Beaujolais Blanc and Beaujolais Rosé – has been both enthusiastic and faultless. South Africa approached with anything like the same energy cannot help but be fascinating, as wines from upcoming Franschhoek, Worcester and Robertson bear witness. Roger also has some fabulous Australian bottlings, focusing heavily on the quality regions of Western Australia. **£5**

Best Buys

- Quando, Sauvignon Blanc, Robertson 2002 (South Africa) £7.55
- Tingle-Wood Wines, The Great Southern, Yellow Tingle Riesling 2001 (Western Australia) £8.95
- Noël Aucoeur, Morgon 2002, (Beaujolais) £9.20

Seckford Wines

Dock Lane, Melton, Suffolk IP12 1PE
Tel: (01394) 446622   Fax: (01394) 446633
Email: mmt@seckfordwines.co.uk
Website: www.seckfordwines.co.uk

If you are willing to buy by the mixed case, this is one of the most exciting wine ranges in the country. Any merchant stocking the elusive right-bank Pomerol, Château Le Pin, earns itself immediate credibility (even if most of us can't afford it), and the rest of the generous Bordeaux stocks look good alongside this expensive oddity. Burgundy comes in from all the best sources: de Vogüé's Chambolle-Musigny, Méo-Camuzet's Vosne-Romanée, La Tache from Domaine de la Romanée-Conti and more. There's a fashionable selection of Italian wines, and a smattering of other stunners such as Opus One from California and The Armagh Shiraz from Australia. Don't miss the 'Oddments' at the back of the list, and remember that Seckford's temperature-controlled bonded warehouse will give your purchases the perfect storage conditions.

Best Buys (exc. VAT)

- Tempier, Bandol Cuvée Classique 2001 (Provence) £11.67
- Duplessis, Chablis Montée de Tonnerre 1994 (Burgundy) £15.00
- Veritas, Heyssen Shiraz, Barossa Valley 1999 (Australia) £16.25

London

Baton Rouge

17 Canonbury Lane, Islington, London N1 2AS
Tel: 020-7226 8382   Fax: 020-7226 9564
Email: enquiries@batonrougewines.com
Website: www.batonrougewines.com

This Islington-based merchant was launched in May 2002 and specialises in the wines of Languedoc-Roussillon, that large and dynamic southern French region. It's good to see a wide range of styles on top of the usual rich reds from this area – for example, a Viognier/Marsanne blend, dry Muscat, some Pinot Noir and rosé. In particular, those looking for pudding wines from the south of France will be pleased – there are several to choose from. As well as southern French options, some Italian and Spanish bottles appear, as do a couple of champagnes, a longer slate of malt whiskies and some mineral waters. Plenty to slake the thirst, then, but mainly from the Med.

Best Buys

- Cave les Costières de Pomerols, Picpoul de Pinet 2002 (Languedoc-Roussillon) £4.95
- Domaine Joliette, Muscat de Rivesaltes 2001 (Languedoc-Roussillon) £7.11
- Cuvée Renaud de Valon, St-Chinian 2000 (Languedoc-Roussillon) £7.13

Bibendum Fine Wine

113 Regents Park Road, London NW1 8UR
Tel: 020-7722 5577   Fax: 020-7722 7354
Email: sales@bibendum-wine.co.uk
Website: www.bibendum-wine.co.uk

The focus over the last few years has been on the top-notch, blue-chip side of this merchant's business, hence the addition of 'Fine Wine' to its title. There are classic wines to explore from: Burgundy, the Rhône, Bordeaux and Champagne (in that order of preference), and smart New World bottles (of which the best are from Australia). This merchant has always catered for customers with more than just a passing interest in wine, so a minimum purchase of one unmixed case will not be a hindrance. Most of Bibendum's sales are direct to the wine trade, but canny buyers will want to shop here too, as this store has access to some truly great wines. The website is very popular and staff offer helpful over-the-counter service.

Best Buys

- M Chapoutier, Rasteau Côte du Rhône-Villages 2002 (Southern Rhône) £5.72
- Albariño, Pazo de Senorans, Rías Baixas 2002 (Spain) £7.73
- Mendoza, Catena Alta Cabernet Sauvignon 2001 (Argentina) £15

Cape Wine & Food

77 Laleham Road, Staines, Middlesex TW18 2EA
Tel: (01784) 451860   Fax: (01784) 469267
Email: capewineandfood@aol.com
Website: www.capewinestores.co.uk

Cape Wine & Food has opened on the site of what used to be Cape Province Wines, and is run by a previous customer, South African Ross Richardson. Ross bought the business in September 2003, renovated the shop and expanded the range of wines by adding bottles from 27 different Cape estates. The welcome result is a range from 60 estates, many of which have limited distribution in the UK. Top of the list must be Vergelegen, Meerlust, Simonsig, Klein Constantia, Thelema and Graham Beck – but there's plenty more to choose from, including spirits, fortified wines and John Platter's indispensable guidebook to Cape wines (£10.49). In time, Ross hopes to stock South African food, deli-style, in the shop. **(£5)**

Best Buys

- Klein Constantia Sauvignon Blanc, Constantia 2001 (South Africa) £8.89
- Graham Beck, Brut NV, Robertson (South Africa) £9.99
- Stellenzicht, Shiraz, Stellenbosch 2000 (South Africa) £11.29

Davy's Wine Shop

161–169 Greenwich High Road, London SE10 8JA
Tel: 020-8858 6014   Fax: 020-8853 3331
Website: www.davy.co.uk

Bordeaux is the special strength here, with the very finest properties available by the bottle in a number of vintages and many more affordable options besides. Vintage port is another speciality. However, don't be entirely fooled by the traditional image of Davy's, which owns 42 wonderfully old-fashioned wine bars around the City of London. The good-value own-label selection now embraces Chilean, Australian and South African varietals and points the way to a list with a broad international outlook. New Zealand has the excellent

wines of Waipara West while Argentina turns up Finca El Retiro, and there are modern Portuguese reds from the Douro to contrast with the ports. Delivery is free of charge for a dozen or more bottles. The special-offer 'New World vs Old World' case seems a good place to start. **(£5)**

Best Buys

- Riesling, Waipara West 2000 (New Zealand) £8.25
- Douro, Prazo de Roriz, Douro Valley 2000 (Portugal) £8.50
- Château Rouquette Cuvée Merigot, Bordeaux Supérieur 2000 (Bordeaux) £9.50

Friarwood

26 New Kings Road, London SW6 4ST
Tel: 020-7736 2628   Fax: 020-7731 0411
Email: sales@friarwood.com
Website: www.friarwood.com

The focus here is on fine wines, with classed-growth clarets going back to 1982. Otherwise the list sticks to ranges from favoured producers, with reliable names such as Antonin Guyon and Roger Belland in Burgundy. The Rhône and Italy take the same approach and California turns up smart bottles like the excellent Zinfandel from Dashe and Cabernet from Clos Pegase. Friarwood has also been actively seeking suppliers of wines under £10 in southern France, South Africa, Chile and Australia, and the list is now well balanced across the price spectrum. Buying by the case will earn you a 10 per cent discount (five per cent if mixed) and it's worth subscribing to the newsletter to keep an eye out for bin-end offers. **(£5)**

Best Buys

- Vin d'Stel, Pinotage 2003 (South Africa) £5.50
- Domaine de la Cour Carrée, Sauvignon de Touraine 2002 (Loire) £6.15
- Viña Haras de Pirque, Carmenère Reserve 2002 (Chile) £7.50

Goedhuis & Co

6 Rudolf Place, Miles Street, London SW8 1RP
Tel: 020-7793 7900   Fax: 020-7793 7170
Email: enquiries@goedhuis.com
Website: www.goedhuis.com

This is a great place to go for Bordeaux from major properties, with a host of offerings from 1986 to the latest vintages. But there's plenty of competition in that arena and more compelling reasons to choose Goedhuis over other merchants can be found in the ranges from Burgundy, the Rhône, the Loire and Italy. This is a merchant that tries hard to track down excellent little-known producers, and the enthusiasm evident from the short profiles on the list is infectious. The minimum buy is an unmixed case, but while these are all serious, elegant wines they are not all seriously expensive. It's well worth getting on the mailing list for *en primeur* offers and regular bin-end sales. **£5**

Best Buys
- Fratelli Tamellini, Soave Superiore, Veneto 2002 (Italy) £7.34
- Domaine le Clos de Cazaux, Cuvée St-Roch, Vacqueyras 2001 (Southern Rhône) £7.63
- Nicolas Potel, Bourgogne Vieilles Vignes Maison Dieu 1998 (Burgundy) £9.69

The London Wine Company

1 Armoury Way, Wandsworth, London SW18 1TH
Tel: 020-8875 9393   Fax: 020-8875 1925
Email: sales@thelondonwine.co.uk

Price, price, price is what drives this switched-on warehouse operation on the Wandsworth one-way system. Champagne and other fizz offers are always worth checking out when you are planning a celebration (especially with generous delivery and sale-or-return terms, glass loan and ice and chill-bin supplies). Multi-buy

discounts apply on most wines but you can still pop in for just one bottle. The list is full of easy-going bottles from all over, many from big brands or major players such as Antinori in Italy, but the policy of importing direct from Europe turns up occasional interesting finds. Australia is taken seriously, with a range that encompasses the likes of Penfold's Bin 707 and Wynns Michael Shiraz.

Best Buys
- Señorio de los Llanos, Valdepeñas Reserva 1998 (Spain) £4.99
- Seaview Edwards & Chaffey, Pinot Noir/Chardonnay Brut 1995 (Australia) £9.99
- Grant Burge, Miamba, Shiraz 1999 (Australia) £9.99

South England

A & A Wines

Manfield Park, Guildford Road, Cranleigh, Surrey GU6 8PT
Tel: (01483) 274666   Fax: (01483) 268460
Email: aawines@aol.com
Website: www.spanishwinesonline.co.uk

The two Andrews, Bickerton and Connor, specialise in Spanish wine and have a comprehensive range that includes plenty of mature and rare bins, with venerable Riojas stretching back to the 1970s plus wines from Ribera del Duero, Navarra, Rueda and Penedès, the latter including a good choice of Cavas. Hidalgo's sherries make a welcome appearance, and there are ciders from the Asturias region, Spanish beers, and even oils, cheeses, olives and other foodstuffs from Spain. A few wines from other parts of the winemaking globe make it on to the A&A list – some De Bortoli bins from Down Under, for example, and a smattering of French country wines – but this list is really for fans of all things Spanish and the country's wonderfully wide range of vinous styles. **£5**

Best Buys

- Manzanilla La Gitana, sherry half bottle (Spain) £3.50
- Albariño Valdamor, Rías Baixas 2003 (Spain) £9.99
- Marqués de Riscal, Gran Reserva, Rioja 1995 (Spain) £19.99

The Bottleneck

7 & 9 Charlotte Street, Broadstairs, Kent CT10 1LR
Tel: (01843) 861095   Fax: (01843) 861095
Email: info@thebottleneck.co.uk
Website: www.thebottleneck.co.uk

Chris and Lin Beckett have gradually built up this business over 16 years, transforming an old-fashioned off-licence, where Liebfraumilch was the best-seller, into the worthwhile modern wine merchant it is today. Australia is the mainstay of the range with producers such as St Hallett, Rockford, Campbells, Moss Wood, Wynn's Coonawarra and De Bortoli, the list makes for an impressive read – and there are half a dozen Australian 'sweeties' for fans of this style. Other countries follow, including England and New Zealand (look out for Hunter's, Jackson Estate and Te Kairanga), and some decent American wines from both north and south are also available. **£5**

Best Buys

- Dr Loosen, Dr L Riesling, Mosel 2002 (Germany) £5.99
- Wynns Coonawarra Estate Riesling, Coonawarra 2001 (Australia) £5.99
- De Bortoli, Noble One Botrytis Semillon, Victoria 2000 half bottle (Australia) £13.99

The Butlers Wine Cellar

247 Queens Park Road, Brighton, East Sussex BN2 9XJ
Tel: (01273) 698724   Fax: (01273) 622761
Email: henry@butlers-winecellar.co.uk
Website: www.butlers-winecellar.co.uk

This neat little Brighton merchant has a modest, middle-rung list of everyday wines: there are enough fairly priced bottles to tempt customers away from the supermarkets but there's generally nothing worth travelling the length of the country to get to (Butlers focuses on supplying to local customers). The Bin End list, however, is another matter, with a great smattering of this and that from around the world: fascinating old 1970s Bordeaux vintages to try out (great celebration wines, leaving change from £30 if you so wish); prestige bottlings from the Mosel, Germany; Italian Amarones; sweet Loire wines; and many more besides. Bin-end shopping here is almost as good as a delve into an Edwardian butler's cellar. **£5**

Best Buys

- P Ducournau, Chapelle l'Enclos, Madiran 1996 (South-west France) £8.95
- Etchart Chardonnay, Cafayate, Salta 1997 (Argentina) £9.99
- Château Messzelato, Tokaji 5 Puttonyos 1993 (Hungary) £10.99

Charles Hennings (Vintners)

The Winecellars, Station Approach, Pulborough, West Sussex RH20 1AQ
Tel: (01798) 872485   Fax: (01798) 873163

Golden Square, High Street, Petworth, West Sussex GU28 0AP
Tel: (01798) 343021   Fax: (01798) 343021

London House, Lowes Street, Pulborough, West Sussex RH20 2BW
Tel: (01798) 872671
Email: sales@chv-wine.co.uk
Website: www.chv-wine.co.uk

This family firm, established for three generations, caters for customers who are keen to experiment or who are looking for something special. To support this laudable aim the wide range pushes beyond a core of familiar names, staff are well trained, and regulars are invited to biannual tastings. Classed-growth Bordeaux and some more affordable alternatives come in a fair range of vintages and there's solid stuff from Burgundy and the Rhône. Australia includes a line-up of Grange among the many offerings. Chile has strong producers and English wines including Nyetimber fizz are a bonus. Hennings has a second branch in Petworth and also a rather good website. Free delivery is available within 30 miles. The firm also stocks a good range of glassware.

Best Buys
● Casa Lapostolle, Merlot 2001 (Chile) £5.99
● Breaky Bottom, Seyval Blanc (England) £6.99
● Domaine des Ballandors, Quincy 2002 (Loire) £8.95

The English Wine Centre

Alfriston, East Sussex BN26 5QS
Tel: (01323) 870164   Fax: (01323) 870005
Email: bottles@englishwine.co.uk
Website: www.englishwine.co.uk

In the wake of the 2003 heatwave vintage, interest in English wine has never been higher, and there's no better place to satisfy your curiosity than here. The centre showcases all the best names – including Breaky Bottom, Hidden Spring and the energetic New Wave Wines group formed from the merger of Carr Taylor, Chapel Down and Lamberhurst – as well as championing the champagne-trouncing sparkling wines of Nyetimber and Ridgeview. Ciders, mead and local beers complete the patriotic range but there are a few wines from around the world too. If you can't make it to the Cuckmere Valley you can always phone in an order or buy online.

Best Buys
● New Wave Wines, Empire Zest 2001 (England) £6.25
● Hidden Spring, Decadence 2001 (England) £7.45
● Ridgeview sparkling, Bloomsbury 2000 (England) £15.95

Le Fleming Wines

19 Spenser Road, Harpenden,
Hertfordshire AL5 5NW
Tel: (01582) 760125   Fax: (01582) 760125
Email: cherry@leflemingwines.co.uk
Website: www.leflemingwines.co.uk

Cherry Jenkins' excellent one-woman wine business celebrates its twentieth birthday in 2005. During previous years her answering machine has always been a hotline to a huge range of interesting wines, although now the website is taking up some of the strain. Particular highlights are a super list from Alsace, featuring Blanck, JosMeyer and Zind-Humbrecht, and a roll-call of top Australian and New Zealand names in red, white and fizz. There's a welcome mix of brand new and more mature vintages, and underpinning the top-quality range is a sound collection of everyday basics, so piecing together a minimum-order mixed case is a real pleasure. A £10 fee buys membership of a customer club with monthly meetings, special offers and guest speakers. **£5**

Best Buys
● Stormy Cape, Chenin Blanc 2003 (South Africa) £5.39
● Gary Crittenden, 'I' Sangiovese 2000 (Australia) £8.12
● JosMeyer, le Kottabe, Riesling 2000 (Alsace) £9.51

Turville Valley Wines

The Firs, Potter Row, Great Missenden,
Buckinghamshire HP16 9LT
Tel: (01494) 868818   Fax: (01494) 868832
Email: chris@turville-valley-wines.com
Website: www.turville-valley-wines.com

This Buckinghamshire wine merchant is home to some of the finest wines in the country: Bordeaux dates back to 1957; Burgundy and Rhône wines not quite so far, but the quality of the domaines involved truly takes the breath away. There are over

150 different wine lots from Domaine de la Romanée-Conti (the largest stocks in the UK apparently), Bonnes Mares from de Vogüé, Richebourg from Leroy and many more to choose from. Not surprisingly, the wines can be expensive, and the minimum sale is still by the case, even at (cheap for Turville) £60 a bottle. France isn't the only contender: Australia, Spain and California feature highly, and Turville has noticed a sudden willingness to pay more for Brunello di Montalcino of late, a boost to the Italian section.

Best Buys
- Château Lafite, Pauillac 1978 (Bordeaux) £20
- Guigal, Côtes du Rhône 2000 (Southern Rhône) £46
- Leflaive, Folatières, Puligny-Montrachet, 1999 (Burgundy) £50

Village Wines

6 Mill Row, High Street, Bexley, Kent DA5 1LA
Tel: (01322) 558772   Fax: (01322) 558772
Email: sales@village-wines.com
Website: www.village-wines.co.uk

Aware of competition from supermarkets and (being in Kent) the French channel ports, this team delves into the world of wine with infectious enthusiasm, and a determination to offer adventurous, good-value wines. From the Rhône and Languedoc the quality–price ratio is superb; more unusual (but no less tempting) is a penchant for red and white Pfalz wines from Germany – also good value. Conventional choices focus on similar smaller, quality-oriented producers but bring in Spanish Navarra, Ribera and Rioja, rich Italian reds from the south, and carefully chosen wines from Western Australia (Palandri Estate), Chile (Montes) and Argentina (Michel Torino). The (no joining fee) customer club offers regular bin-end and discounted cases, Bordeaux *en primeur* options, and mixed cases tailored to suit. (£5)

Best Buys
- Humberto Canale, Black River Merlot/Pinot Noir, Rio Negro 2001 (Argentina) £5.49
- Grand Arte, Alvarinho, Estremadura 2002 (Portugal) £6.49
- Rivola Abadia Retuerta, Sardon de Duero 2001 (Spain) £8.55

East England

Amps Fine Wines

6 Market Place, Oundle, Peterborough PE8 4BQ
Tel: (01832) 273502   Fax: (01832) 273611
Email: info@ampsfinewines.co.uk
Website: www.ampsfinewines.co.uk

Philip Amps and his long-serving team offer a large selection of wines and spirits, and Amps promises to 'taste open bottles with customers to understand exactly what they want' and pledges to take back any wines that are disliked. Some sections of the list are extremely limited (Bordeaux), but Amps' generally wide range includes much of interest from South Africa (Vergelegen, Warwick, Hamilton Russell), Australia (Charles Melton, Petaluma, Mountadam) and New Zealand (Esk Valley, Babich, Alpha Domus), while the sweet wines, ports and fascinating big-format bottles are areas that look especially strong. The tutored tastings by winemakers are well worth signing up for, and a fine wine subscribers' club offers pre-selected cases at monthly, two-monthly or quarterly intervals, with tasting notes provided.

Best Buys
- Albariño, Lagar de Cervera, Rías Baixas 2002 (Spain) £10.25
- Esk Valley, Merlot/Malbec/Cabernet, Hawke's Bay 2002 (New Zealand) £10.50
- Vergelegen, Chardonnay Reserve, Stellenbosch 2001 (South Africa) £11.99

The Cellar d'Or

37 St Giles Street, Norwich NR2 1JN
Tel: (01603) 626246   Fax: (01603) 626256
Email: info@greatestates.co.uk
Website: www.greatestates.co.uk

This newish (1998) Norwich-based company divides business into posh and not-so-posh. In 2003 it created a sister company, Great Estates, to focus on fine wine, and this branch looks after its rare bottles and investment services. The fine wines date back further than 1928, and cover Burgundy, Bordeaux and the Rhône in serious depth: Pauillac, St-Julien, St-Estèphe and Margaux from all the *cru classé* châteaux for a start. Carefully chosen bottles are also available from the rest of the world. For everyday quaffing, the basic Cellar d'Or list (beginning with simple £2.99 wines) works hard to bring in good value. Many of the wines are imported direct from the producer, which keeps costs down. The selection isn't broad, but it does cover as many grape varieties as possible.   **(£5)**

Best Buys

- Chereau Carre, La Griffe, Muscadet Sèvre-et-Maine Sur Lie 2001 (Loire) £4.45
- Terrebianca, Chianti Classico Reserva, Croce, Tuscany 2000 (Italy) £9.86
- Stag's Leap Winery, Chardonnay, Napa 2001 (California) £14.45

Red or White

Evolution House, 46 Castle Street, Trowbridge, Wiltshire BA14 8AY
Tel: (01225) 781666   Fax: (01225) 776505
Email: info@redorwhite.biz
Website: www.redorwhite.biz

This small Wiltshire merchant has the distinct advantage of being able to offer wines to try on-site, at the restaurant and wine lounge. What's more, restaurant-goers directly benefit from the fabulously good-value £6–£7-a-bottle deal (they pop in to the Red or White wine shop next door to select their wine, a £2.50 corkage fee being all the extra they're asked to pay). The wines are a choice, worldwide bunch. Many are from well-known, stellar-quality producers, and others delve into modern eclectic territory: Inniskillin's Canadian sparkling Icewine and Finca el Retiro Argentinian Bonarda for a start. The customer club (£10 joining fee) looks good, offering a 10 per cent discount on any shop purchases and restaurant bills, plus free local delivery and regular personalised mixed cases to suit your taste.   **(£5)**

Best Buys

- Cave de Turckheim, Pinot Gris (Alsace) £6.99
- Chivite, Colleccion 125 Gran Reserva, Rioja 1995 (Spain) £14.99
- Inniskillin, Sparkling Ice Wine, Ontario, half bottle (Canada) £49.98

Great Estates

See The Cellar d'Or, above

South-west England

Cochonnet Wines

See Wine in Cornwall, page 211

Reid Wines

The Mill, Marsh Lane, Hallatrow,
nr Bristol BS39 6GB
Tel: (01761) 452645   Fax: (01761) 453642
Email: reidwines@aol.com

Bill Baker of the buying team has been complaining of late that there are too many 'long-term residents' in the Reid Cellar. By which he means venerable old wines from the 1940s (claret), 1930s (port) and even 1870s (madeira). This isn't a particularly serious complaint, as the wines themselves are ticking over quite nicely, steady in their maturity. It's just that the Reid team need the space to indulge in their more modern fantasies: Cabernet Sauvignon from Western Australia and the Napa Valley, Spanish Ribera del Duero ('Some outstanding kit', says the list), a delicious wealth of Alsace aromatic and late-harvest wines, and others of breathtakingly good quality. Handy and small though the pocket-sized list is, readers will be kept intrigued by the witty quotes and refreshingly frank tasting notes, which completely reflect the enthusiasm of the buyers, who know these wines like old friends.

Best Buys

- Henry Pellé, Menetou Salon Clos des Blanchais 2001 (Loire) £8.95
- Château Potensac, Médoc 1993 (Bordeaux) £13.50
- J-M Pavelot, Savigny-lès-Beaune Narbanton 1996 (Burgundy) £18.75

Savage Selection

The Ox House, Market Place, Northleach, Cheltenham, Gloucestershire GL54 3EG
Tel: (01451) 860896   Fax: (01451) 860996
Email: wine@savageselection.co.uk
Website: www.savageselection.co.uk

Mark Savage MW aims to seek out wines with balance, vitality and genuine originality. To do this he makes the same 'savage selection' at source he always has, weeding out the 'also rans', brands and wannabe wines that lack real quality and fail to reflect their *terroir*. Most of this range comes from France – witness vintages of St-Emilion star Tertre-Rôteboeuf since 1982, carefully selected Languedoc wines, Bandol from Provence, Burgundy from Joseph Drouhin and the gamut of grapes from Alsace. Mark is also proud to list Austria and north-west USA as his specialities – the Oregon Pinot Noirs and Pinot Gris are delicious, if unusual (he is more interested in esoteric wines than in fashionable labels). Mark holds tastings in London and Gloucestershire every year, and offers nationwide delivery.   **£5**

Best Buys

- Weingut Juris, St-Laurent Selection 2001 (Austria) £9.40
- R Stuart & Co, Big Fire Pinot Gris 2001 (Oregon) £9.79
- Domaine Tempier, Bandol Cuvée Speciale 2000 (Provence) £14.20

Wessex Wines

88 St Michael's Estate, Bridport, Dorset DT6 3RR
Tel: (01308) 427177   Fax: (01308) 423400
Email: wessexwines@amserve.com

Wessex Wines' imaginative range of French wines is as good as ever, with Jurançon, Bergerac, Cahors, Madiran, Corbières and Fronsac from the south to delve into for starters – all bottles with a keen eye on price and individuality, not topping the £10 mark unless absolutely necessary (fashionable Burgundy, Bordeaux and Rhône wines overstep this price point, for example). On the whole, this isn't an extensive list, but it's a carefully chosen one, and Dorset residents should be glad of such affordable vinous individuality on their doorstep. Away from France, there are English sparkling wines, offbeat Spanish offerings, and a fair handful of quirky bottles such as rich, sticky Rutherglen Muscat and powerful d'Arenberg Footbolt Shiraz from Australia.   **£5**

Best Buys

- Curious Grape, Flint Dry Sur Lie 2002 (England) £6.35
- Marquis de Pennautier, Collection Privée Rouge, Cabardès 2001 (Languedoc) £7.45
- Lamblin et Fils, Chablis Premier Cru Fourchaumes 2000 (Burgundy) £14.19

Wine in Cornwall

Kernick Business Park, Annear Road,
Penryn, Cornwall TR10 9EW
Tel: (01326) 379426   Fax: (01326) 379486
Email: sales@wineincornwall.co.uk
Website: www.wineincornwall.co.uk

In the last few years the wholesale side of this business has boomed, and Nigel Logan and his team decided that it was only fair that retail customers should benefit from wholesale prices too – a brave and generous decision. Cochonnet Wines has consequently transformed into Wine in Cornwall. Nigel makes sure his list covers all the main wine regions and keeps things quirky and interesting with plenty of Cahors, Collioure and Cairanne-type oddities from southern France, and more adventurous finds from Portugal, southern Italy and even Chile. There are safer choices among the Burgundies, Alsace and Loire wines, although any uncertainties can be ruled out by tasting the wine in the nearby Trengilly Wartha Inn (run by Nigel and team since 1988).

Best Buys

- Quinta de la Rosa White Wine, Douro Valley 2001 (Portugal) £7.48
- J J Maillet, Jasnières, Chenin Blanc 2000 (Loire) £9.62
- Henschke, Innes Pinot Gris, Adelaide Hills 1998 (Australia) £13.62

Midlands

Barrels & Bottles

3 Oak Street, Sheffield S8 9UB
Tel: 0114-255 6611   Fax: 0114-255 1010

There has been a shift towards more exclusive agency listings here, and towards supplying small parcels and bin-end deals, especially from Germany, France and New Zealand. Barrels & Bottles has a relatively small but well-formed collection of pedigree wines, such as Ramos Pinto (port), Pesquera (Spain), Highfield (New Zealand) and Casa Lapostolle (Chile). And it's nice to see wines from

Hungary represented by the excellent Tibor Gal as well as encountering Austria's Brundlmayer and Tement. The list may be concise, but it covers a wide range of exciting, often quirky styles. The company also offers a personalised label service, useful for gifts. Regular tastings are held in Sheffield and samples are open in the shop every day. **(£5)**

Best Buys

- Gilles Ducroux, Regnié 2002 (Beaujolais) £7.75
- Dr Loosen, Riesling Rothai Kabinett, Mosel 2002 (Germany) £8.95
- Highfield Estate, Sauvignon Blanc, Marlborough 2003 (New Zealand) £11.95

Bat & Bottle

9 Ashwell Road, Oakham, Rutland LE15 6QG
Tel: (0845) 108 4407   Fax: (0870) 458 2505
Email: post@batwine.co.uk
Website: www.batwine.co.uk

Bat and Bottle has moved its wicket to Italy over the last year – Ben and Emma Robson in fact spent six months of 2003 trading directly from Italian shores specifically to increase the scope and depth of their range. There are still a few bottles available from Mediterranean France (their previous pitch), and one or two from England and Spain. But it's Italy, particularly its uncharted territory, that the team find so exciting now. Order a mixed case and see what they have learned first-hand from their travels: many of the grower names will be unfamiliar, but the quality is first-class. The itinerant nature of this merchant (it is currently looking for new UK premises) shouldn't be off-putting, as website sales are buoyant and tastings are held across England. **(£5)**

Best Buys

- Vinicola de Felice, Silenus, Puglia (Italy) £8
- Luigi Righetti, Amarone della Valpolicella, Capital de Roari, Veneto (Italy) £14
- Isole e Olena, Syrah, Tuscany (Italy) £18.80

Connolly's Wine Merchants

Arch 13, 220 Livery Street, Birmingham B3 1EU
Tel: 0121-236 9269   Fax: 0121-233 2339
Email: richard@connollyswine.co.uk
Website: www.connollyswine.co.uk

It would be good news if this merchant put as much poetic effort into tasting notes and wine descriptions (there are none of the former) as into the entertaining compilations that introduce the wine list (this year's poem features Posh Spice). What's on offer here is nonetheless an expansive collection of wines spanning stellar Burgundy, Bordeaux and port, smart Rhône, German and Spanish wines, and imaginatively chosen New World listings too. Prices are reasonable, especially if you choose the 'cash and carry' option. And Chris Connolly has a particularly good selection of fizz and champagne – again, from just about everywhere – to whet the appetite, plus a thorough range of post-prandials to finish off many a fine meal.

> **Best Buys**
> - Jordan Estate, Fumé Blanc, Stellenbosch 2002 (South Africa) £7.89
> - Stanton & Killeen, Rutherglen Muscat NV (Australia) £9.99
> - Jaboulet-Aîné, Gigondas 2000 (Southern Rhône) £14.39

Edward Sheldon

New Street, Shipston on Stour, Warwickshire CV36 4EN
Tel: (01608) 661409   Fax: (01608) 663166
Email: finewine@edward-sheldon.co.uk
Website: www.edward-sheldon.co.uk

As befits its heart-of-England location, this merchant (in business since 1842) has all the traditional values and traditional wines you could wish for. Bordeaux is the highlight here, with plenty of fine bottles from old vintages and new – in fact, more clarets are available than the literature declares: 40 or 50 delisted bin-end surprises await discovery by curious callers. Customer service is paramount, and 'all shop sales cases are carried to the car'. Some

of the Sheldon range could do with re-energising (Spain, Italy, California), but on the whole this is a cracking (and well-priced) selection of the world's wines. Don't miss *The Corker*, one of the smartest, most informative merchant newsletters around, with details of the company's 4–6 winemaker dinners a year, tastings and special offers. **£5**

> **Best Buys**
> - O'Fournier, Urban Oak, Tempranillo/Malbec, Valle de Uco 2001 (Argentina) £6.56
> - Perrin & Fils, Rasteau l'Andeol 2001 (Southern Rhône) £8.71
> - Château Talbot, Connetable Talbot 2000 (Bordeaux) £14.10

Evington's Wine Merchants

120 Evington Road, Leicester LE2 1HH
Tel: 0116-254 2702   Fax: 0116-254 2702
Email: evingtonwine@fsbdial.co.uk
Website: www.evingtons-wines.com

Simon March's crusade to get customers to spend more money is all in the interest of encouraging them to drink better wine – and this doesn't mean too dramatic a spend, as many wines are below £10 a bottle. The range reflects a real enthusiasm for wine: everything from the familiar and famous to the eclectic and unusual. Austrian Beerenauslese Chardonnay rubs shoulders with Portuguese white Bairrada, which sits next to Chapoutier's Hermitage (Rhône) and Penfold's Grange from Australia. There aren't the Bordeaux and Burgundy classics to delve into, but plenty of interesting and generously priced wines from elsewhere. Simon is seeing a renewed interest in Riesling and sherry this year, a sure sign that his customers are listening to his message and opting for quality rather than predictability. **£5**

> **Best Buys**
> - Finca el Retiro, Torrontés 2002 (Argentina) £6.90
> - Quinta dos Roques, Touriga Naçional, Dão 1999 (Portugal) £14.70
> - Lustau, VOS 20-year-old amontillado sherry (Spain) £16.44

Inspired Wines

West End, High Street, Cleobury Mortimer,
Worcestershire DY14 8DR
Tel: (01299) 270064   Fax: (01299) 270064
Email: sue@inspired-wines.co.uk
Website: www.inspired-wines.co.uk

Tim and Sue Cowin are still inspired and
still growing their business. What's more,
their customers can still be inspired for less
than £10 a bottle. How many merchants can
say they list 12 different Argentinian grape
varieties? Not many. Here you'll find
Tempranillo, Bonarda, Malbec, Torrontés and
more. Australian wines bring in quality
estates such as Shadowfax and Veritas (again
spanning the full spectrum of grape
varieties), and Austria, Canada and Chile
get a worthy showing too. There are some
affordable French wines here, but things
really get exciting with the Spanish listings:
the Cowins delve into newly fashionable
regions such as Costers del Segre, Utiel
Requena and Campo de Borja with real
relish. Look out for the informative
quarterly newsletter and individually
tailored mixed cases.   **£5**

Best Buys

- Wolfsgraben, Sepp Moser, Grüner
  Veltliner (Austria) £6.99
- Mission Hills, Pinot Blanc, Okanagan
  Valley (Canada) £6.99
- Nieto y Senetiner, Merlot Reserve,
  Mendoza (Argentina) £7.99

To find a wine merchant with
a particular strength in wines
from a certain country or
region, see the regional
chapters in the 'Best wine-
producing countries' section.

John Frazier

Head office: Stirling Road, Cranmore Industrial
Estate, Shirley, Solihull, West Midlands B90 4NE
Tel: 0121-704 3415   Fax: 0121-711 2710

2 Old Warwick Road, Lapworth, Solihull,
West Midlands B94 6LU
Tel: (01564) 784695

Main Road, Tiddington, nr Stratford-upon-Avon,
Warwickshire CV37 7AN
Tel: (01789) 262398
Email: sales@fraziers.co.uk
Website: www.fraziers.co.uk

France is a big deal with John Frazier.
The team have access to some very fine
Bordeaux from key vintages back to
1988 (plus some sensational 1961), decent
champagnes (Dom Pérignon and Krug
among them), good Burgundy names,
respectable Rhône bottlings, and plenty
of regional wines from the Mediterranean
vineyards. Competitively priced Australian
wines feature as strongly as ever, and
imaginatively chosen sparklers are on offer
from everywhere outside Champagne. South
African wines include some stellar properties
(Thelema, Hamilton Russell), and Chilean
and Argentinian wines make a good
showing. On balance, the Old Worlders here
are more exciting, but JF constantly refreshes
its selection and new wines regularly join
the fray. It's always a pleasure to dip in and
see what's on offer among this interesting
lot.   **£5**

Best Buys

- Promessa, Negroamaro, Puglia 1999
  (Italy) £4.50
- Montana, Lindauer Rosé sparkling
  NV (New Zealand) £6.45
- Guigal, Côtes du Rhône 1999
  (Southern Rhône) £8.95

Mills Whitcombe

New Lodge Farm, Peterchurch, Hereford
HR3 6BJ
Tel: (01981) 550028   Fax: (01981) 550027
Email: info@millswhitcombe.co.uk
Website: www.millswhitcombe.co.uk

This Herefordshire merchant just grows and grows. The focus has always been on quality wines, accompanied by plenty of fruit-driven easy drinking in the mix, so balancing your minimum-order mixed case between treats and quaffers will be no problem. Mills Whitcombe has a strong liking for innovative producers in the process of carving out their reputation: think Kim Crawford in New Zealand, the rapidly improving JosMeyer estate in Alsace or Olivier Dumaine in Crozes-Hermitage. While Australia, France and Italy stand out, every country is approached with confidence. Bin-end offers are excellent value, especially the 'lucky sip' surprise mixed cases. Service promises to be 'loud and lively'. Look out for tastings tutored by leading winemakers. **£5**

Best Buys

- Black River, Merlot/Pinot Noir 2000 (Argentina) £5.21
- JosMeyer, le Kottabe, Riesling 1999 (Alsace) £10.73
- Domaine du Vieux Lazeret Châteauneuf-du-Pape (Southern Rhône) £12.99

Noble Rot Wine Warehouses

18 Market Street, Bromsgrove, Worcestershire B61 8DA
Tel: (01527) 575606   Fax: (01527) 833133
Email: info@noble-rot.co.uk
Website: www.noble-rot.co.uk

Noble Rot offers enough low- to mid-price wine to seriously tempt customers away from monotonous supermarket styles. The aim is to be approachable and unpretentious rather than to overwhelm with top quality and inflated prices. All in all, buyer Julie Wyres and her team succeed at this very well. The core, low-risk range is full of generic wines that sum up a region: well-priced Cornas and Châteauneuf-du-Pape from the Rhône, Fleurie from Beaujolais, and a range of Brown Brothers' varietal wines from Australia. (Plus a few Old-Git and Old-Tart-type brands for good cheer.) The more adventurous choices, of which the

team are really proud, include Charlie Melton Shiraz from Australia, Ridge Lytton Springs Zinfandel from California and more. Where Noble Rot really succeeds, however, is with its pre-selected mixed cases.   **£5**

Best Buys

- Dr L Riesling 2003 (Germany) £5.98
- Christa Rolf, Barossa/Shiraz/Grenache, Barossa Valley 2001 (Australia) £8.99
- Jansz, Premium NV sparkling, Tasmania (Australia) £9.99

Parfrements

68 Cecily Road, Cheylesmore, Coventry CV3 5LA
Tel: 024-7650 3646
Email: sales@parfrements.co.uk
Website: www.parfrements.co.uk

This is a short but characterful selection, steering well away from French classics (how refreshing) and bringing in the likes of Argentinian Malbec, Quincy Sauvignon Blanc from the Loire, Marlborough Pinot Gris from New Zealand, and modern Portuguese red from tangy-and-different grapes such as Touriga Nacional. (The latter is actually a key constituent of port, and offers similarly rich, violetty flavours.) Owner/buyer Gerald Gregory keeps his wines well within the affordable £7–£20 price bracket, but finds that many of his customers are spending towards the upper limits of this range – meaning he can afford to bring in even more quirky and interesting bottles. Look out for the customer club with news of monthly tastings and bulletins on the arrival of any new wines.   **£5**

Best Buys

- Ribatejo, Segada, Fernão Pires 2002 (Portugal) £5.34
- Luigi Bosca Paraiso, Tempranillo 2001 (Argentina) £6.34
- Saintsbury, Garnet, Pinot Noir, Carneros 1999 (California) £14.44

Whitebridge Wines

Unit 21, Whitebridge Estate, Stone,
Staffordshire ST15 8LQ
Tel: (01785) 817229   Fax: (01785) 811181
Email: info@whitebridgewines.co.uk
Website: www.whitebridgewines.co.uk

Francis Peel and his team are determined to prove that there's life beyond the supermarkets, and the first few pages of the Whitebridge list should leave customers in no doubt. A hefty handful of sub-£5 wines from southern France bear witness to this, supplemented by juicy Riojas, Portuguese Dão, some crisp (and interesting) Italian whites, and not a few sturdy Chilean bottlings. Whitebridge, however, is also about quality. Impressive allocations from the world's top estates crop up all over this list. Portuguese Redoma from Dirk Niepoort makes an interesting (and good-value) addition to the classy Bordeaux and California wines that grace the upper price brackets here. Francis has a good eye for the eclectic too: don't miss out on the Mexican Zinfandel or chunky Moroccan wine.   **(£5)**

Best Buys

- Dirk Niepoort, Redoma Rosado, Douro 2001 (Portugal) £8.99
- Jim Clendenen, Wild Boy, Chardonnay, Santa Barbera 2000 (California) £12.98
- Inama, Vigneti di Foscarino, Soave, Veneto 2000 (Italy) £12.98

North England

Harrogate Fine Wine Company

Corn Exchange Cellars, The Ginnel, Harrogate,
North Yorkshire HG1 2RB
Tel: (01423) 522270   Fax: (01423) 508315
Email: phil@harrogatefinewinecompany.com
Website: www.harrogatefinewine.co.uk

So far, at this young company, most countries get just a short showing.

Bordeaux, for example, is summed up within 18 wines; there are 7 Rhône wines, 20 Burgundies, and brief glances at North and South America. Despite a professed love of Riesling (it's getting more popular with customers), there's only one each from Austria and Alsace. But real enthusiasm kicks in with a delicious array of interesting grape varieties from Germany, plus a wider selection of Italian (40) and Spanish (38) wines. Things get more exciting with the South African collection – something of a speciality, covering all the main regions. Despite a professed hatred of sherry, owner/buyer Phil Ball stocks 17 rather superb bottles.   **(£5)**

Best Buys

- Paul Cluver, Weisser Riesling, Elgin 2002 (South Africa) £6.99
- Sepp Moser, Von Den Terrassen, Riesling 2001 (Austria) £9.99
- Marqués de Murrieta Ygay, Rioja Reserva 1999 (Spain) £10.99

Nidderdale Fine Wines

High Street, Pateley Bridge, Harrogate,
North Yorkshire HG3 5AW
Tel: (01423) 711703   Fax: (01423) 712239
Email: info@southaustralianwines.com
Website: www.southaustralianwines.com

Nidderdale is a specialist in South Australian wines. All the stars are here: Nepenthe for its Mount Lofty Ranges Chardonnay, d'Arenberg for its burly Rhône-varietal wines, Grosset and Petaluma for their mouth-watering Rieslings, plus of course Henschke, Yalumba, Turkey Flat and Veritas for Cabernets and big reds. But Nidderdale does a fine job of introducing smaller producers and regions too: Wrattonbully, Fleurieu and Limestone Coast are all Aussie *terroirs* due for discovery. Style-wise, everything's here from Australian sparkling reds to dessert and fortified, all at good-value prices. Nidderdale has a fair smattering of wines from other Down-Under regions – all chosen with equal care – but the main collection is the one to watch.   **(£5)**

Best Buys

- Nepenthe, Mount Lofty Ranges, Pinot Gris, Adelaide Hills 2001 (South Australia) £8.99
- d'Arenberg, The Laughing Magpie Shiraz/Viognier 2002 (South Australia) £12.20
- Turkey Flat, Grenache, Barossa Valley 2001 (South Australia) £12.50

R & R Fine Wines

6 Hebburn Drive, Brandlesholme, Bury, Lancashire BL8 1ED
Tel: 0161-762 0022   Fax: 0161-763 4477
Email: fine.wines@btconnect.com

This small, but growing, merchant specialises in offbeat Portugal and any wines from boutique producers who focus on quality – Cullen and Mount Langi Ghiran in Australia for example. R & R takes in wines from just about everywhere. There's a handy selection of sub-£20 claret, some smart Burgundies (including quite a few from the precious 1996 vintage), and one or two delicious dessert wines from Alsace, the Loire and Germany. And from Portugal, R & R's passion, not only are there fashionable red Douro wines (that taste like port without the added spirit), but Portugal's own quirky grapes such as Jaen, Tinto Cão, Encruzado and Alvarinho. This is an ambitious, rigorous team, with quirky taste-preferences: one to watch for the future.   **(£5)**

Best Buys

- Château Langlois, Coteaux du Layon 1997 (Loire) £6.75
- Quinta dos Roques, Tinta Roriz 1997 (Portugal) £13.50
- Arneis, Seghesio, Sonoma 2000 (California) £14.50

For an explanation of the symbols used at the top of some of the merchant entries, see page 118.

Richard Granger

West Jesmond Station, Lyndhurst Avenue, Jesmond, Newcastle upon Tyne NE2 3HH
Tel: 0191-281 5000   Fax: 0191-281 8141
Email: sales@richardgrangerwines.co.uk
Website: www.richardgrangerwines.co.uk

This might look like a short list of wines at first, but peer closely at the fine print and a world of vinous treasures is revealed. Things get better if you visit the Newcastle shop in person: Alastair Stewart and his buying team will advise and suggest new avenues of interest – perhaps steering you towards their ever-growing list of New World wines (cool-climate Pinot Noir, from California's Russian River and New Zealand's Marlborough, feature strongly), or the lengthy (and eminently prestigious) list of Riojas and Ribera del Dueros from Spain. Spicy Alsace wines and robust Italian reds are on offer, and there's a warm welcome for Bordeaux enthusiasts, with a 60-strong range spanning all the 1990s vintages and including top Sauternes. Not a merchant to be underestimated.

Best Buys

- Castell de Remei, Gotim Bru, Costers del Segre 2001 (Spain) £7.52
- Trimbach, Riesling 2001 (Alsace) £9.57
- Shadowfax, Pinot Noir, Geelong/ Yarra Valley 2001 (Australia) £11.75

Scatchard's Wine Merchants

Head Office: 38 Vernon Street, Liverpool L2 2AY
Tel: 0151-236 6468   Fax: 0151-236 6475

21 Victoria Street, Liverpool L1 6BD
Tel: 0151-236 2955   Fax: 0151-236 2955

11 Albert Road, Hoylake, Wirral CH47 2AB
Tel: 0151-632 0507   Fax: 0151-632 0507
Email: jon@scatchard.com

Scatchard's has undergone changes of late, and is now, after selling off the wholesale branch, focusing purely on retail business. What remains is a succinct but quirky global list. Champagne choices are plentiful and diverse, and there are a fair handful of Italian classics and Australian grape varieties, and some tempting vintage ports. Bordeaux and Burgundies look like relative bargains (around the £10 and £15 marks), but beware: at these prices they aren't all of reliable quality. Better to stay with Loire, Rhône and Alsace, where one or two top French names appear. In general, more tasting notes, descriptions and depth to the New World choices would be advantageous, but perhaps these will happen once Scatchard's has completed its second year in business. Watch out for in-store tastings every weekend. **(£5)**

Best Buys

- Señorio de Sarria Viñedo No 9, Cabernet Sauvignon, Navarra 2001 (Spain) £7
- Cave de Turckheim, Pinot Gris Réserve 2002 (Alsace) £7.50
- Clos du Val, Cabernet Sauvignon, Napa Valley 2000 (California) £16.75

Scotland

Gordon & MacPhail

58–60 South Street, Elgin, Moray IV30 1JY
Tel: (01343) 545110   Fax: (01343) 540155
Email: retail@gordonandmacphail.com
Website: www.gordonandmacphail.com

There are some interesting wines here, but also a worrying tendency to focus on bulk suppliers – in particular, of California and South African wines – from whom prices aren't always as cheap as they might be. Australian wines, mistakenly described as 'prestigious', are dreary, all-too-familiar names, and the same can be said for Burgundy and Bordeaux. For a company holding such a large and imaginative range of whiskies, these are disappointing representations of the wine world. Thank goodness things get better in the Rhône and Italian sections: these, along with madeiras, extensive New Zealand coverage, sherry, and offbeat wines from Canada, Uruguay and even Bulgaria, are where the real Gordon & MacPhail vinous passions lie.

Best Buys

- Château Pech-Celeyran, Coteaux du Languedoc La Clape 2002 (Languedoc) £6.29
- A Mano, Primitivo, Puglia 2002 (Italy) £6.99
- Babich Estate, Riesling, Marlborough 2002 (New Zealand) £8.15

Luvians Bottleshop

93 Bonnygate, Cupar, Fife KY15 4LG
Tel: (01334) 654820   Fax: (01334) 654820

66 Market Street, St Andrews, Fife KY16 9NT
Tel: (01334) 477752   Fax: (01334) 477752
Email: info@luvians.com
Website: www.luvians.com

Luvians is particularly proud of its classic Old World wines from big-name, fashionable growers: Lafite, Latour, Domaine de la Romanée-Conti, Raveneau, Sauzet, Mugnier, Sassicaia, Solaia, Huët and Trimbach among them. In fact, this merchant could be justifiably proud of any of its country ranges. Some collections here are shorter than others – such as the Rhône and South Africa – but quality is no less apparent in the wines. Don't miss the spectacular display of champagnes, in large-format bottles too, or the fabulous array of ports, madeiras and sherries. The only things missing are the tasting notes and wine descriptions to guide customers not already in the know. A new branch of Luvians is opening soon in Perth.

Best Buys

- Barbadillo, manzanilla sherry (Spain) £5.99
- Radici, Fiano di Avellino (Italy) £9.99
- Schloss Saarstein, Riesling Spätlese (Germany) £11.99

Wales

Terry Platt Wine Merchants

Council Street West, Llandudno,
Conwy LL30 1ED
Tel: (01492) 874099   Fax: (01492) 874788
Email: info@terryplattwines.co.uk
Website: www.terryplattwines.co.uk

The Terry Platt list starts with 60 wines priced under £5, and thereafter only strays above £10 when there's a real need – for classy bottles to illustrate the classic regions (top Champagne, Bordeaux and Spanish wines, for example). The strength of this list is good value but it still covers interesting wine regions, grapes and vintages, and keeps customers guessing with oddities such as Mexican, Corsican and even Welsh wines. TP can be particularly proud of its newly expanded ranges from Italy, Spain and Chile (with good reason) but Argentinian choices are broader than many too, as are those from Alsace. There's also a useful collection of 26 half bottles and over 20 large-format (magnum and bigger) bottles to enhance celebrations and cater for thirsty friends. **(£5)**

Best Buys

- Pinot Noir Perolière, Vin de Pays de l'Ile de Beauté 1999 (Corsica) £5.11
- Château de la Levraudière, Muscadet de Sèvre-et-Maine Sur Lie 2002 (Loire) £5.49
- L A Cetto, Petite Sirah, Baja California 2000 (Mexico) £5.86

Enjoying wine further

Good wines from top restaurants

This section lists eating establishments that feature in our sister publication *The Good Food Guide 2005* for their outstanding wine cellars as well as for excellent food. All are inspected on a regular basis to ensure that their cuisine meets rigorous standards.

Wine by the glass (the more, the merrier) gives you the opportunity to try a different wine with different items on the menu and match flavours accordingly – a real boon to any restaurant-goer.

The price range at the end of each entry represents the likely charge for one person having a three-course or set meal and includes house wine, coffee and any service or cover charges. We advise you to call ahead and check exact opening times and prices.

London

Bibendum Michelin House, 81 Fulham Road, London SW3 6RD ☎ 020-7581 5817. Conran flagship above eponymous shop, serving modern brasserie cooking. Superb wine list, with good range below and around £20. An enduring collection of France's finest provides the core; Italy, Australia and California head the rest. Just six wines by the glass. £46–£100

Bleeding Heart The Cellars, Bleeding Heart Yard, Greville Street, London EC1N 8SJ ☎ 020-7242 2056. Warm and welcoming restaurant serving the likes of foie gras terrine with roast fig vinaigrette and sea bass on lobster risotto. France dominates the wine list; New World innovators hail from New Zealand, Australia and California. Sub-£20 bottles and 26 wines by the glass are available (£3.75 to £7.95). £36–£65

Chez Bruce 2 Bellevue Road, London SW17 7EG ☎ 020-8672 0114. An appealing modern menu offers generous choice at this restaurant overlooking Wandsworth Common. The effortless wine list reflects trends. Around 30 table wines served by the glass. Expect quality but few bargains, with only 2 wines under £20. £40–£80

The Don The Courtyard, 20 St Swithin's Lane, London EC4N 8AD ☎ 020-7626 2606. Historic character to this twin of Bleeding Heart (above). Features dressed-up classics and spot-on confections like tournedos Rossini

with foie gras. Interesting sherries, wines and ports by the glass; bottles are mostly French plus good Spanish, Italian and New World producers. Not so much choice under £20 – try the owners' Trinity Hill in New Zealand. £37–£68

Enoteca Turi 28 Putney High Street, London SW15 1SQ ☎ 020-8785 4449. Italian regional cuisine, with pasta made in-house. Every menu item has a wine suggested. Affordable starter-point wines and pricier top producers – mostly Italian, also from France and Spain – are on the long list, focusing on Super-Tuscans, Brunellos and Barolos. £32–£61

Fifth Floor Harvey Nichols, 109–125 Knightsbridge, London SW1X 7RJ ☎ 020-7235 5250. Striking, sleek in-store dining room where up-to-the-minute dishes include loin of lamb flavoured with curry spices, finished with roasting juices and watermelon, and coconut tart with roasted pineapple. Twenty-four wines by the glass (£3.50–£13.50) from a 'pleasingly varied' impressive list starting at £13.50. £31–£90

Gordon Ramsay 68–69 Royal Hospital Road, London SW3 4HP ☎ 020-7352 4441. 'Britain's best restaurant' exudes understated confidence. Stratospheric standards underlie dynamic food. The wine list starts at £12 and bristles with big names and steep prices, with forays into interesting regional French, German and Italian whites. Prestige bottles aside, New World selections are brief. Eight wines by the glass from £5. Plentiful half bottles. £51–£131

Great Eastern Hotel, Aurora Liverpool Street, London EC2M 7QN ☎ 020-7618 7000. Spectacular grandeur at hotel dining room serving 'posh' offerings such as lobster and Anjou pigeon – exploited in surprisingly adventurous cooking. Impressive Bordeaux and Burgundy shine on the wine list, and other specialities are the Loire, Rhône, Italy and the New World. The Spanish house red and white (£15) offer good quality. Ten wines by the glass (£3.75–£13.50). £42–£81

Oxo Tower Oxo Tower Wharf, Barge House Street, London SE1 9PH ☎ 020-7803 3888. Invigorating choice and stunning South Bank views. Japanese notes predominate (sea bass saikyo-style) among French paysan, African and even old English influences. The house selection of around 40 wines ranges from £14 to £68.50. For real depth the 'Big List' rounds up hundreds of good, great and cultish wines from Old and New Worlds, for all budgets. £42–£96

Pied-à-Terre 34 Charlotte Street, London W1T 2NH ☎ 020-7636 1178. An unobtrusive, contemporary setting for clear flavours and technical expertise where food is 'expensive but worth it'. Among the wines Burgundy and Bordeaux are the strongest French offerings. California and, unusually, Austria also feature. Bottles under £20 in many regions, but mark-ups are high. £44–£153

Le Pont de la Tour 36D Shad Thames, London SE1 2YE ☎ 020-7403 8403. Glamorous Thames setting for sympathetically treated ingredients like salmon tartare with confit tomatoes and basil, or lamb rump with roasted sweetbreads, gratin and morels. The classy, convincing wine list includes Loire and Rhône heavyweights. Some flavoursome wines under £25; 12 by the glass from £6 are a cut above. £47–£99

Ransome's Dock 35–37 Parkgate Road, London SW11 4NP ☎ 020-7223 1611. Supremely simple scallops, lamb with tarragon jus and al dente pasta typify cooking with character and intention at this canalside eatery. Australia, California and France lead the exciting wine list from

around £14; serious wines by the glass start at £4.50, or treat yourself to a Lustau almacenista sherry. £34–£73

RSJ 33 Coin Street, London SE1 9NR ☎ 020-7928 4554. Delightful nineteenth-century building in revived area; despite occasional misses, food is a technical and aesthetic treat. Superb Loire choices impress on the wine list: great prices and wine notes encourage experimentation. Ten wines by the glass from £2.95. Coverage of other countries is brief. £31–£51

Square 6–10 Bruton Street, London W1J 6PU ☎ 020-7495 7100. Creamy, comforting dishes and well-handled seafood in a spacious, buzzing dining room. A helpful sommelier translates the epic list; Burgundy and Germany lead the whites and worthwhile bottles are obtainable at £20. Classy choices too of champagne, sherry and dessert wine. £47–£124

Tate Britain Restaurant Millbank, London SW1P 4RG ☎ 020-7887 8825. A Whistler mural is the talking-point for gallery diners munching on attractively combined seasonal ingredients. The civilised wine list boasts great names, properly matured vintages and half bottles. Cutting-edge selections include 20 by the glass (£3.95–£9.50). £35–£63

La Trompette 5–7 Devonshire Road, Chiswick, London W4 2EU ☎ 020-8747 1836. Study in brown with intimately spaced tables. Confident cooking. Exciting wines by the glass (£3.70–£11.50) introduce a confident wine list on song in all regions, although France, Italy, Australia and New Zealand stand out. Prices are from £14.50; above £20 the real action starts. £36–£64

Zaika 1 Kensington High Street, London W8 5NP ☎ 020-7795 6533. Made-over banking hall, now Indian restaurant. Fresh and vibrant spicing. A wine list of over 350 includes massive selections of the cream of France and Italy, and some fine dessert wines. Fifteen by the glass range from £4.50 to £7.50, and under £20 there is fair choice. £45–£98

South England

Cherwell Boathouse 50 Bardwell Road, Oxford OX2 6ST ☎ (01865) 552746. Sophisticated conservatory-style restaurant serving dishes such as slow-roast loin of pork and a dessert of lemon, parsley and gin sorbet. Fine clarets and Burgundy accompany the flavoursome food; wines from the rest of France are good value. Well-chosen modern touches. £23–£46

Corse Lawn House Corse Lawn, Gloucestershire GL19 4LZ ☎ (01452) 780771. A calm setting for this bistro and dining room, with summer tables by a large pond (formerly used to wash horse-drawn coaches). Solid French bottles (top-notch Bordeaux and Burgundy) complement the long carte, with several under £20. Lots of half bottles, good sherries and ports add extra interest. £31–£75

Crooked Billet 2 Westbrook End, Newton Longville, Buckinghamshire MK17 0DF ☎ (01908) 373936. A proper local combined with a restaurant, where food is taken seriously and elaboration peaks on the dinner menu. An immaculate collection of nearly 200 wines, including an in-depth French selection with several Alsatian Zind-Humbrechts. Prices, from £14.50 a bottle, are generally high but all are available by the glass. £32–£116

Fat Duck High Street, Bray, Berkshire SL6 2AQ ☎ (01628) 580333. Fun and food fireworks in pretty village at unassuming restaurant offering clean, pure flavours. South African whites, Alsace and Loire wines appeal on list starting around £20, alongside magnificence from Bordeaux, Burgundy and Italy. An exciting range by the glass (£5 to £16), plus aperitifs and dessert sherries. £52–£134

Glasshouse 14 Station Parade, Kew, Surrey TW9 3PZ ☎ 020-8940 6777. 'Neighbourhood' restaurant, serving the best in contemporary food at close-together tables. Modern trends include five sherries by the glass from £3.50 and bottles from Austria and Germany. France, Italy, Australia and California complete the list (few under £20). Some interesting halves and magnums. £31–£80

Gravetye Manor Vowels Lane, East Grinstead, West Sussex RH19 4LJ ☎ (01342) 810567. Deft cooking and flavoursome partnerships at ancient house with famed gardens and panelled rooms. The heavyweight wine list unearths Burgundy and Bordeaux treasures. Modern gems hail from Australia, South Africa,

California and more affordable South America. Fair pricing starts at £16, or £5 by the glass. £39–£88

Hotel du Vin & Bistro 2–6 Ship Street, Brighton, East Sussex BN1 1AD ☎ (01273) 718588. Spacious, galleried bar and buzzing brasserie. Accurate fish cookery and pleasing dishes make up for some inconsistencies. All regions have depth, breadth and length; choice is commendable under £20. £32–£62

Hotel du Vin & Bistro Crescent Road, Tunbridge Wells, Kent TN1 2LY ☎ (01892) 526455. Modern bistro menus offer 'robust flavours, simple ingredients yet sensational results' at this elegant Georgian townhouse hotel. An outstanding global wine range, with fair prices and knowledgeable Gallic service; not many wines are under £20 or by the glass. £33–£63

Hotel du Vin & Bistro Southgate Street, Winchester, Hampshire SO23 9EF ☎ (01962) 841414. Muted, brasserie-style setting for top-notch Sunday lunch roast beef, or chargrilled polenta with wild mushrooms, herbs and truffle oil. Magnificent wines cover the lower reaches as well as the upper crust. France is strongest, followed by Italy, Australia and the USA. House wines start at £13, or from £3 by the glass. £35–£62

Longueville Manor St Saviour, Jersey, Channel Islands JE2 7WF ☎ (01534) 725501. Norman manor with comfortable trappings and cuisine of a high standard. A 'taste of Jersey' version of the menu centres on fish. Classical wines are strong on Burgundy and Bordeaux; prices start at £16 and there's a wealth of vintage champagnes. £27–£88

Le Manoir aux Quat' Saisons Church Road, Great Milton, Oxfordshire OX44 7PD ☎ (01844) 278881. Sumptuous surroundings and knockout food, with impeccable service. The encyclopaedic wine list covers all corners of France and some Bordeaux vintages. Afterthoughts from the rest of the world stretch to Uruguay and Romania. Just six come by the glass, from £6 to £8; bottles are in keeping with the food prices. £68–£151

Le Poussin at Parkhill Beaulieu Road, Lyndhurst, Hampshire SO43 7FZ ☎ 023-8028 2944. Former boys' school offering a burnished style of country-house cooking. The wine list has depth beyond the initial pages of pricy French wines, with short but interesting selections from elsewhere. Thirty wines by the glass (£5 to £25). £50–£87

Read's Macknade Manor, Canterbury Road, Faversham, Kent ME13 8XE ☎ (01795) 535344. Substantial yet homely Georgian manor. Seasonal and local materials on the menu are teamed with 70 'best buy' wines from £16 to £26. Clarets and Burgundy predominate, backed up by other French bottles. Antipodean wines are best of the rest. £34–£95

Sir Charles Napier Spriggs Alley, Chinnor, Oxfordshire OX39 4BX ☎ (01494) 483011. Ancient buildings by beech wood. Walkers can try tomato risotto with squid and Parmesan or roast guinea fowl with confit of shallots, rösti and madeira. A lengthy, immaculate wine list has something for everyone in all regions (including half bottles), and £3.50 to £6 buys adventurous glasses. £35–£77

Vineyard at Stockcross Stockcross, Berkshire RG20 8JU ☎ (01635) 528770. Plush, modern hotel with appealing, luxury-strewn menu. The astonishing wine list stretches to two volumes, with what must be the UK's finest California selection (including owner Sir Peter Michael's own vineyard) and choices from the rest of the world. Some good-value bottles. £36–£94

East England

Old Bridge Hotel 1 High Street, Huntingdon, Cambridgeshire PE29 3TQ ☎ (01480) 424300. Former bank serving fresh, seasonal food of considerable panache and bold flavours. Forty wines are under £20, arranged by style, and a 'top-class' list offers famous, rare and offbeat bottles. £30–£59

South-west England

Gidleigh Park Chagford, Devon TQ13 8HH ☎ (01647) 432367. Characterful, solid house in grounds with flowing river. 'Inspired cooking' exceeds gastronomic expectations. An outstanding European wine selection dominates, though California is also strong. With no bottles below £20 prices are otherwise reasonable. Ten wines by the glass from £6.50 to £13. £56–£116

Hotel du Vin & Bistro The Sugar House, Narrow Lewins Mead, Bristol BS1 2NU ☎ 0117-925 5577. Pan-European food with some challenging combinations in a former sugar warehouse. All wine regions brim with good choices over a broad price range (and there is plentiful choice under £20). Alternatively try the prestige wines or 45 sparklers. £33–£58

Lewtrenchard Manor Lewdown, Devon EX20 4PN ☎ (01566) 783222. Welcoming, ancient house with candlelit dining room. Try terrine of smoked chicken and globe artichoke with goat's cheese beignets, or slow-cooked salmon with smoked salmon won tons in coriander and lemongrass sauce. An intelligent wine list cherry-picks France and South Africa. Seven house wines are £13 a bottle, £2.95 a glass. £29–£58

Seafood Restaurant Riverside, Padstow, Cornwall PL28 8BY ☎ (01841) 532700. Rick Stein flagship, delivering excellent global fishy fare to broad customer base. The extensive wine list is well matched to the cooking, notably in the 14-strong, quality-oriented house selection (£16.50 to £23.75 a bottle / £3.55 to £4.50 a glass). £50–£109

White House 11 Long Street, Williton, Somerset TA4 4QW ☎ (01984) 632777. This Georgian mansion is a haven of good taste. Menus radiate unpretentious vibes and ingredients hail from local producers. Tempting monthly selections on the wine list, offering mature selections at fair prices. Prices start at £14.75, or £4 a glass. £53–£82

Midlands

Hotel du Vin & Bistro 25 Church Street, Birmingham B3 2NR ☎ 0121-200 0600. Sympathetically restored building with wooden floors. The menu sweeps across Europe, while the wine list embraces the globe. Prices – from Languedoc-Roussillon *vin de pays* (£14.50) to 1990 Mas de Daumas Gassac at £105 – cater to all pockets. £32–£56

North England

Chester Grosvenor, Arkle Eastgate, Chester, Cheshire CH1 1LT ☎ (01244) 324024. The pillared Arkle restaurant sports paintings of horses. Luxury ingredients predominate and vegetarians get their own menu. The heavyweight wines range from

£12 to £5,000 (house wines hover around £15.50), and Burgundies are spectacular. Plentiful half bottles. £41–£94

Devonshire Arms, Burlington Restaurant Bolton Abbey, North Yorkshire BD23 6AJ ☎ (01756) 710441. Country-house hotel in Wharfedale countryside. Well-presented dishes include veal layered with foie gras and spinach, and Royal Tokaji jelly and rhubarb. The weighty wine list traverses Burgundy, the Rhône and Italian reds. California's ultra-rare Screaming Eagle vintages start at £1,650; reassuringly, 28 house wines are under £20. £38–£108

Hotel du Vin & Bistro Prospect Place, Harrogate HG1 1LB ☎ (01423) 856800. Interior décor has a hunting theme and a modern brasserie vibe predominates. The place has a real pulse to it, quickened by willing service. The wine list covers the world in detail and depth: over a dozen options in Australian Shiraz; clarets date back to 1982. Prices open at £12.50, around 20 wines come by the glass, but value for money is variable. £40–£59

Sharrow Bay Ullswater, Cumbria CA10 2LZ ☎ (01768) 486301. Touches of gold in this pampering place. Food is varied and attractive, perhaps fillet of brill with lightly spiced aubergine or dark chocolate tart with raspberry sorbet. On the wine list, the rest of the world augments fine Bordeaux and Burgundy. 'Sharrow selection' wines (16 bottles from £16.95 to £36) match the food and are available by glass. £51–£77

Sous le Nez en Ville The Basement, Quebec House, Quebec Street, Leeds LS1 2HA ☎ 0113-244 0108. Appealing modern European cooking at individual venue. From Bordeaux to Australia, wines are suitably bottled-aged, fairly priced (bottles from £10.95, glasses £2.20 to £5) and of outstanding quality. £28–£57

White Moss House Rydal Water, Grasmere, Cumbria LA22 9SE ☎ (015394) 35295. Restrained dining room where the formula never varies (no choice pre-dessert, and fish after soup). Materials are fresh, sometimes organic and often local. Exciting wines feature French regions, their grapes and New World counterparts. Fair prices, with a good range from £2.75 by the glass. £45–£54

Scotland

Cellar 24 East Green, Anstruther, Fife KY10 3AA ☎ (01333) 310378. Warm ambience at restaurant dedicated to good ingredients and seasonality. The wine list is equally at home in Australia, Chile and traditional France (notably Alsace). Fair prices start at £15, or £3.75 to £5.50 for seven by the glass. £31–£63

Champany Inn Champany Corner, Linlithgow, West Lothian EH49 7LU ☎ (01506) 834532. A Chop and Ale House and main dining room mostly serve brilliantly flavoured and sauced steak dishes. South Africa accounts for over 100 wines, plus the six house bottlings (from £15.50/£3.95 a glass). Quality French and Spanish choices are to be found beyond this selection (few are under £20). £37–£96

Forth Floor Harvey Nichols, 30–34 St Andrews Square, Edinburgh EH2 2AD ☎ 0131-524 8350. Magnificent castle views from the formal restaurant. A classical menu has some fashionable touches. The wine excites: glossy New World bottles are whimsically categorised, while Europe is more formally treated by region. Choices under £20 are plentiful. £35–£70

Greywalls Hotel Muirfield, Gullane, East Lothian EH31 2EG ☎ (01620) 842144. Near the golf course, this restaurant feels like a country home. Simple ingredients plus some surprises on the menu. Mastering Burgundy and Bordeaux, the wine list also accommodates the New World. Good choice under £20, but few by the glass. £59–£70

Peat Inn Peat Inn, Fife KY15 5LH ☎ (01334) 840206. Warm and welcoming former coaching inn, with impressive domestic and French menu offerings. The wine selection is structured around French regions, supplemented by global round-ups and a stand-alone German section. Prices are good for the quality, though bottles under £20 are few. House wines are £16 or £3.40 a glass. £33–£75

Summer Isles Hotel Achiltibuie, Highland IV26 2YG ☎ (01854) 622282. White house with conservatory commanding majestic island views. The kitchen uses produce from sea and stream, hill, garden and the local smokehouse. The international, if French-dominated, wine list supplies some affordable bottles (30 red Bordeaux under £30) and an array of post-prandials. £28–£62

Ubiquitous Chip 12 Ashton Lane, Glasgow G12 8SJ ☎ 0141-334 5007. Popular fixture consisting of a bar/brasserie, restaurant and drinking arm. Main dining room comprises a covered courtyard. Food has a strong national identity, with some elaborate embellishments. Wines muster up serious Bordeaux and a worthwhile range from Germany. Five house wines are £14.95 or £3.75 by the glass. £37–£72

Valvona & Crolla Caffè Bar 19 Elm Row, Edinburgh EH7 4AA ☎ 0131-556 6066. Outpost of Italy for 70 years – deli, cookery shop, café and wine merchant (see 'Where to buy wine', page 189) – which also draws on excellent Scottish influences. Perhaps Britain's most exciting Italian list, with 'recommended' wines by the glass (£2.75 to £8) while a £4 corkage charge allows access to the range at retail price. £22–£47

Wales

Fairyhill Reynoldston, Swansea SA3 1BS ☎ (01792) 390139. Fixed-price menus and a simple lunchtime carte bring French touches to local ingredients at this Gower Peninsula house with lake and woodland. Three-figure prices for fine clarets feature, but two pages in the 40-page list host wines under £20. The Rhône, Australia and Austria are worth a look. £32–£63

Penhelig Arms Hotel Terrace Road, Aberdovey, Gwynedd LL35 0LT ☎ (01654) 767215. Seaside inn where food is praised for consistency and reliability. The passionately chosen wine list embraces all regions, with a broad selection by the glass. Value for money is outstanding – 18 house wines are £10.50 to £13.50. £24–£35

Plas Bodegroes Nefyn Road, Pwllheli, Gwynedd LL53 5TH ☎ (01758) 612363. Cream house near woodland, whose modern dining room offers up straightforward, contemporary food with evocative native roots. Bordeaux, Burgundy, Alsace and Italy are strong in a wine list that embraces all regions and offers numerous half bottles. Fair prices mean 80 bottles under £20. £30–£64

St Tudno Hotel, Terrace Promenade, Llandudno, Conwy ☎ (01492) 874411. Flamboyant cooking at discreet hotel overlooking the promenade. Portions are generous, and the spicy Great Orme crab cake wins praise. The enthusiastic, quality-packed wine list is mostly reasonably priced, with prices from £12.50 and a dozen by the glass (£3.50 to £6.20). £27–£63

Tyddyn Llan Llandrillo, Denbighshire LL21 0ST ☎ (01490) 440264. Rural restaurant-with-rooms; food – free of frills and distractions – is characterised by first-class materials (some local) and brilliant handling. Fine California wines run through the innovative range, which lists 'smooth and mature' reds in their prime. Fifty are under £20. £32–£65

Pubs serving good wine

Drinking a good wine in a pub is a more realistic expectation these days. The following pubs, featured in *The Which? Pub Guide 2005*, serve better-than-average wine. All offer fairly priced, imaginative choices and global options that complement the food served. They also have helpful wine lists and a decent selection available by the glass, which you can generally purchase without food. Call ahead to check opening times before visiting these establishments.

London

Anglesea Arms 35 Wingate Road, London W6 0UR ☎ 020-8749 1291. A young crowd throngs this happy hostelry with its wood-panelled bar; food has a touch of intrigue. The wine list of 50 caters to most tastes, with the majority of bottles under £20 and a generous 17 by the glass.

Atlas 16 Seagrave Road, London SW6 1RX ☎ 020-7385 9129. Revamped pub with happy atmosphere, comfortable seating and a patio garden. The carefully chosen, short wine list displays flair and sports modern classics, with a dozen by the glass from £2.70, and dishes are hearty and stylish.

Salusbury Pub & Dining Room 50–52 Salusbury Road, London NW6 6NN ☎ 020-7328 3286. Double-fronted building on busy street, serving rustic Italian dishes. The wine list ranges the world looking for great flavours. Most bottles are over £15.

Victoria 10 West Temple Sheen, London SW14 7RT ☎ 020-8876 4238. Stylish venue with whitewashed floorboards, table football and a delightful conservatory restaurant. The quality-conscious, if pricy, wine list includes eight by the glass, and food sees unusual European combinations.

South England

Bird in Hand Bath Road, Knowl Hill, Berkshire RG10 9UP ☎ (01628) 826622. This old coaching inn is now a modern hotel complex; it offers a varied bar menu and separate ambitious restaurant carte. Innovative wines balance fresh, modern flavours with some serious vintage bottles. Sparkling wines delight and dessert wines impress.

Boar's Head Church Street, Ardington, Oxfordshire OX12 8QA ☎ (01235) 833254. Half-timbered pub-cum-restaurant. Earnest Burgundies and Bordeaux head the wine list, which has rich global pickings for under £20 and eight by the glass. Formal food is inventive while the bar menu is simpler.

Chequers Inn Kiln Lane, Wooburn Common, Buckinghamshire HP10 0JQ ☎ (01628) 529575. Roadside inn in the Chiltern Hundreds, serving old-fashioned pub grub as well as more modern fare. The expensive wine list is supplemented by a cheaper blackboard selection of 12 by the glass, occasionally boosted by bin-ends.

Crooked Billet 2 Westbrook End, Newton Longville, Buckinghamshire MK17 0DF ☎ (01908) 373936. See entry in 'Good wines from top restaurants', page 221.

Griffin Inn Fletching, East Sussex TN22 3SS ☎ (01825) 722890. An upmarket restaurant menu features at this traditional village inn. A dozen wines are under £15; try also the main list of 50 mostly European bottles, with seasonally themed specials and high-priced classics.

Jolly Sportsman Chapel Lane, East Chiltington, East Sussex BN7 3BA ☎ (01273) 890400. Popular eating place with clear, strong flavours on the bistro-style menu. The excellent wine list succeeds at all levels; nine by the glass (in three sizes) exemplify its range. Around 150 wines and extensive half bottles will leave you spoilt for choice.

Knife and Cleaver The Grove, Houghton Conquest, Bedfordshire MK45 3LA ☎ (01234) 740387. Fish is the thrust of the restaurant menu; you can also sample pub favourites. The first wine list has 20 by the glass or 50cl carafe; the restaurant selection is grouped by style and sweeps from £11 basics to French classics.

Lamb at Buckland Lamb Lane, Buckland, Oxfordshire SN7 8QN ☎ (01367) 870484. Cotswold-stone pub with sheep decorative theme. The restful restaurant serves first-class dishes. Six good-quality house wines start at £13.25 (also by the glass); the main list majors on traditional France and also dips a toe in New World waters.

Sir Charles Napier Sprigg's Alley, Chinnor, Oxfordshire OX39 4BX ☎ (01494) 483011. See entry in 'Good wines from top restaurants', page 222.

Star Inn Church Street, Old Heathfield, East Sussex TN21 9AH ☎ (01435) 863570. Adapted fifteenth-century hall house, with an enticing pub menu that uses decent raw materials. Six wines are by the glass from a menu offering 40-plus bottles from £12.50 to £25, with plenty under £15.

Three Chimneys Hareplain Road, Biddenden, Kent TN27 8LW ☎ (01580) 291472. This atmospheric pub with gnarled beams exudes a feeling of great age; the Garden Room dining extension is modern. The eight house wines include Kent's Sandhurst Vineyards. Flavoursome southern hemisphere wines are under £15; French bottles cost more.

Trout at Tadpole Bridge Tadpole Bridge, Buckland Marsh, Oxfordshire SN7 8RF ☎ (01367) 870382. This 'real pub with decent food' has one menu throughout. The wine list features 11 by the glass: all bottles under £25 are on a 'pay for what you drink' basis. Try the home-made sloe gin or cherry plum vodka.

White Horse Inn 1 High Street, Chilgrove, West Sussex PO18 9HX ☎ (01243) 535219. Lots of wood creates a simple, modern look for this wisteria-clad coaching inn. The 'indulgence' wine list showcases classics from France and beyond; there's a good selection by the glass. Bar and restaurant menus take in seasonal game, organic meats and local crab and lobster.

Wykeham Arms 75 Kingsgate Street, Winchester, Hampshire SO23 9PE ☎ (01962) 853834. Venerable establishment set amid cobbled streets. The 90-bin wine list ranges across all styles and – with many bottles under £20, several half bottles, and 20 by the (large or small) glass – pleases most comers. Foodwise, simpler lunch options are followed by more elaborate dinner fare.

East England

Anchor Inn Sutton Gault, Cambridgeshire CB6 2BD ☎ (01353) 778537. This canalside former lodging for fen labourers has a modern, imaginative menu and good British cheeses. The well-rounded (if rather pricy) wine list includes mainstream as well as worthwhile alternative names, with decent options by the glass.

Angel Market Place, Lavenham, Suffolk CO10 9QZ ☎ (01787) 247388. The 1420 building dominates Lavenham's exceptional medieval square. In addition to fine local beers it offers 50 or so good-quality wines and eight house basics from around the world (most reasonably priced at under £20).

Bell Inn High Road, Horndon on the Hill, Essex SS17 8LD ☎ (01375) 642463. Bustling, ancient hostelry with a modern and imaginative restaurant menu featuring complex desserts. An irreverent house list offers 16 wines by the glass, with serious aged Bordeaux and Burgundy buttressed by fair choices from around the world.

Bell Inn Ferry Road, Walberswick, Suffolk IP18 6TN ☎ (01502) 723109. Classic Suffolk coastal pub overlooking the village green, where seafood shows up strongly. Adnams is responsible for the 40-plus wines, including eight by the glass (from £2.35). Some quality reds are to be had for over £20.

Buxhall Crown Mill Road, Buxhall, Suffolk IP14 3DW ☎ (01449) 736521. The classy food is the draw at this warm and welcoming pub. All wines on the list, strong on New World bottles and listed by style, are all available by the glass.

Cornwallis Brome, Suffolk IP23 8AJ ☎ (01379) 870326. Grand sixteenth-century dower house, now a hotel. A booklet of 25 wines by the glass (£2.75 to £5.80) shows serious intent; few of the drinkable bottles on the 100-strong list are under £15.

Crown Hotel 90 High Street, Southwold, Suffolk IP18 6DP ☎ (01502) 722275. Handsome Georgian building on the main street with several eating areas. A monthly selection of 20 wines by the glass or bottle complements the list of 200 interesting, sensibly priced bottles. Long menus feature imaginative flavours.

Lifeboat Inn Ship Lane, Thornham, Norfolk PE36 6LT ☎ (01485) 512236. White inn overlooking salt marshes. A dozen wines by the glass are taken from a 40-strong list which embraces everything from *vins de pays* to a top Super-Tuscan. Fish is prominent on the menu; pub options also feature.

Old Bridge Hotel 1 High Street, Huntingdon, Cambridgeshire PE29 3TQ ☎ (01480) 424300. See entry in 'Good wines from top restaurants', page 223.

Pheasant Inn Loop Road, Keyston, Cambridgeshire PE28 0RE ☎ (01832) 710241. Traditional village inn where one menu is served throughout. The sherries and 14 wines by the glass offer plenty to relish; the list of over 100 wines falls into 'under £20' and 'top class' sections.

Star Inn The Street, Lidgate, Suffolk CB8 9PP ☎ (01638) 500275. Country views are to be had from this pink-washed pub, and wines convey a Spanish theme in keeping with the landlady's nationality. The tempting, well-priced list includes five by the glass. Catalan dishes line up alongside Anglo-Saxon pub staples.

Sun Inn High Street, Dedham, Essex CO7 6DF ☎ (01206) 323351. Constable country coaching inn with a daily-changing menu. The small but perfectly formed wine list is sourced from ambitious modern producers and includes a dozen by the glass from £2.50. Eat Italian, Spanish and Moroccan cuisine here.

Three Horseshoes High Street, Madingley, Cambridgeshire CB3 8AB ☎ (01954) 210221. This thatched pub has a pretty garden. Over 12 house wines are by the glass (£3 to £7.50) and the 100-strong list includes a good selection of sherries and sweet wines. The lively cooking uses bold, modern flavours in forthright combinations with Italian overtones.

Walpole Arms The Common, Itteringham, Norfolk NR11 7AR ☎ (01263) 587258. Village-centre former farmhouse serving East Anglian beers. Fifteen good-value house wines are available by the glass, and there is a selection of sherries, ports and dessert wines.

White Hart Poole Street, Great Yeldham, Essex CO9 4HJ ☎ (01787) 237250. Creature comforts at Tudor building with a

formal restaurant. The outstanding list of 80 exciting wines is a joy whatever your budget, with both modern Europeans and New World classicists. There is a 'light menu' as well as more substantial fare.

White Horse Main Road, Brancaster Staithe, Norfolk PE31 8BW ☎ (01485) 210262. A beautiful marshland setting for this plain pub with a conservatory dining area. Some interesting bottles crop up on the 50-strong wine list (12 by the glass). Just over £20 will bag you Morton Hawke's Bay Pinot Noir, £32.60 a half bottle of rare Mission Hill Icewine. The menu emphasises fish and seafood.

Wildebeest Arms 82–86 Norwich Road, Stoke Holy Cross, Norfolk NR14 8QJ ☎ (01508) 492497. African masks and ethnographica decorate this pub where menus have a strong Anglo-Mediterranean accent. Choose between the fixed-price option and daily specials. Good bottles at reasonable prices pack the wine list, which has a dozen house selections by the glass.

South-west England

Anchor Inn Cockwood, Devon EX6 8RA ☎ (01626) 890203. Atmospheric pub by harbour's edge where traditional pub grub and restaurant food are served, with an emphasis on seafood. Of 30 good-value bottles on the list, about nine are by the glass – or you can plunder the blackboard specials and 'reserve list', which includes some gems.

Angel Inn Upton Scudamore, Wiltshire BA12 0AG ☎ (01985) 213225. Spick-and-span pub with an open-plan restaurant. Modern wines like Wither Hills Sauvignon Blanc mix with Old World counterparts like Vincent Pinard's Sancerre on the upbeat list. Eight are by the glass, and 12 come in half bottles.

Arundell Arms Lifton, Devon PL16 0AA ☎ (01566) 784666. Sporting hotel with fishing rights on the Tamar. France is the focus of the main wine list, which includes some pricy Bordeaux and Burgundy, while Italy, Spain and the New World provide bottles under £20.

Bell at Sapperton Sapperton, Gloucestershire GL7 6LE ☎ (01285) 760298. Cotswold-stone inn converted with style; local food sources inform the brasserie-tinged cooking. The fairly priced wine list ranges from £11.95 up to £47 for good red Burgundy, with Selaks Sauvignon Blanc and Villa Caffagio Chianti offering quality in the middle ground.

Blue Ball Inn Triscombe, Somerset TA4 3HE ☎ (01984) 618242. Three converted barns and a thatched pub form this impressive complex. The 100-strong wine list has good drinking at fair prices, from New Zealand to affordable Burgundy. Eight are also by the glass. Mostly local ingredients, such as Quantock venison and fresh fish, supply the menu.

Culm Valley Inn Culmstock, Devon EX15 3JJ ☎ (01884) 840354. The modern dining area of this former railway inn serves locally sourced (and organic where possible) ingredients in eclectic global combinations. Wines are a mix of good New World names and little-known French producers; all are by the glass and mature vintages are available.

Dartmoor Inn Lydford, Devon EX20 4AY ☎ (01822) 820221. West Country produce tops the list at this country inn. Stars such as William Fèvre and Vincent Girardin stud the 25-strong main list, while nine flavoursome house wines are under £15, six of these by the glass. Fixed-price lunches and suppers are great value.

Falcon Inn London Road, Poulton, Gloucestershire ☎ (01285) 850844. Traditional village pub, with straightforward, consistent cooking. The trim wine list concentrates on quality global flavours, with eight by the glass from £2.85 to £3.95. A monthly-changing menu charts a modern European course.

George and Dragon High Street, Rowde, Wiltshire SN10 2PN ☎ (01380) 723053. Daily supplies of Cornish fish are on the menu at this pub with a walled garden. The wine list includes a 1998 Huët Vouvray, Pol Roger champagne and Domaine Tempier rosé; prices range from £10 to £60 and quality peaks throughout.

Kings Arms Inn Stockland, Devon EX14 9BS ☎ (01404) 881361. One menu serves both bar and dining areas at this thatched inn. A substantial and eclectic list has 21 house wines for £10 (also by the glass) and other exciting options range up to £50.

Museum Inn Farnham, Dorset DT11 8DE ☎ (01725) 516261. Handsome country inn, built by General Pitt-Rivers for visitors to his museum. Nine house wines are by the bottle from £11 or glass from £3, and France is the mainstay of the restaurant list. Vintage ports push the boat out. Features hearty country cooking with bold, fashionable flavours.

New Inn Coleford, Devon EX17 5BZ ☎ (01363) 84242. An Amazonian parrot and ghostly monk are denizens of this thatched inn. The list of around 50 wines, organised by grape variety, efficiently covers a wide range of flavours, with plenty under £15 and decent half bottles.

Nobody Inn Doddiscombsleigh, Devon EX6 7PS ☎ (01647) 252394. Simple country cooking and magnificent West Country cheeses at this thatched inn; the restaurant menu takes a more contemporary approach. The 800-strong wine list excels in terms of range and value, with 20-plus wines by the glass.

Pandora Inn Restronguet Creek, Mylor Bridge, Cornwall TR11 5ST ☎ (01326) 372678. This popular thatched pub has a pontoon and mooring for boats. Eight house wines are by the glass or £11 a bottle – the tempting main list offers good drinking at fair prices.

Pear Tree Inn Top Lane, Whitley SN12 8QX ☎ (01225) 709131. Rough-stone pub decorated with natural colours. Impressive Old and New World names on the wine list include Vincent Pinard's Sancerre and Australia's Nepenthe. At least ten are by the glass, from £2.95.

Rising Sun The Square, St Mawes, Cornwall TR2 5DJ ☎ (01326) 270233. Lively inn overlooking the harbour; menus make good use of fish and local ingredients. Eleven wines are £11 (£2.80 a glass), while 30 or so classy bottles from around the world form a reasonably priced list.

Rock Inn Haytor Vale, Devon TQ13 9XP ☎ (01364) 661305. Gastropub with old-fashioned décor and ambitious dinner options. Serious French wines are followed by cheaper global options and the excellent Nativa Chilean organic Cabernet Sauvignon – six are by the glass.

Seven Stars Bottlesford, Wiltshire SN9 6LU ☎ (01672) 851325. Red-brick, rambling building with Gallic staff. The eight house wines (£10.25) include unusual grapes such as Vermentino and Mauzac. Serious French bottles are costly but there's plenty of global choice for under £20. French classics meet pub food and modern dishes on the menu.

Three Crowns Inn Ullingswick, Herefordshire HR1 3JQ ☎ (01432) 820279. Two interlinked dining rooms at this half-timbered pub have a homely look. Six fruity house wines are by the glass from a quality selection of around 40 bottles (mostly over £15), while a blackboard offers fine-wine options from France and Italy.

Trengilly Wartha Inn Nancenoy, Cornwall TR11 5RP ☎ (01326) 340332. Farmhouse-style décor for pub set in beautiful location: the kitchen uses both local and organic produce. The owners' wine business supplies a mix of trusted names and offbeat discoveries at good prices. Ten are by the glass for £2.70 to £3.90, and a shortlist rounds up the 250-strong bottle selection.

White Horse Cirencester Road, Frampton Mansell, Gloucestershire GL6 8HZ ☎ (01285) 760960. An ambitious modern British menu is served at this pub-restaurant; a bar menu lists simpler dishes. Around 40 wines are arranged by style on the list; six by the glass represent a choice selection. Quality is good, with almost all under £20.

Yew Tree May Hill, Clifford's Mesne, Gloucestershire GL18 1JS ☎ (01531) 820719. The Malvern Hills are the view from this converted cider press whose kitchen uses local produce. Around 20 wines are by the glass from £3.25, and affordable bottles rub shoulders with the great and good on the serious fine wine list.

Midlands

Caunton Beck Main Street, Caunton, Nottinghamshire NG23 6AB ☎ (01636) 636793. Revamped sixteenth-century pub with a beamed bar and traditional dining room (serving the same menu). Wines in descending price order take in Burgundy, the Rhône and New World names. Lots of bottles under £15 and dessert wines.

Falcon Inn Fotheringay, Northamptonshire PE8 5HZ ☎ (01832) 226254. Dine in a conservatory extension at this attractive venue. Try a dozen wines by the glass (£3 to £7.50); the 100-bin main slate is arranged by style and divided into 'under £20' and

'top-class' sections. Sherries and dessert wines bring up the rear. Cooking reflects current trends.

Farmers Arms Welton Hill, Lincolnshire LN2 3RD ☎ (01673) 885671. Restaurant-cum-pub-cum-wine merchant in isolated rural spot. At the last count the engaging, fair-priced wine list ran to 90 bins, including 16 by the glass, plus fizz and dessert wines. Wine-and-food events feature regularly, and popular pub classics are accompanied by roasts on the menu.

Howard Arms Lower Green, Ilmington, Warwickshire CV36 4LT ☎ (01608) 682226. This large inn was once two houses. The wine list offers varied drinking by the glass and bottle, with some well-chosen names above £15.

Hundred House Hotel Bridgnorth Road, Norton, Shropshire TF11 9EE ☎ (01952) 730353. An idiosyncratic Georgian hotel, where the four basic house wines are joined by a dozen at £12.95 or £3.30 a glass, and a list of around 30 bottles.

Inn at Farnborough Farnborough, Warwickshire OX17 1DZ ☎ (01295) 690615. Well-cared-for pub with 'artistic farmhouse' feel. New World wine varieties include emerging specialities like Australian Verdelho and New Zealand Pinot Gris. Classic French bottles and house wines from £9.95 also feature.

Lough Pool Inn Sellack, Herefordshire HR9 6LX ☎ (01989) 730236. Eat at picnic tables in this village by the Wye. The concise, good-value wine list has interesting flavours: eight come by the glass, or try the organically grown champagne.

Olive Branch Main Street, Clipsham, Rutland LE15 7SH ☎ (01780) 410355. Popular pub in small hamlet where boards offer set lunch value, and a printed menu ranges widely. The outstanding and enthusiastic wine list both takes in top clarets and explains wine styles: ten wines are available by the glass.

Roebuck Inn Brimfield, Herefordshire SY8 4NE ☎ (01584) 711230. Cream-coloured building serving straightforward, unpretentious food. The round-the-world wine list has plenty of choice under £20 and four house wines from France and Chile (with around half a dozen by the glass).

Stagg Inn Titley, Herefordshire HR5 3RL ☎ (01544) 230221. Keenly sourced produce is used in appealing dishes at this village pub. Eight house wines at £2.20 a glass kick off a list of around 70 classic and modern bottles – Pedro Ximénez Viejo Napoleon sherry from Hidalgo is not to be missed.

Waterdine Llanfair Waterdine, Shropshire LD7 1TU ☎ (01547) 528214. Drovers' inn with a warren of rooms. French and California bottles lead the field of impressive wines. House wines are £10.50, and 17 half bottles increase the choice. Regional ingredients are astutely handled on the ambitious restaurant menu, alongside familiar pub offerings.

Wig and Mitre 30–32 Steep Hill, Lincoln LN2 1TL ☎ (01522) 535190. Fourteenth-century, family-run eatery between the castle and cathedral. The wine list ranges from French classics to everyday gluggers, with plentiful choice by the glass at all levels and some interesting bottles for around £20.

North England

Abbey Inn Byland Abbey, North Yorkshire YO61 4BD ☎ (01347) 868204. This solid, ivy-covered inn is opposite the haunting abbey ruins. The wine list puts on a modest air but includes some real goodies from South Africa and a 'Fine French' selection, as well as 20 wines by the glass. Expect inventive and modern cooking in the two main eating rooms.

Angel Inn Hetton, North Yorkshire BD23 6LT ☎ (01756) 730263. Classic pub dishes and European specialities feature at this rambling stone inn. Bordeaux, Burgundy and Italy are strong on the wine list, but only the house red and white cost under £15. Bargain seekers should look to half bottles and glasses.

Appletree Marton, North Yorkshire YO62 6RD ☎ (01751) 431457. Village pub on fringes of North York Moors National Park, serving exemplary food. Wine starts at under £10 a bottle on a well-structured, 70-strong list. Ten by the glass are mostly £2.60.

Bay Horse Hotel Canal Foot, Ulverston, Cumbria LA12 9EL ☎ (01229) 583972. Fine views from this eighteenth-century inn with a relaxed, friendly feel. The 100-strong wine list includes French, Australian and choice South African bottles, with a reasonable selection under £20.

Bhurtpore Inn Wrenbury Road, Aston, Cheshire CW5 8DQ ☎ (01270) 780917. Indian-themed gem whose blackboard menu includes baltis/curries. Fruity, everyday drinking on the short, imaginative list starts at £8.50 and the quirky fine wine selection at £15.50. Or check the blackboard for specials.

Black Bull Inn Moulton, North Yorkshire DL10 6QJ ☎ (01325) 377289. Long, low, whitewashed pub that majors on seafood. White wines are well represented, with excellent selections from the Loire, Germany and notably Burgundy. Red Burgundy and claret also feature and prices are fair all round.

Blue Lion East Witton, North Yorkshire DL8 4SN ☎ (01969) 624273. Convivial coaching inn in Dales village. The serious wine list has classic vintages alongside fresh, modern global flavours. Twelve good-value choices are available by the bottle, glass or half-litre.

Cook and Barker Inn Newton-on-the-Moor, Northumberland NE65 9JY ☎ (01665) 575234. This pub lies inland towards the North Sea. Six wines are by the glass from a well-presented list of around 35 bottles: it encompasses some decent flavours under £15 as well as classy, pricier bottles.

Drunken Duck Inn Barngates, Ambleside, Cumbria LA22 0NG ☎ (015394) 36347. This stone pub, popular with walkers, is elegantly styled. The superior wine list of 80 bottles has something for all pockets and offers 20 by the glass, from a simple Sauvignon Blanc (£3) to *premier cru* Chablis (£9). Inventive modern menus make good use of local produce.

Millbank Millbank, West Yorkshire HX6 3DY ☎ (01422) 825588. Rural stone pub with a metropolitan edge. The wine list pairs good-value options with upmarket alternatives, proclaiming 'If you like this, you'll love this'.

Morritt Arms Greta Bridge, County Durham DL12 9SE ☎ (01833) 627232. Georgian coaching inn with a Dickensian theme, housing a bistro and separate restaurant. A dozen wines are offered by the glass from a 160-strong list, arranged by grape variety and region. A set menu and blackboard specials offer wide food choices.

Nag's Head Pickhill, North Yorkshire YO7 4JG ☎ (01845) 567391. Much-extended, 200-year-old country inn: summer meals may be taken under a verandah. Four wines of the month (all under £15) are well above 'house' standards. Mature vintages come at reasonable prices. Dishes range from classic to contemporary fare.

Old Bridge Inn Priest Lane, Ripponden, West Yorkshire HX6 4DF ☎ (01422) 822595. Oak beams and low ceilings abound at this ancient inn. New World bottles show up on the eminently affordable list of around 25 wines, with a decent choice by the glass.

Red Cat 8 Red Cat Lane, Crank, Merseyside WA11 8RU ☎ (01744) 882422. This terraced building feels like a village pub, though the kitchen's ambitions reach higher. Bin-end specials are on a blackboard while the 500-plus fine wine list majors on premium French, Californian and Italian offerings.

Red Lion Burnsall, North Yorkshire BD23 6BU ☎ (01756) 720204. Rambling pub by bridge over River Wharfe, with a hunting theme. The restaurant wine list is available in the bar on request; otherwise, the bar list is a slate of a dozen-plus wines. Several menus operate – from light lunches to bar blackboards and formal restaurant dishes.

Red Lion 2 Red Lion Street, Stathern, Leicestershire LE14 4HS ☎ (01949) 860868. Gem of a pub with stone-flagged, beamed bar. A concise wine list cherry-picks global bottles from £9.95 to £38.50; there are plenty under £15 and around six by the glass. Local sourcing marks the brasserie-tinged modern British cooking.

Ring O' Bells 212 Hill Top Road, Thornton, West Yorkshire BD13 3QL ☎ (01274) 832296. Honey-coloured moorland pub with a congenial atmosphere. The extensive wine list includes both classics and up-to-date bottles: many of the 100 or so bins are under £15. Six half bottles and six by the glass complete the selection.

Rose and Crown Romaldkirk, County Durham DL12 9EB ☎ (01833) 650213. This restaurant and country hotel is first and foremost a pub. The ten wines by the glass (£3 to £4.95) are full of flavour; the wine list adds 50-odd bottles, arranged by grape

variety. Food ranges through simple starters to enterprising main courses.

Star Inn Harome, North Yorkshire YO62 5JE ☎ (01439) 770397. Good cheer at this fourteenth-century longhouse in a picture-postcard village. Ten interesting house wines by the glass cost £3 to £4.95; the non-budget main list of 100 bins concentrates on quality from the New World and France. Skilfully crafted local supplies are on the menu.

Stone Trough Inn Kirkham Priory, North Yorkshire YO60 7JS ☎ (01653) 618713. A classic local that doubles as an adventurous dining pub, with a patriotic line-up of Yorkshire beers. Nine house wines (£9.95 to £10.95) touch all points of the flavour compass; the main list is good on middle-ground producers like Spain's Enate and New Zealand's Saint Clair.

Wellington Inn 19 The Green, Lund, East Riding of Yorkshire YO25 9TE ☎ (01377) 217294. Upmarket dishes are on the blackboard menu at this hostelry with flagstone floors. Wines range from £15 to £40: South Africa is good at all levels, and Robert Arnoux's Burgundy is outstanding.

White Hart 51 Stockport Road, Lydgate, Greater Manchester OL4 4JJ ☎ (01457) 872566. Revamped coaching inn with a brasserie and restaurant extension. The wines fall into 'France' and 'Rest of the World' (including Spain's sought-after Vega Sicilia), with plenty of choices by the glass and half bottle.

White Swan Market Place, Pickering, North Yorkshire YO18 7AA ☎ (01751) 472288. Sixteenth-century inn with contemporary-styled interior. The first wine list roams the world, finding good drinking for £20; the second reflects the owner's passion for expensive St-Emilion clarets.

Scotland

Burt's Hotel Market Square, Melrose, Borders TD6 9PL ☎ (01896) 822285. Comfortable inn run by the same family for over 30 years. Five tempting house wines start at £12.25 (also by the glass) and the list runs to 80 well-chosen, good-value bottles – including a page of fine wines.

Creggan's Inn Strachur, Argyll and Bute PA27 8BX ☎ (01369) 860279. Inn overlooking Loch Fyne where you can enjoy the fruits of the sea (and loch). The well-assembled wine list runs to 90 bins, majoring on France and the rest of Europe. Six good house wines start at £3.20 a glass or £12.50 a bottle.

Killiecrankie Hotel Killiecrankie, Perthshire & Kinross PH16 5LG ☎ (01796) 473220. Local whiskies and ales are on offer at this elegant dower house with an informal feel. The wine list offers extensive choice from excellent producers around the world, with eight by the glass; plenty are under £20 or you can splash out with confidence.

Ubiquitous Chip 12 Ashton Lane, Glasgow G12 8SJ ☎ 0141-334 5007. See entry in 'Good wines from top restaurants', page 224.

Wales

Bell at Skenfrith Skenfrith, Monmouthshire NP7 8UH ☎ (01600) 750235. An atmospheric setting for this seventeenth-century inn near the castle. The 100-strong wine list races confidently through easy-drinkers for under £15 to first-growth clarets from the amazing 1989 and 1990 vintages. Food has traditional pub appeal.

Clytha Arms Clytha, Monmouthshire NP7 9BW ☎ (01873) 840206. Former dower house, done up in a rural style. The list of 100 bottles travels the world, and

includes trophy wines Tignanello and Cloudy Bay. Two Welsh wines are among the under-£15 selection.

Nantyffin Cider Mill Inn Brecon Road, Crickhowell, Powys NP8 1SG ☎ (01873) 810775. This sixteenth-century pub occupies some of Wales' finest walking country. An admirable and clearly set out wine list includes many interesting bottles, although just four come by the glass. The kitchen is passionate about local flavours.

Penhelig Arms Hotel Aberdovey, Gywnedd LL35 0LT ☎ (01654) 767215. This terraced hotel overlooks the Dovey Estuary. The wine list runs to over 300 bins: all the world's regions are covered in depth (famous names and old vintages included), and prices are superb whether you spend £13 or £40. Food is smart and up to date.

West Arms Llanarmon Dyffryn Ceiriog, Wrexham LL20 7LD ☎ (01691) 600665. Low beams, slate floors and inglenooks set the tone at this former drovers' inn. Traditional classics like Burgundy and Bordeaux sit alongside newcomers from Spain and Italy on the wine list, which also numbers respectable New World bottles; only three or four are by the glass. Menus have enterprising touches.

Wine courses

For a helping hand with getting to know wine, or for more in-depth learning, the following organisations run courses for beginners and wine lovers. Some of them offer formal qualifications, but these are by no means obligatory for getting the most out of a glass.

Association of Wine Educators
166 Meadvale Road, London W5 1LS
☎ 020-8930 0181, website
www.wineeducators.com. A UK-wide register of wine educators. Courses are also offered to the general public.

Christie's Wine Courses 153 Great Titchfield Street, London W1W 5BD
☎ 020-7665 4350, website *www.christies.com*. Now with a brand-new suite of lecture rooms, Christie's offers introductory wine courses for £210 (one evening a week, for five weeks), and more in-depth master classes run by leading wine specialists (£80 each). There are also summer courses held on two evenings a week (£110 for two lectures) covering different regional wine styles.

Connoisseur 10 Wedderburn Road, London NW3 5QG ☎ 020-7328 2448, website *www.connoisseur.org*. A small, sociable wine school offering a beginners' course of five sessions (£169) or a day's introduction to wine at £75. Intermediate classes – taking a closer look at the world's regions and styles – cost £95 for three evening sessions, £190 for six. Lectures are for a maximum of 20 people, so book ahead (allow a month in advance). Tailor-made wine courses and tastings are also offered.

Heart of England School of Wine
18 Gilbert Scott Court, Towcester, Northamptonshire NN12 6DX ☎ (01327) 350711, website *www.hoesow.aol.com*. Linked with the Association of Wine Educators (see above), this is a group of about 16 teachers providing wine courses and tutored tastings for customers anywhere in the UK. Activities include dinners, wine weekends and a ten-week appreciation course. The emphasis is on tailor-made, informal learning but Wine and Spirit Education Trust qualifications are also available.

Vineyard visits (e.g. to Bordeaux and Austria) are offered too.

Leith's School of Food and Wine
21 St Albans Grove, London W8 5BP
☎ 020-7229 0177, website *www.leiths.com*. As well as cookery courses, Leith's runs wine-tasting evening classes, costing £295 for five weekly introductory lessons. You can take an optional exam at the end of the course to gain Leith's own wine qualification. Food-and-wine-matching courses are available at £60, as is a 'learn about champagne' evening (£75).

The Lincoln Wine Course Mark Baker, 6 Main Street, Ashby-de-la-Launde, Lincolnshire LN4 3JG ☎ (01526) 320142. These two-term wine courses of two hours a week (starting in September each year) are based at the North Hykeham Evening Institute near Lincoln. Participants gain a good general knowledge of wine and a Wine and Spirit Education Trust qualification (Intermediate or Advanced Certificate) for £70 (plus a fee of £5 a week for the wines).

Northern Ireland Wine and Spirit Institute Peter Morris Wilson, 16 Cromlech Court, Port Stewart, County Londonderry BT55 7QU ☎ 028-7083 5531, email *petermorriswilson@yahoo.co.uk*. The Institute provides an interesting and varied monthly programme of talks, tastings and wine-related activities for members throughout the year (excluding July and August). Membership costs £60 and is open to all; members can invite guests to tastings for an extra charge. Regular study tours are organised to wine-producing areas such as Rioja or Navarra.

Plumpton College Chris Foss, Ditchling Road, Plumpton, near Lewes, East Sussex BN7 3AE ☎ (01273) 890454, website *www.plumpton.ac.uk*. Plumpton offers winegrowers' and winemakers' courses as well as an introduction to vine growing, sessions on the sensory evaluation of wine, and seminars on other aspects of wine. The college is an approved centre for the Wine and Spirit Education Trust, and also offers an HND qualification. A commercial vineyard and winery are run with the assistance of students.

Sotheby's Wine Department
34–35 New Bond Street, London W1A 2AA ☎ 020-7293 5727, website *www.sothebys.com*. Learn about wine by grape variety or by region, with alternate courses throughout the academic year on Monday evenings. The price is £240 for six sessions, or £450 to take part in the two consecutive courses.

Vinopolis, City of Wine 1 Bank End, London SE1 9BU ☎ (0870) 241 4040, website *www.vinopolis.co.uk*. An informative and interactive wine exhibition (travelling the world's wine regions) which also offers an hour-long introductory course (£25) and a food-and-wine-matching course (£50). Fine wine classes are a little more advanced, and cost £75. The price of the courses also includes a tour of the exhibition. Tempting wine accessories and bottles (through a branch of Majestic) are on sale too.

Wine Education Service Sandy Lecke, Vanguard Business Park, Alperton Lane, Western Avenue, Greenford, Middlesex UB6 8AA ☎ 020-8991 8212/3, website *www.wine-education-service.co.uk*. The biggest wine education centre in the UK offers a variety of courses. Classes are available UK-wide: the WES can hire venues on request.

Introductory sessions cost £195, intermediate classes are £120 for short courses of five sessions (on wines of the New World, or wines of Italy, Spain and Portugal) or £220 for the longer course of 10 sessions (covering classic wines of France). Advanced classes, wine tastings and one-day workshops (including a themed lunch) are also offered.

Wine & Spirit Education Trust Five Kings House, 1 Queen Street Place, London EC4R 1QS ☎ 020-7236 3551, website *www.wset.co.uk*. The Trust was set up to educate members of the wine trade, but courses are now available to the general public too. The Intermediate Certificate costs £283 and the Advanced Certificate £503, while Diploma-level studies cost £1,260 per year for two years or £2,468 for evening classes over one year. (Courses include the cost of wine samples and lead to trade-recognised qualifications.) Also offered are a Foundation Course – a one-day introduction to wine for £98 – tutored tastings and tailor-made seminars, and a spirits qualification (the Professional Certificate in Spirits, costing £283).

Winewise Michael Schuster, 107 Culford Road, London N1 4HL ☎ 020-7254 9734. Classes are run on two levels: the beginners' course costs £170 for six weekly evening sessions (40 wines are tasted from around the world); the Fine Wine course costs £275 and focuses on the classic wines of France. Both courses emphasise tasting technique in rigorous detail.

Magazines and books

To delve a bit further into any of the subjects raised in *The Which? Wine Guide*, or to keep up to date with new vintages, new wines and the ongoing issues covered in this book, the following are useful sources of wine information.

Magazines

Decanter
A monthly magazine providing major wine reviews by teams of regional experts, plus in-depth features, interviews, news, views and recommendations. The publication assumes some prior wine knowledge. To subscribe, call (0845) 676 7778.

The World of Fine Wine
This new publication is headed by the world's favourite wine writer, Hugh Johnson (see 'Books', right). It is a beautifully written, detailed bimonthly magazine for lovers of tasting notes and in-depth wine buffery – contributing authors are among the world's finest wine critics. To subscribe, call 020-7700 6700.

Harpers
The 'wine and spirit weekly' is published for the wine trade and covers all the news and commercial issues of the day. Of interest to the general wine lover are the direct news snippets straight from the vineyards, and the regular regional supplements that offer real insight into the featured vineyards – everywhere covered from Austria to Australia. To subscribe, call (01353) 654427.

Wine
With more of an easy, introductory feel than *Decanter*, this is a better read for the beginner. It covers similar ground, with major wine reviews each month, as well as interviews, get-to-know-the-region features, wine news and gossip in a chatty style. To subscribe, call (01795) 414880.

Wine Spectator
For an all-American perspective, this bimonthly is about as glossy as magazines get. As well as wine reviews (complete with marks out of 100, if that's your thing) there's plenty of restaurant and food information. Don't expect news of bargain bottles; this is all about the glamorous, big-money wines. To subscribe, call 001 212 684 4224.

Books

The Art and Science of Wine
How is wine made and how do winemakers achieve the flavours they do? This is a step-by-step guide to the choices made in the winery, revealing style by style what makes wine taste the way it does. (James Halliday and Hugh Johnson, Mitchell Beazley, reprinted 2003)

Bordeaux: People, Power and Politics
Why do Bordeaux and its people wield the power they do? The complexities behind the world's most pivotal wine region are unravelled – the high prices explained! (Stephen Brook, Mitchell Beazley, 2001)

Classic Wine Library Series
Each title in the series describes the wines of a particular region or country, lovingly rendered by a renowned expert in the field. The books are ideal reading for seekers of quality wine. Newest titles include *The Wines and Vineyards of Portugal* and *Port and the Douro* (both by Richard Mayson), *Rioja* (by John Radford) and *Biodynamics* (by Monty Waldin). Other recommended titles are *The Wines of California* (by Stephen Brook, 1999), *Barolo to Valpolicella* (1999) and *Brunello to Zibibbo* (2001) (both by Nicolas Belfrage MW). (Series published by Mitchell Beazley, latest titles published 2004)

Essential Wine Tasting
An authoritative guide to tasting wine, explaining in detail how to get the most out of every glass, and what to look for when seeking to identify a wine blind. Fascinating for beginners and buffs alike. (Michael Schuster, Mitchell Beazley, 2000; paperback due out March 2005)

The Oxford Companion to Wine
Alphabetical listings of every wine term, wine region, grape and wine guru you could ever wish to know about are contained in this book. Thoroughly researched and meticulously detailed, this is a reference

source you'll never want to be without. (Jancis Robinson, second edition, Oxford University Press, 1999)

Planet Wine

A rip-roaring romp around the world explaining, by grape variety, why a wine will taste different in France or California despite being made from the same fruit: in essence, how geography affects the wine in your glass. A rock 'n' roll approach to learning about wine. (Stuart Pigott, Mitchell Beazley, 2004)

Riesling Renaissance

If you love Riesling, this is an essential new guide to where in the world the best is grown. (Freddy Price, Mitchell Beazley, 2004)

The Story of Wine

This book charts every stage of wine's evolution – from its Black Sea origins, via Bacchanalian rituals and ancient trading allegiances, to its present-day sophistication. The 2004 edition adds in new archive photography and an update into the twenty-first century. (Hugh Johnson, second edition, Mitchell Beazley, 2004)

Wines of the World

A global introduction to the world's wine enclaves, this book explains in full colour where the best wines come from and gives detailed profiles of the growers who make them taste the way they do. Maps, photographs and clear diagrams make this one of the most visual wine books available. (Dorling Kindersley, 2004)

The World Atlas of Wine

This classic wine title is full of maps to help you visualise the world's wine regions, and elegantly worded to explain geographically the wine styles they produce. (Hugh Johnson, latest edition updated by Jancis Robinson, Mitchell Beazley, 2001)

Vintage Wine

The mysteries behind the vintage revealed. Michael Broadbent's extensive and entertaining notes show how beguiling a wine can be if you give it time. Burgundy is charted back to 1858, Bordeaux to 1784, and Madeira even further. (Michael Broadbent, Websters, 2002)

Wine with Food

The best guide to food-and-wine matching, with the essential guidelines clearly explained, and tricks for soothing even the fiercest of clashes. (Joanna Simon, Mitchell Beazley, 1999)

Wine on the Web

The present time is something of a golden age for wine on the Internet. Not only is a plethora of new independent wine merchants adding diversity to our wine shopping options, but the mine of wine information available online has never been so productive. As a source of wine information and communication, the Web has really grown up, and this is reflected with pin-sharp clarity in the world of wine online.

There are some brand-new sites that are well worth a visit, covering a whole range of wine interest areas. For the wine buff, London wine merchant and enthusiast Neal Martin offers a wonderfully comprehensive and occasionally quixotic view of the greatest wines of Bordeaux at *www.wine-journal.com*, while the knowledgeable and affectionate magazine of Switzerland-based Yorkshireman Bill Nanson, *www.burgundy-report.com*, carries in-depth profiles and tasting assessments for the region.

Among the 'old guard' of online magazines, Jancis Robinson says that her eponymous site is her principal occupation these days (and confesses to a certain frustration that some old buffers refuse to believe it can be anything more than a trivial distraction from her more 'serious' books and articles). Robert Parker has added a downloadable Palm version of his tasting notes database to *www.erobertparker.com*, and Wine International magazine finally has a Web presence worthy of note, complete with International Wine Challenge data, at *www.wineint.com*.

The site *www.UKwineforum.com* also had a makeover at the tail-end of 2003, which has given the UK and Europe a wine discussion site that can hold its own against global rivals. Great fun.

General information and online magazines

www.bath.ac.uk/~su3ws/wine-faq
Long in the tooth for sure, but this site clings on to its entry in *The Which? Wine Guide* because the simple, text-based resource of Frequently Asked Questions (and answers) is still one of the most thorough wine resources on the Internet.

www.bullworks.net/virtual.htm
The Corkscrew Museum. It houses a vast pictorial celebration of corkscrews.

www.burgundy-report.com
Bill Nanson is a passionate Burgundy lover who, living in Switzerland, can make regular visits to the best domaines. This very stylish journal is published online once per quarter, with tastings and features. Best of all, it is free. (For purists it is also free of advertising.)

www.cephas.com
The website of specialist wine photographer Mick Rock. Rock's photography graces a huge number of wine magazines and books,

and this site makes for a nice bit of browsing distraction. You can purchase prints.

www.decanter.com
A companion site to Britain's best-known wine magazine in print (see 'Magazines and books'), the online version is strong on news and contains features and reports in an archive of magazine articles. There are also extensive reference files in the 'Learning Route' section. The 'Fine Wine Tracker' catalogues auction prices on a portfolio of wines of your own selection.

www.englishwine.com
There's not a lot to this site, but it does have a very useful list of links to English wine producers and other helpful English wine sites.

www.foodandwinematching.co.uk
Writer Fiona Beckett's site has recipes, guides and articles. While it has no great depth of content, updates seem quite regular.

www.harpers-wine.com
The online version of *Harpers* (see 'Magazines and books') has an archive of

news and feature articles that is available free of charge. Also free is a comprehensive set of 'wine reports', giving all sorts of useful statistics, information, and maps for every major wine-producing country. Subscription to the weekly print magazine buys access to extended features on the Internet, including a comprehensive directory of wine businesses.

www.investdrinks.org
Wine writer Jim Budd's crusade against wine-related investment scams and rip-offs names names and issues sound advice for those thinking of putting cash into fine wine.

www.jancisrobinson.com
Few would have imagined that Britain's best-known and most respected authority on wine (editor of *The Oxford Companion to Wine*, creator of BBC2's *Wine Course*, etc.) would become so immersed in her website that she says it is now her main focus of attention. It still looks a little amateurish compared to some, and the juiciest content is available only within the subscription-based 'Purple Pages' section (£49 per annum), but Jancis' stature makes this one of the world's most important wine information sites.

www.ozclarke.com
Unlike Jancis Robinson's site, this is mostly just a promotional site for Oz Clarke's books and CD-Rom, but a regular 'wine of the week' and some editorial content make it worth listing.

www.thevintageportsite.com
This site is produced by the Symington group of Port producers, but is crammed with excellent general information, including a very detailed vintage search that goes all the way back to 1900.

www.thewinedoctor.com
The minimalist design makeover for wine-loving medic Chris Kissack's site does not convince, but good content includes articles, wine tips and educational material.

www.ukwinejobs.com
Fancy making a break into the wine trade? This recruitment-service site lists opportunities, and you can sign up to lodge your own CV online.

www.vine2wine.com
A huge resource, with hundreds of reviews for wine-related sites. Sites are categorised and rated from one to three stars. Updates appear to be becoming less frequent.

www.wine-encore.com
This site highlights discount deals on wine available in UK supermarkets and chains such as Oddbins or Thresher. There isn't much to inspire the enthusiast, but it seems to be regularly updated.

www.wine-journal.com
There's a sense of irreverence about Neal Martin's new site. An earnest homage to fine wines – particularly Bordeaux – containing fantastically extensive information, it is quirky and offbeat when you start to explore its furthest corners. Well worth a look.

www.wine-pages.com
Established in 1995, this is one of the most comprehensive wine e-zines. Updated daily, the site includes a six-part wine appreciation course, tricky quizzes, guides to the world's wine regions, tens of thousands of tasting notes, a BYO directory, and expert columnists such as Tom Stevenson and Rosemary George MW.

www.wine-searcher.com
This retains its place as arguably the most useful wine site out there. Its huge database of retailers and what they stock allows you to search for specific wines and see a list of stockists sorted in ascending price order. A limited data-set is available free, and the full catalogue of over one million wines requires a US $24.95 subscription (though the site is a joint UK/New Zealand venture).

www.wineanorak.com
Jamie Goode is carving a name for himself as an expert on wine science (his day job is as a science editor), but his well-established, British-based e-zine covers wine much more broadly, with pertinent features, wine tips and editorials.

www.winedine.co.uk
This long-established site from Tony le Ray Cook offers a hedonist's diary of fine food, wine and 'lifestyle' features. A bit of a mish-mash, but worth checking out.

www.wineint.com
A resource-packed online companion to *Wine International* magazine. It includes the results of the International Wine Challenge (for the wine trade only).

www.winelabels.org
Peter May once appeared on the BBC's *Food & Drink* chastising restaurants for bottled water rip-offs. A man of strong passions, he

indulges his lighter side here in a quirky and fun site that celebrates the odd, unusual and downright weird in wines and wine labelling.

www.wineontheweb.co.uk
The main thing going for this rather patchy site is a series of 'Radio Postcard' audio reports on wine-related topics – ideal for visually impaired surfers.

www.winespectator.com
This is the sprawling online edition of the top US wine magazine (see 'Magazines and Books'); some will find it too US-centred and commercial. There's a wealth of information on wine and 'gracious living' here, including travelogues, tasting reports and online discussion. Extended features – such as accessing all 100,000 wine reviews instead of a small sample – require a paid subscription ($49.95 per annum).

Tasting notes and wine recommendations

Most of the sites listed above feature tasting notes and recommendations, but the following are dedicated to the task of tasting, grading and cataloguing wines.

www.erobertparker.com
Robert Parker is the world's most prominent wine critic, and his bimonthly newsletter, *The Wine Advocate*, is hugely influential. *www.erobertparker* presents a database of 70,000 tasting notes, with powerful and efficient search facilities and new notes added continually. For this, an annual subscription of $99 is charged. (The print edition requires a separate subscription, but retains the crucial advantage of notes appearing two months before making it on to the Internet.) A free trial subscription is available. Recently added is 'Parker in Your Palm', a version of the tasting notes database for use on hand-held PDA devices. This requires an additional subscription.

www.finewinediary.com
The Edinburgh- and Oxford-based Bailey brothers have amassed a formidable collection of tasting notes, almost exclusively on fine wines. Scores are awarded for current drinking quality and development potential in this huge, searchable archive. This simple, relatively uncommercial site keeps up a high standard.

www.superplonk.com
Malcolm Gluck's site is a fund of snappy assessments of low- and medium-priced wines available on the high street and in cyberspace. Attempts to move the most valuable content to a subscription-only service during 2004 appear to have been abandoned.

www.tastings.com
This professional US site claims 40,000 wine notes in its database. All notes are dated and give a score out of 100.

Wine talk

The opportunity to interact with others is one of the joys of the Internet as a medium. These are two of the best sites for online wine discussion.

www.wldg.com
This is an established and friendly US-centred discussion group, but some may find it too biased to a North American viewpoint.

www.ukwineforum.com
Many forums are severely under-used, but the friendly, civilised and lively group that constitutes the UK Wine Forum makes it the number-one spot for online discussion of wine from a distinctly British angle. A relaunch in December 2003 has really brought the forum alive. There's a community-built tasting notes archive on thousands of wines, non-commercial space for buying, selling and swapping wines, and a dedicated area for planning 'offline' get-togethers.

Glossary

almacenista (Spain) a small-scale sherry stockholder

Amarone (Italy) dry PASSITO wine from Valpolicella

amontillado (Spain) an aged FINO sherry on which FLOR yeast has stopped growing but which is matured further without *flor* to develop delicate, nutty flavours; commercial 'medium amontillados' are not made in this way but are blended, sweetened sherries

appellation a regional category that provides an indication of the style and also the quality of the wine.

appellation d'origine contrôlée (AOC) (France) the best-quality category of French wine, with regulations defining the precise vineyard area according to soil, grape varieties, yields, alcohol level, and sometimes vineyard and cellar practices. Below AOC come VDQS (an intermediate step for wines wishing to become AOC), *VIN DE PAYS* and basic *VIN DE TABLE*. The AOC rules are countrywide – each region then adds its own *CRU*, *PREMIER CRU* and *GRAND CRU* categories (for details, see chapters on Burgundy, Bordeaux, Alsace and Champagne)

aromatic wines usually refers to wines made from highly perfumed grapes, for example, Gewürztraminer, Muscat and Pinot Gris

aromatics the perfumes released by AROMATIC WINES

Ausbruch (Austria) dessert wine, between BEERENAUSLESE and TROCKENBEERENAUSLESE, from nobly rotten grapes (see BOTRYTIS)

Auslese (Germany, Austria) usually sweet wine from selected ripe grapes, possibly with noble rot (see BOTRYTIS)

barrique 225-litre barrel, of French or American oak, in which both red and white wines are matured and white wines sometimes fermented. Normally replaced every 2–3 years, as new *barriques* have a more pronounced effect on taste

bâtonnage (France) the operation of stirring the LEES

Beerenauslese (BA) (Germany, Austria) wine from specially selected ripe berries, probably with noble rot (see BOTRYTIS)

bin end the last few bottles or cases of wine left in a shipment; merchants often sell them off at bargain prices

biodynamics (Burgundy, and elsewhere) an extreme form of organic viticulture, based on the teachings of Rudolf Steiner, which takes into account the influence of the cosmos (for example, the phases of the moon) on a vine

blanc de blancs white wine or champagne made from white grapes only

blanc de noirs white wine or champagne made from red grapes vinified without skin contact (the juice of most red grapes is colourless; all the colouring matter is in the skins)

bodega (Spain) cellar, winery

Botrytis cinerea a form of grape bunch rot that shrivels grapes and concentrates their sugars (AKA 'noble rot')

boutique wines small-production wines, made with the utmost care; frequently expensive

brut (Champagne) dry or dryish (up to 15g sugar/litre)

Bual (Madeira) sweetest style of madeira after MALMSEY

carbonic maceration fermentation of whole bunches of grapes in a vat filled with carbon dioxide to give fruity wines with low tannin

Cava (Spain) champagne-method sparkling wines; now a DO in its own right

chaptalisation the addition of sugar to the MUST to increase the final alcohol content of the wine

classico (Italy) heartland of a DOC zone, producing its best wines, e.g. Soave

clos (France) vineyard site that was walled in the past, and may still be walled

Colheita (Portugal) vintage table wine; single-vintage TAWNY PORT

cream (Spain) sweet sherry

crianza (Spain) basic wood-aged wine, with a minimum of six months' oak-cask ageing and one year's bottle- or tank-ageing; can be released only after two full calendar years

cru (France) literally 'growth', meaning either a distinguished single property (as in Bordeaux) or a distinguished vineyard area (as in Beaujolais, Burgundy, the Rhône or Languedoc)

cru bourgeois (Bordeaux) classification system of the Médoc just below classed growth (CRU CLASSÉ) status. In descending order: *cru bourgeois exceptionnel, cru bourgeois supérior, cru bourgeois*

cru classé (Bordeaux) 'classed growth', indicating a wine from the Médoc's primary classification system, divided into five strata (*premiers, deuxièmes, troisièmes, quatrièmes* and *cinquièmes crus classés*); or from the classification systems of the Graves, Sauternes or St-Emilion. (See also GRAND CRU CLASSÉ)

crusted/crusting (Portugal) a blend of port from different years for short-term cellaring; needs decanting

cuvée (France) term applied to a batch of wine, usually of superior quality but with no precise legal definition

demi-sec (Champagne, Loire) sweet (up to 50g sugar/litre)

denominação de origem controlada (DOC) (Portugal) the Portuguese equivalent to France's AOC category

denominación de origen (DO) (Spain) wines of controlled origin, grape varieties and style

denominación de origen calificada (DOCa) (Spain) as DO (see above), but entails stricter controls including bottling at source; so far, only Rioja has been given a DOCa status

denominazione di origine controllata (DOC) (Italy) wine of controlled origin, grape varieties and style

denominazione di origine controllata e garantita (DOCG) (Italy) wine from an area with stricter controls than DOC (see above)

domaine (Burgundy) estate, meaning the totality of vineyard holdings belonging to a grower or NÉGOCIANT

doux (Champagne, Loire) sweet to very sweet (over 50g sugar/litre)

Eiswein (Germany) wine made from frozen grapes

en primeur (Bordeaux) agreeing to buy in advance of a wine's being released for sale

entry-level wine cheapest wine made by any one producer (the starting point in the range)

Erstes Gewächs (Germany) 'first growths', a regions' own system of classification of vineyards

extra-brut (Champagne) absolutely dry (no added sugar)

extra-dry (Champagne) off-dry (12–20g sugar/litre)

fino (Spain) pale, dry sherry matured under FLOR

flor (Spain, Jura) the layer of yeast growing on wine or sherry in a part-empty butt

frizzante (Italy) lightly sparkling

garrafeira (Portugal) better-than-average table wine given longer-than-average ageing

'garage' style wines wines made on a small scale; the original garage wines were made by winemakers who had nothing but a garage to work in. (See also BOUTIQUE WINES)

grand cru (Alsace) classified vineyard site

grand cru (Burgundy) finest category of named vineyard site

grand cru classé (Bordeaux) 'fine classed growth'; in St-Emilion indicates wine from the second level of the classification system

grand vin (Bordeaux) 'fine wine': the top wine of a Bordeaux château, blended from selected CUVÉES only, as opposed to the 'second wine', which is blended from less successful *cuvées*, is perhaps the wine of younger vines, and is generally sold at a lower price

gran reserva (Spain) wine aged for a minimum of two years in oak cask and two years in bottle; can be released only after five full calendar years

'green wines' wines made from organic, BIODYNAMIC or holistically managed vineyards. (See also LUTTE RAISONÉE)

Halbtrocken (Germany) semi-dry

hang-time the length of time the grapes are on the vine, from formation to harvest time

Icon wines (New World especially) wines made with no expense spared, to be top of their field

indicação de proveniência regulamentada (IPR) (Portugal) below DOC; similar to France's VDQS status

indicazione geografica tipica (IGT) (Italy) wine of controlled origin, grape varieties and production methods, with less stringent regulations than DOC. Now covers many SUPER-TUSCANS

Kabinett (Germany, Austria) first category of PRÄDIKAT wine, light, dry and delicate in style

late-bottled vintage (LBV) (Portugal) a medium-quality red port of a single year

late harvest sweet wine made from grapes picked in an over-mature or maybe BOTRYTISED condition

lees dregs or sediment that settle at the bottom of a container

lutte raisonée (France) a balanced approach to vine growing that respects the environment. A long way along the road to organic viticulture

maceration process of leaving grapes to 'stew' on their skins before, during and after fermentation

Malmsey (Madeira) the most sweet and raisiny of madeiras

malolactic fermentation a secondary, non-alcoholic 'fermentation' that converts malic acid into lactic acid. The process is accomplished by bacteria rather than yeast

manzanilla (Spain) salty FINO from Sanlúcar de Barrameda

manzanilla pasada (Spain) aged MANZANILLA

méthode traditionnelle (France) the Champagne method of producing sparkling wines

micro-cuvée wine of which only small amounts are made

mis en bouteille par (France) 'bottled by'

mis-en-cave (France) literally, 'put in cellar'. Refers to the place where the wine was aged, or cellared; usually in barrel

moelleux (France) medium-sweet to sweet

monopole vineyard wholly owned by one grower, usually in Burgundy

mousse (France) term used to describe the effervescence in sparkling wine

mousseux (France) sparkling

mouthfeel the texture of the wine; the way it feels in the mouth. For example, a Chilean Merlot might feel velvety, a Gewürztraminer oily or fat

must a mixture of grape juice, stem fragments, grape skins, seeds and pulp prior to fermentation

MW Master of Wine (UK qualification)

négociant (France) wholesale merchant and wine trader

noble rot see BOTRYTIS

non vintage (NV) a wine or champagne made from a blend of wines from different years

oloroso (Spain) sherry aged oxidatively rather than under FLOR

organic wine wine produced according to eco-friendly principles in both the vineyard and the winery, and which has received accreditation from one of a number of official bodies

palo cortado (Spain) light and delicate style of OLOROSO

passito (Italy) dried or semi-dried grapes or wine made from them

petits châteaux (Bordeaux) properties modest in reputation and price, but which can provide some of the best value wine in the region

phylloxera aphid that kills vines by attacking their roots. Phylloxera devastated Europe's vineyards in the second half of the nineteenth century, since which time vines have had to be grafted on to disease-resistant rootstock

Prädikat (Germany, Austria) a category of wine with a 'special attribute' based on natural sugar levels in MUST, such as KABINETT, SPÄTLESE, AUSLESE, BEERENAUSLESE, TROCKENBEERENAUSLESE or EISWEIN

premier cru (Burgundy) second highest category of named vineyard site. If no vineyard name is specified, wine made from a number of different *premiers crus* sites

premier grand cru classé (Bordeaux) 'first fine classed growth', indicating a wine from the top level of the St-Emilion classification system

Prosecco (Veneto, Italy) refers both to the grape and to the wine (usually sparkling), characterised by fresh fruit flavours with a faintly bitter twist

Qualitätswein bestimmter Anbaugebiete (QbA) (Germany) quality wine from a specific region

Qualitätswein mit Prädikat (QmP) (Germany) quality wine with a 'special attribute' (*see* PRÄDIKAT)

quinta (Portugal) farm, estate. In the port context, any style may be branded with a quinta name, but *single quinta* port generally refers to a single-farm port from a lesser year

recioto (Italy) sweet PASSITO wine from the Veneto

récolte (France) harvest

reserva (Portugal) better-than-average wine; slightly higher (0.5%) in alcohol than the legal minimum; at least one year old

reserva (Spain) wine aged for a minimum of one year in oak cask and one year in bottle; can be released only after three full calendar years

riserva (Italy) wines aged for longer than normal

sec (Champagne, Loire) medium-dry (17–35g sugar/litre); (other areas) dry *secco* (Italy) dry

seco (Portugal, Spain) dry

second wine (Bordeaux) *see* GRAND VIN

Sekt (Germany, Austria) sparkling wine

sélection des grains nobles (Alsace) wine made from BOTRYTIS-affected grapes

semi-seco (Spain) medium-dry

sercial (Madeira) the driest madeira, though cheap examples are rarely fully dry

sin crianza (Spain) without wood-ageing

solera (Portugal, Spain) ageing system which, by fractional blending, produces a consistent and uniform end product

Spätlese (Germany, Austria) wine from late-picked grapes, possibly with noble rot (see BOTRYTIS)

special reserve (Madeira) madeira with a minimum age of ten years

spumante (Italy) sparkling

sulfites (USA) sulphur dioxide, present in all wines (including organic wines), used as a preservative and disinfectant

supérieur (France) higher alcohol content than usual

superiore (Italy) wine with higher alcohol than usual, and sometimes more age

Super-Tuscan (Italy) usually non-DOC wine of high quality from Tuscany. Most now fall under IGT category

sur lie (Loire) refers to a wine (generally Muscadet) bottled directly from its LEES, without having been racked or filtered. It may contain some carbon dioxide

Tafelwein (Germany) table wine

tawny port (Portugal) basic light port. True wood-aged tawny ports are either marketed as COLHEITAS or as 'ports with an indication of age'

terroir (France) term encompassng a number of factors, including the soil, climate, aspect, altitude and gradient of a vineyard, all of which can affect the way a vine grows and therefore the taste of the ultimate wine

Trocken (Germany) dry

Trockenbeerenauslese (TBA) (Germany, Austria) very sweet wine from grapes affected by noble rot (see BOTRYTIS)

ullage the air space at the top of an unopened bottle of maturing wine – can increase through evaporation as the wine ages

varietal a wine based on a single grape variety

vin délimité de qualité supérieure (VDQS) (France) covers the very much smaller category than APPELLATION D'ORIGINE CONTRÔLÉE (AOC), below AOC but with very similar regulations

vecchio (Italy) old

velho (Portugal) old

vendange tardive (Alsace) 'late harvest', meaning wine made from especially ripe grapes

Verband Deutscher Prädikatsweingüter e.V. (VDP) (Germany) group of estates whose members have agreed to a set of regulations

verde (Portugal) 'green', meaning young

Verdelho (Madeira) medium-dry madeira

viejo (muy) (Spain) old (very)

Vieilles vignes indicates wine made from old wines (literally), which tends to be richer and more concentrated

vigneron (France) wine grower

viña (Spain) vineyard

vin de paille (France) sweet wine made from grapes that have been allowed to dry out, traditionally on straw (*paille*)

vin de pays (France) literally translates as country wine, and describes wine that is better than basic VIN DE TABLE, with some regional characteristics. Usually *vins de pays* are determined by administrative geography, with more flexible regulations than for APPELLATION D'ORIGINE CONTRÔLÉE

vin de table (France) the most basic category of French wine, with no specific provenance other than country of origin given on the label

vin doux naturel (France) sweet wine made by adding spirit part-way through the fermentation process before all the grape sugar has been converted to alcohol

vinho de mesa (Portugal) table wine

vinho regional (VR) (Portugal) equivalent to France's VIN DE PAYS

vino da tavola (VdT) (Italy) table wine

vino de la tierra (Spain) country wine

vino de mesa (Spain) table wine

vin santo (Italy) type of PASSITO wine from Trentino, Tuscany and Umbria

vintage champagne champagne made from a blend of grapes from a single year, sold after at least three years' ageing

vintage character (Portugal) medium- to premium-quality ruby port

vintage madeira (Madeira) the finest madeira from one specific year

vintage port (Portugal) very fine port, bottled young and requiring long cellaring (8–40 years); needs decanting

Vitis vinifera the species of the *Vitis* genus in which virtually all of the major wine grape varieties are found

Index of wine merchants

Index